FOURTH EDITION
CITIES IN A
WORLD ECONOMY

Sociology for a New Century Series

SOCIOLOGY FOR A NEW CENTURY

FOURTH EDITION

CITIES IN A WORLD ECONOMY

SASKIA SASSEN

Columbia University

Los Angeles | London | New Delhi
Singapore | Washington DC

Los Angeles | London | New Delhi
Singapore | Washington DC

FOR INFORMATION:

Pine Forge Press
An Imprint of SAGE Publications, Inc.
2455 Teller Road
Thousand Oaks, California 91320
E-mail: order@sagepub.com

SAGE Publications Ltd.
1 Oliver's Yard
55 City Road
London EC1Y 1SP
United Kingdom

SAGE Publications India Pvt. Ltd.
B 1/I 1 Mohan Cooperative Industrial Area
Mathura Road, New Delhi 110 044
India

SAGE Publications Asia-Pacific Pte. Ltd.
33 Pekin Street #02-01
Far East Square
Singapore 048763

Acquisitions Editor: David Repetto
Editorial Assistant: Maggie Stanley
Production Editor: Karen Wiley
Copy Editor: Kim Husband
Typesetter: C & M Digitals (P) Ltd.
Proofreader: Jennifer Gritt
Indexer: William Ragsdale
Cover Designer: Candice Harman
Marketing Manager: Erica DeLuca
Permissions Editor: Karen Ehrmann
Cover Image: Hilary Koob-Sassen, Still
from "Transcalar Investment Vehicles"
Film London, FIAMIN Productions 2011

Printed in the United States of America

Library of Congress Cataloging-in-Publication Data

Sassen, Saskia.

Cities in a world economy / Saskia Sassen. — 4th ed.

p. cm.
— (Sociology for a new century series)

Includes bibliographical references and index.

ISBN 978-1-4129-8803-2 (pbk.)

1. Urban economics. 2. Metropolitan areas—Cross-
cultural studies. 3. Cities and towns—Cross-cultural
studies. 4. Sociology, Urban. I. Title.

HT321.S28 2012
330.9173'2—dc23   2011027766

This book is printed on acid-free paper.

11 12 13 14 15 10 9 8 7 6 5 4 3 2 1

Brief Contents

Detailed Contents

Preface to the Fourth Edition

The last few years have seen the rise of an acute sense of crisis—financial, environmental, and of urban violence. There has been extreme growth in inequality and extreme growth in financial profits. The sons and daughters of the middle classes earn less than their parents, get less education, and are less likely to own a home. The number of global cities has grown, with both a massively internationalized very rich professional class and a very low-wage service class. We have seen the emergence of a global labor market. We have seen new global alignments, with the rise of China, Brazil, India, and others. The failure of interstate climate negotiations has brought to the forefront the importance and effectiveness of urban leaderships in addressing the environmental challenge. Asymmetric war has continued to urbanize war; global insecurity has strengthened racisms of all sorts and engendered new forms of urban violence.

Through it all, the city has strengthened its role as strategic space where our major challenges become acute and visible—a lens to see a larger world that remains difficult to grasp.

In this new edition, I have taken in all these transformations and the pertinent texts are incorporated throughout all the chapters. I have also added a new chapter that focuses on cities as strategic sites for asymmetric war, the financial crisis that exploded in 2008, and the environmental challenge. Cities play an increasingly significant role in all three. Among the new subjects addressed throughout the book are the new types of global labor markets that are emerging throughout the world, from China to Peru, and the new types of geographies of global migrations and remittances. I maintained much of the original structure and content, except for updates and better data presentations where better data became available. And the prefaces to the preceding editions remain part of the basic preface to the book.

As always, there are many persons to thank. The editors of the series and the editorial team at SAGE/Pine Forge, David Repetto, Maggie Stanley,

Karen Wiley, and Kim Husband. A special thank you goes to my exceptional research assistants at Columbia University: Natan Dotan, Ifeoma Ajunwa, Walker Kahn, Joan Robinson, Kate Glynn-Broderick, Priti Narayan, Sara Partridge, and in Los Angeles, Jonathan Nettler. Olivia Nicol and Marta Walinska, both from Columbia University, worked with me on the report *The Global Labor Market at a Tipping Point* for the Economist Intelligence Unit, which helped me shape some of the new sections on global labor markets in the book. Besides general research, Natan Dotan worked with me on an article, now published, on cities and the environmental crisis; it helped me write the section on the environment in the new Chapter 8. Finally, I would like to thank the teachers who have used the book in their classes. As with every edition, their comments, critiques, and suggestions were enormously important to me.

Preface to the Third Edition

L ittle did I know that 15 years after the original version I would find
myself working on a third edition of this book. The two earlier prefaces
contain much of what I would like to repeat here, but the occasion demands
brevity. Besides a thorough updating, bringing in the latest available data, this
new edition addresses some of the critical questions about a range of processes that have gained prominence over the last several years. One of these
is international migrations, examined in Chapter 7, a whole new chapter, and
through new material in several other chapters. Women have emerged as key
actors in migration processes and in some of the labor markets growing fast
in global cities. When it comes to new trends, the second edition showed a
strengthening of patterns that had been only dimly detected in the first edition. The data for the late 1990s and into 2005 examined in this third edition
show a further strengthening of some of those patterns, such as the sharp
concentration of global wealth and the growth of various forms of inequality,
as well as the emergence of new patterns. Perhaps most notable among the
latter is the rapid growth in the network of global cities and the addition of
several new major centers at the top of the system. Further, some of the leading centers, such as Tokyo, have lost ground, while others, such as New York
after the attacks of September 11, 2001, have regained power. The data covering social variables show a sharpening in several alignments, further suggesting the emergence of new types of social formations inside these cities.

Much was said already in the prefaces to the two preceding editions,
particularly the first, about the genesis of the book and all the institutions and
people who made it possible. They made all the difference, and I remain
grateful to them. Here, I would like to acknowledge the encouragement
of teachers and students who have used the book. Their praise and their
comments mean a lot to me. I would like to single out several users of the
book for their most helpful suggestions: Professors Rhacel Parrenas (University
of California, Davis), Jan Nijman (University of Miami), Daniel Monti
(Boston University), Gerry Sussman (State University of New York, Oswego),

and Peter Taylor (Loughborough University, United Kingdom). They wrote detailed comments and suggestions that I have tried to follow.

Finally, the people who made this third edition happen: I am most grateful to the editors of the Series, York Bradshow (University of South Carolina, Upstate), Vincent Roscigno (Ohio State University), and Joya Misra (University of Massachusetts, Amherst), for asking me to do a third edition. It is not really easy or comfortable to go back to an old book, and to do so word by word, number by number. They persuaded me it was a good idea. Ben Penner, the Pine Forge editor of the series, was contagious in his enthusiasm and was a generous supporter of the project, especially of the vast research necessary to do the updates. Annie Louden of Pine Forge was extremely helpful. The single largest thank you goes to David Lubin, who did much of the research for the tables and their final preparation; it could not have been done, certainly not on time, without him. Zachary Hooker, Vikas Chandra, Danny Armanino, and Nilesh Patel were enormously helpful at various stages of the work. Last but not least, copy editor Teresa Barensfeld made all the difference.

Preface to the Second Edition

Since I completed this book in the early 1990s, the world has seen a recession come to an end, a boom in global financial transactions, and a major crisis in Southeast Asia, parts of Latin America, and Russia. Yet throughout these often sharp and massive shifts, we have also seen the continuation of the major developments that I used to specify the features of the global economy that have made cities strategic. Indeed, many of the updated tables in this edition show the accentuation of some of the trends identified in the earlier edition. They also show the growth of the cross-border network of cities that constitutes a transnational space for the management and servicing of the global economy. As countries adopt the new rules of the global game, their major business centers become the gateways through which capital and other resources enter and exit their economies.

A major new trend that is becoming evident over the last few years is the strengthening of the networks connecting cities, including a novel development: the formation of strategic alliances between cities through their financial markets. The growth of global markets for finance and specialized services, the need for transnational servicing networks due to sharp increases in international investment, the reduced role of the government in the regulation of international economic activity, and the corresponding ascendance of other institutional arenas, notably global markets and corporate headquarters—all these point to the existence of a series of transnational networks of cities. We can see here the formation, at least incipient, of transnational urban systems. To a large extent, it seems to me that the major business centers in the world today draw their importance from these transnational networks. The global city is a function of a network—and in this sense, there is a sharp contrast with the erstwhile capitals of empires. This subject is sufficiently new and so little known that I have added a whole new section on it in Chapter 5.

These networks of major international business centers constitute new geographies of centrality. The most powerful of these new geographies of centrality at the global level bind the major international financial and business centers: New York, London, Tokyo, Paris, Frankfurt, Zurich, Amsterdam, Los Angeles, Sydney, and Hong Kong, among others. But this geography now also includes cities such as Bangkok, Seoul, Taipei, São Paulo, Mexico City, and Buenos Aires. The intensity of transactions among these cities, particularly through the financial markets, trade in services, and investment, has increased sharply, and so have the orders of magnitude involved. At the same time, there has been a sharpening inequality in the concentration of strategic resources and activities between each of these cities and others in the same country.

One of the more controversial sections of the first edition of this book proved to be my analysis and conceptualization of the growth of inequality within these cities. Then and now, the data are inadequate to have definitive proof. Yet I would argue that we continue to see this trend toward inequality. There is an ongoing growth of the highly paid professional classes connected to leading sectors of the global economy and of national economies. And there is also continuing growth of low-wage service workers, including industrial services. In many of these cities, we continue to see a fairly large middle class. But on closer examination, a good part of this middle class is still living at the level of prosperity it gained in the earlier economic phase. It is not certain at all that the sons and daughters of these aging middle classes in various cities around the world will have the, albeit modest, prosperity enjoyed by their parents. Furthermore, the growth of disadvantaged sectors, many excluded from a growing range of institutional worlds—of work, education, and politics—continues to be evident in many of these cities.

It has been fascinating to revisit the earlier empirical information and bring it up to date. The strengthening of many of these patterns took even me a bit by surprise.

Preface to the First Edition

Sociologists have tended to study cities by looking at the ecology of urban forms and the distribution of population and institutional centers or by focusing on people and social groups, lifestyles, and urban problems. These approaches are no longer sufficient. Economic globalization, accompanied by the emergence of a global culture, has profoundly altered the social, economic, and political reality of nation-states, cross-national regions, and—the subject of this book—cities. Through the study of the city as one particular site in which global processes take place, I seek to define new concepts useful to understand the intersection of the global and the local in today's world—and tomorrow's.

It is helpful in this context to recall Janet Abu-Lughod, a leading urban sociologist, who has commented that it is impossible to study the city only from a sociological perspective because it requires an understanding of many other realities. Manuel Castells, another major urban sociologist, has added that it is impossible to study the city only from an urban perspective. These two observations mark an empty space in urban sociology, which I seek to address in this book.

Although there has been an international economic system for many decades and a world economy for many centuries, the current situation is distinct in two respects. On the one hand, we have seen the formation of transnational spaces for economic activity where governments play a minimal role, different from the role they once had in international trade, for instance. Examples of such spaces are export processing zones, offshore banking centers, and many of the new global financial markets. On the other hand, these transnational spaces for economic activity are largely located in national territories under the rule of sovereign states. There is no such entity as a global economy completely "out there," in some space that exists outside nation-states. Even electronic markets and firms operating out of the World Wide Web have some aspect of their operation partly embedded in actual national territories. Yet the location of the global largely in the national happens through a significant new development: a change in the ways in which the national state regulates and governs at least part of its economy. Deregulation and privatization are but partial descriptions of this change. The outcome is the formation of transnational spaces inside the national. This new configuration is increasingly being called a global economy to distinguish it from earlier formations such as the old colonial empires or the international economic system of the immediate post–World War II period, in which governments played a crucial regulatory role in international trade, investment, and financial markets.

Understanding how global processes locate in national territories requires new concepts and research strategies. The global city is one such new concept; it draws on and demands research practices that negotiate the intersection of macroanalysis and ethnography. It presumes that global processes, from the formation of global financial markets to the rapid growth of transnational labor markets, can be studied through the particular forms in which they materialize in places.

This book shows how some cities—New York, Tokyo, London, São Paulo, Hong Kong, Toronto, Miami, and Sydney, among others—have evolved into transnational "spaces." As such cities have prospered, they have come to have more in common with one another than with regional centers in their own nation-states, many of which have declined in importance. Such developments require all those interested in the fate of cities to rethink traditionally held views of cities as subunits of their nation-states or to reassess the importance of national geography in our social world. Moreover, the impact of global processes radically transforms the social structure of cities themselves—altering the organization of labor, the distribution of earnings, the structure of consumption, all of which in turn create new patterns of urban social inequality. In *Cities in a World Economy*, I seek to provide the vocabulary and analytic frames with which students and the general reader can grasp this new world of urban forms.

List of Exhibits

1

Place and Production in the Global Economy

In the late twentieth century, massive developments in telecommunications and the ascendance of information industries led analysts and politicians to proclaim the end of cities. Cities, they told us, would become obsolete as economic entities. The growth of information industries allows firms and workers to remain connected no matter where they are located. The digitizing of both services and trade shifts many economic transactions to electronic networks, where they can move instantaneously around the globe or within a country. Indeed, from the 1970s onward, there have been large-scale relocations of offices and factories to less congested and lower-cost areas than central cities, as well as the growth of computerized clerical work that could be located anywhere—in a clerical "factory" in the Bahamas or China or a home in a nearby suburb. Although these trends may be sharpest in the United States, they are evident in a growing number of countries around the world. Finally, the emergent globalization of economic activity seems to suggest that place—particularly the type of place represented by cities—no longer matters.

But, as I argue in this book, the spatial dispersion of the economy is only half of the story of today's global and digital age. Alongside the well-documented spatial dispersal of economic activities and the increased digitizing of the sphere of consumption and entertainment are the growing spatial concentration of a wide range of highly specialized professional

1

activities, top-level management, and control operations, as well as, perhaps most unexpectedly, a multiplication of low-wage jobs and low-profit economic sectors. More analytically, these trends point to the development of novel forms of territorial centralization amid rapidly expanding economic and social networks with global span.

Given the generalized trends toward dispersal—whether at the metro-politan or global level—and given the widespread conviction that this is the future, what needs explaining is that at the same time, centralized territorial nodes are growing. In this book, I examine why and how firms and markets that operate in multisited national and global settings require central places where the top-level work of running global systems gets done. I also show why information technologies and industries designed to span the globe require a vast physical infrastructure containing strategic nodes with hyper-concentrations of material facilities. Finally, I show how even the most advanced information industries, such as global finance and the specialized corporate legal and accounting services, have a production process that is partly place-bound: Not all of the activities of these industries circulate in electronic networks.

Once these place-centered processes are brought into the analysis of the new global and electronic economy, surprising observations emerge. These centralized territorial nodes of the digitized global economy turn out to be not only the world of top-level transnational managers and professionals but also that of their secretaries and that of the janitors cleaning the build-ings where the new professional class works. Further, it is also the world of a whole new workforce, increasingly made up of immigrant and minori-tized citizens, who take on the functions once performed by the mother/wife in the older middle classes: the nannies, domestic cleaners, and dog walkers who service the households of the new professional class also hold jobs in the new globalized sectors of the economy. So do truck drivers and indus-trial service workers. Thus emerges an economic configuration very differ-ent from that suggested by the concept of *information economy*. We recover the material conditions, production sites, and place-boundedness that are also part of globalization and the information economy. To understand the new globalized economic sectors, we actually need detailed examinations of a broad range of activities, firms, markets, and physical infrastructures that go beyond the images of global electronic networks and the new globally circulating professional classes.

These types of detailed examinations allow us to see the actual role played by cities in a global economy. They help us understand why, when the new information technologies and telecommunications infrastructures were introduced on a large scale in all advanced industries beginning in the

1980s, we saw sharp growth in the central business districts of the leading cities and international business centers of the world—New York, Los Angeles, London, Tokyo, Paris, Frankfurt, São Paulo, Hong Kong, and Sydney, among others. For some cities, this era took off in the 1980s, and for others, in the 1990s and into the new century. But all experienced some of their highest growth in decades in the form of a vast expansion of the actual area covered by state-of-the-art office districts, high-end shopping, hotel, and entertainment districts, and high-income residential neighborhoods. The numbers of firms opening up in these downtown areas grew sharply.

These trends in major cities in the 1980s, 1990s, and onward go against what was expected according to models emphasizing territorial dispersal; this is especially true considering the high cost of locating a business enterprise in a major downtown area. Complicating the understanding of the new global economy and also often receiving most of the attention from the media and commentators was the fact that the departure of large commercial banks, insurance firms, and corporate headquarters was far more visible than the growth of smaller, highly specialized, and high-profit firms that was happening at the same time. This suggests that the growth trends were part of a new type of economic configuration. Thus, explaining the place of cities simply in terms of the departure of large corporate firms and the growing dispersal trends was evidently missing a key new component of the story.

But this still leaves us with the question, if information technologies have not made cities obsolete, have they at least altered the economic function of cities—have cities lost some of their old functions and gained new ones we could not quite understand when this new phase was taking off? And if this is so, what does it tell us about the importance of place and its far greater mix of diverse economic sectors and social groups than is suggested by the prevalent imagery of high-level corporate economic globalization and information flows? Is there a new and strategic role for major cities, a role linked to the formation of a truly global economic system, a role not sufficiently recognized by analysts and policymakers? And could it be that the reason this new and strategic role has not been sufficiently recognized is that economic globalization—what it actually takes to implement global markets and processes—is not only about massive dispersal of operations around the world but also about thick places?

The notion of a global economy has become deeply entrenched in political and media circles all around the world. Yet its dominant images—the instantaneous transmission of money around the globe, the information economy, the neutralization of distance through telematics—are partial, and hence profoundly inadequate, representations of what globalization and the rise of information economies actually entail for the concrete life of cities. Missing from this abstract model are the actual material processes, activities, and infrastructures crucial to the implementation of globalization. Overlooking the spatial dimension of economic globalization and overemphasizing the virtual information dimensions have served to distort the role played by major cities in the current phase of economic globalization.

A focus on cities almost inevitably brings with it recognition of the existence of multiple social groups, neighborhoods, contestations, claims, and inequalities. Yet this raises its own questions. Where does the global function of major cities begin, and where does it end? How do we establish what segments of the thick and complex environment of cities are part of the global? These issues are difficult to measure and determine with precision. But that does not mean that we can overlook them and simply focus on the economic core of advanced firms and the households of top-level professionals. We need to enter the diverse worlds of work and social contexts present in urban space, and we need to understand whether and how they are connected to the global functions that are partly structured in these cities. This requires using analytic tools and concepts that come from the scholarship on class and inequality, immigration, gendering, the politics of culture, and so on. These are scholarships not easily associated with the prevalent imagery about the information economy. At the same time, these kinds of inquiries also help us specify the question of globalization in more than its economic forms and contents. They help us specify the fact of multiple globalizations—economic, political, and cultural. Cities are good laboratories for these types of inquiries because they bring together vast mixes of people, institutions, and processes in ways that allow us to study them in great detail. Few, if any other places, contain such a mix of people and conditions and make their detailed study as possible as cities do.

One way of addressing the question of where the global begins and ends in this dense urban environment is to focus in detail on the multiple shapes and contents of globalization rather than assuming it consists of global firms and global professionals.

Beginning in the late 1970s and taking off in the mid-1980s, there have been pronounced changes in the geography, composition, and institutional framework of the world economy. Although cross-border flows of capital, trade, information, and people have existed for centuries, the world economy has been repeatedly reconstituted over time. A key starting point for this book is the fact that in each historical period, the world economy has consisted of a distinct configuration of geographic areas, industries, and institutional arrangements. One of the most important changes in the current phase has been the increase in the mobility of capital at both the national and especially the transnational levels. This transnational mobility of capital has brought about specific forms of articulation among different geographic areas and transformations in the role played by these areas in the world economy. This trend in turn has produced several types of locations for international transactions, the most familiar of which are export processing zones and offshore banking centers; these began to be developed in the late 1960s, precisely a time when national states exercised strong regulatory powers over their economies. One question for us is, then, the extent to which major cities are yet another type of *location* for international transactions in today's world economy, although clearly one at a very high level of complexity compared with those zones and centers.

A key focus in studies of the global economy has been the increased mobility of capital, particularly in the shape of the changing geographic organization of manufacturing production and the rapidly expanding number of financial markets becoming part of global networks. These are critical dimensions, and they emphasize the dispersal of firms and markets worldwide. What such studies leave out is the fact that this dispersal itself generates a demand for specific types of production needed to ensure the management, control, and servicing of this new organization of manufacturing and finance. These new types of production range from the development of telecommunications to specialized services—legal, accounting, insurance—that are key inputs for any firm managing a global network of factories, offices, and service outlets, and for any financial market operating globally. The mobility of capital also generates the production of a broad array of innovations in these sectors. These types of service production have their own locational patterns; they tend toward high levels of agglomeration in cities with the needed resources and talent pools. Thus, the fact itself that a manufacturing multinational firm produces its goods partly in export processing zones in ten, twenty, or even thirty countries creates a demand for new types of accounting, legal, and insurance services. It is these increasingly specialized and complex services that can benefit from the many state-of-the-art firms and experienced professionals concentrated in cities.

We will want to ask whether a focus on the *production* of these service inputs illuminates the question of place in processes of economic globalization, particularly the kind of place represented by cities. In fact, specialized services for firms and financial transactions, as well as the complex markets connected to these economic sectors, are a layer of activity that has been central to the organization of major global processes beginning in the 1980s. To what extent is it useful to add the broader category of cities as key production sites for such services for firms to the list of recognized global spaces, that is, headquarters of transnational corporations, export processing zones, and offshore banking centers? These are all more narrowly defined locations compared with cities. But I show in this book that to further our understanding of major aspects of the world economy's organization and management, we cannot confine our analysis to these narrow and self-evident "global" locations. We need to enter and explore the more complex space where multiple economies and work cultures come together to produce the complex organizational and management infrastructure necessary to handle the running of global operations. Further, we need to understand the new types of tensions, segmentations, and inequalities that are generated in this process and become visible in the space of the city.

However, this way of thinking about cities as a site for empirical research about economic, political, and cultural globalization has tended to fall between the cracks of existing scholarship. On the one hand, much of the research on cities focuses on internal social, economic, and political conditions, and it views cities as parts of national urban systems. International matters have typically been considered the preserve of nation-states, not of cities. On the other hand, the literature on international economic activities has traditionally focused on the activities of multinational corporations and banks and has seen the key to globalization in the *power* of multinational firms and the new telecommunications capabilities. This leaves no room for a possible role for cities. Finally, the scholarship on international relations has confined itself to a focus on states as the key actors in the global realm.

All of these approaches contain much useful and important empirical and analytical material. But they are not enough to allow us to understand cities as strategic global sites. Twenty years of empirical and theoretical struggles by a small but growing number of researchers from many parts of the world have now produced a novel type of scholarship that gets precisely at this issue. Usually referred to as the *world cities* or *global city* scholarship, it provides many of the materials examined and discussed in this book.

Including cities in the analysis adds three important dimensions to the study of globalization. First, it breaks down the nation-state into a variety of components and thereby allows us to establish whether and how, some of these components are articulated with global processes, and others are not at all. Second, our focus is not only on the power of large corporations over governments and economies but also on the range of activities and organizational arrangements necessary for the implementation and maintenance of a global network of factories, service operations, and markets; these are all processes only partly encompassed by the activities of transnational corporations and banks. Third, it contributes to a focus on place and on the urban social and political order associated with these activities. Processes of economic globalization are thereby reconstituted as concrete production complexes situated in specific places containing a multiplicity of activities and interests, many unconnected to global processes. As with other production complexes—mines, factories, transport hubs—the narrowly economic aspects are only one, even if crucial, component. The organization of labor markets, their gendering, new inequalities, and local politics can variously be part of this new urban production complex. Including these dimensions allows us to specify the micro-geographies and politics unfolding within these sites places. Finally, focusing on cities allows us to specify a variety of transnational geographies that connect specific groups of cities—depending on economic activity, migration flows, and the like.

Bringing all of these elements together is a central thesis organizing this book: Since the 1980s, major transformations in the composition of the world economy, including the sharp growth of specialized services for firms and finance, have renewed the importance of major cities as sites for producing strategic global inputs. In the current phase of the world economy, it is precisely the combination of, on the one hand, the global dispersal of factories, offices, and service outlets, *and* on the other, global information integration—under conditions of continued concentration of economic ownership and control—that has contributed to a strategic role for certain major cities. These I call *global cities* (Sassen [1991] 2001), of which there are by now about seventy worldwide, covering a broad variety of specialized roles in today's global economy. Some of these, such as London, Amsterdam, Mumbai, and Shanghai, have been centers for world trade and banking for centuries. Others have not, notably São Paulo, Singapore, Chicago, and Los Angeles. Today's global cities are (1) command points in the organization of the world economy, (2) key locations and marketplaces for the leading industries of the current period—finance and specialized services for firms, and (3) major sites of *production*, including the production of innovations, for these industries as their products are not simply a function of talent but are made. Several cities also fulfill equivalent functions on the smaller geographic scales of both trans- and subnational regions. Furthermore, whether at the global or the regional level, these cities must inevitably engage each other in fulfilling their functions, as the new forms of growth in these cities partly result from the proliferation of inter-urban networks. There is no such entity as a single global city.

Once we focus on places, whether cities or other types of places, rather than whole national economies, we can easily take account of the fact that some places even in the richest countries are becoming poorer, or that a global city in a developing country can become richer even as the rest of the country becomes poorer. An analysis of places rather than national indicators produces a highly variable mosaic of results. Alongside these new global and regional hierarchies of cities lies a vast territory that has become increasingly peripheral and is excluded from the major processes that fuel economic growth in the new global economy. Many formerly important manufacturing centers and port cities have lost functions and are in decline, not only in the less developed countries but also in the most advanced economies.[1] This is yet another meaning of economic globalization. We can think of these developments as constituting new geographies of centrality that cut across the old divide of poor versus rich countries, or, as in my preferred usage in this book, the global South versus global North divide. But there are also new geographies of marginality cutting across the poor–rich country divide, as growing numbers of people in global cities of both the north and the south are now poorer and work in casual rather than unionized jobs.

The most powerful of these new geographies of centrality binds together the major international financial and business centers: New York, London, Tokyo, Paris, Frankfurt, Chicago, Seoul, Hong Kong, Shanghai, São Paulo, Mumbai, Zurich, Amsterdam, Sydney, and Toronto, among others. But this geography now also includes cities such as Buenos Aires, Shenzen, Kuala Lumpur, Istanbul, and Budapest. The intensity of transactions among these cities, particularly through financial markets, flows of services, and investment, has increased sharply, and so have the orders of magnitude involved. At the same time, there has been a sharpening inequality in the concentration of strategic resources and activities between each of these cities and others in their respective countries. For example, Paris now concentrates a larger share of leading economic sectors and wealth in France than it did as recently as 1980, whereas Marseilles, once a major economic center, has lost some of its share in France's economy. Frankfurt's financial center has gained sharply over the other six financial centers in Germany; given the rather decentralized political organization of this country, we might have expected to see multiple equally strong financial centers. Some national capitals, for example, have lost central economic functions and power to the new global cities, which have taken over some of the coordination functions, markets, and production processes once concentrated in national capitals or in major regional centers. A case in point, São Paulo has gained immense strength as a business and financial center in Brazil over Rio de

Janeiro—once the capital and most important city in the country—and over the once powerful axis represented by Rio and Brasilia, the current capital. This is one of the consequences of the formation of a globally integrated economic system.

These economic dynamics are partly constituted in social and cultural terms. For example, foreign or native migrant workforces supply the new types of professional households with nannies and cleaners; these same migrants also bring cultural practices that add to a city's life, and they bring political experiences that can help with union organizing. Further, the new economic dynamics have often sharp and visible effects on urban space, notably the expansion of luxury housing and office districts at the cost of displacing lower-income households and low-profit firms. The city brings together and makes legible the enormous variety of globalities that are emerging and the many different forms—social, cultural, spatial—they assume.

More generally, what is the impact of this type of economic growth on the broader social and economic order of these cities? Much earlier research on the impact of dynamic, high-growth manufacturing sectors in developed and developing countries shows that these sectors raised wages, reduced economic inequality, and contributed to the formation and expansion of a middle class. There is less research on the distributive outcomes of the new economic sectors that dominate global cities, partly because these are still relatively new processes. But the available evidence does show much more inequality than that associated with dynamic manufacturing-based economies. Indeed, much of the new prosperity in China originated from the rapid growth of manufacturing.

These somewhat hidden features of the globalized core in complex cities become legible when we emphasize the material conditions for and the work of producing the specialized services that are a key component of all such cities. It means, as indicated earlier, bringing into the analysis nonprofessional workers and work cultures: for example, bringing in the truckers that deliver the software, not only the high-level professionals that use it. Such an emphasis is not typical in research on these specialized services; they are usually seen as a type of output: high-level technical expertise. Thus, insufficient attention has gone to the actual array of jobs, from high paying to low paying, involved in the production of even the most sophisticated and complex services. A focus on production displaces the emphasis from expertise to work. Services need to be produced, and the buildings that hold the workers need to be built and cleaned. The rapid growth of the financial industry and of highly specialized services generates not only high-level technical and administrative jobs but also low-wage unskilled jobs.

This is one type of inequality we are seeing within cities, especially within global cities. Since this same inequality is also evident in global cities of developing and even poor countries, it contributes to the formation of new geographies of centrality and marginality that cut across the North–South divide and exclude the increasing numbers of poor in both the North and the South.

This new urban economy is in many ways highly problematic, particularly in global cities, where it assumes its sharpest forms given the large concentrations of high-profit firms and high-income households. The new growth sectors of specialized services and finance contain capabilities for profit making vastly superior to those of more traditional economic sectors. Many of these more traditional sectors remain essential for the operation of the urban economy, including the new globalized core, and for the daily needs of residents, but their survival is threatened in a situation in which finance and specialized services can earn super-profits. This sharp polarization in the profit-making capabilities of different sectors of the economy has always existed. But today it is much sharper, and it is engendering massive distortions in the operations of various markets, from housing to labor. We can see this effect, for example, in the unusually sharp increase in the earnings of high-level professionals in the corporate sector and in the falling or stagnating wages of low-skilled manual and clerical workers. We saw the same effect in the retreat of many real estate developers from the low- and medium-income housing market in the 1980s and 1990s as the rapidly expanding demand for housing by the new highly paid professionals rose and delivered higher profits through overpricing. These trends are all evident in cities as diverse as New York and Dublin, Oslo and São Paulo, Shanghai and Istanbul.

The rapid development of an international property market has made this disparity even worse. It means that real estate prices at the center of New York City are more connected to prices in central London or Frankfurt than to the overall real estate market in New York's metropolitan area. In the 1980s, powerful institutional investors from Japan, for example, found it profitable to buy and sell property in Manhattan or central London. In the 1990s, this practice multiplied, involving a rapidly growing number of cities around the world. German, Dutch, French, and US firms invested heavily in properties in central London and in other major cities. Increasingly, the city itself became the object of investment. And even after the attacks of September 2001 and the financial crisis of 2008, New York City real estate has been bought by a growing number of foreign investors, partly due to the weak dollar, which made these acquisitions profitable. These practices generally forced prices up because of the competition among very powerful and rich investors and buyers. Because much of the purpose was to sell at a profit rather than actually to use the property, it further raised prices. How can a low- or medium-profit local commercial operation compete with such powerful investors for space and other resources, no matter how long and successful its record in the older economy?

The high profit-making capability of the new growth sectors, of which finance is emblematic, rests partly on speculative activity. The extent of this dependence on speculation can be seen in the regular crises in many developed countries. Notable is the crisis in the late 1980s and early 1990s that followed the unusually high profits in finance and real estate in the 1980s. That real estate and financial crisis, however, left the basic dynamic of the sector untouched, and we saw prices and stock market values reach new highs by the mid-1990s—only to have yet another crisis in 1997–98, though by then most of the highly developed countries had learned how to protect themselves, and the costs of the crisis were largely borne by countries that had been considered emerging markets for financial investments. As had happened before, this crisis was followed by enormous increases in profits, only to be followed by yet another series of crises in the 2000s, culminating in the massive crisis of 2008. These crises do generate a temporary adjustment to more reasonable (i.e., less speculative) profit levels, but for only brief periods of time. The overall dynamic of polarization in profit levels in the urban economy remains in place across these various crises, as do the distortions in many markets, well illustrated by super-profits in finance and simultaneous massive unemployment in most global North economies.

The typical informed view about the global economy, cities, and the new growth sectors does not incorporate the multiple dimensions examined in this book. Elsewhere, I have argued that the dominant narrative or mainstream account about economic globalization is a narrative of eviction (Sassen 1996). In the dominant account, the key concepts—globalization, information economy, and high-level professional outputs—all suggest that place no longer matters and that the only type of worker that matters is the highly educated one. That account favors (1) the capability for global transmission over the concentrations of material infrastructure necessary to make that transmission possible; (2) information outputs over the workers producing those outputs, whether they be specialists or secretaries; and (3) the new transnational corporate culture over the multiplicity of cultural environments, including reterritorialized immigrant cultures within which many of the *other* jobs of the global information economy take place. In brief, the dominant narrative concerns itself with the upper circuits of capital, not the lower ones, and with the fact of hyper upward mobility while ignoring downward mobility and deepening inequalities.

This narrow focus in the mainstream account has the effect of excluding the *place*-boundedness of significant components of the global information economy; it thereby also excludes a whole array of activities and types of workers from the story of globalization that in their own way are as vital to that story as are international finance and global telecommunications. Failing to include those activities and workers ignores the variety of cultural contexts within which the advanced sectors function. That diversity is as present in processes of globalization as is the new global corporate culture. When we focus on place and production, we can see that globalization is a process involving the corporate side and the immigrant economies and work cultures, the new importance of craftworkers, the cultural sector, and global tourism evident in global cities. And all these sectors include lowly paid workers and low-profit-making firms.

These new empirical trends and theoretical developments are making the study of cities prominent once again for a growing number of social scientists and cultural theorists. Cities have re-emerged not only as objects of study but also as a lens for research and theorization on a broad array of major social, cultural, economic, technological, and political processes central to the current era: (1) economic globalization and international migration, (2) the emergence of specialized services and finance as the leading growth sector in advanced economies, (3) new types of inequality, (4) the new politics of identity and culture, (5) new types of politically and ideologically radicalizing dynamics, (6) the urbanizing of a broad range of high-technology systems, and (7) the politics of space, notably the growing movement for claiming rights to the city.

Many of these processes are not urban per se, but they have an urban moment; in many cases, the urban moment has become increasingly important and/or capable of illuminating key features of the larger process involved. In this context, it is worth noting that we are also seeing the beginning of a repositioning of cities in policy arenas. Two instances of this recent trend stand out in particular. One is the programmatic effort to develop analyses that can show how important urban economic productivity is to macroeconomic performance; in the past, economic growth was measured simply in terms of overall national and regional indicators. The other is the explicit effort by the leadership of a growing number of cities to bypass national states and gain direct access to global investment and tourism markets as well as to recruit firms, cultural projects (such as international festivals and science exhibitions), sports events, and conventions. The mayors of a growing number of cities worldwide have set up offices for foreign economic affairs in multiple countries and appear increasingly interested in dealing directly with the mayors, firms, and cultural institutions of other countries.

The subject of the city in a world economy is extremely broad. The body of literature on cities is enormous, but it focuses mostly on single cities and on domestic issues; further, international studies of cities have leaned toward the comparative. Lacking until recently was a transnational perspective on the subject: that is to say, one that takes as its starting point a dynamic system or set of transactions that by their nature entail multiple locations involving more than one country. This contrasts with a comparative international approach, which focuses on two or more cities that may have no connections to each other.

This book focuses particularly on recent empirical and conceptual developments because they are an expression of major changes in urban and national economies and in modes of inquiry about cities. Such a choice is inevitably limited and certainly cannot account for the many cities in the world that may *not* have experienced any of these developments. This book's focus on the urban impact of economic, political, and cultural globalization; the new inequalities among and within cities; and the new urban socio-spatial order is justified by the major characteristics of the current historical period and the need for social scientists to address these changes.

Chapter 2 examines the key characteristics of the global economy that matter for an understanding of globalization and cities. In many cities, these global presences are weak or nonexistent. But they are becoming increasingly strong in a growing number of cities. Understood as tendencies, they reveal new formations and indicate future trends. Chapter 3 analyzes the new interurban inequalities, focusing on three key issues: (1) the diversity of urbanization patterns across continents, (2) the impact of globalization, particularly the internationalization of production and the growth of tourism, on so-called primate urban systems in less developed countries, (3) the impact of economic globalization on so-called balanced urban systems, and (4) the possible formation of transnational urban systems, including the emergence of hundreds of cities across the world with significant immigrant populations. Chapter 4 focuses on the new urban economy, where finance and specialized services have emerged as driving engines for profit-making. One important aspect examined in this chapter is the sharp increase in the linkages binding cities that function as production sites and marketplaces for global capital. Chapter 5 explores these issues in greater detail through case studies of the turning point that led some cities into global city status from the 1980s to the 1990s. It further examines a more recent set of turning points in the 2000s, illustrated through very diverse cases: Hong Kong and Shanghai, the Gulf city-states, and the repositioning of a 3,000-year-old imperial capital, Istanbul, in the re-emerging global East–West axis. Chapter 6 focuses on new urban social forms resulting from growing inequalities and segmentations in labor markets and urban space. The effort here is to understand whether the changes documented in this book are merely a quantitative transformation or also a qualitative one. Is it simply a matter of more poor and more inequality, or are we seeing emerging types of poverty and inequality that constitute new social forms? Chapter 7 takes one particular case as a lens to get at a more detailed and focused account of the issues introduced in Chapter 6: women immigrants who increasingly constitute global care-chains as they become the nannies, nurses, maids, and sex workers in global cities. Chapter 8 considers the larger transnational social, cultural, and political dynamics that are becoming mobilized through the variety of processes examined in this book.

Note

1   The city of Detroit, Michigan, once a hub of automobile manufacturing and now in economic decline, is one prime example.

2

The Urban Impact
of Economic Globalization

Profound changes in the composition, geography, and institutional framework of the world economy over the centuries have had major implications for cities. In the 1800s, when the world economy consisted largely of extracting natural resources and trade, the global function of cities was as servicing centers, typically developed alongside harbors. Then as now, trading companies depended on multiple industrial, banking, and other commercial services located in cities. Many of the major cities in the colonial empires of Britain, the Netherlands, France, Germany, Spain, and Portugal were international gateways. Yet, cities were not the key production sites for the leading industries in the 1800s; they were centers for administration and commerce. The material production that fed the wealth-making circuits, notably trade, was centered in harbors, plantations, factories, and mines.

Today's global economy still consists of international trade, agribusiness, manufacturing, and extraction of natural resources, but these have all been overshadowed, both in value and in power, by the development of vast global financial markets as well as a proliferation of global markets for highly specialized corporate services. These markets are today's leading wealth-making circuits, and they have subjected material production to their logics; for instance, gold is no longer simply traded as metal but is today also traded through a series of financial instruments. In the 1980s, finance and services generally emerged as the major components of international transactions: They service all the other components of the global economy; thus, as the global economy grows, so does the value of finance and services. Further, finance has invented its own wealth-producing markets, as have some of the specialized services, such as consulting services of various kinds. The shift to electronic financial markets and the lifting of national barriers to capital flows, both features taking off in the late 1980s, allowed finance to reach values that dwarfed those of other major components of the global economy. Thus, by the end of 2004, the value of global trade stood at US$1 trillion, compared with US$262 trillion for global finance—as measured through the value of traded derivatives. By 2008, the value of finance had jumped to US$600 trillion, further lengthening the distance between its value and the value of trade.

The crucial sites for financial and services transactions are financial markets, advanced corporate service firms, banks, and the headquarters of transnational corporations (TNCs). Today, it is these sites that lie at the heart of the global economy rather than mines, factories, and plantations; in fact, the latter are increasingly subordinated to the logic of financial profit and shareholder value. The most specialized and least routinized of these markets and firms are disproportionately concentrated in global cities and constitute key components of what I have conceptualized as the "global city production function." Thus, one of the variables influencing the role of cities in the new global economy is the composition of international transactions. Although standard analyses of the world economy focus in great detail on these transactions, they do not pick up on their spatial correlates and hence on the significance of cities in the global economy. It took the scholarship on global cities and world cities to arrive at this conceptualization.

In the first half of this chapter, I present a somewhat detailed account of today's geography, composition, and institutional framework of the global economy with an eye to capturing the implications for cities. In the second half, I focus on two types of strategic places for international financial and service transactions: global cities and offshore banking centers. Finally, I consider the impact of the collapse of the Pax Americana on the world economy and the subsequent shift in the geography of international transactions from the North–South axis of much of the twentieth century to an increasingly East–West axis. To this should be added China's recent development of a new transversal axis, best illustrated through massive investments in Africa, ranging from enormous acquisitions of land to the building of large-scale infrastructures—notably roads and ports.

The Global Economy Today

The emphasis here is on new investment patterns and the major features of the current period. The purpose is not to present an exhaustive account of all that constitutes the world economy today. It is rather to discuss what distinguishes the current period from the immediate past. Trade and primary industries, the dominant sectors of the prior hundred-plus years of the world economy, were rapidly outdistanced in the 1980s and onward by finance, foreign direct investment, and specialized services for firms. Besides the already cited sharper growth of the value of financial transactions compared to that of trade, foreign direct investment (FDI) grew three times faster in the 1980s than the export trade. By the mid-1980s, investment in services had become the main component in FDI flows, whereas before most of the FDI flows were for manufacturing and raw materials extraction. From 1990 through 2007, the services and manufacturing sectors comprised approximately 90% of FDI stock worldwide, but with increasingly diverging shares: that of services grew from approximately 48% to 64%, while that of manufacturing fell from approximately 41% to 27%. The numbers are even more striking for developing economies (see Exhibit A.2.3), though by the end of 2000s, investments in mining, land, and oil rose sharply and investments in manufacturing mostly fell (see Exhibit A.2.4), especially in Africa.

Geography

Geography is a key empirical feature of the world economy regardless of the century or what empire dominates. It depends on multiple factors ranging from the number of competing empires to the composition of global transactions. When international flows consist of raw materials, agricultural products, or mining goods, the geography of transactions is in part determined by the location of natural resources. Historically, this has meant that a large number of countries in Africa, Latin America, and the Caribbean were key sites in this geography. When finance and specialized services became the dominant component of international transactions in the early 1980s, the role of many of these areas declined in importance and that of financial and service centers increased, even though much of finance consists of instruments that are a financial version of those goods.

Compared with the 1950s, the 1980s saw an increase in the values but a narrowing in the geography of the global economy. The result was a strengthened East–West axis with a sharp growth of investment and trade within what at the time was referred to as *the triad:* the United States, Western Europe, and Japan. In contrast, developing countries lost share in overall international investment in the 1980s even as absolute values rose; as a group, though not individually, these countries had regained their share by the mid-1990s but typically through novel articulations with the world economy.

The fact of a new geography of international transactions becomes evident in FDI flows—that is, investors acquiring a firm, wholly or in part, or building and setting up new firms in a foreign country (see UNCTAD 1992; 2009b for a full definition). Recently, extreme forms of foreign direct investment have involved direct large-scale land acquisitions by corporations and governments—for growing food, for accessing water supplies, and for extracting so-called "rare earths," critical metals for our electronic revolution (see generally Exhibits 2.4 and 2.5; Sassen 2010). This accelerated search for resources has reactivated a North–South flow, but one that is different from the old European and American colonial empires. As already indicated, China leads in these investments and does so through a transversal global geography that bypasses the old centers of power in the west.

Notwithstanding these realignments, foreign direct investment flows remain highly differentiated in their destination because they consist of a vast number of individual investments in all economic sectors and through a large number of firms and government. These investment flows can be constituted through many different kinds of economic processes, a subject I discuss throughout this book. Thus, in the 1980s and 1990s, the growth in FDI took place through the internationalization of production of goods and services and of portfolio investment (buying firms). In the late 1990s and up to the late 2000s, it is services, the globalization of finance, and the financializing of more and more economic sectors that is the dominant pattern. One clear trend is the sharp and ongoing growth of FDI up to the financial and economic crisis that took off in 2008. Worldwide FDI inflows went from US$638 billion for the period 1985–90 to US$1.7 trillion for 1990–94, then rose further to US$4.1 trillion for 2000–04 and began to fall after 2007 down to US$1.7 trillion in 2008 (see Exhibit A.2.1). Investment in the tertiary sector grew consistently over this period (see Exhibit A.2.2).

The geography of FDI shows clearly that by far the largest share of FDI went and continues to go to developed countries, with an average annual growth of 24% from 1986 to 1990, reaching a value of US$129.6 billion in 1991, out of a total worldwide FDI inflow of US$159.3 billion, and rising to US$1.1 trillion in 2000 out of a world total of US$1.38 trillion. From 2005–08, the developed world received 63.93% of FDI inflows (see Exhibits A.2.1 and A.2.2). On average, the share of developed countries has hovered around 70%, albeit with fluctuations across the years; this is also reflected in the cumulative FDI stock of developed

Exhibit 2.1   Foreign Direct Investment Inflows by Sector, 1989–1991 and
2005–2007

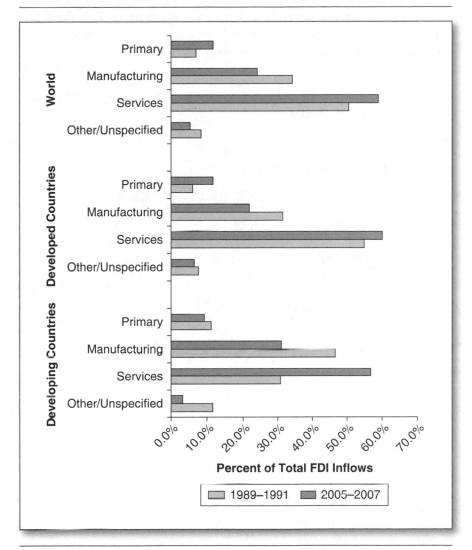

Source: Compiled from data in UNCTAD (2009b): 220–21.

countries (see Exhibits A.2.3 and A.2.4). There was sharp concentration in
the destination of flows even among developed countries. Four countries
tend to be the major capital importing and exporting countries (United
States, United Kingdom, France, and Germany); together, they account for
about half of world inflows and outflows. Financial concentration across

these decades is also evident in a ranking of the top banks in the world, with only eight countries represented (see Exhibits 2.3 and A.2.5; see also Chapter 5). The rise of China as an investor will not necessarily alter these rankings, even as it develops its own North–South investment axis, with Africa and South America as key destinations.

Exhibit 2.2   Foreign Direct Investment Outflows by Sector, 1989–1991 and 2005–2007

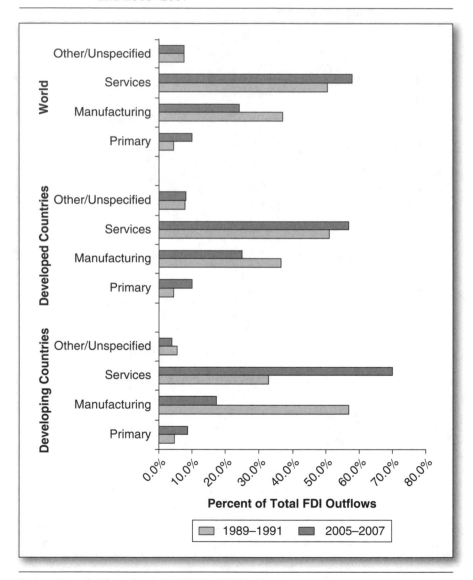

Source: Compiled from data in UNCTAD (2009b): 220–21.

Exhibit 2.3 Cities Ranked by Revenues of the World's Largest Commercial and Savings Banks, 2005 and 2009 (US$ millions)

Rank	City	Number of Firms	Revenues	Profits
1	Paris	4	189,294	16,850
2	New York	2	165,207	21,512
3	London	3	140,822	22,264
4	Frankfurt	4	121,615	4,450
5	Brussels	3	120,211	7,796
6	Zurich	2	115,743	11,039
7	Edinburgh	2	107,506	13,868
8	Charlotte	2	91,391	19,357
9	Tokyo	3	86,055	6,808
10	Beijing	4	75,738	8,896
11 to 21		27	517,801	47,272
Total:	—	56	1,731,383	180,112

2009 (US$ millions)

Rank	City	Number of Firms	Revenues	Profits
1	Paris	5	427,190	12,061
2	New York	5	361,581	−15,351
3	Brussels	2	299,043	3,646
4	London	4	272,818	18,673
5	Beijing	4	227,925	45,939
6	Amsterdam	1	226,577	−1,067
7	Frankfurt	4	188,991	−11,269
8	Edinburgh	2	175,488	−56,918
9	Tokyo	3	126,862	−12,136
10	Madrid	1	117,803	12,992
11 to 20		16	762,400	28,930
Total:	—	47	3,186,677	25,500

Source: Calculations based on "Global 500" (2005) and "Global 500" (2009).

The growth of investment flows into developing countries in the 1990s did not even come near the levels for developed countries, but it did represent a historic high—a fact that reflects the growing internationalization of economic activity generally (see Exhibits A.2.1 to A.2.4). From 1985 to 1990, FDI grew at an annual rate of 22% compared with 3% from 1980 to 1984 and 13% from 1975 to 1979. Yet the share of worldwide flows going to developing countries as a whole fell from 32.23% to 17.7% between the early 1980s and the late 1980s, pointing to the strength of flows within the triad (United States, Western Europe, and Japan). From 1992 to 1997, the average share grew to 38% of world inflows before falling again with the Asian financial crisis of 1997–98. After a low of 18% of world inflows, the share of developing countries was up to 36.57% in 2008. (Exhibits A.2.1 to A.2.4)

When the flows to developing countries are disaggregated for the 1980s and 1990s, it becomes clear that they went mostly into East, South, and Southeast Asia, where the annual growth rate on average was about 37% a year in the 1980s and 1990s. These figures point to the emergence of this Asian region as a crucial transnational space for production; in the 1980s, it surpassed Latin America and the Caribbean for the first time ever as the largest host region for FDI in developing countries. This is also evident in the dominance of China as a capital-receiving country: it has the largest number of affiliates of global firms (see Exhibit A.2.6). There was a time when Latin America was the single largest recipient region of FDI. But the 1980s marked the end of that phase. Between 1985 and 1989, Latin America's share of total flows to developing countries fell from 49% to 38%, and Southeast Asia's rose from 37% to 48%. However, the absolute increase in FDI has been so large that, even with a falling share, Latin America had considerable increases in the amount of FDI, especially toward the end of the 1980s and in the 1990s. But again, when the flows to Latin America are disaggregated, we see that most investment went to Brazil, Argentina, and Chile (see Exhibit 3.5 on p. 69).

One rapidly growing component of foreign direct investment by rich country governments and firms is land. More than thirty million hectares have been bought or leased since 2006 by foreign governments and firms. (See generally Exhibits 2.4 and 2.5.) While the old empires already were in the business of buying and appropriating land, the post-2006 patterns are, in my view, a new phase in this old practice (Sassen 2010). The world is today divided into sovereign states, which, at least nominally, have authority over their land. This has meant complex contractual arrangements because it is not that simple for one state to buy land from another state (Sassen 2008a: chap. 5; 2010). Africa is a major destination for these investments, but so are Russia, Ukraine, and Latin America. Buyers are governments (as diverse as Sweden, South Korea, or China) and global firms (mining firms, food growers, financial firms). In short, FDI is growing in both scale and scope.

The other two major components of the global economy are trade and financial flows other than FDI. By its very nature, the geography of trade is less concentrated than that of direct foreign investment—wherever there are buyers, sellers are likely to go. Finance, on the other hand, is enormously concentrated, as I show in Chapters 4 and 5.

Composition

In the 1950s, the major international flow was world trade, especially of raw materials, other primary products, and resource-based manufacturing. In the 1980s, the gap between the values mobilized through trade and those mobilized through financial flows began to widen sharply, as I described earlier. Notwithstanding severe measurement problems, it is clear that the value reached by financial transactions dwarfs that of other flows. Finally, within FDI stock and flows, the tertiary sector raised its share over that of primary and secondary sector investments, reaching about sixty of global FDI inflows and outflows (see Exhibit A.2.4).

Many factors feed the composition of international transactions. For example, in the 1980s, (1) several developed countries became major capital exporters, most notably Japan; (2) the number of cross-border mergers and acquisitions grew sharply; and (3) the flow of services and transnational service corporations emerged as major components in the world economy. Services, which accounted for about 24% of worldwide stock in FDI in the early 1970s, had grown to 50% of stock and 60% of annual flows by the end of the 1980s. The single largest recipient of FDI in services in the 1980s was the European Community, yet another indication of a very distinct geography in world transactions (UNCTAD 2009b:219–20). But investment in services also increased in absolute terms for developing countries. In the 1990s and into the early years of the twenty-first century, the second and third trends continued to shape the global economy. Services accounted for 60% of FDI inflows to developed countries by 2005–07. Mergers and acquisitions took off in the European Union and most recently in some of the most developed Asian countries, especially after the 1997–98 financial crisis. As for the first trend identified for the 1980s, the role of developed countries as the major capital exporters, it continues, including for Japan, which remains probably the leading exporter of capital; what is different is the absence of any new major capital exporter among the developed

Exhibit 2.4   Land Investments to Secure Food Supplies, Select Cases 2006–2009

Country Investor	Country Target	Plot Size (hectares)
Bahrain	Philippines	10,000
China (with private entities)	Philippines	1,240,000
China (ZTE International)	D.R. Congo	2,800,000
China (Chongqing Seed Corp.)	Tanzania	300
China	Zambia	2,000,000
Jordan	Sudan	25,000
Libya	Ukraine	250,000
Libya	Mali	100,000
Qatar	Kenya	40,000
Qatar	Philippines	100,000
Saudi Arabia	Tanzania	500,000
Saudi Arabia (Hail Agricultural Dev. Co.)	Sudan	10,117
Saudi Arabia (Bin Laden Group)	Indonesia	500,000
South Korea (with private entities)	Sudan	690,000
United Arab Emirates (Abraaj Capital)	Pakistan	324,000
United Arab Emirates	Sudan	378,000
Vietnam	Cambodia	100,000
Vietnam	Laos	100,000

Source: IFPRI "Land Grabbing" by Foreign Investors in Developing Countries: Risks and Opportunities, April 2009. http://www.ifpri.org/sites/default/files/publications/bp013all.pdf.

countries and the rise of China as an investor, including a buyer of US government debt (Treasury bonds); by 2005, China was the second largest owner of dollars in the world after Japan, and today it is the largest.

Another major transformation beginning in the 1980s and continuing today is the sharp growth in the numbers and economic weight of transnational corporations (TNCs) firms that operate in more than one country

Exhibit 2.5   Farmland Acquired by Selected Investors, 2006–2009 (in hectares)

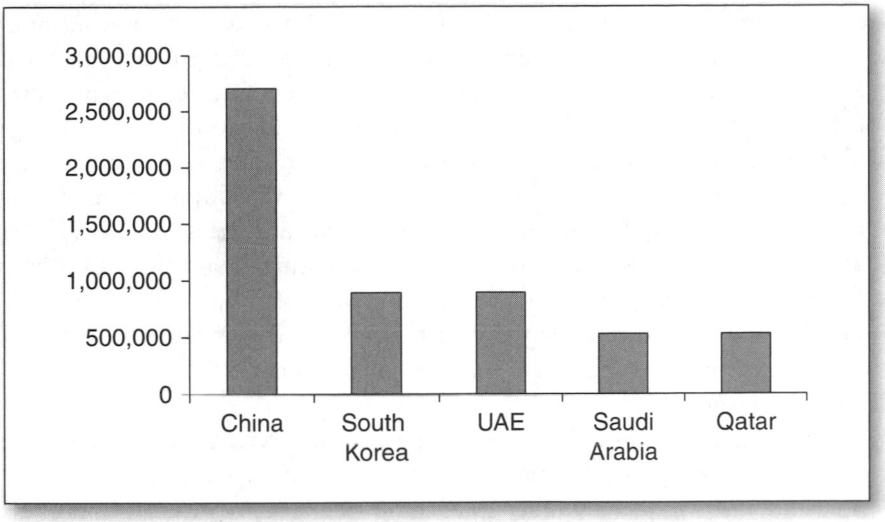

Source: Graph by IFPRI, obtained from "Buying farmland abroad: outsourcing's third wave," a news report published by *The Economist,* May 21, 2009, http://www.economist.com/world/international/displaystory.cfm?story_id=13692889.

through affiliates, subsidiaries, or other arrangements. This invites us to rethink the meaning of the "market" for global trade, since so much of it is actually managed by TNCs. The central role played by TNCs is illustrated by the fact that 80% of US international trade in the late 1980s was in the hands of US and foreign TNCs (UNCTC 1991, chap. 3). By 1997, global sales generated by foreign affiliates of TNCs were valued at US$9.5 trillion, larger than the US$7.4 trillion of global trade, of which one-third was itself intrafirm trade (UNCTAD 1998). By 2008, all these figures had grown, signaling the ongoing weight of TNCs and their affiliates and other forms of subcontracting in global trade. And this role keeps expanding. One important example is the recent growth of defense contracting by TNCs: in 2009, TNC employees and subcontractors made up 53% of the American Department of Defense workforce in Iraq and Afghanistan (Schwartz 2009).

Institutional Framework

How does the *world economy* cohere as a system? We cannot take the world economy for granted and assume that it exists simply because international transactions do. One question raised by the developments described earlier is whether today's global economic activities represent a mere quantitative change or actually entail a different international configuration, including changes in the regimes governing the world economy. Elsewhere, I have argued that the ascendance of international finance and services produced a new type of world economy with deregulation regimes that often have sharply negative effects on other industries, especially manufacturing, and on regional development insofar as regions tend to be dominated by nonfinancial industries (Sassen [1991] 2001, part 1; 2008a: chap. 5). These are structural conditions that lead to particular conceptions about how to govern and how to ensure profitability for certain sectors; the effect has been to privilege the needs of certain sectors, notably high finance, over others, such as traditional manufacturing.

One consequence of this new regime is that TNCs have become even more central to the organization and governance of the world economy, and new and vastly expanded older financial exchanges are now an important element in the institutional framework. In addition to financing huge government deficits, the financial firms and exchanges largely serve the needs of TNCs. These in turn emerged as a source of financial flows to developing countries, both through FDI and indirectly because FDI stimulates other forms of financial flows. In some respects, TNCs replaced the traditional transnational banks.[1] The bank crisis of 1982 sharply cut traditional bank loans to developing countries, with more financial resources leaving the region than coming in during much of the 1980s. For better or for worse, TNCs and new types of global financial firms and exchanges stepped into the picture and became strategic organizers of what we now call the global economy.

Affiliates of TNCs and other contracting arrangements have become a key mechanism for organizing and governing the globalization of production and the delivery of services. The growth in their numbers has been sharp (see Exhibit A.2.6). From a world total of 174,900 in 1990, the number of affiliates reached 807,363 by 2008. Partly reflecting the massive FDI flows among developed countries, the number of affiliates in developed countries grew from 81,800 in 1990 to 96,620 in 1996 and 366,881 in 2008. The United States, the United Kingdom, France, Germany, and Japan were the developed countries with the largest numbers. But by far the largest numbers of affiliates are in developing countries, because they are a mechanism for TNCs to access global South markets and resources and to outsource jobs to low-age areas. Their number went from 71,300 in 1990 to 580,638 in 2003. This number fell to 425,258 in 2008 due to the crisis, but above all due to the growing number of foreign firms setting up headquarter offices rather than merely working through affiliates. Not surprisingly, the largest single concentration is in China, with 16,000 in 1989 to 424,196 in 2002. By 2007, this number was down to 286,232, in good part because the number of foreign firms with headquarter offices in China had risen from 350 in 2002 to 3,429 in 2007. A third area of sharp growth is Central and Eastern Europe, where the total went from 21,000 affiliates in 1990 to 243,750 in 2003, followed by declines in 2008.

Global financial exchanges have emerged as yet another crucial institution for organizing and governing the world economy (see Exhibits 2.6 to 2.8). The central role of financial markets, a key component of the world economy today, was in part brought about by the so-called third-world bank crisis which was formally declared in 1982. This was a crisis for the major transnational banks in the United States, with their massive loans to third-world countries and firms that failed to be repaid. The crisis created a space that small, highly competitive financial firms, which were far less subject to regulation than the traditional transnational banks, moved into. This launched a whole new era in the 1980s in financial speculation, innovation, and levels of profitability. The result was a highly unstable period but one with almost inconceivably high levels of profits that fed a massive expansion in the volume of international financial transactions. Deregulation was another key mechanism facilitating this type of growth, centered in internationalization and speculation, as it opened up one country after another to these and other firms. Markets provided an institutional framework that organized these massive financial flows. Notwithstanding two financial crises, one in 1990–91 and the second in 1997–98, the end of the 1990s saw a steep growth in the value of financial transactions. And although the terrorist attacks of September 2001 in New York City created a temporary crisis, by the end of 2001, stock market capitalization had reached the levels it had attained before September 2001. Since then, the escalation in the value and in the types of financial assets has been even sharper, a subject I return to in Chapter 5 (see Exhibit A.2.5). Considerable effort and resources have gone into the development of a framework for governing global finance, including the development of new institutional accounting and financial reporting standards, minimum capital requirements for banks, and efforts to institute greater transparency in corporate governance. But generally, the leading exchanges and financial centers seem to be able to innovate their way out of regulatory constraints time after time.

Exhibit 2.6 Largest Markets by Domestic Equity Capitalization, 1997, 2000, 2004, 2008

Ten Largest Stock Markets Members in 1997	1997 Market Capitalization (in US$ bn)	1997 Percentage of WFE Members Capitalization	Ten Largest Stock Markets in 2000	2000 Market Capitalization (in US$ bn)	2000 Percentage of WFE Capitalization
NYSE	8,879.6	41.0	NYSE	11,534.6	37.1
Tokyo	2,160.6	10.0	NASDAQ	3,597.1	11.6
London	1,996.2	9.2	Tokyo	3,157.2	10.2
NASDAQ	1,737.5	8.0	London	2,612.2	8.4
Germany	825.2	3.8	Euronext Paris	1,446.6	4.7
Paris	676.3	3.1	Deutsche Börse	1,279.2	4.1
Switzerland	575.3	2.7	Switzerland	792.3	2.6
Canada (Toronto)	567.6	2.6	Toronto	770.1	2.5
Amsterdam	468.9	2.2	Italy	768.4	2.5
Hong Kong	413.3	1.9	Euronext Amsterdam	640.5	2.1% of
Total WFE[a]			% of Total WFE[a]		
Capitalization for Top Ten	84.5		Capitalization for Top Ten		85.6

Ten Largest Stock Markets Members in 2004	2004 Market Capitalization (in US$ bn)	2004 Percentage of WFE Members Capitalization	Ten Largest Stock Markets in 2008	2008 Market Capitalization (in US$ bn)	2008 Percentage of WFE Members in 1997 Capitalization
NYSE	12,707.6	34.45	NYSE Euronext (US)	9,208.9	
Tokyo SE	3,557.7	9.7	Tokyo SE Group	3,115.8	
NASDAQ	3,532.9	9.6	NASDAQ OMX	2,396.3	
London SE	2865.2	7.8	NYSE Euronext (Eur.)	2,101.7	
Euronext	2,441.3	6.6	London SE	1,868.2	
Deutsche Börse	1,184.5	3.2	Shanghai SE	1,425.4	
TSX Group	1,177.5	3.2	Hong Kong Exchanges	1,328.8	
BME Spanish Exchanges	940.7	2.6	Deutsche Börse	1,110.6	
Hong Kong Exchanges	861.5	2.3	TSX Group	1,033.4	
Swiss Exchange	826.0	2.2	BME Spanish Exchanges	948.4	
% of Total WFE[a]			% of Total WFE[a]		
Capitalization for Top Ten		81.7	Capitalization for Top Ten		

Notes:

a. World Federation of Exchanges, formerly the Federation Internationale des Bourses de Valeurs (FIBV).

Source: Compiled from World Federation of Exchanges (2004, 2008a, b), year-end figures with calculations of percentages added.

Exhibit 2.7   Total Value of Share Trading for Selected Major Stock Markets, in US$ Billions, 1990–2008

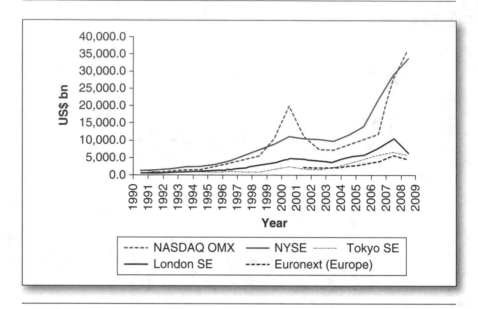

Notes: Euronext (Europe) was formed in late 2000 following a merger of the Amsterdam Stock Exchange, Brussels Stock Exchange, and the Paris Bourse. In 2002, the Lisbon Stock Exchange also merged with Euronext.

Source: Compiled by author using data from World Federation of Exchanges (2008a).

Trade has provided a third set of institutional framings. In 1993, the World Trade Organization (WTO) was set up to oversee cross-border trade, and almost all countries today are members. It has the power to adjudicate in cross-border disputes between countries and represents a potentially key institutional framework for the governance of the global economy. A second component in cross-border trade is the formation of transnational trading blocs. The three major blocs are the European Union (EU; which arose from the erstwhile European Economic Community), the Association of Southeast Asian Nations (ASEAN), and the North American Free Trade Agreement (NAFTA). But beyond these three massive blocs, the number of trade agreements both within and outside the framing of WTO grew sharply in a few years, with more than 70 regional trade agreements by the late 1990s and about 150 by 2004. The role of FDI in international trade also grew sharply: by the mid-1990s, 143 countries had adopted special regimes to attract FDI, up from twenty in 1982 (UNCTAD 1998, chap. 3).

Exhibit 2.8   Total Number of Listed Companies for Selected Major Stock
Markets, 1990–2008

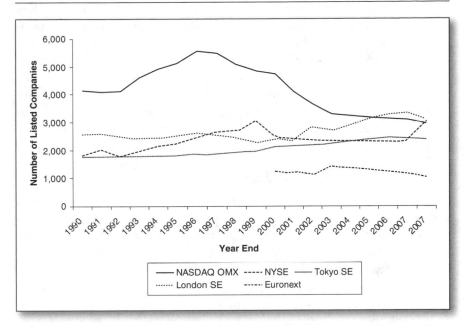

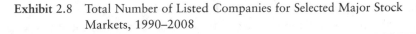

Notes: Euronext (Europe) was formed in late 2000 following a merger of the Amsterdam Stock Exchange, Brussels Stock Exchange, and the Paris Bourse. In 2002 the Lisbon Stock Exchange also merged with Euronext.

Source: Compiled by author using data from World Federation of Exchanges (2008b).

The specifics of the major trading agreements and probably most of the other agreements vary sharply, but they all provide for the cross-border mobility of capital and, importantly, an emphasis on the free movement of financial services as part of the international trade in services. Although trade has received far more attention, it is in many ways a less significant factor in changing the institutional apparatus of the world economy than is finance. There has long been considerable trade among the countries in each major bloc, and many import tariffs were already low for many goods in many countries. Beyond trade, the EU, NAFTA, and ASEAN blocs represent a further formalization of capital as a transnational entity, one that operates through TNCs and global trade.

These realignments have had pronounced consequences. The extremely high level of profitability in the financial industry, for example, has devalued manufacturing *as production* and shifted investors' focus toward its value as a financial investment. This is illustrated by the rise of the notion of shareholder value: a shift in emphasis from production to securing good stock market valuations of a manufacturer's publicly listed shares. Second, much of the policy around deregulation has had the effect of making finance so profitable that it takes investment away from manufacturing. Third, finance can deliver super-profits merely by maximizing the circulation of and speculation in money—that is, multiplying buying and selling transactions over a given period of time with each such transaction a possible source of profit. Manufacturing does not have this option because capital for production is caught in much longer cycles (from six to nine months to produce a car or a plane), and resale values are not where a company makes its profits. Fourth, beginning in the 1980s, a variety of financial instruments were created that made it possible to sell an increasingly broad range of household debts such as, credit cards, mortgages, student loans, at a profit. A simple illustration is the bundling of a large number of home mortgages so as to reach certain value thresholds, no matter that these are negative values (debts), into instruments that can be sold many times over, even though the number of houses involved stays the same. *Securitization* is the general term used to describe this and other innovations that made it possible to transform various types of financial assets and debts into marketable instruments. This trend continues today with the invention of ever more complex and speculative instruments, such as credit default swaps; these grew from US$1 trillion in 2001 to US$62 trillion in 2007, more than the value of global GDP at US$54 trillion, and became the immediate source of the 2008 financial crisis (see Chapter 8). These new financial instruments create new types of risks and a potential for greater volatility. In contrast, manufactured goods do not allow (at least till now) such speculative options; they can become the source of speculative profits via shareholder value, but this takes us back to banking and finance. The good is made and sold once; when the good enters the realm of circulation, it enters another set of industries, for example, trading firms and wholesalers, and the profits from subsequent sales accrue to these sectors.

These changes in the geography and composition of international transactions and the framework through which these transactions are implemented have contributed to the formation of new strategic sites in the world economy. This is the subject of the next section.

Strategic Places

Four types of places, above all others, symbolize the new forms of economic globalization: export processing zones, offshore banking centers, high-tech districts, and global cities. There are also many other locations where international transactions materialize. Harbors continue to be strategic in the world of growing international trade, and the major global harbors in the world contribute to a large demand for highly specialized legal, accounting, financial, and similar services. Massive industrial districts in major manufacturing export countries, such as the United States, Japan, and Germany, are in many ways strategic sites for international activity and specifically for production for export. None of these locations, however, captures the prototypical image of today's global economy the way the first four do.

Here, I do not examine export processing zones, an innovation that began in the 1960s and took off in the 1980s (e.g., Lim 1982) or high-tech districts (e.g., Saxenian 1996) because their activities have a highly intermediated relationship to cities. My argument is, briefly, that this intermediated relationship is there when manufacturing is part of a corporate organization: the more it gets off-shored or, in the case of high-tech, the more global its markets and innovative its products, the more its umbrella corporation will need highly specialized legal, financial, accounting, and other such services to manage the manufacturing part. This is the indirect growth effect for the urban specialized services sector; for this effect to occur, it matters less where manufacturing is located than whether it is part of a corporate organization. I return to these issues when I examine the role of manufacturing in the expansion of the specialized corporate services sector in Chapter 4.

Export processing zones, a less familiar entity than high-tech districts (made famous by California's Silicon Valley), deserve a brief description; I develop this at length in Sassen (1988, 2008c). Such zones tend to be located in low-wage countries where firms from developed countries can secure low wages for highly labor-intensive or high-health-risk work. Labor-intensive manufacturing, processing, and assembling can be done at lower costs and with far less demanding environmental, workplace, and labor regulations than in the home countries of the firms. What gets worked on typically is brought in from and re-exported to the home countries of these firms. Developed countries had to implement a variety of legislative pieces to make this possible at a time when Keynesian tariffs and protections were the norm in developed countries. The central rationale for these zones is access to cheap labor for the labor-intensive stages of a firm's production process. Tax breaks and lenient workplace standards in the zones are additional incentives, whose granting also required legislative changes in the developing countries. These zones became a key mechanism in the internationalization of production that took off in the 1980s; but the first such zones were implemented in the late 1960s, partly as a response to the strength of labor unions at the time in developed countries and the emergence of strong legislatures willing to impose stricter environmental, workplace, and worker health standards. In addition to these zones, less formalized arrangements proliferated in the 1990s; those other arrangements are usually referred to as *outsourcing*. The growth in the number of affiliates described earlier is one element in the infrastructure for outsourcing.

Now we turn to global cities and offshore banking centers, two sites of more direct concern to the analysis in this book.

Global Cities

Global cities are strategic sites for the management of the global economy and the production of the most advanced services and financial operations that have become key inputs for that work of managing global economic operations. The growth of international investment and trade and the need to finance and service such activities have fed the growth of these functions in major cities. The erosion of the role of the government in the world economy, which was much larger when trade was the dominant form of international transaction, has shifted some of the organizing and servicing work from governments to specialized service firms and global markets in services and finance.

A second, much less noted, shift of functions to this specialized service sector concentrated in cities comes from the headquarters of global firms. The added complexity and uncertainties involved in running global operations and the need for highly specialized knowledge about the law, accounting, business cultures, and so on, of large numbers of countries has meant that a growing component of headquarter functions is now being outsourced to specialized corporate services firms. Therefore, today there are two sites for the production of headquarter functions of global firms: one is the headquarters proper, and the other is the specialized service sector disproportionately concentrated in major cities. Thus, when firms globalize their operations, they are not necessarily only exporting jobs, as is usually argued. They export certain jobs, for example, labor-intensive manufacturing and clerical work, but they actually may be adding jobs to their top headquarter functions. To illustrate, when Detroit lost many of its manufacturing jobs, New York City gained specialized service jobs. This was in response to the work of major auto manufacturing headquarters becoming increasingly complicated and the increased demand for state-of-the-art legal, accounting, finance, and insurance advice, not to mention consulting of various kinds and new types of public relations efforts. Headquarters of firms that operate mostly globally tend to be located in global cities. But given the option to outsource the most complex and variable headquarter functions to the specialized services sector in a global city, headquarters can actually locate anywhere, a trend evident in the United States; it is less common in countries where there is only one major internationally connected city.

Here, I briefly examine these developments, first by presenting the concept of the global city and then some of the empirical evidence showing the concentration of major international markets and economic sectors in various cities.

Since the 1980s, the specific forms of the world economy have created particular organizational requirements that differ from those of the preceding phase, which had been dominated by large US transnational corporations and banks seeking to develop markets for American products and bank accounts worldwide. The emergence of global markets for finance and specialized services, along with the growth of investment as a major type of international transaction, has created a demand for new types of organizational forms. These have contributed to the expansion in command functions and the demand for specialized services for firms, whether the firm is in agriculture, mining, transport, finance, or any other major sector. Much of this activity is not encompassed by the organizational form of the transnational firm or bank, even when these types of firms account for a disproportionate share of international flows. Furthermore, much of this activity goes beyond the power of TNCs, a power often invoked to explain the fact itself of economic globalization.

Of interest at this point are some of the hypotheses that launched the world city and global city analyses, especially those that examine the spatial and organizational forms of economic globalization and the actual work of running transnational economic operations. The aim of these hypotheses was to recover organizational forms other than that of the headquarters of powerful firms, which is the typical approach. Thus, these hypotheses also include particular types of places and work processes as part of the organizational framings for the current forms of economic globalization. In one of the first formulations that launched this new type of analysis, Friedmann and Wolff (1982) started from cities and emphasized the concentration of command and coordination functions of operations (see also Friedmann 1986). I proposed similar hypotheses but started from a somewhat different angle: the central proposition in the global city model (Sassen [1991] 2001) is that it is precisely the *combination* of geographic dispersal of economic activities with simultaneous system integration that gave cities a strategic role in the current phase of the world economy. Rather than becoming obsolete because of global geographic dispersal and integration made possible by information technologies, cities became strategic. In a very early formulation (Sassen-Koob 1982), I emphasized the growing need for long-distance management and how, ironically, this new need would also generate all kinds of new professional jobs and firms, even though at the time most major cities in the United States and Europe were in severe economic and fiscal crisis. To the concentration of command and coordination functions emphasized by Friedmann and Wolff (1982), I added two additional functions: (1) cities are post-industrial production sites for the leading industries of this period—finance and specialized services—and (2) cities are transnational marketplaces where firms and governments from all over the world can buy financial instruments and specialized services. These early formulations emerged long before this type of analysis exploded into a rapidly growing scholarship from the 1990s onward.[2]

The territorial dispersal of economic activity at the national and world scale implied by globalization has created new forms of territorial centralization. One critical and often overlooked fact is that this territorial dispersal is happening under conditions of ongoing concentration in ownership and control. Dispersal might have contributed to a parallel decentralization, even democratizing, of ownership and control. It did not. One way of understanding this empirically is to examine some of the figures on the growth of transnational enterprises and their affiliates. Exhibit A.2.6 shows the vast number of TNC affiliates. This is evidence of dispersal along with ongoing central ownership and appropriation of profits. Further, as already discussed, the transactions among firms and their affiliates and other types of contracting account for a good share of global trade; this intrafirm trade is not, strictly speaking, *free* market trade, even though the imagery around the growth of global trade is centered on the expansion of free markets. That this is managed trade becomes critical for understanding the role of cities in the global economy because global management requires a mix of specialized servicing and command functions generated in global cities. There is not much of an invisible hand there.

The financial industry has a similar dynamic of dispersal and global integration: a growth in the number of cities integrated in the global financial network and a simultaneous increased concentration of value managed at the top of the hierarchy of centers (see Exhibits 2.6 to 2.8 and A.2.5). We can identify two distinct phases. Up to the end of the 1982 third-world debt crisis, the large transnational banks dominated the financial markets in terms of both the volume and the nature of financial transactions. After 1982, this dominance was increasingly challenged by other financial institutions and the major innovations they produced. These challenges led to a transformation in the leading components of the financial industry, a proliferation of financial institutions, and the rapid internationalization of financial markets. The marketplace and the advantages of agglomeration— and, hence, cities—assumed new significance beginning in the mid-1980s. These developments led simultaneously to (1) the incorporation of a multiplicity of worldwide markets into a global system that fed the growth of the industry after the 1982 debt crisis and (2) new forms of concentration, specifically the centralization of the industry in a network of leading financial centers. Hence, in the case of the financial industry, to focus only on the large transnational banks would exclude precisely those sectors of the industry where much of the new growth and production of innovations was launched in the 1980s and is continuing today. It would also leave out an examination of key components of finance—activities, firms, and markets—located in cities.

In brief, the geographic dispersal of plants, offices, and service outlets and the integration of a growing number of stock markets around the world could have been accompanied by a corresponding decentralization in control and central functions. But that did not occur.

If some of the evidence on financial flows is organized according to the places where the markets and firms are located, we see both distinct patterns of concentration and a larger number of cities that become part of this concentration. For example, thirty-nine of the 100 largest banks and twenty-three of the twenty-five largest securities houses in 1991 were located in only three countries (Japan, the United States, and the United Kingdom; see Exhibit A.2.5a), mostly in Tokyo, New York and London. This pattern persisted throughout the late 1990s, notwithstanding multiple financial crises in the world and particularly in Japan, and has only recently declined (see Exhibits A.2.5a and b). Thus between 2003 and 2009, the United States actually went from having ten of the largest banks to having only six. The top three countries went from holding twenty-three of the largest banks to sixteen in 2009.

The full impact of deregulation and the growth of financial markets can be seen in the increases in value and numbers of firms listed in all the major stock markets in the world (see Exhibit 2.6 to 2.8). The market value of listings rose from US$2.8 trillion in 1990 to US$9.4 trillion in 1997 and US$12.9 trillion in 2004 in the New York Stock Exchange, and from US$1 trillion to US$2 trillion and $2.8 trillion in the London Exchange for those same years. Similar patterns, although at lower orders of magnitude, are evident in the other stock markets listed in Exhibits 2.7 and 2.8. The concentration in the operational side of the financial industry is made evident by the fact that most of the stock transactions in the leading countries are concentrated in a few stock markets. The Tokyo exchange accounts for 90% of equities traded in Japan; New York accounts for about two-thirds of equities traded in the United States; and London accounts for most of the trading in the United Kingdom. There is, then, a disproportionate concentration of worldwide capitalization in a few cities and of national capitalization typically in one city in each country.

Certain aspects of the territorial dispersal of economic activity may have led to some dispersal of profits and ownership. Large firms, for example, have increased their subcontracting to smaller firms worldwide, and many national firms in the newly industrializing countries have grown rapidly, thanks to investment by foreign firms and access to world markets, often through arrangements with transnational firms. Yet this form of growth is ultimately part of a chain in which a limited number of corporations continue to control the end product and reap most of the profits associated with selling on the world market. Even industrial homeworkers in remote rural areas are part of that chain (e.g., Beneria and Roldan 1987; Russell and Rath 2002). Subprime loans, for example, can be seen as an effort by high finance to capture low-end wealth into the chain. Simultaneously, new instruments extend the chain upward. For instance, the securitization of US home mortgages in Euros makes them directly accessible to European investors.

But this geographic dispersal of a corporation's activities is organized centrally and hence creates a need for expanded central control and management work, much of it produced in cities. It thereby feeds the strategic role of cities in the world economy. The mix of globally dispersed operations of firms and the concentration of management functions enables a worldwide process of capture of more and more low-end wealth and the capital of small national firms.

Offshore Banking Centers and Onshore Preferential Tax Regimes

Offshore banking centers are yet another important spatial point in the worldwide circuits of financial flows, although they are less complex than global cities (see Exhibit A.2.7). Such centers are, above all else, tax shelters, a response by private-sector actors to government regulation.[3] The implementation of these centers began in the 1970s. Diverse types of international tax shelters have existed for a long time. But the 1970s marked a juncture—a growing gap between economic internationalization and government control over the economy in developed countries. These centers, both in the form of tax havens and of onshore preferential tax regimes, emerged as one option for avoiding government control in a context of expanding globalization. They are, to a large extent, paper operations.

The Cayman Islands illustrate an early phase in this development (Roberts 1994; IMF 1999, 2009). By 1997, they were ranked as the seventh largest international banking operation in the world and the fifth largest financial center after London, Tokyo, New York, and Hong Kong, according to International Monetary Fund (IMF) data (IMF 1999). They also were still the world's second largest insurance location with gross capital of US$8 billion in 1997. The value of deposits held in banks in the Cayman Islands grew from US$250 billion in 1990 to US$640 billion in 1997. Its 593 banks in 1997 included forty-seven of the world's top fifty banks. But even though that tiny country supposedly has well over 500 banks from all around the world, only sixty-nine banks have offices there, and only six are "real" banks for cashing and depositing money and other transactions. Many of the others exist only as folders in a cabinet (Walter 1989; Roberts 1994). As of 2008, there were a total of 9,000 investment fund entities operating in the Cayman Islands with assets of up to $1.8 trillion. There were also 279 banks with assets of about $35 billion and a total of 777 insurance entities (IMF 2009: Table 2).

These centers are located in many parts of the world. The majority of Asian offshore centers are located in Singapore and Hong Kong; Labuan (Malaysia) and Macau are also significant centers. In the Middle East, Bahrain took over from Beirut in 1975 as the main offshore banking center, with Dubai close behind. In the South Pacific, major centers are located in Australia and New Zealand, and smaller offshore clusters are in Vanuatu, the Cook Islands, Nauru, and Samoa. In the Indian Ocean, centers cluster in the Seychelles and in Mauritius. In Europe, Switzerland tops the list, and Luxembourg is a major center; others are Cyprus, Madeira, Malta, the Isle of Man, and the Channel Islands. Several small places are also struggling to compete with the established centers: Gibraltar, Monaco, Liechtenstein, and Andorra. The Caribbean has Bermuda, the Cayman Islands, Bahamas, Turks and Caicos, and the British Virgin Islands.

Why do such centers exist? This question is especially pertinent given the massive deregulation of major financial markets beginning in the 1980s, which included the establishment of de facto "free international financial zones" in several major cities in highly developed countries. Some of these are basically onshore preferential tax regimes. The Tax Justice Network (2007) has tracked these developments closely, preparing, among other documents, a list of narrowly defined tax havens and offshore banking centers, as well as a list of a more broadly defined range of countries offering preferential tax regimes with negative consequences for the larger social order, for example, tax losses for governments that can translate into cuts of social programs.

Both offshore and onshore centers were set up to side-step the system for regulating exchange rates and balance-of-payments imbalances contained in the Bretton Woods agreement of 1945. The Bretton Woods agreement set up a legal framework for the regulation of international transactions, such as foreign currency operations, for countries or banks wanting to operate internationally. In finance, *offshore* does not always mean overseas or foreign; basically, the term means that less regulation takes place than *onshore*—the latter describing firms and markets not covered by this special legislation. Compared with the major "international zones" and onshore preferential tax regimes, offshore banking centers offer certain types of additional flexibility: secrecy, openness to *hot* money and to certain quasilegitimate options not quite allowed in the deregulated markets of major financial centers, and tax minimization strategies for international corporations.

The best early example of onshore preferential tax regimes for financial activity is the Euromarket, which started in the 1960s and expanded rapidly, with London at the center of the Euromarket system. Euromarkets were initially Eurodollar markets, where banks from the United States and other countries could do dollar transactions and avoid US regulations. They eventually expanded to include other currencies and more assets have been made liquid through securitization and denomination in Euros. The Euromarkets are significant in international finance. According to the Bank for International Settlements, the Eurocurrency markets grew from US$9 billion in 1964 to US$57 billion in 1970, US$661 billion in 1981 to US$17 trillion in 2004 (BIS 2005). The oil crisis was important in feeding this growth. In the 1980s, much growth came through Eurobonds and Eurosecurities—bonds and securities traded offshore, that is, outside the standard regulatory framework. Securitization was crucial to launch the new financial era by making liquid what had been formerly illiquid forms of debt. Since the launch of the euro in January 1999, Euromarkets have changed and grown rapidly, with the current value of outstanding international debt in both euro and legacy currencies reaching US$1.6 trillion in 1998 (IMF 1999, part 2) to 2.3 trillion in 2005 (BIS 2005).

Other early onshore examples, as of 1981, were international banking facilities in the United States, mostly in New York City, that allowed US banks to establish special adjunct facilities to accept deposits from foreign entities free of reserve requirements and interest rate limitations. Tokyo, finally, saw the development of a facility in 1986 that allowed transactions in the Asian dollar market to be carried out in that city; this meant that Tokyo got some of the capital being transacted in Hong Kong, Singapore, and Bahrain—all Asian dollar centers.

The first phase of the current deregulation regime was implemented in the 1980s in some countries, notably the United States, the UK, and France. London's much-noted "big bang" and the less-noted "petit bang" in Paris are instances of such a process of deregulation of financial markets. It brought much offshore capital back into onshore markets, especially in New York and London. The return flow of capital helped convince reluctant governments worldwide to proceed with deregulation of the financial markets in the 1990s. This in turn led to a large number of so-called "adjustment" crises in those countries, which began to decimate small-scale national firms and the older traditional middle-class sectors (Sassen [1991] 2001: chap. 4).

In brief, offshore centers represent a highly specialized location for certain types of international financial transactions. They are also buffer zones in case the governments of the leading financial centers in the world should decide to re-regulate the financial markets. On the broader scale of operations, however, they represent a fraction of the financial capital markets now being managed from the growing network of global cities.

Impact of the US War on Terrorism on Off-Shore Banking Secrecy

In September of 2006, an article appeared in the The Wall Street Journal revealing that the Treasury Department and the CIA, United States government agencies, had created and used a program to access the Society for Worldwide Interbank Financial Telecommunication (SWIFT) transaction database after the September 11 attacks.[4] This program was named Terrorist Finance Tracking Program. SWIFT quickly came under pressure for compromising the data privacy of its customers by letting a foreign government agency access sensitive personal data, and the Belgian government declared that the SWIFT dealings with US government authorities were, in fact, a breach of Belgian and European privacy laws (Brand 2006).

In response, the European Union negotiated an agreement with the United States government to permit the transfer of intra–EU SWIFT transaction information to the United States under certain circumstances. An interim agreement was signed without European Parliamentary approval by the European Council on November 30, 2009, the day before the Lisbon Treaty—which would have prohibited such an agreement from being signed under the terms of the Codecision procedure—formally came into effect. On February 11, 2010, the European Parliament decided to reject the interim agreement between the EU and the USA with 378 to 196 votes (Constant 2010).

Conclusion: After the Pax Americana

The world economy has never been a planetary event; it has always had more or less clearly defined boundaries. Moreover, although most major industries were involved throughout, the cluster of industries that dominated any given period changed over time, contributing to distinct structurations of the world economy. Finally, the institutional framework through which the world economy coheres has also varied sharply, from the earlier empires through the quasi-empire of the Pax Americana—the period of US political, economic, and military dominance, especially the two decades after World War II—and its decay in the 1970s.

It is in this decaying Pax Americana, with the rebuilt economies of Western Europe and Japan reentering the international markets, that we see emerging a new phase of the world economy. There is considerable agreement among specialists that in the mid-1970s, new patterns in the world economy became evident. First, the geographical axis of international transactions changed from North–South to East–West. In this process, significant parts of Africa and Latin America became unhinged from their hitherto strong ties with world markets in commodities and raw materials. Second, there was a sharp increase in the weight of FDI in services and the role played by international financial markets. Third, there was the breakdown of the Bretton Woods agreement, which had established the institutional framework under which the world economy had operated since the end of World War II. This breakdown was clearly linked to the decline of the United States as the single dominant economic power in the world. Japanese and European multinationals and banks became major competitors with US firms. The financial crises in Asia in the 1990s once again strengthened the role of the North Atlantic system in the global economy. But the rise of China, the massive indebtedness of the United States, and its growing dependence on Japan and China for financing that debt point to the possibility of a final blow to the remnants of the Pax Americana that once provided a United States–centered global order.

This does not mean that US global firms are suffering. While there is disagreement on this point, I argue that a key feature of the current phase of globalization is that global firms, whether American, European, or Asian, are increasingly exiting the old arrangements that connected them to their respective nation-states through protectionisms of various sorts and strong-hand politics by their governments aimed at protecting their national firms whenever possible. These arrangements were a critical part of the Pax Americana, with the United States playing a key role in enabling its firms to dominate the world economy. By the end of the 1990s, the global economy had become largely structured in terms of global markets and multiple protections for global firms in all the countries that had deregulated their economies to become part of the global economy. Although the US government remains the major military and economic power in the world, its government is in a far more dubious position: It continues to extract exceptions from other governments and international institutions for itself and major US global firms. But it collects a declining share of taxes from US global firms. And all along, many US industries are in fast decline.

These realignments are the background for understanding the position of different types of cities in the current organization of the world economy. A limited but growing number of global cities are the sites for the major financial markets and the leading specialized services necessary to manage global operations. And a large number of other major cities have lost their role as top export centers for manufacturing precisely because of the worldwide dispersal of factories. This shift in roles among major cities in the new world economy will be the focus of Chapter 3.

Notes

1 Foreign direct investments by TNCs may be financed through transnational banks or the international capital markets. In the mid-1980s, the share of the latter began to grow sharply (see Sassen [1991] 2001: chap. 4), and it continues to do so today.

2 For one of the best examinations of the evolution of several distinct strands in urban research since the 1980s, see Paddison's Introduction in the *Handbook of Urban Studies* (Paddison 2001); see also Taylor et al. 2007; Banerjee-Guha 2010.

3 There is no definitive list of tax havens and offshore financial centers. Exhibit A.2.7 shows the listings produced by OECD (Organisation for Economic Cooperation and Development) and by the Tax Justice. The main listings of tax havens have been developed by the OECD as part of the "harmful tax practices" of its Committee on Fiscal Affairs, a project launched in 1998. The ambiguity of the notion of a tax haven is partly due to the fact that almost any jurisdiction can have some tax haven or onshore preferential tax regime; a smaller number are usually identified as "pure" tax havens.

4 The Society for Worldwide Interbank Financial Telecommunication (SWIFT) operates a worldwide financial messaging network that exchanges messages between banks and other financial institutions. SWIFT also markets software and services to financial institutions, much of it for use on the SWIFTNet Network, and ISO 9362 bank identifier codes (BICs) are popularly known as "SWIFT codes." The majority of international interbank messages use the SWIFT network. As of September 2010 SWIFT linked 9,000+ financial institutions in 209 countries. SWIFT transports financial messages but does not hold accounts for its members and does not perform any form of clearing or settlement. See http://www.swift.com/about_swift/company_information/index.page?lang=en.

Chapter 2 Appendix

Exhibit A.2.1 Inflows and Outflows of Foreign Direct Investment (FDI), 1980–2008

	Year	Developed Countries		Developing Countries		Transition and Eastern Europe		All Countries	
		Inflows	Outflows	Inflows	Outflows	Inflows	Outflows	Inflows	Outflows
Value (US$bn)	1980–1984	195.69	206.25	93.08	11.61	0.05	—	288.81	217.86
	1985–1989	525.66	665.30	113.07	47.52	0.03	—	638.76	712.82
	1990–1994	693.37	1,035.04	308.57	135.51	6.81	2.93	1,008.75	1,173.48
	1995–1999	2,091.82	2,682.22	872.70	311.92	36.81	8.68	3,001.33	3,002.82
	2000–2004	2,930.98	3,520.36	1,122.63	433.31	78.22	35.40	4,131.83	3,989.07
	2005	613.09	741.97	329.29	122.71	30.95	14.31	973.33	878.99
	2006	972.76	1,157.91	433.76	215.28	54.55	23.72	1,461.07	1,396.92
	2007	1,358.63	1,809.53	529.34	285.49	90.87	51.50	1,978.84	2,146.52
	2008	962.26	1,506.53	620.73	292.71	114.36	58.50	1,697.35	1,857.73
	2005–2008	3,906.74	5,215.94	1,913.13	916.19	290.72	148.03	6,110.59	6,280.16
Share of Total	1980–1984	67.76%	94.67%	32.23%	5.33%	0.02%	—	100%	100%
	1985–1989	82.29%	93.33%	17.70%	6.67%	0.00%*	—	100%	100%
	1990–1995	68.74%	88.20%	30.59%	11.55%	0.67%	0.25%	100%	100%

Year	Developed Countries		Developing Countries		Transition and Eastern Europe		All Countries	
	Inflows	Outflows	Inflows	Outflows	Inflows	Outflows	Inflows	Outflows
1995–2000	69.70%	89.32%	29.08%	10.39%	1.23%	0.29%	100%	100%
2000–2004	70.94%	88.25%	27.17%	10.86%	1.89%	0.89%	100%	100%
2005	62.99%	84.41%	33.83%	13.96%	3.18%	1.63%	100%	100%
2006	66.58%	82.89%	29.69%	15.41%	3.73%	1.70%	100%	100%
2007	68.66%	84.30%	26.75%	13.30%	4.59%	2.40%	100%	100%
2008	56.69%	81.09%	36.57%	15.76%	6.74%	3.15%	100%	100%
2005–2008	63.93%	83.05%	31.31%	14.59%	4.76%	2.36%	100%	100%
Growth Rate (from previous year)								
2001	–46.74%	–38.65%	–16.14%	–38.51%	38.98%	–13.96%	–40.62%	–38.57%
2002	–25.67%	–26.93%	–18.33%	–40.10%	16.12%	69.20%	–23.25%	–28.04%
2003	–18.35%	5.16%	4.58%	–8.26%	76.23%	129.76%	–10.25%	5.00%
2004	14.65%	56.76%	57.83%	164.48%	52.30%	32.39%	30.03%	65.01%
2005	48.02%	–6.68%	13.39%	1.88%	2.11%	1.22%	32.45%	–5.45%
2006	58.67%	56.06%	31.73%	75.44%	76.26%	65.81%	50.11%	58.92%
2007	39.67%	56.28%	22.04%	32.61%	66.58%	117.10%	35.44%	53.66%
2008	–29.17%	–16.74%	17.26%	2.53%	25.86%	13.57%	–14.22%	–13.45%

Note: Asterisk (*) denotes less than .005.

Source: Calculations based on UNCTAD (2009a).

Exhibit A.2.2 Sectoral Distribution of Foreign Direct Investment Stock for the Largest Developed Home Countries and the Largest Developed and Developing Host Countries, Select Years, 1970–1990 (US$ billions and percentage)

Group of Countries and Sectors	Billions of Dollars					Average Annual Growth Rate in Percentage					Share in Percentage				
	1970	1975	1980	1985	1990	1971-1970	1976-1975	1981-1980	1986-1985	1981-1990	1970	1975	1980	1985	1990
A. Outward stock															
Developed countries[a] Primary	29	58	88	115	160	6.2	14	8.7	5.5	6.8	22.7	25.3	18.5	18.5	11.2
Secondary	58	103	208	240	556	10.3	11.7	15.1	2.9	18.3	45.2	45	43.8	38.7	38.7
Tertiary	41	68	179	265	720	14.9	10.4	21.4	8.2	22.1	31.4	27.7	37.7	42.8	50.1
Total	129	229	475	620	1436	11.7	11.7	15.7	5.5	18.3	100	100	100	100	100
B. Inward stock															
Developed countries[b] Primary	12	17	18	39	94	18	4.7	5.9	16.7	19.2	16.2	12.1	6.7	9.2	9.1
Secondary	44	79	148	195	439	11.5	10.7	13.4	5.7	17.6	60.2	56.5	55.2	46.2	42.5
Tertiary	17	44	102	188	499	17.2	16.5	18.3	13	21.6	23.7	31.4	38.1	44.5	48.4
Total	73	140	268	422	1032	14.4	11.3	13.9	9.5	19.6	100	100	100	100	100

Group of Countries and Sectors	Average Annual Growth, Billions of Dollars				Rate in Percentage				Share in Percentage				
	1971-1975	1976-1980	1981-1985	1986-1990	1971-1975	1976-1980	1981-1985	1986-1990	1970	1975	1980	1985	1990
Developing countries/economies[c]													
Primary	7	17	31	46	19.4	12.8	8.2	10.5	—	20.6	22.7	24	21.9
Secondary	19	41	64	102	16.5	9.3	9.8	9.5	—	55.9	54.6	49.6	48.6
Tertiary	8	17	34	62	16.3	14.9	12.8	13.8	—	23.5	22.7	26.4	29.5
Total	34	75	129	210	17.1	11.4	10.2	10.8	—	100	100	100	100

a. Australia, Canada, France, Federal Republic of Germany, Italy, Japan, Netherlands, United Kingdom, and United States; together these countries accounted for almost 90% of outward FDI stock in 1990. 1970 and 1971-1975 growth data exclude Australia and France.

b. Australia, Canada, France, Federal Republic of Germany, Italy, Japan, Netherlands, United Kingdom, Spain, and United States; together these countries accounted for approximately 72% of total inward FDI stock in 1990. 1970 and 1971-1975 growth data exclude Australia, France, and Spain.

c. Argentina, Brazil, Chile, China, Colombia, Hong Kong, Indonesia, Malaysia, Mexico, Nigeria, Philippines, Republic of Korea, Singapore, Taiwan Province of China, Thailand, and Venezuela. Together these countries accounted for 68% of total inward FDI in developing countries.

Source: UNCTAD (1993:62)

Exhibit A.2.3   Distribution of Inward and Outward Foreign Direct Investment Stock by Sector, 1990 and 2007

	Inward Stock		Outward Stock	
	1990	2007	1990	2007
World:				
Primary	9.4%	7.5%	8.8%	7.2%
Manufacturing	41.1%	27.0%	43.5%	26.0%
Services	48.8%	63.8%	47.4%	64.9%
Private buying & selling of property	0.0%	0.0%	0.0%	0.0%
Unspecified	0.7%	1.6%	0.2%	1.9%
Developed Economies:				
Primary	9.6%	7.5%	8.8%	7.8%
Manufacturing	40.6%	28.1%	43.6%	28.4%
Services	49.3%	63.0%	47.4%	61.9%
Private buying & selling of property	0.0%	0.1%	0.0%	0.0%
Unspecified	0.6%	1.4%	0.2%	0.0%
Developing Economies:				
Primary	8.4%	6.3%	12.7%	2.4%
Manufacturing	43.6%	24.0%	35.5%	8.6%
Services	46.7%	67.8%	48.5%	87.3%
Private buying & selling of property	—	—	—	—
Unspecified	1.4%	1.9%	3.3%	1.8%
Transition Economies:[a]				
Primary	—	22.9%	—	27.6%
Manufacturing	—	26.0%	—	8.1%
Services	—	45.0%	—	59.2%
Private buying & selling of property	—	0.0%	—	
Unspecified	—	6.1%	—	5.2%

a. Transition Economies include non-EU countries in Eastern and Southeast Europe and the former Soviet Republics that comprise the CIS.

Source: Compiled from data contained in UNCTAD (2009b): 219–20

Exhibit A.2.4   Foreign Direct Investment Flows by Sector, 1989–1991 and 2005–2007

	Inflows		Outflows	
	1989–1991	2005–2007	1989–1991	2005–2007
World:				
Primary	6.9%	11.6%	4.5%	10.0%
Manufacturing	34.2%	24.0%	37.3%	24.4%
Services	50.4%	59.0%	50.4%	57.9%
Other/Unspecified	8.4%	5.4%	7.8%	7.8%
Developed Economies:				
Primary	5.9%	11.7%	4.5%	10.0%
Manufacturing	31.4%	21.9%	36.8%	25.1%
Services	54.9%	60.0%	50.8%	56.7%
Other/Unspecified	7.7%	6.4%	7.8%	8.2%
Developing Economies:				
Primary	11.2%	9.2%	4.7%	8.8%
Manufacturing	46.5%	31.0%	56.9%	17.3%
Services	30.8%	56.7%	32.9%	69.9%
Other/Unspecified	11.5%	3.2%	5.5%	4.0%
Transition Economies:[a]				
Total	—	100.0%	—	100.0%
Primary	—	30.1%	—	325.6%
Manufacturing	—	16.4%	—	36.3%
Services	—	52.3%	—	−228.9%
Other/Unspecified	—	1.3%	—	−33.0%

Notes:

a. Transition Economies include non-EU countries in Eastern and Southeast Europe and the former Soviet Republics that comprise the CIS.

Source: Compiled from data contained in UNCTAD (2009b): 220–21

Exhibit A.2.5a   A Concentration of World's Fifty Largest Banks, 1991 and 1997 (US$ billions and percentage)

1991				
Number of Firms	*Assets (US$ bn)*	*% of Top 50*	*Capital (US$ bn)*	*% of Top 50*
Japan	27	6,572.42	40.7	975.19	40.6
United States	7	913.01	5.7	104.73	4.4
United Kingdom	5	791.65	4.9	56.75	2.4
Subtotal	39	8,277.08	51.3	1,136.67	47.4
Total for Top 50	50	16,143.35	100.0	2,400.44	100.0

1997				
Number of Firms	*Assets (US$ bn)*	*% of Top 50*	*Capital (US$ bn)*	*% of Top 50*
Japan	12	6,116.31	36.4	1,033.42	45.8
United States	6	1,794.82	10.7	242.00	10.7
United Kingdom	5	1,505.69	9.0	130.59	5.8
Subtotal	23	9,416.81	56.0	1,406.01	62.3
Total for Top 50	50	16,817.69	100.0	2,257.95	100.0

Note: 1997 data ranked by assets as determined by Dow Jones Global Indexes in association with WorldScope; figures are based on each company's 1997 fiscal-year results, except data on Japanese banks, which are based on fiscal 1998 results.

Source: Author's calculations based on "World Business" (1992; 1998).

Exhibit A.2.5b A Concentration of World's Fifty Largest Banks, 2003 and 2009 (US$ billions and percentage)

2003			
Number of Country	*Combined Assets Top Banks*	*% of (US$ bn) Top 50*	
United States	10	5,047.25	20.1
Japan	6	3,955.17	15.8
Germany	7	3,322.50	13.2
Total for Top 3 Countries	23	12,324.92	49.1
Total for Top 5 Countries[a]	34	17,931.62	71.4
Total for Top 50 Banks	50	25,108.73	100

2009			
Number of Country	*Combined Assets Top 50 Banks*	*% of (US$ bn)*	*Top 50*
United Kingdom	5	11,729	18.9
United States	6	9,278	15.0
France	5	8,614	13.9
Total for Top 3 Countries	16	29,262	47.7
Total for Top 5 Countries[b]	27	42,097	67.8
Total for Top 50 Banks	50	62,050	100.0

Notes:

a. In addition to top three countries listed, the top five in 2003 includes the UK with six of the top fifty banks with US$ bn 3,166.65 in combined assets and France with five of the top fifty banks with US$ bn 2,440.05 in combined assets.

b. In addition to the top three countries listed, the top five in 2009 includes Germany with seven of the top fifty banks with US$ bn 6,850 in combined assets and Japan with four of the top fifty banks with US$ bn 5,626 in combined assets.

Source: Compiled from Global Finance (2003, 2009).

Exhibit A.2.6   Number of Parent Transnational Corporations and Foreign
Affiliates, by Region and Country, Select Years, 1985–2008

		Parent Corporations	Foreign Affiliates
	Year	Based in Country	Located in Country
Developed Countries	1990[a]	33,500	81,800
	1996[a]	43,442	96,620
	2003[a]	45,007	102,560
	2008[a]	58,783	366,881
Select developed countries:			
Australia	1992	1,306	695
	1997	485	2,371
	2001	682	2,352
	2006	1,380	1,991
Canada	1991	1,308	5,874
	1996	1,695	4,541
	1999	1,439	3,725
Germany	1990	6,984	11,821
	1996	7,569	11,445
	2002	6,069	9,268
	2007	6,115	11,750
France	1990	2,056	6,870
	1996	2,078	9,351
	2002	1,267	10,713
Japan	1992	3,529	3,150
	1996	4,231	3,014
	2001	3,371	3,870
	2006	4,663	4,500
Sweden	1991	3,529	2,400
	1997	4,148	5,551
	2002	4,260	4,656
	2007	1,268	11,944
Switzerland	1985	3,000	2,900
	1995	4,506	5,774
	2008	2,616	6,852

	Year	Parent Corporations Based in Country	Foreign Affiliates Located in Country
United Kingdom	1991	1,500	2,900
	1996	1,059	2,609
	2003	2,607	13,176
	2005	2,360	13,667
United States	1990	3,000	14,900
	1995	3,379	18,901
	2000	3,235	15,712
	2002	2,418	5,664
	Year	Parent Corporations Based in Country	Foreign Affiliates Located in Country
Developing Countries	1990[a]	2,700	71,300
	1996[a]	9,323	230,696
	2003[a]	14,192	580,638
	2008[a]	21,425	425,258
Select developing countries:			
Brazil	1992	566	7,110
	1995	797	6,322
	1998	1,225	8,050
	2008	226	4,172
China	1989	379	15,966
	1997	379	145,000
	2002	350	424,196
	2007	3,429	286,232
Colombia	1987	—	1,041
	1995	302	2,220
	2008	71	645
Hong Kong, China	1991	500	2,828
	1997	500	5,067
	2001	948	9,132

(Continued)

Exhibit A.2.6   (Continued)

		Parent Corporations	Foreign Affiliates
	Year	Based in Country	Located in Country
Indonesia	2007	1,167	9,712
	1988	—	1,064
	1995	313	3,472
	2004	313	721
Philippines	1987	—	1,952
	1995	—	14,802
	2004	—	311
Republic of Korea	1991	1,049	3,671
	1996	4,806	3,878
	2002	7,460	12,909
	2008	7,460	16,953
Singapore	1986	—	10,709
	1995	—	18,154
	2002	—	14,052
		Parent Corporations	Foreign Affiliates
	Year	Based in Country	Located in Country
Transition Economies [b]	1990[a]	400	21,800
	1996[a]	842	121,601
	2003[a]	2,313	243,750
	2008[a]	1,845	3,990
World Total	1990[a]	36,600	174,900
	1996[a]	53,607	448,917
	2003[a]	61,582	926,948
	2008[a]	82,053	807,363

Notes:

a. Aggregate of numbers for latest available year to given date for countries in category.

b. Transition Economies include non-EU countries in Eastern and Southeast Europe and the former Soviet Republics that comprise the CIS.

Source: Based on UNCTAD (1998: 3–4; 2004: 273–74; 2009a: 222–24).

Exhibit A.2.7   Tax Justice Network: Tax Havens and Noxious Preferential Tax Regimes (2005)

Jurisdiction	Country Code	OECD	FSF-IMF 2000	TJN 2005
1. Andorra	AD	■	■	■
2. Anguilla	AI	■	■	■
3. Antigua & Barbuda	AG	■	■	■
4. Aruba	AW	■	■	■
5. Australia	AU	□		
6 Austria	AT	□		
7 Bahamas	BS	■	■	■
8. Bahrain	BH	■	■	■
9. Barbados	BB	*	■	■
10. Belgium	BE	□		■
11. Belize	BZ	■	■	■
12. Bermuda	BM	■	■	■
13. British Virgin Islands	VG	■	■	■
14. Canada	CA	□		
15. Cayman Islands	KY	■	■	■
16. Cook Islands	CK	■	■	■
17. Costa Rica	CR		■	■
18. Cyprus	CY	■	■	■
19. Domnica	DM	■	■	■
20. Dubai	AE			■
21. Finland (Åland)	FI	□		
22. France	FR	□		
23. Germany (Frankfurt)	DE	□		■
24. Gibraltar	GI	■	■	■
25. Greece	GR	□		
26. Grenada	GD	■	■	■
27. Guernsey, Sark & Alderney	GG	■	■	■
28. Hong Kong	HK		■	■
29. Hungary	HU	□		■

(Continued)

Exhibit A.2.7   (Continued)

Jurisdiction	Country Code	OECD	FSF-IMF 2000	TJN 2005
30. Iceland	IS	◻		■
31. Ireland	IE	◻	■	■
32. Isle of Man	IM	■	■	■
33. Israel (Tel Aviv)	IL			■
34. Italy (Campione d'Italia & Trieste)	IT	◻		■
35. Jersey	JE	■	■	■
36. Korea	KR	◻		
37. Latvia	LV			
38. Lebanon	LB		■	■
39. Liberia	LR	■		■
40. Liechtenstein	LI	■	■	■
41. Luxembourg	LU	◻	■	■
42. Macao	MO		■	■
43. Malaysia (Lubuan)	MY		■	■
44. Maldives	MV	*		■
45. Malta	MT	■	■	■
46. Marshall Islands	MH	■	■	■
47. Mauritius	MU	■	■	■
48. Monaco	MC	■	■	■
49. Montserrat	MS	■	■	■
50. Nauru	NR	■	■	■
51. Netherlands	NL	◻		■
52. Netherlands Antilles	AN	■	■	■
53. Niue	NU	■	■	■
54. Northern Mariana Islands	MP			■
55. Palau			■	
56. Panama	PA	■	■	■
57. Portugal (Madeira)	PT	◻		■
58. Russia (Ingushetia)	RU			■
59. Saint Kitts & Nevis	KN	■	■	■
60. Saint Lucia	LC	■	■	■

Jurisdiction	Country Code	OECD	FSF-IMF 2000	TJN 2005
61. Saint Vincent & the Grenadines	VC	■	■	■
62. Samoa	WS	■	■	■
63. San Marino	SM	■		
64. São Tomé e Principe	ST			■
65. Seychelles	SC	■	■	■
66. Singapore	SG		■	■
67. Somalia	SO			■
68. South Africa	ZA			■
69. Spain (Melilla)	ES	◘		■
70. Sweden	SE	◘		
71. Switzerland	CH	◘	■	■
72. Taiwan (Taipei)	TW			■
73. Tonga	TO	*		■
74. Turkey (Istanbul)	TR	◘		
75. Turkish Rep. of Northern Cyprus				■
76. Turks & Caicos Islands	TC	■	■	■
77. United Kingdom (City of London)	UK			■
78. Uruguay	UY			■
79. US Virgin Islands	VI	■		■
80. USA (New York)	US	◘		■
81. Vanuatu	VU	■	■	■

■   Tax Haven OECD, TJN 2007 / Offshore Financial Centre FSF/IMF 2000

◘   OECD member country with potentially harmful preferential tax regime as distinguished by OECD 2000

■   No longer regared a tax haven according to the OECD 2006

Note: OECD and other mainstream sources only count tax havens in the narrow geographic sense of the term; they do not include the Tax Justice Network's list of noxious preferential tax regimes.

Source: http://www.taxjustice.net/cms/upload/pdf/Identifying_Tax_Havens_Jul_07.pdf (pp. 8–9). Reprinted with permission.

3

National and Transnational Urban Systems

The trends described in Chapter 2 point to the emergence of a new kind of urban system, one operating at the global and transnational regional levels (Marcotullio and Lo 2001; Taylor 2004; RPA 2007; Derudder et al. 2010; Xu and Yeh 2010; Fainstein and Campbell 2011; Mori Foundation 2011; Bridge and Watson 2011). This is a system in which cities are crucial nodes for the international coordination and servicing of firms, markets, and even whole economies that are increasingly transnational. This global urban map of the *organizational* side of the world economy needs to be distinguished from the far wider global map of the consumption of globally distributed goods and services; consumer outlets of global brands are more or less everywhere, but this does not mean that these places are part of the organizational map of the global economy. And it needs to be distinguished from the global map of foreign direct investment; the fact that several buildings in a city are foreign owned does not necessarily make it part of the organizational map of the global economy. First, the foreign direct investment and, especially, the consumption map are far wider and more diffuse than the organizational map; the latter is strategic and dominated by about seventy global cities in a world with millions of cities. Second, global cities also emerge as strategic places in an emergent transnational political and cultural geography. The number of global cities grew sharply during the 1990s because the global economy expanded vastly as more and more countries, often under pressure, adopted the deregulatory and privatizing policies required for joining the global corporate system. Many other processes—global culture, migrations, global civil society—were part of the making of some cities into global cities, as I discuss later in this chapter.

Most cities, including most large cities, are not part of the new transnational urban systems. Typically, urban systems are coterminous with nation-states, and most cities exist within these national geographies. Correspondingly, studies of city systems in the 1980s and 1990s, when this new global phase was in full swing, generally took the nation-state as the unit of analysis. But there were important exceptions (Chase-Dunn 1984; Timberlake 1985; Savitch 1988; GaWC [Globalization and World Cities Study Group and Network]; Sassen [1991] 2001; Santos et al. 1994). Although this is still the most common view, there is now a growing scholarship that allows for the possibility that intercity networks can cross national borders directly, bypassing national states as these entities now have reduced gatekeeping functions.

This chapter examines the impact of economic globalization on national urban systems in order to understand if the globalization of major industries, from auto manufacturing to finance, has had distinct effects on different types of national urban systems. I focus especially on balanced and primate urban systems, the two major types identified in urban research. Western European countries have typically been regarded as a good example of balanced urban systems and Latin American countries as a good example of primate systems—where much of a country's population, jobs, and firms are concentrated in one city, typically the national capital. But we find this pattern also in developed economies, as exemplified with London and Tokyo. The second half of this chapter examines the emergence of transnational urban systems.

Global Patterns of Urbanization

Before entering into the detailed discussion of primate and balanced urban systems, focused on respectively Latin America and Europe, I briefly introduce some general growth trends for the world's urban population and for Africa and Asia, two continents with some of the highest population growth rates. Since 1988, the United Nations' Population Division has issued estimates and projections on the world's urban population growth, on countries' urbanization rates, and on cities' size—three different measures.[1] Some of the largest cities are in China and India, two countries with low urbanization rates, and some of the most urbanized countries have no megacities, for example, the Netherlands and Canada. Mexico is more urbanized than China, even though the latter has several megacities.

Exhibits 3.1 and 3.2 point to a future leveling off in the rate of urban population growth, though not in its absolute numbers, and a decline in the global share of the rural population has slowed between 1970 and 2010, though in absolute numbers it only declined in the developed world (see Exhibit 3.4). The developed world had its highest urban population growth rates in the 1970s, a process that can combine multiple different urban trends; in the United States, for instance, it took the form of massive suburbanization, growth in smaller cities, and declines in some of the largest cities. In Japan, some of the highest growth rates in the urban population happened in its period of accelerated industrialization in the 1960s when up to 60% of the rural population moved and was moved to cities (the government moved whole villages to the cities, grandmothers and all). As this process proceeded, inevitably the *rate* of growth would decline and eventually level off, and in the future, the rate of growth may well become negative—that is, if significant numbers leave cities and suburbs to live in exurbs and rural areas. But a declining urban population does not preclude a mostly urban population.

Exhibit 3.1 Average Annual Growth Rate for Urban Population, 1970–2010

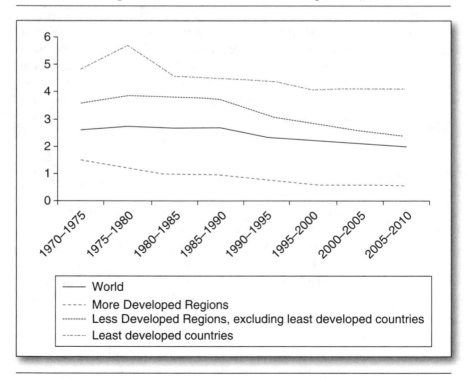

Source: Compiled from data in Population Division of the Department of Economic and Social Affairs of the United Nations Secretariat (2008).

Exhibit 3.2   Average Annual Growth Rate for Rural Population, 1970–2010

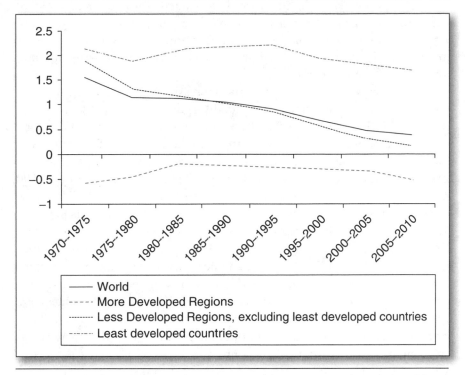

Source. Compiled from data in Population Division of the Department of Economic and Social Affairs of the United Nations Secretariat (2008).

In the developing world, this leveling off in urban population growth rates coexists with estimated ongoing increases in the actual number of urban dwellers up to 2030, along with an increased share of national GDP concentrated in the major cities (see Exhibits 3.3 and 3.4; see also Exhibit A.3.5). Although cities and suburbs in Africa are continuing to grow, overall, the rate of growth is declining from 5% growth between 1960 and 1965 to 3% in 2005 through 2010 and a projected 2% in 2045 through 2050 (UN 2010). In Asia, which today has one of the fastest-growing urban populations in the world, the actual rate of growth is declining, from 3.9% in 1960 through 1965 to a projected nominal 1% for 2045 through 2050 (UN 2010). Multiple conditions are likely to be at work, and they are likely to vary greatly across continents and across countries. India's unequal development and sharp inequality keep most of the poor in rural areas and villages—they are too poor even to migrate. China's tens of millions of rural migrants working in cities and metro areas are actually counted as nonurban because a city residence permit is required to be a permanent resident, and most of these workers are on a temporary work permit. Generally, Asia and Africa are home to very large slums, and many of those urban residents are not included in official counts, though multiple estimates abound about their rapid growth rate.

Finally, many of the large cities and increasingly some of the mid-sized cities are reaching the limits of their absorption capacity; this also happened earlier in Latin America, where Mexico City and Sao Paulo, among others, had been projected to reach thirty million residents by 1990 but in fact leveled off at about twenty million. It is clear that many parts of Asia are in desperate need of whole new cities. China is planning to build 100 new cities over the next few decades. But the massive costs of building new cities or significantly expanding existing cities, and the enormous planning and engineering challenges, make this an option only for some countries. What China can do, a country such as India, with its enormous concentrated wealth, cannot. India has the engineering talent and, in principle, the resources, but these are mostly and increasingly in private profit-seeking hands. Ineffectiveness and widespread corruption in the government are additional obstacles. The evidence suggests that for the hundreds of millions of poor in China, there is a bit of hope. But for those in India, there seems to be none. Brazil, without the resources and central planning powers of China, has done far more than India, through a simple government initiative: a flat grant to millions and millions of mostly urban poor families, which helped reduce poverty by thirty million people in only a few years. Nigeria's government commands massive wealth (derived from oil revenues) but that wealth has only enriched a small elite and has been employed to build a luxurious new capital city with prices sufficiently high so as to keep out most Nigerians; the government has chosen not to invest in massive infrastructure to provide reliable electricity, water and housing to its people.

A major issue for research and policy is urban primacy. Many regions in the world—Latin America, the Caribbean, large parts of Asia, and (to some extent) Africa—have long been characterized by urban primacy as older scholarship has established (Hardoy 1975; Linn 1983; Dogan and Kasarda 1988; Abreu et al. 1989; Lee 1989; Stren and White 1989; Lozano and Duarte 1991; Feldbauer et al. 1993). Primate cities account for a disproportionate share of population, employment, and gross national product (GNP; see Exhibit 3.4). For example, in 2007 to 2008, Buenos Aires had 32.4% of the national population but accounted for 63.3% of national GDP (see Exhibit 3.3).

Exhibit 3.3   National Share of Population and GDP for Select Primary Cities
2007–2008

City[a]	Country	City Share of National Population 2007 (%)	City GDP 2008 (US$ bn at PPP)[b]	National GDP 2008 (US$ bn at PPP)	City Percent of National GDP, PPP 2008
Algiers	Algeria	9.9	45	276	16.3%
Bogota	Columbia	16.8	100	396	25.3%
Buenos Aires	Argentina	32.4	362	572	63.3%
Casablanca Greater	Morocco	10.2	33	137	24.1%
Mexico City	Mexico	17.9	390	1,542	25.3%
Istanbul	Turkey	13.4	182	1,029	17.7%
Karachi	Pakistan	7.4	78	439	17.8%
Khartoum	Sudan	12.3	35	89	39.3%
Lagos	Nigeria	6.4	35	315	11.1%
Lima Metro	Peru	28.7	109	245	44.5%
Bangkok	Thailand	10.5	119	519	22.9%
Metro Manila	Philippines	12.6	149	317	47.0%
Mumbai	India	1.6	209	3,388	6.2%
Nairobi	Kenya	8.0	12	61	19.7%
Santiago	Chile	34.4	120	242	49.6%
Sao Paolo	Brazil	9.8	388	1,977	19.6%
Seoul	South Korea	20.3	291	1,358	21.4%

a. Cities include urban agglomeration.

b. GDP for urban agglomerations is estimated.

Source: Population statistics from Population Division of the Department of Economic and Social Affairs of the United Nations Secretariat (2008); city GDP estimates from PricewaterhouseCoopers (2009); National GDP from World Bank (2009).

Exhibit 3.4 Urban Growth Patterns in Select Developing Countries, 2008, and Projections for 2030

Country	Per capita GNI 2008 (US$)	Size of Population in Thousands				Urban Percentage of Population	
		2008		2030			
		Urban	Rural	Urban	Rural	2008	2030
Argentina	7,200	36,686	3,190	2,544	2,544	92.0	94.6
Mexico	9,980	82,103	24,248	106,689	21,436	77.2	83.3
Colombia	4,660	33,178	11,356	46,610	10,967	74.5	81.0
Brazil	7,350	164,289	27,682	215,492	20,988	85.6	91.1
Algeria	4,260	22,411	11,951	34,096	10,630	65.2	76.2
Morocco	2,580	17,494	13,735	25,883	13,376	56.0	65.9
Malaysia	6,970	18,992	8,001	28,994	6,276	70.4	82.2
Senegal	970	5,175	7,036	10,403	9,152	42.4	53.2
Côte d'Ivoire	980	10,044	10,547	17,632	10,456	48.8	62.8
Nigeria	1,160	73,178	78,141	144,246	82,609	48.4	63.3
Kenya	770	8,323	30,211	20,739	42,022	21.6	33.0
India	1,070	336,746	803,219	611,407	894,341	29.5	40.6
Indonesia	2,010	117,457	110,792	192,805	86,861	51.5	68.9
People's Republic of China	2,940	571,351	754,289	879,892	578,529	43.1	60.3

Source: Compiled from data in World Bank (2009) and Population Division of the Department of Economic and Social Affairs of the United Nations Secretariat (2008).

Primacy, the overwhelming dominance of one city in a county, is not about absolute size, nor is large size a marker of primacy. Algiers and Lima (see Exhibit 3.4), both primate cities, are not necessarily among the largest in the world. Primacy is a relative condition that holds within a national urban system. Some of the largest urban agglomerations in the world do not necessarily entail primacy: New York, for example, is among the twenty largest cities in the world, but it is not a primate city, given the multipolar nature of the urban system in the United States. The same can be said about Beijing or Mumbai. Furthermore, primacy is not an exclusive trait of developing countries, even though its most extreme forms are to be found in the developing world: Tokyo and London are primate cities in highly developed countries. Finally, the emergence of so-called megacities may or may not be associated with primacy.

Primacy and megacity status are clearly fed by urban population growth, a process that is expected to continue. But they combine in multiple patterns; there is no single model. The evidence worldwide points to the ongoing urbanization of the population, especially in developing countries, but not necessarily a decline in the share of the rural population (see generally Exhibit 3.3). Exhibit 3.4 shows rates of urban growth in select developing countries from the 1990s onward, a period that has seen the beginning of today's sharp urbanization of the world's population. The higher the level of development, the higher the urbanization rate, though not necessarily the urban population growth rate. It is important to note that there are countries such as India and China that have vast urban agglomerations, notwithstanding their very low rate of urbanization. As a result, the information conveyed by an indicator such as the urbanization rate in these countries differs from that of countries with more average population sizes. In 2008, the share of the urban population in India and in China was, respectively, 29.5% and 43.1%.

Urbanization in Africa Today

The Growth of Large Cities in Africa

Judging from UN records, both urbanization and megacities have been slow to arise in most of Africa. As of 1950, Al-Qahirah (Cairo) had 2.49 million people and was the only African city to appear in the list of "the 30 largest urban agglomerations" (UN 2010). We might want to keep in mind that Egypt became independent in 1922, while most African states were still subject to European colonial powers until the 1960s. But also, African countries that gained independence in 1950 had a low urbanization rate of 14.7%, and it was not until 2000 that it reached 37% and Africa had several megacities (UN 2002). Egypt has kept urbanizing, and Cairo has kept growing and is estimated to reach 13.5 million people by 2025 (UN 2010).

Lagos, the commercial center of the most populous African country, Nigeria, first joined the list of the world's thirty largest cities in 2000 (UN

2010); its population was 7.2 million and is expected to reach 15.8 million by 2025—the size of New York City today. It would make Lagos the world's 11th largest city (UN 2010). Starting in 2010, Kinshasa, capital of the Democratic Republic of Congo, joined the list of global megacities, with an estimated 8.75 million residents, projected to nearly double by 2025 at 15 million (UN 2010). Other large cities in Africa include Luanda, in Angola, which is expected to reach 8 million by 2025, Khartoum, Sudan, projected at almost 8 million in 2025, and Nairobi, Kenya, projected at 6 million by 2025. Nigeria has several cities of more than 4 million people, including Ibadan in the southwest and Kano in the north. South Africa's major cities are also growing, with Johannesburg projected to reach more than 4 million people in 2025 and its legislative capital, Cape Town, will outgrow its current population of 3 million (UN 2010). African cities are increasingly the commercial powerhouses for their respective countries (see Exhibit 3.3). For example, Algiers has 9.9% of Algeria's population but accounts for 16.3% of the country's GDP. Casablanca has 10.2% of Morocco's population but accounts for 24.1 % of its GDP. Nairobi has 8.0% of Kenya's population but accounts for 19.7% of Kenya's GDP.

Urbanization in Asia Today

Asia's Projected Urban Growth

As early as 1950, several Asian cities already appeared on the UN list of the world's largest cities. With 11.27 million inhabitants, Japan's Tokyo was then the world's second largest city. Another city from Japan, Osaka-Kobe, more than one city from India, Kolkata (Calcutta) and Mumbai (Bombay), and two more from China, Tianjin and Shenyang, also made the list. By the year 2010, Tokyo's population had grown to 36.7 million and so did other Asian cities, notably Delhi in India with 22 million and Mumbai with 20 million people. By the year 2025, the top three largest cities of the world are expected to be in Asia: Tokyo, Delhi, and Mumbai. By the year 2025, fifteen out of the world's thirty largest cities will be in Asia: Five of those are in China: Beijing, Shanghai, Guangzhou, Chongqing, and Shenzhen (UN 2010; see generally Exhibit A.3.2).

As with Africa, Asia's declining urban population growth rate does not preclude the rapid growth of cities and the absolute numbers of urban dwellers. Nor does it preclude their major role in the global economy and in global culture. Bangkok accounts for 10.5% of Thailand's population but for 22.9% of national GDP. Manila has 12.6% of the population but 47% of the Philippines' GDP (see Exhibit 3.4). Asia's cities also rank high in business connectivity, which refers to the density of business transactions connecting a city to other cities (see Exhibits 4.1 to 4.4). This accounts for five of the top ten cities on this variable. Hong Kong is the third most connected business city of the world, surpassed only by New York and London. Singapore ranks fifth, Tokyo sixth, Shanghai eighth, and Beijing tenth. China is the only country with three cities in the top ten in terms of business connectivity, although this can still mean that it has less than London or New York. I return to some of these issues later in the book (pp.111–127; A.4.1–A.4.6).

Impacts on Primate Systems:
The Case of Latin America and the Caribbean

On the subject of primacy, the literature about Latin America shows considerable convergence in the identification of major patterns, along with multiple interpretations of these patterns. Many studies in the late 1970s and early 1980s found sharper primacy rather than the emergence of the more balanced national urban systems forecast by *modernization* theory (for critical evaluations, see Edel 1986; El-Shakhs 1972; Roberts 1976; Smith 1985; Walters 1985). The disintegration of rural economies, including the displacement of small landholders by expanding large-scale commercial agriculture, and the continuing inequalities in the spatial distribution of institutional resources are generally recognized as key factors strengthening primacy (PREALC [Regional Employment Program for Latin America and the Caribbean] 1987; Kowarick, Campos, and de Mello 1991).

Less widely known and documented is that in the 1980s, there was a deceleration in primacy in several, although not all, countries in Latin America. This trend will not eliminate the growth of megacities, but it is worth discussing in some detail because it resulted in part from specific aspects of economic globalization—specifically, concrete ways in which global processes implant themselves in particular localities. The overall shift in growth strategies toward export-oriented development and large-scale tourism enclaves created growth poles that emerged as alternatives to the primate cities for rural-to-urban migrations (Landell-Mills, Agarwala, and Please 1989; Portes and Lungo 1992a, 1992b; Gilbert 1996; Roberts and Portes 2006).[2] This shift was substantially promoted by the expansion of world markets for commodities and the foreign direct investments of transnational corporations, both in turn often stimulated by World Bank and IMF programs.

One of the best sources of information on the emergence of these patterns in the 1980s is a large, collective, multicity study directed by Portes and Lungo (1992a, 1992b) that focused on the Caribbean region, including Central America.[3] The Caribbean has a long history of urban primacy. Portes and Lungo studied the urban systems of Costa Rica, the Dominican Republic, Guatemala, Haiti, and Jamaica. In the 1980s, export-oriented development, a cornerstone of the Caribbean Basin Initiative, and the intense promotion of tourism began to draw workers and firms. Expanded suburbanization has also had the effect of decentralizing population in the primate cities of the Caribbean while adding to the larger metropolitan areas of these cities. The effect of these trends can be seen clearly in Jamaica, for example, where the primacy index declined from 7.2 in 1960 to 2.2 in 1990, largely as a result of the development of the tourist industry on the northern coast of the island, the revival of bauxite production for export in the interior, and the growth of satellite cities at the edges of the broader Kingston metropolitan area. (See McMichael 2004 generally on development.)

In some Caribbean and Latin American countries, however, the new growth poles have had the opposite effect. Thus, in Costa Rica, a country with a far more balanced urban system, the promotion of export manufacturing and tourism has tended to concentrate activities in the metropolitan area of the primate city of San José and its immediate surrounding cities, such as Cartago. Finally, Guatemala has one of the highest levels of urban primacy in Latin America because a violent political situation hindered the development of alternative growth poles until the 1990s (Jonas 1992). Only in the 1990s did efforts to develop export agriculture promote some growth in intermediate cities, with coffee and cotton centers growing more rapidly than the capital, Guatemala City. (See generally Exhibits 3.3 to 3.5 and A.3.5.)

At the same time, deregulation and the associated sharp growth of foreign direct investment since the early 1990s (see Exhibit 3.5) has further strengthened the role of the major Latin American business centers, particularly in Brazil and Mexico. Also, as discussed in Chapter 2, privatization, FDI, and the financial system have been key components of this growth. The central role of financial firms and exchanges in these increasingly complex investment processes has raised the economic importance of the major cities where these institutions are concentrated—most prominently, Mexico City, Buenos Aires, and Sao Paulo.[4] We see in these cities the emergence of conditions that resemble patterns evident in major Western cities: highly dynamic financial markets and specialized service sectors; the overvaluing of the output, firms, and professionals in these sectors; and the devaluing of the rest of the economic system (Ciccolella and Mignaqui 2002; Parnreiter 2002; Schiffer 2002). This is a subject I return to in Chapter 4.

Exhibit 3.5   Foreign Direct Investment Inflows in Select Latin American Countries, 1985–2008 (Annual Averages in US$ millions)

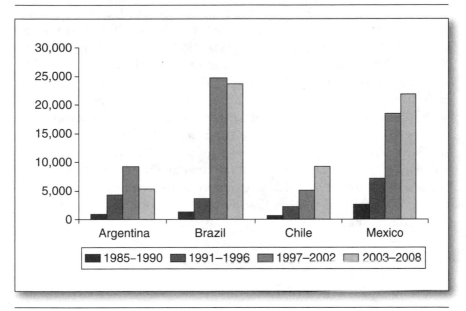

Source: Author's calculations based on UNCTAD (2009a).

In brief, economic globalization has had a range of impacts on cities and urban systems in Latin America and the Caribbean. In some cases, it has contributed to the development of new growth poles outside the major urban agglomerations. In others, it has actually raised the importance of primate urban agglomerations, in that the new growth poles were developed right in those areas. A third case is that represented by the major business and financial centers in the region, several of which saw a sharp strengthening in their linkages with global markets and with the major international business centers in the developed world.

Production zones, centers for tourism, and major business and financial centers are three types of sites for the implantation of global processes. Beyond these sites is a vast terrain containing cities, towns, and villages that are either increasingly unhinged from this new international growth dynamic or are part of the low-profit end of long chains of production (for one of the most detailed accounts, see the larger project summarized in Beneria 1989; Buechler 2007). The character of the articulation or dissociation is not simply a question of city size, since there exists long subcontracting chains connecting workers in small villages to the world markets. It is, rather, a question of how these emergent transnational economic systems are articulated, how they connect specific localities in less developed countries with markets and localities in highly developed countries (see, e.g., Beneria 1989; Ward 1991; Chaney and Castro 1993; Gereffi and Korzeniewicz 1994; Gereffi, Humphrey, and Sturgeon 2005; Chen 2009; Derudder et al. 2010; Bonacich et al. 1994; Bose and Acosta-Belen 1995). The implantation of global processes seems to have contributed to sharpening the separation between cities or sectors within cities which are articulated with the global economy and those that are not. This is a new type of interurban inequality, one not predicated on old hierarchies of city size. The new inequality differs from the long-standing forms of inequality present in cities and national urban systems because of the extent to which it results from the *implantation* of a global dynamic, be it the internationalization of production and finance or international tourism.

Impacts on Balanced Urban Systems: The Case of Europe

One of the most interesting findings of a major multiyear, multicountry study on cities in Europe, sponsored by the European Economic Community (EEC), was the renewed demographic and economic importance of Europe's large cities in the 1980s. (For a summary, see Kunzmann and Wegener 1991; European Institute of Urban Affairs 1992; see also Eurocities 1989; INURA 2003; Kazepov 2005.) In the 1960s and 1970s, most, if not all, of these large cities had experienced declines in population and in economic activity, whereas smaller cities experienced growth in both dimensions. We saw a similar pattern in the United States, where this process took the form of suburbanization.

Many analysts, both in Europe and in the United States, asserted that central cities, with the exception of old historical centers with cultural importance, had lost much of their use to people and to the economy. The widespread growth of small cities in Europe in those two earlier decades was seen as a strong indication of how balanced the urban systems of Western European nations were and continue to be. And, indeed, compared with almost any other major continental region, Western European nations had and continue to have the most balanced urban systems in the world. Nonetheless, it is now clear that beginning in the 1980s and continuing today, major cities in Europe have gained population and experienced significant economic growth (see Exhibits 3.6, A.3.4, and A.3.6). The exceptions were some of Europe's large cities in more peripheral areas: There were continuing losses in Marseilles, Naples, and England's old industrial cities, Manchester and Birmingham. But some of these cities have also seen new population and economic gains as of the late 1990s (see Kazepov 2005). Marseilles in particular displayed a major increase while Naples and Manchester only experienced minor growth between 2005 and 2010. At the same time, compared with the 1960s, the sharpest growth has occurred in the larger metropolitan areas. Smaller cities slowed down, often markedly, in the 1980s and continue to do so today. Indeed, there is now an emergent field of research focused on "shrinking cities" in older industrial areas of Europe.

These trends can be interpreted in several ways. On one hand, these could be mild demographic shifts that leave the characteristics of the urban system basically unaltered; that is, urban systems remain balanced at the levels of the nation and of Western Europe as a whole. On the other hand, the trends could indicate a renewed importance of major cities because the economic changes evident in all developed countries have organizational and spatial implications for such cities. The EEC study mentioned earlier found that the second of these interpretations fits the data gathered for twenty-four cities in Europe for the 1980s. The evidence shows clearly that the period 1985 to 1990 marks the crucial turnaround from negative to positive population growth in the urban core after consistent losses in the preceding periods (see Exhibit 3.6; see also Eurocities 1989; Kazepov 2005; for critical accounts of the contents of this growth, see Hitz et al. 1995; Bodnar 2000; INURA 2003). Further, in the 2005 to 2010 period, cities like Barcelona, Dublin, and Madrid experienced rapid growth. Finally, the evidence also signals that the new organization and composition of the economy of core cities can accommodate high economic growth with little, and even negative, population growth (see also Sassen [1991] 2001: chaps. 8–9; 2007: chap. 4).

The organizational and spatial implications of the new economic trends assume distinct forms in various urban systems. Some cities become part of transnational networks, whereas others become unhinged from the main centers of economic growth in their regions or countries. A review of the EEC report, as well as other major studies on cities in Europe, suggests that there are at least three tendencies in the reconfiguration of urban systems in

Exhibit 3.6 Annual Average Rate of Population Change in Select European Cities, 1970–2010

City[a]	1970–1975	1975–1980	1980–1985	1985–1990	1990–1995	1995–2000	2000–2005	2005–2010
Amsterdam	1.07	−0.79	−0.73	0.62	1.09	0.34	0.36	0.41
Antwerpen	0.30	0.28	0.01	0.28	0.28	0.13	0.14	0.05
Athens	1.94	1.74	0.39	0.15	0.34	0.37	0.31	0.17
Barcelona	1.10	0.84	0.68	0.65	1.03	1.09	1.09	0.98
Berlin	−0.48	−0.48	0.03	2.23	0.29	−0.51	0.04	0.19
Birmingham	−0.04	−0.07	−0.23	−0.25	−0.09	−0.05	−0.02	0.07
Bordeaux	1.00	0.63	0.91	1.04	0.88	0.88	0.78	0.60
Brussels	0.54	0.53	0.00	0.32	0.41	0.21	0.10	0.02
Cologne	1.33	1.33	−1.08	0.66	0.31	−0.04	0.28	1.19
Copenhagen	−3.27	−1.33	−0.74	−0.41	0.25	0.54	0.14	0.04
Dublin	1.55	1.62	0.36	−0.08	0.65	0.87	0.96	1.14
Glasgow	−1.60	−1.83	−1.82	−1.82	−0.52	−0.26	−0.19	0.07
Hamburg	−0.82	−0.82	−0.81	0.66	0.81	0.04	0.34	0.43
Helsinki	2.75	2.93	1.45	3.7	1.57	1.56	1.42	0.81
Lille	0.66	0.01	0.20	0.31	0.47	0.47	0.50	0.50
Lisbon	2.93	3.04	0.56	0.15	0.49	0.55	0.66	0.91
Liverpool	−4.52	−5.23	0.11	1.06	−0.05	−0.26	−0.18	0.11
London	0.10	0.30	0.02	−0.03	0.65	0.79	0.67	0.24
Lyon	1.00	0.60	0.48	0.44	0.74	0.73	0.66	0.50
Madrid	2.00	1.78	0.47	0.27	1.26	1.41	1.41	1.25

City[a]	1970–1975	1975–1980	1980–1985	1985–1990	1990–1995	1995–2000	2000–2005	2005–2010
Manchester	-0.22	-0.23	-0.26	-0.26	-0.18	-0.16	-0.12	0.04
Marseilles	1.16	0.66	0.18	-0.03	0.39	0.39	0.43	0.46
Milan	0.76	0.22	-0.25	-0.42	-0.28	-0.23	-0.21	-0.09
Munich	0.04	0.04	-0.49	-0.79	0.37	-0.62	0.85	0.72
Naples	0.94	0.84	0.21	-0.01	0.09	0.13	0.12	0.06
Newcastle	-1.10	-1.20	0.87	1.24	0.14	-0.07	-0.01	0.16
Nice-Cannes	1.85	0.97	1.44	1.60	0.46	0.46	0.50	0.52
Oslo	0.04	-0.04	0.60	0.64	1.28	1.19	1.07	0.99
Paris	0.49	0.26	0.65	0.82	0.38	0.38	0.33	0.21
Porto	1.73	1.81	0.63	0.43	0.72	0.77	0.86	1.05
Rome	1.03	0.54	0.23	0.12	-0.14	-0.24	-0.22	-0.10
Rotterdam	-0.85	-0.33	0.37	0.47	0.62	0.19	0.19	0.28
Stockholm	-0.39	-0.46	0.41	0.51	1.83	1.16	0.69	0.58
Thessaloniki	2.57	2.35	0.86	0.59	0.66	0.67	0.59	0.39
Toulouse	1.82	0.85	1.81	2.26	1.75	1.74	1.34	0.72
Turin	0.86	0.25	-0.36	-0.58	-0.48	-0.45	-0.40	-0.16
Valencia	1.50	1.38	0.47	0.34	0.25	0.24	0.24	0.29
Vienna	-0.1	-0.1	0.2	0.26	0.29	0.29	0.96	1.04
Zurich	0.08	-0.18	3.37	3.69	0.83	0.56	0.39	0.35

a. Population statistics for cities refer to greater metropolitan areas.

Source: Compiled from data in Population Division of the Department of Economic and Social Affairs of the United Nations Secretariat (2008).

Western Europe that began in the 1980s. First, several sub-European regional systems have emerged (CEMAT [European Conference of Ministers Responsible for Regional Planning] 1988; Kunzmann and Wegener 1991). Second, within the territory of the EEC and several immediately adjacent countries (Austria, Denmark, and Greece) in the 1980s, the new European Union in the 1990s, and the enlarged union as of 2005, a limited number of cities have strengthened their role in an emergent European urban system. Finally, a few of these cities are also part of an urban system that operates at the global level.

National European urban systems are also being affected by these developments. The traditional national urban networks are changing. Cities that were once dominant in their countries may lose that importance, while cities in border regions or transportation hubs may gain a new importance. Furthermore, the new European global cities may capture some of the business, demands for specialized services, and investments that previously went to national capitals or major provincial cities. Cities at the periphery will feel the widening gap with the newly defined and positioned geography of centrality.

Cities in peripheral regions and old port cities began to lose ground in the 1970s and 1980s in their national urban systems as a result of the new hierarchies (van den Berg et al. 1982; Siebel 1984; Hausserman and Siebel 1987; Castells 1989; Parkinson, Foley, and Judd 1989; Roncayolo 1990; Vidal et al. 1990). By the 1990s, many cities were increasingly disconnected from the major European urban systems. Some of these peripheralized cities with outmoded industrial bases have reemerged with new functions and as part of new networks in the 1990s—for example, Lille in France as a major transportation hub, especially for the Eurostar transport system, and Glasgow in the United Kingdom as a major tourism and cultural destination. Others have lost politico-economic functions and are unlikely to regain them in the foreseeable future. Yet others are becoming centers for tourism or places for second homes; for example, a growing number of high-income Germans and English have bought country houses—indeed, whole "castles"—in rural Ireland, inducing other continental Europeans to do the same. In an ironic twist, much of the beauty and current value of the Irish countryside—whole regions untouched by industrialization—is a legacy of poverty; it also became the site for much of Ireland's high-tech manufacturing. Changes in military defense policies resulting from the fall of the Soviet Union and its recomposition into a series of smaller nation-states have brought decline in cities that were once crucial production centers or control centers for an earlier phase of national security systems. Smaller port cities, or large ones that have not upgraded and modernized their infrastructures, are at a great disadvantage in competing with the large, modernized port cities in Europe. Marseilles was once a great port, strategically located on the Mediterranean; today, it has been left behind by Rotterdam and a few other major European ports that constitute a cluster of state-of-the-art ports. Nothing in the near future seems to secure the revitalization of old industrial centers on the basis of the industries that once were their economic core. The most difficult cases are small and medium-size cities in somewhat isolated or peripheral areas dependent on coal and steel industries. They are likely to have degraded their environments and hence do not even have the option of becoming tourist centers.

The shifts that took off in the 1980s were sufficiently dramatic to engage a whole series of scholars into painting new urban scenarios for Europe. Kunzmann and Wegener (1991) asserted that the dominance of large cities would continue in part because they would be more competitive in getting both European and non-European investors' preferences for the larger high-tech industrial and service cities (see also Deecke, Kruger, and Lapple 1993). Furthermore, according to some researchers, this spatial polarization would deepen because of the development of high-speed transport infrastructure and communications corridors, which would help to connect major centers or highly specialized centers essential to the advanced economic system (Masser, Sviden, and Wegener 1990; Castells and Hall 1994; Graham and Marvin 1996). Much of this forecasting is turning out to be correct. We see massive concentrations of resources in some cities (e.g., Abrahamson 2004; Rutherford 2004) and peripheral cities that are literally shrinking: Their built environment is severely underutilized and in some cases fully abandoned (see, e.g., Giesecke 2005). However, an old mining and steel city such as Lille is now one of Western Europe's major transportation and communications hubs. This has radically changed this once-dying industrial city. This is but one of many such cases. European cities have a capacity to reinvent themselves through energetic government support and civic leadership that is rare in the rest of the world.

A process of recentralization may be occurring in certain cities that have been somewhat peripheral. Some of the smaller cities in Europe (such as Aachen, Strasbourg, Nice, Liege, and Arnheim) are likely to benefit from the single European market insofar as they can expand their hinterland and function as a nexus to a broader European region. Changes in Eastern Europe are likely to strengthen the role of Western European cities that used to have extensive interregional linkages before World War II—notably Hamburg, Copenhagen, and Nuremberg—which in turn may have the effect of weakening the position of other peripheral cities in those regions. Cities bordering Eastern Europe may assume new roles or resume old ones;

Vienna and Berlin are emerging as international business platforms for the whole central European region.[5]

Finally, major Eastern European cities such as Budapest, Prague, and Warsaw may regain some of their prewar importance. Budapest is a good example: Toward the late 1980s, it emerged as the leading international business center for the Eastern European region, a role illustrated by the fact that Hungary has since consistently been a major recipient of foreign direct investment in Eastern Europe (see Exhibit 3.7; Bodnar 2000). Although the absolute investment levels were lower than those in the Russian Federation (with its vastly larger territory and economy than Hungary), in relative terms, these figures represent a greater internationalization than in the former Soviet Union. Western European and non-European firms seeking to do business in Eastern Europe established offices in Budapest to launch operations for a large transnational Central European region. By the early 1990s, Budapest had a rather glamorous Western-looking international business enclave that offered the requisite comforts, hotels, restaurants, and business services to an extent that most other major

Exhibit 3.7   Foreign Direct Investment Inflows in Select Central and Eastern European Countries, 1991–2008 (Annual Averages in US$ millions)

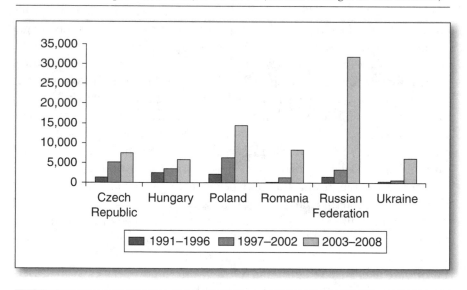

Notes: Annual average for 1993–1996 in Czech Republic and 1992–1996 for Ukraine and Russian Federation.

Source: Author's calculations based on UNCTAD (2009a).

Eastern European cities did not have at the time. More recently, however, the Russian Federation received significantly more FDI than the rest of Eastern Europe.

Europe, once a continent of emigration, has become a major receiver of immigrants since the 1960s, albeit that it has had small immigration flows for centuries (Sassen 1999). Immigration was seen by many as a partial solution to Europe's demographic deficit and it has become a major factor in demographic and labor-force growth. Today, given high unemployment and virulent anti-immigration sentiment in many quarters, this role becomes less likely. An initial scholarship that engaged the new migration phase that took off in the 1980s argued that immigration would continue (Brown 1984; Gillette and Sayad 1984; Cohen 1987; Blaschke and Germershausen 1989; Balbo and Manconi 1990; Canevari 1991; Tribalat et al. 1991; SOPEMI [Systeme d'Observation Permanente pour les Migrations] 1999–2005).[6] In fact, cities that function as gateways into Europe receive, and continue to, immigration flows from Eastern Europe, Africa, and the Middle East. This led to increasingly strong political divisions as many of these cities, particularly old port cities such as Marseilles, Palermo, and Naples, were already experiencing economic decline and were seen as unable to absorb the additional labor and costs (for critical examinations of some of these assumptions, see Mingione 1991; Pugliese 2002). Although these cities may have functioned largely as entrepôts, with variable shares of immigrants expected to move on to more dynamic cities, resident immigrant populations also took root.

One concern in these cities has been that having their infrastructures and services overburdened would further peripheralize these gateway cities in the emerging European urban hierarchy connecting leading cities in Europe and contribute to socio-spatial polarization. However, some of Europe's global cities, such as Paris and Frankfurt, which are at the center of major transportation networks and are final destinations for many immigrants, have recognized the often major benefits associated with significant shares of immigrants in their populations and workforces. In Frankfurt, for example, 24% of the workforce is foreign born, including significant shares of top-level professionals (City of Frankfurt, 2011). In other cases, it is older imperial geographies that have made certain cities key destinations, with often positive dispositions towards immigrants. Thus, Berlin, an emerging global city in a variety of highly specialized sectors (culture, new media, software design), is also a preferred destination of many new migrations, as is Vienna. In the past, Berlin and Vienna were centers of vast regional migration systems, and they seem to be recapturing that old role. The enlarging of the European Union in 2004 has created a new perimeter for

Europe with growing concerns that the Eastern edge cities in that perimeter will have to take on immigration control and gateway functions for which they are not fully equipped or prepared. Elsewhere (Sassen 1999, 2007: chap. 5), I have argued that Europe has had immigration for centuries, with steep up and down cycles of positive and negative dispositions toward immigrants, and has always wound up with significant levels of integration—as is suggested by, for example, a third of France's native-born population having a foreign-born ancestor two or three generations back, a figure that goes up to 40% in the case of a city such as Vienna. I return to immigration issues in some of the later chapters.

There are, then, a multiplicity of economic and demographic geographies of centers and margins in Europe at this time. A central urban hierarchy connects major cities, many of which in turn play key roles in the wider global system of cities: Paris, London, Frankfurt, Amsterdam, Zurich, Madrid, and Milan. Paris, for example, hosted twenty-seven of the top 500 corporations in addition to a number of banking and service firms in 2009 (see Exhibit A.3.9). Somewhat less oriented to the global economy is a major network of European financial/cultural/service capitals, such as Edinburgh, Berlin, Dublin, Rome, Stockholm, Prague, and Warsaw—some with only one and others with several of these functions, which articulate the European region. And then there are several geographies of margins: the East–West divide and the North–South divide across Europe as well as new micro-divisions. In Eastern Europe, certain cities and regions are rather attractive for European and non-European investment, whereas others will increasingly fall behind (notably, those in the former Yugoslavia and Albania). A similar differentiation exists in the south of Europe: Madrid, Barcelona, and Milan are gaining in the new European hierarchy; Naples and Marseilles much less.

Transnational Urban Systems

A rapidly growing and highly specialized research literature began to focus in the 1980s on different types of economic linkages binding cities across national borders (Friedmann and Wolff 1982; Sassen-Koob 1982, 1984; Leyshon, Daniels, and Thrift 1987; Noyelle and Dutka 1988; Sassen 1988; Castells 1989; Daniels 1991; Graham and Marvin 1996; GaWC 1998). Today, this has emerged as a major issue of interest to a variety of disciplines (Taylor 2004; Derudder et al. 2010; Xu and Yeh 2010; Mori Foundation 2011), even though the data are partial and often problematic. Prime examples of such linkages are the multinational networks of affiliates and subsidiaries typical of major firms in manufacturing and specialized services (see Exhibits 2.5 and 4.7). The internationalization and deregulation of various financial markets is yet another very recent development that binds cities across borders, to be discussed in Chapter 4. An increasing number of stock markets around the world now participate in a global equities market. There are also a growing number of less directly economic linkages, notable among which are a variety of initiatives launched by urban governments that amount to a type of foreign policy by and for cities. In this context, the long-standing tradition of designating sister cities (Zelinsky 1991) has recently been reactivated, taking on a whole new meaning in the case of cities eager to operate internationally without going through their national governments (Eurocities 1989; Sassen 2002; Toly 2008; Burdett and Sudjic 2011)

Some of the most detailed data on transnational linkages binding cities come from studies on corporate services firms. These firms have developed vast multinational networks containing special geographic and institutional linkages that make it possible for client firms—transnational firms and banks—to use a growing array of service offerings from the same supplier (Daniels 1991; Ernst 2005; Bryson and Daniels 2007). There is good evidence that the development of transnational corporate service firms was associated with the needs of transnational firms for global servicing capabilities (Ernst 2005; Sassen [1991] 2001: chap. 5). One of the best data sets on the global networks of affiliates of leading firms in finance, accounting, law, and advertising is the Globalization and World Cities Study Group and Network, usually referred to (including in this book) as GaWC. Recent GaWC research shows that the network of affiliates in banking/finance and law firms closely follows the relative importance of world cities in those two sectors (see Exhibits 3.8 and 3.9 and A.3.11 to A.3.14). The transnational banking/finance or law firm, therefore, can offer global finance and legal services to a specific segment of potential customers worldwide. And so can the global communications firms. Global integration of affiliates and markets requires making use of advanced information and telecommunications technology that can come to account for a significant share of costs—not only operational costs but also, and perhaps most importantly, research and development costs for new products or advances on existing products.

The need for scale economies on all these fronts helps explain the recent increase in mergers and acquisitions, which has consolidated the position of a few very large firms in many of these industries and has further strengthened cross-border linkages between the key locations that concentrate the needed telecommunications facilities. These few firms can now control a significant share of national and international markets. The rapid increase in foreign direct investment in services is strongly linked with the high level of concentration in many of these industries and a strong tendency toward increasing market share among the larger firms. This is particularly true for firms servicing large corporations. At the same time, subcontracting by larger firms and a proliferation of specialized markets has meant that small independent firms can also thrive in major business centers. The link between international law firms and financial firms has contributed to a centralization of law firms in major financial centers.

Derudder et al. (2010) and Taylor et al. (2010) have developed a methodology and several data sets that allow them to measure intercity networks (Exhibit 3.8 and 3.9). They gathered data on the locational strategies of 175 advanced producer services (APS) firms in 525 cities, with full details provided in the cited texts. For each of the 175 firms, they measured a city's importance as a location for the firm; the city's score can range from 0 (when the firm has no office in that city) to 5 when it has the firm's global corporate headquarters. They computed the overall connectivity of each city in the office networks of globalized APS firms by applying a network model to this data set—175 corporate services firms in 525 cities, which delivers 91,875 pieces of information. For ease of interpretation, business connectivities are presented as percentages of the most connected city. Clearly, these connectivities are not a measure of a city's international communication technologies capacity but rather a measure of how they fit in global business networks of high-level economic sectors.

Exhibit 3.8 shows the connectivity results for cities in 2000 and in 2008, with data gathered basically in the same way for each year. New York and London were the cities with the highest level of connectivity in 2000 and stayed so in 2008. Hong Kong increased its connectivity as did rapidly rising cities like Paris, Singapore, Sydney, Shanghai, Beijing, Seoul, and Moscow. Major connectivity losses were found in Los Angeles and San Francisco. They found that in North America, only New York, Toronto, and Chicago remain among the world's most well-connected cities. These outcomes confirm the data presented in Chapter 4 (Exhibits 4.1 to 4.5), with a decline in the position of US cities except for New York and Chicago and a rise of especially Asian cities, but also, and less noticed, smaller European cities and some Latin American cities. Exhibit 3.9 points to the complexity of the world city network based on the business links of these APS firms bus, which signal potential workflows. The graph shows intercity links that scored more than 450, a number that indicates that these cities share about fifty of the sample's 175 firms in the 2008 data set. A city's size in the graph represents its overall connectivity, and the lines represent the size of their links.

Exhibit 3.8   Comparative Business Connectivity of Cities, 2000 and 2008
(percentages)

	2000			2008	
1	London	100.00	1	New York	100.00
2	New York	97.10	2	London	99.32
3	Hong Kong	73.08	3	Hong Kong	83.41
4	Tokyo	70.64	4	Paris	79.68
5	Paris	69.72	5	Singapore	76.15
6	Singapore	66.61	6	Tokyo	73.62
7	Chicago	61.18	7	Sydney	70.93
8	Milan	60.44	8	Shanghai	69.06
9	Madrid	59.23	9	Milan	69.05
10	Los Angeles	58.75	10	Beijing	67.65
11	Sydney	58.06	11	Madrid	65.95
12	Frankfurt	57.53	12	Moscow	64.85
13	Amsterdam	57.10	13	Brussels	63.63
14	Toronto	56.92	14	Seoul	62.74
15	Brussels	56.51	15	Toronto	62.38
16	Sao Paulo	54.26	16	Buenos Aires	60.62
17	San Francisco	50.43	17	Mumbai	59.48
18	Zurich	48.42	18	Kuala Lumpur	58.44
19	Taipei	48.22	19	Chicago	57.57
20	Jakarta	47.92	20	Taipei	56.07

Source: Derudder et al. (2010) and Taylor et al. (2010).

When we disaggregate by sector, we can see shifts in the overall connectivity of cities. For instance, Hong Kong is as well connected in the financial services sectors, as are New York and London. And Brussels is very well connected in legal services, mostly due to the European Union and its

Exhibit 3.9 Top Dyads 2010

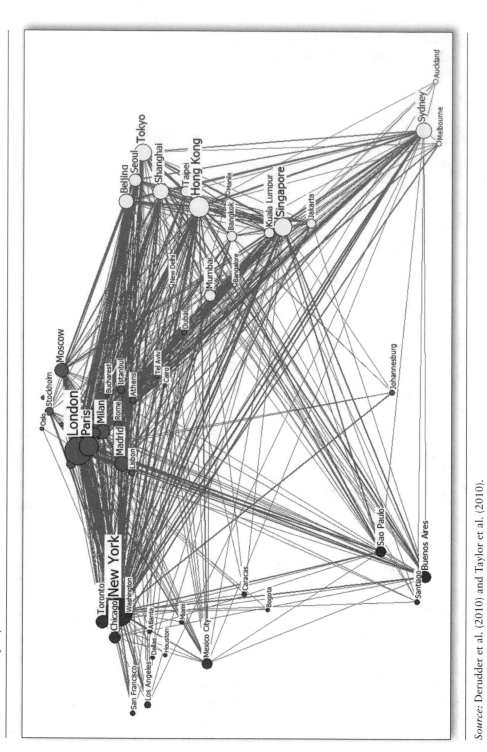

Source: Derudder et al. (2010) and Taylor et al. (2010).

central role in legal matters. (For several sectoral exhibits, see Exhibits A.3.10 to A.3.14.) This again confirms the evidence presented in Chapter 4 (Exhibits 4.1 to 4.5) showing the many different positions cities have in global networks depending on what factor is being considered.

Whether these links have engendered transnational urban systems is less clear and is partly a question of theory and conceptualization. So much of social science is profoundly rooted in the nation-state as the ultimate unit for analysis that conceptualizing processes and systems as transnational is bound to create controversy. Much of the literature on world and global cities does not necessarily proclaim the existence of a transnational urban system: in its narrowest form, this literature posits that global cities perform central place functions at a transnational level. But that leaves open the question of the nature of the articulation among global cities. If we accept that they basically compete with each other for global business, then they do not constitute a transnational system. Studying several global cities then falls into the category of traditional comparative analysis. If, however, we posit that in addition to competing with each other, global cities are also the sites for transnational processes with multiple locations (Taylor 2004), then we can begin to explore the possibility of a systemic dynamic binding these cities.

Elsewhere (Sassen [1991] 2001, chaps. 1 and 7; 2002), I have argued that in addition to the central place functions performed by these cities at the global level as posited by Hall (1966), Friedmann and Wolff (1982), and Sassen-Koob (1982), these cities relate to one another in distinct systemic ways. For example, already in the 1980s, when the notion of global multi-sited systems was barely developed, I found that the interactions among New York, London, and Tokyo, particularly in terms of finance, services, and investment, consisted partly of a series of processes that could be thought of as "chains of production" and international divisions of labor. Thus, in the case of global finance in the mid-1980s, I argued that Tokyo functioned as the main exporter of the raw material we call money, while New York was the leading financial processing and innovation center in the world. Many of the new financial instruments were invented in New York; and money, either in its raw form or in the form of debt, was transformed into instruments aimed at maximizing the returns on that money. London, the world's major banking entrepôt, had the network to centralize and concentrate small amounts of capital available in a large number of smaller financial markets around the world, partly as a function of its older network for the administration of the British Empire. More recently, I have replicated this type of analysis focusing on the specialized differences of major global cities (RPA 2007; Urban Geography 2008; Xu and Yeh 2010: chap. 5).

These are examples suggesting that cities do not simply compete with each other for the same business. There is an economic system that rests on the distinct types of locations and specializations each city represents. Furthermore, it seems likely that the strengthening of transnational ties among the leading financial and business centers is accompanied by a weakening of the linkages between each of these cities and its hinterland and national urban system (Sassen [1991] 2001). Cities such as Detroit, Liverpool, Manchester, Marseilles, the cities of the Ruhr, and now Nagoya and Osaka have been affected by the territorial decentralization of many of their key manufacturing industries at the domestic and international levels. But this same process of decentralization has contributed to the growth of service industries that produce the specialized inputs to run spatially dispersed production processes and global markets for inputs and outputs. Such specialized inputs—international legal and accounting services, management consulting, and financial services—are heavily concentrated in business and financial centers rather than in manufacturing cities. In brief, the manufacturing jobs that Detroit began to lose in the 1970s and 1980s fed a growing demand for specialized corporate services in New York City to coordinate and manage a now globally distributed auto manufacturing system. This is a mix of outcomes that is evident in many different cases.

Global Cities and Immigration

The United Nations data on immigrants has focused generally on the number of foreign-born residents in countries. Given that immigrants comprise an integral part of every city's workforce and social sphere, obtaining a specific account of the foreign-born residents in cities would be helpful in understanding what the world's top urban immigrant destinations are and whether leading global cities are also magnets for immigrants. But obtaining adequate information is a challenge. Professors Marie Price and Lisa Benton-Short of George Washington University (2007) have produced a data set that covers some of these issues from a global perspective. In their larger project, they focus on urban immigration and settlement to discover how immigrant flows are driven by income differentials, social networks, and the varying immigration regulation policies of sovereign states. For their analysis, the authors employ a census-based methodology. They use data from national censuses (which counts the entire population of any given city) rather than just track the yearly immigration rates as documented by various state governments, covering largely the 2000 through 2007 years for a total of 150 cities and 52 countries. The cities listed here are host to at least 1 million or more foreign residents, with at least 100,000 of those residents being foreign born.

The authors find twenty cities with at least 1 million or more foreign residents. Some are established immigrant gateways—Sydney, New York, London,

Chicago, and Toronto. Others, such as Dubai, Houston, Washington, DC, Dallas-Ft. Worth, and San Francisco, have only recently become immigrant hubs. These "million immigrant cities"[7] account for about 37 million foreign-born residents, which amounts to about 19% of the world's immigrant population. They are scattered throughout the globe, with nine in North America, three in Europe, four in the Middle East, two in Asia, and two in Australia/Oceania. There are no Latin American and African cities among them. Many of these million immigrant cities are also hyperdiverse; as the immigrants make up almost 10% of the population, they hail from all regions of the world, and no one country provides 25% or more of the immigrant in-flow.

Exhibit 3.10   Cities With More Than 1 Million Foreign-born Residents as of 2005 (unless indicated otherwise)

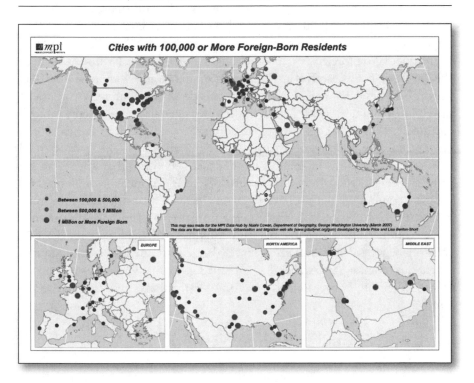

Cities With at Least 100,000 Immigrants

European cities predominate in this category. Exhibit A.3.12 shows that there are thirty European cities that have more than 100,000 foreign-born residents, and it is significant that immigrants account for 10% or more of their urban population. All Western European cities have at least one immigrant hub city of at least 100,000 immigrants, and countries such as Germany, France, and the United Kingdom play host to several such cities. The authors note, however, that the recent "increase" of immigrants in Eastern Europe might not necessarily be the result of any migratory movement but rather might stem from political reclassifications. For example, Moscow, St. Petersburg, Kyiv, and Tbilisi have significant numbers of "foreign-born" residents. While some "new" or "nontraditional" immigrants such as Afghans, Angolans, and Chinese might explain a small amount of this augmentation, the break-up of the Soviet Union accounts for most of it. The demise of the Soviet Union resulted in the phenomenon of former Soviet citizens being reclassified as "foreign-born" residents because the republic they reside in was no longer part of the republic in which they had been born.

This category also includes other regions of the world that have experienced rapid immigrant growth in the past century due to immigrant-friendly state policies. For example, in response to the temporary worker programs offered by Persian Gulf cities, thousands of workers from North Africa and Asia have migrated there. Dubai, in particular, is an extreme case, with more than 80% of the population foreign-born and holding high-level jobs all the way down to the lowest-paid jobs. Israel is also a country of immigrants with more than one-third of the residents having been born outside of the country. Two African cities, Johannesburg, South Africa, and Accra, Ghana, are represented in this category. As the most fiscally sound country in sub-Saharan Africa, South Africa should continue to receive more African immigrants. This upward trend of immigration stands in contrast to the Asian countries that appear in this same category. Although there has been an accelerated increase of immigrants to Asian countries in the last fifteen years, foreigners still only make up a small percentage of Asian cities. For example, less than 1% of Seoul's population is foreign born. The authors note that this could be attributed to "limited access to permanent residency and citizenship." Also, Latin America has seen more of an exodus of immigrants rather than an influx, with many residents leaving for North American, European, and also Asian destinations.

Global Cities and Diasporic Networks

A particular type of transnational urban system is slowly emerging from a variety of networks concerned with transboundary issues such as immigration, asylum, international women's agendas, antiglobalization struggles, and many others. Although these networks are not necessarily urban in their orientation or genesis, their geography of operations is partly inserted in a large number of cities. The new network technologies, especially the Internet, ironically have strengthened the urban map of these transboundary networks. It does not have to be that way, but at this time, cities and the networks that bind them function as anchors and enablers of cross-border transactions and struggles. Global cities especially already have multiple intercity transactions and immigrants from many different parts of the world. These same developments and conditions also facilitate the globalizing of terrorist and trafficking networks. But they also facilitate the development of activist and civil society networks; for instance, the international activist network Avaaz.org has 3.5 million members. (See generally Lustiger-Thaler and Dubet 2004; Latham and Sassen 2005; Dean et al. 2006; Fraser 2007; Daniels 2009; Lovink and Dean 2010.)

Global cities and the new strategic geographies that connect them and partly bypass national states are becoming a factor in the development of globalized diasporic networks. This is a development from the ground up, connecting a diaspora's multiple groups distributed across various places. In so doing, these networks multiply the transversal transactions among these groups and destabilize the exclusive orientation to the homeland typical of the older radial pattern (Axel 2002). Furthermore, even a partial reorientation away from national homeland politics can ease these groups' transactions in each city with that city's other diasporas and nondiasporic groups involved in diverse types of transnational activities and imaginaries (Bartlett 2007). In such developments, in turn, lies the possibility that at least some of these networks and groups can become part of the infrastructure for global civil society rather than being confined to deeply nationalistic projects. These dynamics can then be seen as producing a shift toward globalizing diasporas by enabling transversal connections among the members of a given worldwide diaspora and by intensifying the transactions among diverse diasporic and nondiasporic groups within a given city.

Cities are concentrated enabling environments for these types of activities, even when the networks themselves are not urban per se. In this regard, these cities enable the experience of participation in global nonstate networks. One might say that global civil society is enacted partly in the microspaces of daily life rather than on some putative global stage. Groups can experience themselves as part of a globalized diaspora even when they are in a place where there might be few conationals, and thus the term *diaspora* hardly applies. In the case of global cities, there is the added dimension of the global corporate economy and its networks and infrastructures enabling cross-border transactions and partially denationalizing urban space.

Both globalization and the international human rights regime have contributed to create operational and legal openings for nonstate actors to enter international arenas once exclusive to national states. Various yet very minor developments signal that the state is no longer the exclusive subject for international law or the only actor in international relations. Other actors—from NGOs (nongovernmental organizations) and first-nation peoples to immigrants and refugees who become subjects of adjudication in human rights decisions—are increasingly emerging as subjects of international law and actors in international relations. Therefore, these nonstate actors can gain visibility as individuals and as collectivities, and they can emerge from the invisibility of aggregate membership in a nation-state exclusively represented by the state. For example, the environment is becoming highlighted as such a supranational subject.

The nexus in this configuration is that the weakening of the exclusive formal authority of states over national territory facilitates the ascendance of sub- and transnational spaces and actors in politico-civic processes. The *national* as a container of social process and power is cracked, enabling the emergence of a geography of politics and civics that links subnational spaces. Cities are foremost in this new geography. The density of political and civic cultures in large cities and their daily practices roots, implants, and localizes global civil society in people's lives. Insofar as the global economic system can be shown to be partly embedded in specific types of places and partly constituted through highly specialized cross-border networks connecting today's global cities, one research task to help understand how this all intersects with immigrants and diasporas is, then, to find out about the specific contents and institutional locations of this multiscalar globalization, the subject of this book. Further, it means understanding how the emergence of global imaginaries changes the meaning of processes that may be much older than the current phase of globalization but that today are inscribed by the latter. Thus, immigrant and diasporic communities are much older than today's globalization. But that does not mean that they are not altered by various specific forms of globalization today.

As discussed in preceding chapters and again later in Chapter 7, recapturing the geography of places involved in economic political globalization allows us to recapture people, workers, communities, and the many different political projects in and of these communities (e.g., Espinoza 1999; Mele 1999). The global city can be seen as one strategic research site regarding these processes and the many forms through which global processes become localized in specific arrangements. This localizing includes a broad range of processes: the new, *very*-high-income, gentrified urban neighborhoods of the transnational professional class and rich exiles, and the work lives of the foreign nannies and maids in those same neighborhoods and of the poor refugees concentrated in asylum housing. Although the formation of the network of global cities is largely driven by corporate economic globalization, multiple political and cultural processes have localized in these complex, partly denationalized environments. This is an old history for cities, but it has received a whole new life through the formation of today's networks of global cities.

The next subsection briefly addresses some general issues of an emergent global politics centered on local struggles and actors.

A Politics of Places on Global Circuits

The space constituted by the worldwide grid of global cities—a space with new economic and political potentialities—is perhaps one of the most strategic spaces for the formation of transnational identities and communities. This is a space that is both place-centered, in that it is embedded in particular and strategic cities, and transterritorial because it connects sites that are not geographically proximate yet are intensely connected to each other. It is not only the transmigration of capital that takes place in this global grid but also that of people, both rich (i.e., the new transnational professional workforce) and poor (i.e., most migrant workers). It is also a space for the transmigration of cultural forms and the reterritorialization of local subcultures.

An important question is whether it is also a space for a new politics, one going beyond the politics of culture and identity, though likely to be embedded partly in these. The politics of diasporic groups may be grounded in shared identities, but these politics do not necessarily conform to the politics of identity in our Western societies. The possibility of transnational identity formation among politicized diasporic groups is an interesting question, given a history of homeland orientation. It is one of the questions running through this book, particularly because global cities are enabling environments in this regard. One of the most radical forms assumed today by the linkage of people to territory is the loosening of selfhood from traditional sources of identity, such as the nation or the village. This unmooring in the process of identity formation can engender new notions of community of membership and of entitlement, though it can also feed in-group/out-group mentalities.

Immigration is one major process through which a new transnational political economy is being constituted, largely embedded in major cities because most immigrants are concentrated in major cities. It is one of the constitutive processes of globalization today, even though not recognized or represented as such in mainstream accounts of the global economy. Immigration becomes part of a massive demographic transition in these cities with a growing presence of women, native minorities, and immigrants in the population of more and more cities. Global capital and immigrants are two major examples, each a unified cross-border actor (or aggregate of actors) who find themselves in contestation with each other inside global cities. Insofar as immigration is one of the forces shaping diasporas, these current features of immigration can be expected, first, at least partly to transnationalize diasporas, moving them away from an exclusive orientation to the homeland; and, second, to urbanize at least some of their contestatory politics, moving them away from an exclusive focus on national states—either their homeland state or the state that has robbed them of having a homeland state. In the case of high-level professional diasporic groups, the dynamics are not dissimilar, and indeed the tendency to form global networks is strong.

These two major types of actors—global corporate capital and the mix of disadvantaged and minoritized people—find in the global city a strategic site for their economic and political operations. The leading sectors of corporate capital are now global in their organization and operations. And many of the disadvantaged workers in global cities are women, immigrants, and people of color—all people whose sense of membership is not adequately captured in terms of the national.

There is an interesting correspondence between great concentrations of corporate power and large concentrations of *others*. Large cities in both the global South and global North are the terrains where a multiplicity of globalization processes assume concrete, localized forms. A focus on cities allows us to capture, further, not only the upper but also the lower circuits of globalization. This points to the possibility of a new politics of traditionally disadvantaged and excluded actors, a politics that arises out of actual participation as workers in the global economy but under conditions of disadvantage and lack of recognition—whether factory workers in export-processing zones or cleaners on Wall Street.

The cross-border network of global cities is a space where we are seeing the formation of new types of global politics of place. These vary considerably: They may involve contesting corporate globalization or involve homeland politics. The demonstrations by the antiglobalization network have signaled the potential for developing a politics centered on places understood as locations on global networks. Some of the new globalizing diasporas have become intensive and effective users of the Internet to engage in these global politics of place. We see here the potential transformation of a whole range of local conditions or institutional domains (such as the household, community, neighborhood, school, and health care clinics) into localities situated on global networks. From being lived or experienced as nonpolitical or domestic, these places are transformed into microenvironments with global span. *Microenvironments with global span* are small local entities in which technical connectivity creates a variety of links with similar entities in other neighborhoods—whether located in the same city or other cities in the same country or abroad. A community of practice can emerge that creates multiple lateral, horizontal communications, collaborations, solidarities, and supports. This can enable local political or nonpolitical actors to enter into cross-border politics.

The space of the city is a far more concrete space for politics than that of the national state system. It becomes a place where nonformal political actors can be part of the political scene in a way that is much easier than at the national level. Nationally, politics needs to run through existing formal systems: whether the electoral political system or the judiciary (taking state agencies to court). Nonformal political actors are rendered invisible in the space of national politics. The city accommodates a broad range of political activities—squatting, demonstrations against police brutality, fighting for the rights of immigrants and the homeless, the politics of culture and identity, gay and lesbian politics, and the homeland politics that many diasporic groups engage in. Much of this becomes visible on the street. This makes possible the formation of new types of political subjects that do not have to go through the formal political system. The city also enables the operations of illegal networks.

Beyond the impact on immigrants and diasporas, these various conditions are a crucial building block for a global civil society that can incorporate both the micropractices and microobjectives of people's political passions. The possibility of transnational identities emerging as a consequence of micropolitics is crucial for strengthening global civil society; the risk of nationalism and fundamentalism is, clearly, present in these dynamics as well.

Conclusion: Urban Growth and Its Multiple Meanings

Major recent developments in urban systems point to several trends. In the developing world, we see the continuing growth of megacities and primacy, as well as the emergence of new growth poles resulting from the internationalization of production and the development of tourism. In some cases, these new growth poles emerge as new destinations for migrants and thereby contribute to a deceleration in primacy; in other cases, when they are located in a primate city's area, they have the opposite effect.

In the developed world, and particularly in Western Europe, we see the renewed strength of major cities that appear to concentrate a significant and often disproportionate share of economic activity in leading sectors. In the 1970s, many of the major cities in highly developed countries were losing population and economic activity. Much was said at the time about the irreversible decline of these cities. But beginning in the mid-1980s, there has been a resurgence that results in good part from the intersection of two major trends in all advanced economies: (1) the shift to services, including, importantly, services for firms, such as finance and corporate services, and (2) the increasing transnationalization of economic activity. This transnationalization can operate at the regional, continental, or global level. These two trends are interlinked. The spatial implication is a strong tendency toward agglomeration of the pertinent activities in major cities. A fact typically overlooked in much of today's commentary about cities is that this dynamic of urban growth is based largely on the locational needs or preferences of firms and does not necessarily compensate for population losses due to suburbanization. Urban growth in less developed countries, by contrast, results largely from population growth, especially in-migration. However, beneath the megacity syndrome, we now also see, as of the 1990s, the two trends mentioned earlier in emergent global cities; in the case of very large cities, these trends are easy to overlook, and the focus is often confined to the megacity syndrome.

The transnationalization of economic activity has raised the intensity and volume of transaction among cities. The growth of global markets for finance and specialized services, the need for transnational servicing networks in response to sharp increases in international investment, the reduced role of the government in the regulation of international economic activity, and the corresponding ascendance of other institutional arenas, notably global markets and corporate headquarters—all these point to the existence of transnational economic arrangements with multiple urban locations in more than one country. Here is the formation, at least incipiently, of a transnational urban system.

The pronounced orientation to the world markets evident in such cities raises questions about the articulation with their hinterlands and nation-states. Cities typically have been and still are deeply embedded in the economies of their region, often reflecting the characteristics of the latter. But cities that are strategic sites in the global economy tend, in part, to disconnect from their region. This phenomenon also conflicts with a key proposition in traditional scholarship about urban systems—notably, that these systems promote the territorial integration of regional and national economies.

Two tendencies contributing to the new forms of inequality among cities are visible in the geography and characteristics of urban systems. On one hand, there is growing transnational articulation among an increasing number of cities. This is evident at both a regional transnational level and the global level; in some cases, there are overlapping geographies of articulation or overlapping hierarchies that operate at more than one level; that is, there are cities such as Paris or London that belong to a national urban system or hierarchy, transnational European system, and global system. On the other hand, cities and areas outside these hierarchies tend to become peripheralized.

A second major trend is for powerless groups in global cities to become active in transnational activities, producing a whole series of new, and newly invigorated, intercity networks. Although economic transactions among cities many have launched the formation of emergent transnational urban systems, a proliferation of people networks began to emerge in the late 1980s and has grown rapidly since then. Generally, those networks with a key basing point in cities originate from two types of conditions. One type derives from immigration and diasporic politics. Although these have long existed across the centuries and the world, the new information technologies have made a significant difference in the intensity and simultaneity of transactions they make possible and in the multiplication of transversal linkages, beyond the radial pattern centered in the homeland. The second type originates from a variety of activist and information-sharing networks concerned largely with localized politico-social struggles: it produces a kind of horizontal globality anchored in localities. Even individuals and organizations that are not mobile—too poor or persecuted or simply not interested in traveling—can become part of these new global networks. The marking condition is the recurrence of certain issues that touch upon the environmental, political, social—in many localities across the world.

These transnational networks of powerless groups are especially experiencing large growth in the megaslums that exist in the peripheries of major cities. These are slums in which a globally articulated subjectivity is emerging through the emergence of activist organizations and the use of communication technologies. These global slums are discussed in more detail in Chapter 6.

Notes

1   See http://esa.un.org/unpd/wup/index.htm.

2   See also the special case of border cities such as Tijuana, by now with a long history of growth and migration driven by the outsourcing of manufacturing jobs south of the United States–Mexico border by US firms, and eventually by firms from more than seventy countries (Fernandez-Kelly 1984; Sassen 1988; Sanchez and Alegria 1992; Herzog 2006). Another type of case is represented by the new export manufacturing zones in China that have drawn large numbers of migrants from many regions of the country (Sklair 1985; Solinger 1999: 277–90; Chen 2005). For one of the best accounts of border cities, see Herzog 1990.

3   This region is here defined as consisting of the island nations between the Florida peninsula and the north coast of South America and the independent countries of the Central American isthmus; it excludes the large nations bordering on the Caribbean Sea.

4   There are several new excellent global city analyses of these cities (e.g., Ciccolella and Mignaqui 2002; Schiffer 2002; see various chapters in Gugler 2004 and in Amen et al. 2006).

5   The strengthening of Berlin, both through reunification and the regaining of the role of capital, may alter some of the power relations among Budapest, Vienna, and Berlin. Indeed, Berlin could become a major international business center for Central Europe after the recent 2004 enlargement, with possibly corresponding reductions in the roles of Budapest and Vienna. However, these three cities may create a regional transnational urban system for the whole region—a multinodal urban center of gravity in which both competition and a division of functions have the effect of strengthening the overall international business capability of the region.

6   This is not an exceptional situation. All developed countries in the world now have immigrant workers. Even Japan, a country known for its anti-immigration stance, became a destination for migrant workers in the late 1980s, a role that has continued since, albeit with ups and downs and a changing nationality composition in the flows (AMPO 1988; Asian Women's Association 1988; Morita and Sassen 1994; Iyotani 1998; Sassen 1998: chap. 4; [1991] 2001: chap. 9; Iyotani, Sakai and de Bary 2005).

7   This is my original coined term for cities with a million or more foreign-born residents.

Chapter 3 Appendix

Exhibit A.3.1   Africa's Largest Cities (2010)

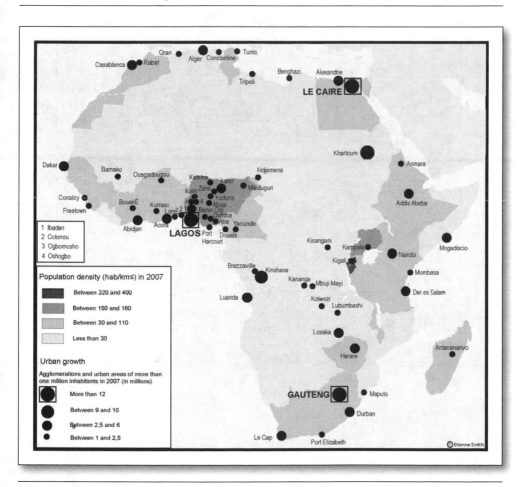

Source: Smith, Etienne. 2009. L'Afrique: historie et defis: 50 cartes et fiches. Paris: Ellipses.

Exhibit A.3.2 Asia's Largest Cities (2010)

Exhibit A.3.3   Latin America's Largest Cities (2010)

Exhibit A.3.4 Europe's Largest Cities (2010)

Exhibit A.3.5 Urban Growth Patterns in Select Developing Countries, Select Periods, 1980–2030 (numbers and percentage)

Country	Per Capita GNP Level 2003 (US$)[a]	Size of Population (000s)[b] Urban 2003	Rural 2003	Urban 2030	Rural 2030	Urban Pop. (%) 2003	Urban Pop. (%) 2030	Avg. Rate of Growth Urban 1980–1985	Urban 1995–2000	Urban 2000–2005	Rural 1980–1985	Rural 1995–2000	Rural 2000–2005
Argentina	3,372	34,642	3,786	45,568	3,043	90.1	93.7	1.88	1.39	2.00	-0.87	-0.88	-1.10
Mexico	6,052	78,100	25,357	110,770	22,821	75.5	82.9	3.36	2.39	1.80	0.34	-0.07	0.40
Colombia	1,779	33,808	10,414	51,860	8,982	76.5	85.2	3.11	2.29	2.20	0.28	-0.07	-0.50
Brazil	2,759	148,270	30,201	202,686	19,392	83.1	91.3	3.71	2.28	2.00	-1.27	-1.00	-2.40
Algeria	2,092	18,711	13,089	32,032	12,087	58.8	72.6	3.71	3.85	2.60	2.51	1.25	0.30
Morocco	1,431	17,564	13,002	30,824	11,680	57.5	72.5	4.28	3.42	2.80	1.40	0.50	0.10
Malaysia	4,247	15,611	8,814	27,324	7,867	63.9	77.6	4.51	3.32	3.00	1.06	0.15	0.10
Senegal	644	5,008	5,086	11,350	5,577	49.6	67.1	3.34	4.26	3.90	2.11	1.52	1.00
Cote d'Ivoire	826	7,464	9,167	14,054	9,204	44.9	60.4	6.63	5.24	2.60	2.54	2.26	0.80
Nigeria	471	57,907	66,102	134,398	72,298	46.7	65.0	6.07	5.33	4.40	2.22	2.02	1.00
Kenya	449	12,593	19,394	25,807	15,334	39.4	62.7	8.06	6.72	4.40	3.17	2.78	-0.40
India	564	301,260	764,202	586,052	830,525	28.3	41.4	3.91	3.96	2.30	1.65	0.93	1.20
Indonesia	946	100,294	119,859	187,846	89,721	45.6	67.7	4.60	3.62	3.90	1.13	0.14	-0.90
China	1,086	503,740	800,456	877,623	572,898	38.6	60.5	1.44	2.95	3.20	1.18	0.58	-0.80

Sources:

a. World Bank (2005).

b. United Nations Department for Economic and Social Affairs, Policy Analysis (2003).

Exhibit A.3.6 Population Change in Select European Cities, Select Periods, 1970–2005 (percentages)

Core City[a]	1970–1975		1975–1980		1980–1985		1985–1990		1990–1995		1995–2000		2000–2005[b]	
	Core	Ring	CORE	Ring	Core	Ring	Core	Ring	Core	Ring	Core	Ring	Core	Ring
Hamburg	-0.77	0.85	-0.91	0.36	-0.77	0.06	0.24	0.06	0.65	—	0.33	—	0.13	—
Frankfurt	—	—	—	—	-1.01	-0.04	1.62	0.11	—	—	—	—	—	—
Dortmund	-0.41	0.08	-0.79	-0.27	-1.15	-0.56	0.54	0.37	—	—	—	—	—	—
Berlin	-0.47	-0.25	-0.02	-0.07	0.21	0.03	2.19	0.09	0.18	—	0.05	—	0.02	—
Paris	-1.48	1.93	-0.69	0.66	-1.02	0.78	1.01	2.06	0.38	—	0.38	—	0.33	—
Lyons	-1.79	4.25	-1.23	-1.18	0.07	-0.04	0.07	1.21	0.74	—	0.74	—	0.67	—
Marseilles	0.27	4.47	-0.48	2.91	-1.10	1.57	-1.10	2.84	0.39	—	0.39	—	0.39	—
Milan	-0.14	1.06	-1.17	1.07	-2.02	0.6	-1.03	0.35	-1.05	—	-0.86	—	-0.86	—
Amsterdam	-1.84	1.51	-1.11	0.81	-1.18	0.57	0.34	0.47	0.9	—	0.46	—	0.53	—
Rotterdam	-1.99	1.1	-1.38	0.81	-0.28	0.56	0.22	0.28	0.57	—	0.29	—	0.34	—
Brussels	-1.99	0.48	-1.38	0.15	-0.95	0.02	-0.17	0.04	-0.04	—	0.04	—	1.31	—
London	-1.89	-0.37	-1.6	-0.14	-0.38	-0.06	0.56	-0.32	-0.03	—	-0.03	—	-0.03	—
Birmingham	-0.3	0.35	-1.01	-0.66	-0.33	0	-0.37	0.06	-0.25	—	-0.25	—	-0.25	—

Core City[a]	1970–1975		1975–1980		1980–1985		1985–1990		1990–1995		1995–2000		2000–2005[b]	
	Core	Ring	CORE	Ring	Core	King	Core	Ring	Core	Ring	Core	Ring	Core	Ring
Glasgow	-3.38	-1.47	-1.84	-0.11	-1.06	-0.17	-1.41	-0.32	—	—	—	—	—	—
Dublin	-0.41	—	-0.41	—	-1.61	—	—	—	0.65	—	0.87	—	0.88	—
Copenhagen	-2.28	2	-1.47	0.46	-0.59	-0.12	-0.72	0.14	0.3	—	-4.61	—	0.23	—
Thessaloniki	2.06	—	1.44	—	0.93	0.54	—	—	0.66	—	0.67	—	0.67	—
Athens	1.09	—	-0.16	—	-1.43	1.45	—	—	0.34	—	0.37	—	0.37	—
Madrid	0.45	8.28	-0.2	8.19	-0.63	3.16	0.28	0.07	0.51	—	0.43	—	0.43	—
Barcelona	-0.07	3.4	0.13	2.27	-0.58	0.71	0.04	-0.04	0.62	—	0.21	—	0.21	—
Valencia	1.44	1.47	1.11	1.73	-0.41	1.26	0.6	-0.48	—	—	—	—	—	—
Seville	1.24	-0.02	1.81	1.23	0.16	1.19	0.75	0.52	—	—	—	—	—	—

Notes:

a. Core City refers to cities in growth or dynamic regions in Western Europe.

b. Estimated.

Source: Data for 1970–1990 taken from European Institute of Urban Affairs (1992:56); data for 1990–2005 taken from United Nations Department for International Economic and Social Affairs (2003, Table A.14).

101

Exhibit A.3.7   Location of Top Banking, Industrial, and Commercial Firms by City, Select Years, 1960–2009

City, Country[a]	2009[b]	1997[c]	1990[c]	1980[c]	1970[c]	1960[c]
Tokyo, Japan	7 (1)[d]	18 (5)	12 (2)	6	5 (1)	1
New York, USA	3	12 (1)	7 (5)	10 (4)	25 (8)	29 (8)
Paris, France	8	11 (1)	5	7 (2)	0	0
Osaka, Japan	2	7 (3)	2 (1)	1	1	0
Detroit, USA	2 (2)	4 (2)	2 (2)	2 (2)	3 (3)	5 (2)
London, UK	3 (1)	3 (1)	7 (2)	8 (3)	7 (3)	7 (3)
Chicago, USA	0	3	2	4 (2)	5	6 (2)
Munich, Germany	4 (1)	3	2	1	1	1
Amsterdam, Netherlands	1 (1)	3	0	0	0	0
Seoul, South Korea	4	3	0	0	0	0

Notes:

a. After ranking cities according to the number holding the world's 100 largest corporation headquarters (in 1999), the list was trimmed to the top forty cities, of which ten are listed in the table above.

b. Author's calculations based on "Global 500" (2009).

c. Short and Kim (1999: 26).

d. The figure in parentheses gives the number of the world's top 20 corporations for that city.

Exhibit A.3.8   Top Five Global Command Centers Based on Corporations, Banks, Telecommunications, and Insurance Agencies, 2005

Rank	City[a]	Corporations	Banks	Telecommunications	Insurance Agencies
1	Tokyo	56	3	2	6
2	Paris	26	4	2	3
3	London	23	3	0	5
4	New York	22	2	1	4
5	Beijing	12	4	2	1

Note:

a. Cities with the most "high-revenue" multinational corporations.

Source: Calculations based on "Global 500" (2005).

Exhibit A.3.9   Top Five Global Command Centers Based on Number of Companies, Banks, Telecommunications, and Insurance Agencies Among the Top 500 Global Companies by Revenue, 2009

Rank[a]	City	Total No. of Top Companies	Banks[b]	Telecommunications[c]	Insurance Agencies[d]
1	Tokyo	51	3	3	6
2	Paris	27	5	2	3
3	Beijing	26	4	2	1
4	New York	18	5	1	4
5	London	15	4	1	1

Notes:

a. Cities are ranked by the number of the 500 highest-revenue companies in the world that are located there.

b. Out of sixty-two banks ranked among the 500 highest-revenue companies in the world.

c. Out of twenty-one telecommunications companies among the 500 highest-revenue companies in the world.

d. Out of thirty-seven insurance companies among the 500 highest-revenue companies in the world.

Source: Calculations based on "Global 500" (2009).

Exhibit A.3.10   Advertising Network Connectivity (2008)

Rank	City	NC
1	New York	1.00
2	London	0.74
3	Paris	0.73
4	Hong Kong	0.68
5	Tokyo	0.68
6	Singapore	0.65
7	Moscow	0.65
8	Shanghai	0.64
9	Warsaw	0.63

(Continued)

Exhibit A.3.10   (Continued)

Rank	City	NC
10	Sydney	0.63
11	Brussels	0.62
12	Buenos Aires	0.62
13	Taipei	0.62
14	Mumbai	0.61
15	Athens	0.61
16	Toronto	0.61
17	Stockholm	0.60
18	Bangkok	0.60
19	Beijing	0.60
20	Madrid	0.60
21	Seoul	0.59
22	Budapest	0.57
23	Vienna	0.56
24	Istanbul	0.56
25	Kuala Lumpur	0.55
26	Helsinki	0.55
27	Dubai	0.55
28	Milan	0.54
29	Lisbon	0.54
30	Mexico City	0.53
31	Amsterdam	0.53
32	Jeddah	0.53
33	Copenhagen	0.52
34	Bucharest	0.52
35	Rome	0.51
36	Prague	0.51
37	Caracas	0.50

Exhibit A.3.11   Law Network Connectivity (2008)

Rank	City	NC
1	London	1.00
2	New York	0.89
3	Paris	0.70
4	Frankfurt	0.59
5	Washington	0.58
6	Brussels	0.54
7	Hong Kong	0.53
8	Moscow	0.50

Exhibit A.3.12   Financial Network Connectivity (2008)

Rank	City	NC
1	New York	1.00
2	Hong Kong	0.99
3	London	0.99
4	Tokyo	0.84
5	Singapore	0.84
6	Shanghai	0.83
7	Sydney	0.82
8	Paris	0.81
9	Seoul	0.75
10	Beijing	0.75
11	Madrid	0.73
12	Milan	0.70
13	Taipei	0.69

(Continued)

Exhibit A.3.12   (Continued)

Rank	City	NC
14	Frankfurt	0.65
15	Toronto	0.64
16	Mumbai	0.63
17	Zurich	0.62
18	Moscow	0.59
19	Dublin	0.59
20	Kuala Lumpur	0.58
21	Jakarta	0.58
22	Bangkok	0.58
23	Brussels	0.57
24	Sao Paulo	0.56
25	Amsterdam	0.56
26	Buenos Aires	0.53
27	Warsaw	0.51
28	Istanbul	0.50

Exhibit A.3.13   Accountancy Network Connectivity

Rank	City	NC
1	London	1.00
2	New York	0.78
3	Hong Kong	0.70
4	Sydney	0.69
5	Milan	0.67
6	Singapore	0.64
7	Beijing	0.64
8	Buenos Aires	0.63
9	Paris	0.62

Rank	City	NC
10	Kuala Lumpur	0.62
11	Toronto	0.61
12	Tel Aviv	0.61
13	Shanghai	0.60
14	Jakarta	0.60
15	Moscow	0.60
16	Brussels	0.59
17	Auckland	0.59
18	Tokyo	0.59
19	Seoul	0.59
20	Lisbon	0.57
21	Rome	0.57
22	Mumbai	0.57
23	Mexico City	0.57
24	Sao Paulo	0.56
25	Berlin	0.56
26	Madrid	0.56
27	Istanbul	0.56
28	Caracas	0.56
29	Oslo	0.55
30	New Delhi	0.55
31	Kuwait	0.55
32	Bogota	0.55
33	Barcelona	0.55
34	Vienna	0.53
35	Jeddah	0.52
36	Santiago	0.52
37	Dublin	0.52
38	Warsaw	0.51
39	Guadalajara	0.51
40	Riyadh	0.50
41	Johannesburg	0.50
42	Zurich	0.50
43	Hamburg	0.50
44	Chicago	0.50
45	Athens	0.50

Exhibit A.3.14   Management Consultancy Connectivity

Rank	City	NC
1	New York	1.00
2	London	0.67
3	Paris	0.65
4	Hong Kong	0.61
5	Chicago	0.57
6	Singapore	0.56
7	Tokyo	0.56
8	Zurich	0.55
9	Madrid	0.55
10	Beijing	0.53
11	Mumbai	0.50
12	Atlanta	0.50

4

The New Urban Economy

The Intersection of Global Processes and Place

As recently as the 1970s, many of our great cities worldwide were in physical decay and losing people, firms, key roles in the national economy, and share of national wealth. New York and Tokyo were officially bankrupt; London was informally bankrupt. As we moved into the last decade of the twentieth and into the first of the twenty-first century, a rapidly growing number of cities had re-emerged as strategic places for a wide range of activities and dynamics. Underlying all the other dimensions has been the critical new economic role of cities in national economies and in an increasingly globalized world.

Much is known about the wealth and power of global firms and financial exchanges. Their ascendance in a globalizing world is no longer surprising. And the new information and communication technologies are generally recognized as the handmaiden of economic globalization—both tool and infrastructure. Now we are also learning about the fact that these firms and exchanges are highly susceptible to crisis. Since the 1980s, there have been five major financial crises that have affected most firms, in good part due to the high level of financializing in more and more economies.

Less clear is why cities should matter more in the globalized world that began in the 1980s than they did in the Keynesian world of the mid-1900s.

Nor is it clear in what ways the financializing of a growing range of economic sectors affects cities, especially global cities. Finally, while inequality has long been a feature of cities, major structural trends in today's phase generate novel types of social and spatial inequality that begin to alter the meaning of the civic and urbanity itself. This is especially evident in global cities, which become the site for new kinds of political practices and political actors.

From the Keynesian City to the Global City

In that earlier period, cities were above all centers for administration, small-scale manufacturing, and commerce. Cities were mostly the space for rather routinized endeavors. The strategic spaces where the major innovations were happening were the government (the making of social contracts, such as the welfare state) and mass manufacturing, including mass construction of suburban regions and national transport infrastructure.

The most common and easiest answers as to why cities became strategic in a global corporate economy are the ongoing need for face-to-face communications and the need for creative classes and inputs. Both are part of the answer. But in my reading, these are surface conditions and cannot fully explain the new phase.

The rise of cities as strategic economic spaces is the consequence of a deeper structural transformation evident in all developed economies. It affects cities at multiple levels, from provincial to global. At the heart of this deep structural trend is the fact that even the most material economic sectors (mines, factories, transport systems, hospitals) today are buying more insurance, accounting, legal, financial, consulting, software programming, and other such services for firms. These so-called intermediate services tend to be produced in cities, no matter the nonurban location of the mine or the steel plant that is being serviced. Thus, even an economy centered in manufacturing or mining will feed the urban corporate services economy. Firms operating in more routinized and subnational markets increasingly buy these service inputs from more local or regional cities, which explains why we see the growth of a professional class and the associated built environments also in cities that are not global. The difference for global cities is that they are able to handle the more complex needs of firms and exchanges operating globally. It is only in its most extreme forms that this structural transformation feeds into the growth of global cities.

The outcomes of this structural condition get wired into urban space. The growth of a high-income professional class and high-profit corporate service firms becomes legible in urban space through the growing demand of state-of-the-art office buildings and all the key components of the residential sphere and consumption. The growing demand of both leads to often massive and visible displacements of the more modest-income households and modest-profit-making firms, no matter how healthy these may be from the perspective of the economy and market demand. In this process, urban space itself is one of the actors producing the outcome. This partly explains why architecture, urban design, and urban planning have each played such critical roles. Beginning in the 1980s, we see the partial rebuilding of cities as platforms for a rapidly growing range of globalized activities and flows, from economic to cultural and political. But it also explains why global cities became an object of investment when this global phase took off in the 1980s, beyond being a place for investment. And it partly explains why the number and types of cities that became such objects expanded rapidly as globalization expanded in the 1990s and onward.

When I first developed the global city model in the 1980s, my starting points were the global networks of affiliates of firms, global financial exchanges, global trade routes, and global commodity chains. The emergent scholarship on globalization examining these global operations emphasized geographic dispersal, decentralization, and deterritorialization. This was indeed all happening. But I was interested in the territorial moment of all these increasingly electronic and globally dispersed operations. At that time, my idea was to focus on New York and Los Angeles. They seemed to be major territorial nodes. But sticking to my own methodology—starting with the global operations of firms and exchanges and tracking the sites where they hit the ground—forced me to recognize that in the 1980s, it was New York, London, and Tokyo that stood out, with Los Angeles far from the top of the list.

Applying this methodology today leads one to a vastly expanded global geography of sites. There is more of everything—export processing zones, off-shore banking centers, massive warehouses that are one stop on global trade routes, and many more global cities.

The Multiple Circuits of the Global Economy

There is no such entity as "the" global economy. There are global formations, such as electronic financial markets and firms that operate globally. But the key feature of the current era is a vast number of highly particular global circuits that crisscross the world, some specialized and some not, that connect specific areas, most of which are cities. While many of these global circuits have long existed, what began to change in the 1980s was their proliferation and their increasingly complex organizational and financial framings. These emergent intercity geographies begin to function as an infrastructure for globalization. And they increasingly urbanize global networks.

Different circuits contain different groups of countries and cities. For instance, Mumbai is today part of a global circuit for real estate development that includes investors from cities as diverse as London and Bogotá. Coffee is mostly produced in Brazil, Kenya, Indonesia, but the main trading place for futures on coffee is Wall Street, even though New York does not grow a single bean. The specialized circuits in gold, coffee, oil, and other commodities each involve particular places, which will vary depending on whether it is a production circuit, a trading circuit, or a financial circuit. And then there are the types of circuits a firm such as Wal-Mart needs to outsource the production of vast amounts of products, including manufacturing, trading, and financial/insurance servicing circuits. If we were to track the global circuits of gold as a financial instrument, it is London, New York, Chicago, and Zurich that dominate. But the wholesale trade in the metal brings São Paulo, Johannesburg, and Sydney into the map, and the trade in the commodity, much of it aimed at the retail trade, adds Mumbai and Dubai. New York and London are the biggest financial centers in the world. But they do not dominate all markets. Thus, Chicago is the leading financial center for the trading of futures, and in the 1990s, Frankfurt became the leading trader for, of all things, British treasuries. These cities are all financial leaders in the global economy, but they lead in different sectors and they are different types of financial centers.

Yet another pattern, the combination of global dispersal and ongoing spatial concentration of certain functions, becomes evident in the fact that the 250,000 multinationals in the world together have more than a million affiliates and partnership arrangements worldwide, but they tend to keep their headquarters in their home countries. And so do the 100 top global advanced services firms that together have operations in 350 cities outside their home bases. While financial services can be bought everywhere electronically, the major headquarters of leading global financial services firms tend to be concentrated in a limited number of cities, and these are the ones that directly experience the unemployment crisis of the sector. Each of these financial centers is particularly specialized and strong in specific segments of global finance, even as they also engage in routinized types of transactions that need to be executed by all financial centers.

Not only global economic forces feed this proliferation of circuits. Migration, cultural work, and civil society struggle to preserve human rights, the environment, and social justice and also to feed the formation and development of global circuits. Thus, NGOs fighting for the protection of the rainforest function in circuits that include Brazil and Indonesia as homes of the major rainforests, the global media centers of New York and London, and the places where the key forestry companies selling and buying wood are headquartered, notably Oslo, London, and Tokyo. There are particular music circuits that connect specific areas of India with London, New York, Chicago, and Johannesburg; and even more particular music circuits that connect parts of China with Los Angeles.

Adopting the perspective of one of these cities reveals the diversity and specificity of its location on some or many of these circuits. These emergent intercity geographies function as an infrastructure for multiple forms of globalization. The critical nodes in these intercity geographies are not simply the cities but, more specifically, the particular, often highly specialized capabilities of each city. Further, a critical trend is that, ultimately, being a global firm or market means entering the specificities and particularities of national economies. This explains why such global firms and markets need more and more global cities as they expand their operations across the world. Handling these national specificities and particularities is a far more complex process than simply imposing global standards.

This process is easier to understand if we consider consumer sectors rather than the organizational/managerial side of global firms. Thus, even such a routinized operation as McDonald's adjusts its products to the national cultures in which it operates, whether that is France, Japan, or South Africa. When it comes to the managerial and organizational aspects, matters become complicated. The global city contains the needed resources and talents to bridge between global actors and national specifics. Even a highly imperfect global city is better for a global firm or exchange than no such city. And this, then, explains why the many and very diverse global cities around the world do not just compete with each other but also collectively form a globally networked platform for the operations of firms and markets.

The network of global cities has expanded as more and more firms go global and enter a growing range of foreign national economies. The management and servicing of much of the global economic system takes place in this growing network of global cities and city-regions. And while this role involves only certain components of urban economies, it has contributed to a repositioning of cities both nationally and globally.

This repositioning of cities and the move away from intercity competition is further strengthened by the emerging fact that cities are at the forefront of a range of global governance challenges. Because of this, many cities have had to develop capabilities to handle these challenges long before national states signed international treaties or passed national laws. The air quality emergency in cities such as Tokyo and Los Angeles back in the 1980s is one instance: these cities could not wait until an agreement such as Kyoto might appear, nor could they wait till national governments passed mandatory laws for car fuel efficiency and zero emissions. With or without a treaty or law, they had to address air quality urgently. And they did. Cities have even shown a willingness to go against national law when the urgency of confronting particular conditions demands it. For instance, in 2006, more than 800 municipal governments in the United States signed on to a declaration for joint action banning carbon dioxide that the US Environmental Protection Agency had designated as safe.

Finally, the urgency of such global challenges in cities takes on a further practical character by the urbanizing of war. The new military asymmetries arising out of conventional armies confronting networked insurgencies tend to produce an increasingly urban geography of warring. Within this context, the expanding presence of cities in global networks and the expanding number of intercity networks take on added meanings.

The Specialized Differences of Cities Matter: There Is No Perfect Global City

While there is competition among cities, there is far less of it than is usually assumed. A global firm does not want one global city but many. However, given the level of specialization of globalized firms, what are preferred cities will vary according to the firm. Firms thrive on the specialized differences of cities, and it is this that gives a city its particular advantage in the global economy. This also points to the possibility of an urban global politics of reclamations among cities on similar circuits that confront similar corporate giants.

Recognizing the value of the specialized differences of cities and urban regions in today's global economy shows how the deep economic history of a place matters for the type of knowledge economy that a city or a city-region ends up developing. This goes against the common view that globalization homogenizes economies. How much this deep economic history matters varies and partly depends on the particulars of a city's or a region's economy. It matters more than is commonly assumed, and it matters in ways that are not generally recognised. Globalization homogenizes standards—for managing, for accounting, for building state-of-the-art office districts, and so on. But it needs diverse specialized economic capabilities.

The capabilities needed to trade, finance, service, and invest globally need to be produced. They are not simply a by-product of the power of global firms and telecommunications advances. Different cities have different resources and talents for producing particular types of capabilities. The global city is a platform for producing such global capabilities, even when this requires large numbers of foreign firms, as is the case in cities as diverse as Beijing and Buenos Aires. Each of the seventy plus major and minor global cities in the world contributes to the production of these capabilities in its home country and thereby functions as a bridge between its national economy and the global economy.

The other side of this dynamic is that for a firm to go global, it has to operate in multiple cities that function as entry points into national economies. This bridging capacity is critical: the multiple circuits connecting major and minor global cities are the live infrastructure of the global economy. It indicates that cities do not simply compete with each other. A global firm does not want one global city, even if it is the best in the world. Different groups of cities will be desirable, even if they have some serious negatives. This helps explain why there is no one "perfect" global city. Today's global phase does not function through one imperial global capital that has it all. A large study rates the top cities for worldwide commerce using a large number of variables.1 Not one of them ranks at the top in all of the sixty-five variables used to measure diverse aspects of cities relevant to global firms. None of the top seventy-five cities gets the perfect score of 100. The scores for the top two cities are seventy-nine for London and seventy-three for New York; further down, the tenth-ranked city, for instance, which is Amsterdam, scores sixty, followed by Madrid at fifty-eight (see Exhibit 4.1). London and New York, the two leading global cities, rank low in several aspects—neither is in the top ten when it comes to starting a business or closing a business or even political and legal frameworks (see Exhibits 4.2 and 4.3a) If we consider a critical variable in the "ease of doing business" indicator, part of which is "ease of entry and exit," London ranks forty-third and New York ranks fifty-sixth (see Exhibit 4.3b). Perhaps most surprising, London ranks thirty-seventh on "contract enforcement" and twenty-first on "investor protection." It is Singapore that ranks number one in relation to all three variables. Less surprising is that New York ranks thirty-fourth on one of the data points for "livability": health and safety (see Exhibit 4.4). In the global South, cities like Mumbai and São Paulo are in the top group for financial and economic services but are brought down in their overall score by their low rankings in factors related to the ease of doing business and livability, given their especially low levels of well-being for vast sectors of the population (see Exhibits A.4.1 and A.4.2).

Exhibit 4.1   WCOC 2008 Overall Ranking

Rank	City	WCOC Index
1	London	79.17
2	New York	72.77
3	Tokyo	66.60
4	Singapore	66.16
5	Chicago	65.24
6	Hong Kong	63.94
7	Paris	63.87
8	Frankfurt	62.34
9	Seoul	61.83
10	Amsterdam	60.06
11	Madrid	58.34
12	Sydney	58.33
13	Toronto	58.16
14	Copenhagen	57.99
15	Zurich	56.86
16	Stockholm	56.67
17	Los Angeles	55.73
18	Philadelphia	55.55
19	Osaka	54.94
20	Milan	54.73

Note: 100 is the top score.

Source: Exhibit prepared by Saskia Sassen, based on MasterCard. 2008. *2008 Worldwide Centers of Commerce Index*. Purchase, NY: MasterCard.

The growing number of global cities, along with their differences, signals a shift to a multipolar world. The loss of position of US cities compared with the 2006 survey is part of this shift (see Exhibit 4.5). Los Angeles

Exhibit 4.2 Political and Legal Frameworks and Selected Subindicators

Rank	Indicator 1: Political and Legal Frameworks	Dealing with Licenses	Registering Property	Trading Across Borders	EX-IM Bank Exposure Premiums for Sovereign and Nonsovereign Risk Transactions
1	Stockholm	Copenhagen	Riyadh	Hong Kong	London
2	Copenhagen	Bangkok	Stockholm	Copenhagen	New York
3	Singapore	Tokyo	Atlanta	Singapore	Singapore
4	Atlanta	Stockholm	Boston	Berlin	Tokyo
5	Boston	Singapore	Washington, DC	Frankfurt	Chicago
6	Washington, DC	Dublin	Chicago	Munich	Hong Kong
7	Chicago	Paris	Houston	Montreal	Paris
8	Houston	Berlin	Los Angeles	Toronto	Seoul
9	Los Angeles	Frankfurt	Miami	Vancouver	Frankfurt
10	Miami	Munich	New York	Stockholm	Amsterdam
11	New York	Atlanta	San Francisco	Vienna	Madrid
12	San Francisco	Boston	Zurich	Dubai	Sydney
13	Montreal	Washington, DC	Geneva	Atlanta	Toronto
14	Toronto	Chicago	Dubai	Boston	Copenhagen
15	Vancouver	Houston	Singapore	Washington, DC	Zurich
16	Berlin	Los Angeles	London	Chicago	Stockholm

(Continued)

Exhibit 4.2   (Continued)

Rank	Indicator 1: Political and Legal Frameworks	Dealing with Licenses	Registering Property	Trading Across Borders	EX-IM Bank Exposure Premiums for Sovereign and Nonsovereign Risk Transactions
17	Frankfurt	Miami	Montreal	Houston	Philadelphia
18	Munich	New York	Toronto	Los Angeles	Los Angeles
19	London	San Francisco	Vancouver	Miami	Osaka
20	Tokyo	Seoul	Beijing	New York	Milan
21	Zurich	Montreal	Chengdu	San Francisco	Taipei
22	Geneva	Toronto	Shanghai	Amsterdam	Boston
23	Vienna	Vancouver	Shenzhen	London	Atlanta
24	Melbourne	Mexico City	Bangkok	Tel Aviv	Berlin
25	Sydney	Melbourne	Amsterdam	Barcelona	Miami
26	Amsterdam	Sydney	Santiago	Madrid	Munich
27	Barcelona	Santiago	Copenhagen	Melbourne	Vienna
28	Madrid	Zurich	Moscow	Sydney	San Francisco
29	Dublin	Geneva	St. Petersburg	Paris	Dublin
30	Dubai	Copenhagen	Vienna	Tokyo	Brussels

Note: Top ten cities from WCOC indicated

Source: Exhibit prepared by Saskia Sassen, based on MasterCard. 2008. 2008 Worldwide Centers of Commerce Index. Purchase, NY: MasterCard.

Exhibit 4.3a Ease of Doing Business and Subindicators (Part 1 of 2)

Rank	Indicator 3: Ease of Doing Business	Starting a Business	Employing Workers	Getting Credit	Closing a Business	Conventions/ Exhibitions/ Meetings
1	Vancouver	Sydney	New York	KualaLumpur	Singapore	London
2	Toronto	Melbourne	Chicago	London	Tokyo	Paris
3	Montreal	Toronto	Philadelphia	Edinburgh	Osaka	Berlin
4	Singapore	Montreal	Los Angeles	Frankfurt	Toronto	Vienna
5	London	Vancouver	Boston	Berlin	Montreal	Singapore
6	Dublin	Dublin	Atlanta	Munich	Vancouver	Hong Kong
7	Copenhagen	Brussels	Miami	Hamburg	Copenhagen	Prague
8	San Francisco	Singapore	San Francisco	Dusseldorf	Amsterdam	New York
9	New York	Paris	Houston	Sydney	Brussels	Istanbul
10	Los Angeles	Stockholm	Dallas	Melbourne	Dublin	Munich
11	Washington, DC	New York	Washington, DC	New York	London	Shanghai
12	Hong Kong	Chicago	Singapore	Chicago	Edinburgh	Barcelona
13	Boston	Philadelphia	Copenhagen	Toronto	Seoul	Dubai
14	Chicago	Los Angeles	Sydney	Philadelphia	Taipei	Seoul

(Continued)

Exhibit 4.3a (Continued)

Rank	Indicator 3: Ease of Doing Business	Starting a Business	Employing Workers	Getting Credit	Closing a Business	Conventions/ Exhibitions/ Meetings
15	Stockholm	Boston	Melbourne	Los Angeles	Sydney	Madrid
16	Tokyo	Atlanta	Hong Kong	Boston	Melbourne	Tokyo
17	Miami	Miami	Toronto	Atlanta	Hong Kong	Bangkok
18	Brussels	San Francisco	Montreal	Miami	New York	Moscow
19	Sydney	Houston	Vancouver	San Francisco	Chicago	Sao Paulo
20	Atlanta	Dallas	London	Montreal	Philadelphia	Beijing
21	Houston	Washington, DC	Edinburgh	Houston	Los Angeles	Milan
22	Melbourne	Hong Kong	Tokyo	Dallas	Boston	Budapest
23	Zurich	Copenhagen	Osaka	Washington, DC	Atlanta	Chicago
24	Frankfurt	London	Dublin	Vancouver	Miami	Edinburgh
25	Geneva	Edinburgh	Zurich	Buenos Aires	San Francisco	San Francisco
26	Amsterdam	Zurich	Geneva	Dublin	Houston	Brussels
27	Munich	Geneva	Kuala Lumpur	Tel Aviv	Dallas	Amsterdam
28	Berlin	Tel Aviv	Bangkok	Hong Kong	Washington, DC	St. Petersburg
29	Paris	Lisbon	Riyadh	Madrid	Stockholm	Sydney
30	Vienna	Amsterdam	Santiago	Barcelona	Madrid	Dublin

Note: Top ten cities from WCOC indicated

Source: Exhibit prepared by Saskia Sassen, based on MasterCard. 2008. 2008 *Worldwide Centers of Commerce Index.* Purchase, NY: MasterCard.

Exhibit 4.3b Ease of Doing Business and Subindicators (Part 2 of 2)

Rank	Indicator 3: Ease of Doing Business	Banking Services	Ease of Entry and Exit	Investor Protection	Corporate Tax Burden	Contract Enforcement
1	Vancouver	London	Singapore	Singapore	Singapore	Singapore
2	Toronto	New York	Hong Kong	Hong Kong	Hong Kong	Hong Kong
3	Montreal	Singapore	Frankfurt	Kuala Lumpur	Dubai	Vienna
4	Singapore	Hong Kong	Amsterdam	New York	Riyadh	Sydney
5	London	Paris	Toronto	Chicago	Dublin	Melbourne
6	Dublin	Frankfurt	Copenhagen	Philadelphia	London	New York
7	Copenhagen	Amsterdam	Stockholm	Los Angeles	Edinburgh	Chicago
8	San Francisco	Madrid	Berlin	Boston	Copenhagen	Philadelphia
9	New York	Copenhagen	Munich	Atlanta	Santiago	Los Angeles
10	Los Angeles	Zurich	Vienna	Miami	Stockholm	Boston
11	Washington, DC	Stockholm	Hamburg	San Francisco	Toronto	Atlanta
12	Hong Kong	Berlin	Montreal	Houston	Montreal	Miami
13	Boston	Munich	Vancouver	Dallas	Vancouver	San Francisco
14	Chicago	Vienna	Dusseldorf	Washington, DC	Amsterdam	Houston
15	Stockholm	Dublin	Prague	Tel Aviv	Johannesburg	Dallas

(Continued)

Exhibit 4.3b (Continued)

Rank	Indicator 3: Ease of Doing Business	Banking Services	Ease of Entry and Exit	Investor Protection	Corporate Tax Burden	Contract Enforcement
16	Tokyo	Brussels	Paris	Toronto	Zurich	Washington, DC
17	Miami	Hamburg	Seoul	Montreal	Geneva	Seoul
18	Brussels	Barcelona	Zurich	Vancouver	Lisbon	Paris
19	Sydney	Dusseldorf	Shanghai	Dublin	Beirut	Dublin
20	Atlanta	Geneva	Milan	Johannesburg	Sydney	Budapest
21	Houston	Dubai	Taipei	London	Melbourne	Tokyo
22	Melbourne	Edinburgh	Dublin	Edinburgh	New York	Osaka
23	Zurich	Tokyo	Brussels	Tokyo	Chicago	Brussels
24	Frankfurt	Sydney	Geneva	Osaka	Philadelphia	Frankfurt
25	Geneva	Toronto	Dubai	Brussels	Los Angeles	Berlin
26	Amsterdam	Los Angeles	Lisbon	Copenhagen	Boston	Munich
27	Munich	Osaka	Rome	Bogota	Atlanta	Hamburg
28	Berlin	Milan	Santiago	Lisbon	Miami	Dusseldorf
29	Paris	Montreal	Beijing	Mumbai	San Francisco	Moscow
30	Vienna	Dallas	Budapest	Santiago	Houston	St. Petersburg

Note: Top ten cities from WCOC indicated

Source: Exhibit prepared by Saskia Sassen, based on MasterCard. 2008. *2008 Worldwide Centers of Commerce Index.* Purchase, NY: MasterCard.

Exhibit 4.4 Livability and Selected Subindicators

Rank	Indicator 7: Livability	Quality of Life	Basic Services	Health and Safety	Personal Freedom
1	Vancouver	Los Angeles	Singapore	Zurich	New York
2	Dusseldorf	Sydney	Copenhagen	Geneva	Tokyo
3	San Francisco	San Francisco	Munich	Stockholm	Chicago
4	Frankfurt	Melbourne	Frankfurt	Frankfurt	Paris
5	Vienna	London	Vancouver	Amsterdam	Frankfurt
6	Munich	New York	Dusseldorf	Toronto	Amsterdam
7	Zurich	Paris	Tokyo	Copenhagen	Toronto
8	Tokyo	Milan	Zurich	Munich	Copenhagen
9	Paris	Rome	Stockholm	Vienna	Zurich
10	Copenhagen	Boston	Vienna	Dublin	Stockholm
11	Sydney	Berlin	London	Montreal	Philadelphia
12	Berlin	Washington, DC	Osaka	Vancouver	Los Angeles
13	Toronto	Vancouver	Montreal	Dusseldorf	Osaka
14	Boston	Tokyo	Dallas	Berlin	Milan
15	Geneva	Chicago	Paris	Brussels	Boston

(Continued)

Exhibit 4.4 (Continued)

Rank	Indicator 7: Livability	Quality of Life	Basic Services	Health and Safety	Personal Freedom
16	Stockholm	Vienna	Sydney	Hamburg	Atlanta
17	Los Angeles	Dallas	Toronto	Edinburgh	Berlin
18	Amsterdam	Dusseldorf	Atlanta	Singapore	Miami
19	Montreal	Johannesburg	Hamburg	Tokyo	Munich
20	Melbourne	Frankfurt	Amsterdam	Osaka	Vienna
21	Washington, DC	Toronto	Philadelphia	Boston	San Francisco
22	Brussels	Atlanta	Boston	San Francisco	Brussels
23	Osaka	Miami	Brussels	Paris	Hamburg
24	London	Brussels	Washington, DC	Melbourne	Montreal
25	New York	Amsterdam	Geneva	Chicago	Houston
26	Chicago	Philadelphia	Melbourne	Sydney	Dallas
27	Hamburg	Osaka	New York	Philadelphia	Washington, DC
28	Dallas	Munich	Chicago	Washington, DC	Vancouver
29	Philadelphia	Houston	Berlin	London	Dusseldorf
30	Milan	Barcelona	Los Angeles	Madrid	Geneva

Note: Top ten cities from WCOC indicated

Source: Exhibit prepared by Saskia Sassen, based on MasterCard. 2008. *2008 Worldwide Centers of Commerce Index.* Purchase, NY: MasterCard.

Exhibit 4.5   WCOC Index, 2006

Rank	City	WCOC Index
1	London	77.79
2	New York	73.80
3	Tokyo	68.09
4	Chicago	67.19
5	Hong Kong	62.32
6	Singapore	61.95
7	Frankfurt	61.34
8	Paris	61.19
9	Seoul	60.70
10	Los Angeles	59.05
11	Amsterdam	57.30
12	Toronto	57.11
13	Boston	56.47
14	Sydney	56.26
15	Copenhagen	56.14
16	Madrid	56.06
17	Stockholm	54.51
18	San Francisco	54.36
19	Zurich	54.33
20	Atlanta	54.19

Note: 100 is the top score.

Source: Exhibit prepared by Saskia Sassen, based on MasterCard. 2008. *2008 Worldwide Centers of Commerce Index.* Purchase, NY: MasterCard.

dropped from the tenth to the seventeenth rank, and Boston from thirteenth to twenty-third, while European and Asian cities moved up in the top ranks, notably Madrid going from sixteenth to eleventh. In 2006, the US had six cities in the top twenty; in 2008, it had four. These shifts give added content to the loss of position of the United States as the dominant economic and military power. It is not that the United States is suddenly poorer, it is that other regions of the world are rising and that there are multiple forces feeding these multisited economic, political, and cultural strengths.

Urban/Rural Specificity Feeds the Knowledge Economy

The specific global circuits on which a city is located will vary from city to city, depending on a city's particular strengths, just as the groupings of cities vary on each circuit. All of this also shows us that the specialized differences of cities matter and that there is less competition among cities and more of a global or regional division of functions than is commonly recognised. For example, the knowledge economies of São Paulo, Chicago, and Shanghai all share a long history of servicing major heavy manufacturing sectors; theirs are economic histories that global cities such as New York and London never developed. Out of these specialized differences comes a global division of functions. Thus, a steel factory, a mining firm, or a machine manufacturer that wants to go global will, depending on its location, go to São Paulo, Shanghai, or Chicago for its legal, accounting, financial, insurance, economic forecasting, and other such specialized services. It will not go to New York or London for this highly particular servicing. Increasingly, these urban economies are part of a networked global platform.

The deep economic history of a place and the specialized economic strengths it can generate increasingly matter in a globalized economy. This goes against the common view that globalization homogenizes economies. How much this specificity matters will vary, partly depending on that region's economy. Establishing how a city/region becomes a knowledge economy requires highly detailed research. So let me use a case I researched, Chicago, to illustrate this. Chicago is usually seen as a latecomer to the knowledge economy—almost fifteen years later than New York and London. Typically, the answer is that Chicago had to overcome its heavy agro-industrial past: its economic history was seen as a disadvantage compared to old trading and financial centers such as New York and London. But I found that its past was not a disadvantage. It was one key source of its competitive advantage. This is most visible in the fact of its preeminence as a futures market built on pork bellies. The complexity, scale, and international character of Chicago's historical agro-industrial economy required highly specialized financial, accounting, and legal expertise. But these were/ are quite different from the expertise required to handle the sectors

New York specialized in—service exports, finance, and trade. It was Chicago's past as a massive agro-industrial complex that gave it some of its core and distinctive knowledge economy components and has made it the leading global futures financial center and global provider of specialized services (accounting, legal, insurance, etc.) for handling heavy industry, heavy transport, and large-scale agriculture. Chicago, São Paulo, Shanghai, Tokyo, and Seoul are among the leading producers of these types of specialized corporate services, not in spite of their economic pasts as major heavy industry centers, but because of them. Thus, when Boeing decided that it needed to enter the knowledge economy, it did not move its headquarters to New York but to Chicago.

The Global City as a Postindustrial Production Site

We are seeing the formation of a new producer–services complex in major cities. But how is this complex of management, financing, and servicing processes of internationalization actually constituted in cities? And what are the actual components of the larger work of running the global operations of firms and markets that get done in these cities? The answers to these two questions help us understand the new or sharply expanded role of a particular kind of city in the phase of the world economy that took off in the mid-1980s.

At the heart of this development lie two intersecting processes critical to the current phase. The first process is the sharp growth in the globalization of economic activity (see Chapter 2) and the concomitant increases in the scale and the complexity of international transactions, which in turn feeds the growth of top-level multinational headquarters' functions and of advanced corporate services. Although globalization raises their scale and complexity, these operations are also evident at smaller geographic scales and lower orders of complexity, as is the case with firms that operate regionally or nationally. Also, these firms run increasingly dispersed operations, albeit not global, as they set up chains and/or buy up the traditional single-owner shops that sell flowers, food, or fuel or run chains of hotels and a growing range of service facilities. Though operating in simpler contexts, these firms also need to centralize their control, management, and specialized servicing functions. National and regional market firms need not negotiate the complexities of international borders and the regulations and accounting rules of different countries, but they do create a growing demand for corporate services of all kinds, feeding economic growth in second-order cities as well.

The second process we need to consider is the growing service intensity in the organization of all industries (Sassen [1991] 2001: chap. 5). This development has contributed to a massive growth in the demand for services (legal, accounting, insurance, etc.) by firms in all industries, from mining and manufacturing to finance and consumer industries. Cities are key sites for the production of services for firms. Hence, the increase in service intensity in the organization of all industries has had a significant growth effect on cities beginning in the 1980s. This growth in services for firms is evident in cities at different levels of a nation's urban system. Some of these cities cater to regional or subnational markets, others cater to national markets, and yet others cater to global markets. In this context, the specific effect of globalization is a question of scale and added complexity. The key process from the perspective of the urban economy is the growing demand for services by firms in all industries and across market scale—global, national, or regional.

As a result of these two intersecting processes, we see in cities the formation of a new urban economic core of high-level management and specialized service activities that comes to replace the older, typically manufacturing-oriented office core. In the case of cities that are major international business centers, the scale, power, and profit levels of this new core suggest the formation of a new urban economy in at least two regards. First, even though these cities have long been centers for business and finance, since the mid-1980s there have been dramatic changes in the structure of the business and financial sectors, as well as sharp increases in the overall magnitude of these sectors and their weight in the urban economy. Second, the ascendance of the new finance and services complex engenders a new economic regime; that is, although this sector may account for only a fraction of the economy of a city, it imposes itself on that larger economy. Most notably, the possibility for superprofits in finance has the effect of devalorizing manufacturing because manufacturing cannot generate the superprofits typical in much financial activity.

This does not mean that everything in the economy of these cities has changed. On the contrary, these cities still show a great deal of continuity and many similarities with cities that are not global nodes. Rather, the implantation of global processes and markets has meant that the internationalized sector of the economy has expanded sharply and has imposed a new valorization dynamic—that is, a new set of criteria for valuing or pricing various economic activities and outcomes. This has had devastating effects on large sectors of the urban economy. High prices and profit levels in the internationalized sector and its ancillary activities, such as top-of-the-line restaurants and hotels, have made it increasingly difficult for other sectors to compete for space and investments. Many of these other sectors have experienced considerable downgrading and/or displacement; for example, neighborhood shops tailored to local needs have been replaced by upscale boutiques and restaurants catering to the new high-income urban elite.

Although at a different order of magnitude, these trends also took off in the early 1990s in a number of major cities in the developing world that have become integrated into various world markets: São Paulo, Buenos Aires, Bangkok, Taipei, and Mexico City are a few examples. Also in these cities, the new urban core was fed by the deregulation of financial markets, the ascendance of finance and specialized services, and integration into the world markets. The opening of stock markets to foreign investors and the privatization of what were once public-sector firms have been crucial institutional arenas for this articulation. Given the vast size of some of these cities, the impact of this new core on their larger urban area is not always as evident as in central London or Frankfurt, but the transformation is still very real.

Producer Services

The expansion of producer services is a central feature of growth in today's advanced urban economies and, to a lesser degree, in national economies as well. The critical period for the rise of producer services in the developed countries was the 1980s, and their rise can in fact function as a lens on the underlying structural transformations in the economy. The concern here is to capture this shift rather than to track the evolution of producer services since then. In the 1980s, developed countries mostly experienced a decline or slowdown in manufacturing alongside sharp growth in producer services. Elsewhere, I have posited that the fundamental reason for this growth lies in the increased service intensity in the organization of all industries (Sassen [1991] 2001: 166–68). Whether in manufacturing or in warehousing, firms are using more legal, financial, advertising, consulting, and accounting services. These services can be seen as part of the supply capacity of an economy because they facilitate adjustments to changing economic circumstances (Marshall et al. 1986: 16). They are a mechanism that organizes and adjudicates economic exchange for a fee (Thrift 1987) and are part of a broader intermediary space of economic activity (Bryson and Daniels 2007).

Producer services are services for firms, from the most sophisticated to the most elementary ones. They include financial, legal, general management matters, innovation, development, design, administration, personnel, production technology, maintenance, transport, communications, whole-sale distribution, advertising, cleaning services, security, and storage. Central components of the producer–services category are a range of industries with mixed business and consumer markets. They are insurance, banking, financial services, real estate, legal services, accounting, and professional associations.[2]

Although disproportionately concentrated in the largest cities, pro-ducer services are actually growing at faster rates at the national level in most developed economies. The crucial process feeding the growth of producer services is the increasing use of service inputs by firms in all industries. Consumption of services has also risen in households, either directly (such as the growing use of accountants to prepare tax returns) or indirectly via the reorganization of consumer industries (buying flowers or dinner from franchises or chains rather than from self-standing and privately owned "mom-and-pop" shops). Services directly bought by consumers tend to be available, often through mere outlets, wherever population is concentrated. In that regard, they are far less geographically concentrated than producer services, especially those catering to top firms. The demand for specialized services by households, from account-ing to architects, may be a key factor contributing to the growth of these mixed-market services at the national level.

National employment trends for the crucial period of the shift show that some of the mixed-market producer services (usually categorized as "mostly producer services") make up the fastest-growing sector in most developed economies even though they account for a small share of total jobs. Generally, these trends continue today. Total employment in the United States grew from 82 million in 1970 to 154.2 million in 2009 (see Exhibit 4.6), but the mostly producer services grew well above average, especially miscellaneous business services and financial activities. In contrast, employ-ment in manufacturing dropped. The other major growth sectors included health, education, and personal services (care, leisure, hospitality). Parallel patterns are emerging in other developed economies, including Japan, the UK, and France, among others.

A focus on cities reveals the same, though sharper, trends in the critical period of the mid-1980s. Producer services linked to the expansion of a global economy became the most dynamic, fastest-growing sector in many cities. Particularly notable here is the United Kingdom, where overall employment actually fell and manufacturing suffered severe losses. Yet in only three years, between 1984 and 1987, producer services in Central London raised their numbers even as relative and absolute declines hit all other major employment sectors there; their share rose from 31% to 40%

Exhibit 4.6 National Employment Trends by Industry in Germany, Japan, and the United States, 1970–2008 (in thousands)[a]

	Germany					Japan					United States				
	1970	1980	1990	2000	2008	1970	1980	1990	2000	2008	1970	1980	1990	2000	2008
Total	26,610.1	26,684	30,369	39,731	41,875	53,320	57,231.1	63,595.3	67,660	63,850	82,048.8	106,085	126,424	140,863	154,287
Agriculture, hunting, forestry, and fishing	1,990.4	1,528	990	982	872	10,151.4	6,111	4,391.3	3,260	2,680	2,955.8	3,117.1	3,566	3,650	2,306
Mining and quarrying	380.4	339	190	152	109	216.1	108	63.4	60	30	655.2	1,989.8	766	543	845
Manufacturing	9,992	9,106	8,841	8,542	8,517	13,716.6	13,246.1	14,642.7	13,210	11,740	20,823.9	23,550.8	22,464	20,681	16,869
Electricity, gas, and water	214.8	231	254	290	346	289.9	348.6	333.6	350	320	1,011.1	1,413.2	1,614	1,470	1,254
Construction	2,163.8	1,964	1,847	3,118	2,521	3,963.9	5,282.2	5,342	6,530	5,370	4,967.4	6,664.9	8,471	9,977	12,140
Wholesale and retail trade and restaurants and hotels	4,034.8	3,788	4,636	6,409	6,751	10,137.5	12,731.1	13,801.7	14,740	15,030	16,047.5	21,292.3	25,811	29,245	32,551

Exhibit 4.6 (Continued)

	Germany					Japan					United States				
	1970	1980	1990	2000	2008	1970	1980	1990	2000	2008	1970	1980	1990	2000	2008
Transport, storage, and communication	1,443	1,520	1,620	2,008	2,147	3,235.9	3,504.3	3,674.7	4,150	3,910	4,325.4	5,990.3	6,814	8,547	6,831
Financing, insurance, real estate, and business	1,234.9	1,445	2,375	4,256	5,473	1,384.1	2,003.4	2,661.8	6,160	9,350	6,421.2	10,424.2	13,953	17,197	27,197
Community, social, and personal services	5,039.3	6,027	7,733	10,671	11,755	9,457.4	12,314	15,949.6	15,630	14,660	22,519.3	30,175.4	42,215	49,106	54,294
OTHER		677		203	6,552	39.9	61.5	320.9	390	1,480	2,072.6	1,677.7	30	447	0

Notes:

a. Excludes unemployment numbers.

b. Labor statistics for Germany for years 1970, 1980, and 1990 are from the Federal Republic of Germany.

Source: Compiled from ILO (2010).

of all employment in Central London by 1989 (Frost and Spence 1992). Similar developments took place in New York City: in 1987, at the height of the 1980s boom, producer services accounted for 37.7% of private-sector jobs and grew sharply, including the 62% growth in legal services jobs. In contrast, employment fell by 22% in manufacturing and by 20% in transport. (For detailed accounts, see Sassen 1991: chap. 8).

Accompanying these sharp growth rates in producer services was an increase in the level of employment specialization in business and financial services in major cities throughout the 1980s. For example, more than 90% of jobs in finance, insurance, and real estate (FIRE) in New York City were located in Manhattan, as were 85% of business service jobs. By 1990, after large-scale suburbanization of households and firms, the finance and business services in the New York metropolitan area were more concentrated in Manhattan than they had been in the mid-1950s (Harris 1991).[3]

In the 1990s, the mostly producer services began to grow faster at the national level than in major cities. This is commonly interpreted as cities losing producer-services jobs to larger metropolitan areas and small towns. I interpret the data differently: the fact of growth nationwide is an indicator of the growing importance of producer services for all sectors of the economy (see Sassen [1991] 2001: chap. 5). If we consider only those components of producer services that may be described as information industries, we can see a steady growth in jobs across the United States. But the incidence of these industries does not decline in major cities. New York City posted a significantly higher concentration than any other major American city. From 1970 to 2000, employment in professional and business services grew from 24.2% of jobs in New York City to 37.2%, from 24.1 to 33.2% in Los Angeles, and from 19.2% to 33.5% in Chicago. All three cities show a higher incidence of these specialized services throughout this period of transformation of the urban economy than their average growth of 15.1% to 17.6% in the national economy. High concentration of finance and certain producer services in the downtowns of major international financial centers around the world, from Toronto and Sydney to Frankfurt and Tokyo, all have increasingly specialized in these services even as their share of the global market declined as new international centers joined the global network.

These cities emerged as important producers of services for firms, including for export to the rest of their national economies and worldwide. There is a strong tendency toward hierarchy and specialization. New York and London are the leading producers and exporters of accounting, advertising, management consulting, international legal, and other business services. In fact, New York, London, Tokyo, Paris, Zurich, and Munich accounted for

Exhibit 4.7 Cities Ranked by Assets of the World's Top Fifty Publicly Listed Financial TNCs, 2008[a]

Rank	Average GSI[b]	No. of Top Financial TNCs	City	Total Assets (US$ millions)	Total Employees	Affiliates Total	Affiliates Number Foreign	No. of Host Countries
1	52.3	5	Paris	8,679,654	553,951	2,498	1,630	217
2	43.9	7	New York	7,422,354	842,192	2,966	1,854	235
3	40.0	5	London	6,797,451	641,201	2,419	1,290	166
4	30.8	3	Tokyo	4,167,163	145,442	311	175	51
5	55.2	4	Zurich	3,602,362	194,752	1,337	1,240	126
6	32.6	1	Edinburgh	3,511,187	199,000	1,169	388	32
7	43.3	3	Amsterdam	3,270,013	225,833	2,412	1,436	100
8	52.4	1	Frankfurt	3,150,820	80,456	934	713	36
9	39.1	2	Bilbao	2,277,942	282,897	660	402	51
10	43.7	3	Munich	2,275,604	228,860	1,330	824	105
11	42.4	3	Brussels	1,572,522	97,983	973	736	71
12	56.7	1	Milan	1,495,868	174,519	1,111	1,052	34

Rank	Average GSI[b]	No. of Top Financial TNCs	City	Total Assets (US$ millions)	Total Employees	Affiliates Total	Affiliates Number Foreign	No. of Host Countries
13	37.2	3	Toronto	1,319,023	166,372	350	286	53
14	32.2	3	Stockholm	1,285,432	66,132	388	295	47
15	38.9	1	Turin	910,062	108,310	218	127	26
16	26.2	1	Copenhagen	680,095	23,624	73	50	10
17	59.5	1	Trieste	549,269	84,063	396	342	41
18	25.8	1	Dublin	277,705	16,026	197	101	13
19	33.5	1	Omaha, NE	267,399	246,000	570	200	32
20	31.1	1	Oslo	263,592	14,057	33	32	10

Notes:

a. Top financial companies as determined by Geographical Spread Index (see note b below). Data on total assets and employees, from Bloomberg, currency (US$) millions, period 2008. Data on affiliates is based on Dun and Bradstreet's "Who Owns Whom" database.

b. GSI, the Geographical Spread Index, is calculated as the square root of the Internationalization Index multiplied by the number of host countries. Average GSI is the average for all top financial companies in city.

Source: Calculations based on UNCTAD (2009b: 234).

a large share of the world's top 100 largest publicly listed financial company assets in 2008 (see Exhibits A.4.3 to A.4.5) and also did for the world's top fifty largest insurer assets in 2009, together with Amsterdam, now ranked at the top (see Exhibit A.4.6). These and a few other cities are the most important international markets for these services. Some of the cities have long been major exporters of these services, notably New York, London, Paris, and Hong Kong. Others only became major exporters in them when the new global phase began in the 1980s; for example, it was not until the late 1980s that Tokyo emerged as an important center for the international trade in services, going beyond its initial restricted role of exporting only the services required by its large international trading houses. Beginning early on, Japanese firms gained a significant share of the world market in certain producer services, namely construction and engineering, but not in others, such as advertising and international legal services (Rimmer 1988). For instance, in the late 1970s, the United States accounted for sixty of the top 200 international construction contractors and Japan for ten (Rimmer 1986). By 1985, in a sharp reversal, each accounted for thirty-four (see Sassen [1991] 2001: 174–75).

There are also tendencies toward specialization among different cities within a country. In the United States, New York is more narrowly specialized as a financial, business, and cultural center; thus, it leads in banking, securities, manufacturing administration, accounting, and advertising. Washington, DC, leads in legal services, computing and data processing, management and public relations, research and development, and membership organizations; at the same time, some of the legal activity concentrated in Washington, DC, is actually serving New York businesses that have to go through legal and regulatory procedures, lobbying, and so on. Such services are bound to be found in the national capital, and many are oriented to the national economy and to noneconomic purposes. Furthermore, in another contrast with New York City, much of the specialized activity in Washington is aimed not at the world economy but at the national economy in sectors such as medical and health research. Thus, adequate understanding requires we specify the composition of a city's producer-services complex and whether it is oriented to world markets and integration into the global economy or whether it responds largely to domestic demand.[4]

It is important to recognize that manufacturing remains a crucial sector in all of these economies, even when it may have ceased to be a dominant sector in major cities. Indeed, when these new trends began to emerge in cities in the 1980s and even more strongly in the 1990s, there was quite a debate about the place of manufacturing in urban economies dominated by advanced services. Several scholars argued that the producer-services sector could not exist without manufacturing (Cohen and Zysman 1987; Markusen 1994). The weakening of the manufacturing sector in the broader New York region could be seen as a threat to the city's status as a leading financial- and producer-services center (Markusen and Gwiasda 1994). A key proposition for this argument is that producer services depend on a strong manufacturing sector for growth (Noyelle and Dutka 1988; Sassen [1991] 2001; Drennan 1992). Drennan (1992), the leading analyst of the producer-services sector in the 1980s and 1990s in New York City, argued that a strong finance- and producer-services sector is possible notwithstanding decline in its industrial base, partly because of their strong integration into the world markets so that articulation with their hinterland becomes secondary.

In a variant on both positions (Sassen [1991] 2001), I argue that manufacturing is one factor feeding the growth of the producer-services sector but that it does so whether located in the area in question or overseas. Even though manufacturing—and mining and agriculture, for that matter—feeds growth in the demand for producer services, its actual location is of secondary importance for global-level service firms. Thus, whether manufacturing plants are located offshore or within a country is irrelevant as long as they are part of a multinational corporation likely to buy the needed legal and accounting services from top-level firms. Second, in my research, I find that the territorial dispersal of plants, especially if international, actually raises the demand for producer services (see the section on "Global Cities" in Chapter 2). This is yet another meaning, or consequence, of globalization: the growth of producer service firms headquartered in New York or London or Paris can be fed by manufacturing located anywhere in the world as long as it is part of a multinational corporate network. Thus, Detroit's manufacturing job losses due to outsourcing are New York's job gains in advanced producer services. Third, a good part of the producer-services sector is fed by financial and business transactions that have nothing to do with manufacturing, as in many of the global financial markets, or for which manufacturing is incidental, as in much merger and acquisition activity (which is centered on buying and selling firms no matter what they do) and, above all, financial innovation of speculative instruments.

The Formation of a New Production Complex

According to standard conceptions about information industries, the rapid growth and disproportionate concentration of many of the producer services in central cities should not have happened. This is especially so for advanced corporate services, because they are thoroughly embedded in the most advanced information technologies; they would seem to have locational options that bypass the high costs and congestion typical of major cities. But cities offer agglomeration economies and highly innovative environments. Some of these services are produced in-house by firms, but a large share is outsourced to specialized service firms. The growing complexity, diversity, and specialization of the services these firms require make it more efficient to buy them from specialized firms rather than hiring in-house full-time professionals. The growing demand for these services has enabled a freestanding specialized service sector to become economically viable in cities.

The work of producing these services benefits from proximity to other specialized services, especially in the leading and most innovative sectors of these industries. Complexity and innovation often require highly specialized inputs from several industries. The production of a financial instrument, for example, requires inputs from accounting, advertising, legal services, economic consulting, public relations, software innovations, design, and printing. In this regard, these are highly networked firms. These particular characteristics of production explain the centralization of management and servicing functions that has fueled the economic boom in major cities beginning in the mid-1980s.

The commonly heard explanation that high-level professionals require face-to-face interactions needs to be refined in several ways. Producer services, unlike other types of services, are not necessarily dependent on spatial proximity to buyers—that is, firms served. Rather, economies occur in such specialized firms when they locate close to others that produce key inputs or whose proximity makes possible joint production of certain service offerings. The accounting firm can service its clients at a distance, but producing that service depends on proximity to specialists, from lawyers to programmers. My interpretation is that so-called face-to-face communication is actually a production process that requires multiple simultaneous inputs and feedbacks. At the current stage of technical development, having immediate and simultaneous access to the pertinent experts is still the most effective way to operate, especially when dealing with a highly complex product. Moreover, concentration arises out of the needs and expectations of the people likely to be employed in these new high-skill jobs that tend to be attracted to the amenities and lifestyles that large urban centers can offer.

A critical variable in the most advanced and specialized segments of the sector is speed. Time replaces weight as a force for agglomeration. In the past, the weight of inputs from iron ore to unprocessed agricultural products was a major constraint that encouraged agglomeration in sites where the heaviest inputs were located. Today, the combination of added complexity and acceleration of economic transactions has created new forces for agglomeration; that is, if there were no time pressures and little complexity, the client could conceivably make use of a widely dispersed array of cooperating specialized firms. And this is often the case in routine operations. Where time is of the essence, however, as it is today in many of the leading sectors of these industries, the benefits of agglomeration in the production of specialized services are still extremely high—to the point where whatever the costs of urban agglomeration, the concentration of multiple state-of-the-art specialized service firms has become an indispensable arrangement. Central here has been the general acceleration of all transactions, especially in finance (where minutes and seconds count), the stock markets, the foreign-currency markets, the futures markets, and so on. Speed in these types of sectors puts a premium not just on competence among lawyers, accountants, financiers, and so on, but also on the knowledge that emerges from the interactions among talented and experienced professionals.

This combination of constraints and advantages has promoted the formation of a producer-services complex in all major cities. The producer-services complex is intimately connected to the world of corporate headquarters, leading to the formation of a joint headquarters–corporate-services complex. But the two need to be distinguished. Although headquarters still tend to be disproportionately concentrated in cities, many have moved out during the last two decades. Headquarters can indeed be located outside cities, but they need a producer-services *complex* somewhere in order to gain access to the needed specialized services and financing. Headquarters of firms with very high overseas activity or in highly innovative and complex lines of business still tend to locate in major cities. In brief: on the one hand, firms in more routinized lines of activity, with predominantly regional or national markets, appear to be increasingly free to move or install their headquarters outside cities. On the other hand, firms in highly competitive and innovative lines of activity and/or with a strong world-market orientation appear to benefit from being located at the center of major international business centers, no matter how high the costs.

Both types of firms, however, need access to a corporate-services complex; access to individual firms is not enough. Where this complex is located is increasingly unimportant from the perspective of many, though not all, headquarters. However, from the perspective of producer-services firms, such a specialized complex is most likely to be in a city rather than, for example, in a suburban office park. The latter will be the site for producer-services firms but not for a services complex. And only such a complex is capable of handling the most advanced and complicated corporate needs.

These issues are examined in the next two sections. The first discusses how the spatial dispersal of economic activities engenders an increased demand for specialized services; the transnational corporation is one of the major agents in this process. The second section examines whether and, if so, under what conditions corporate headquarters need cities.

Corporate Headquarters and Cities

It is very common in the general literature and in some more scholarly accounts to use the concentration of major headquarters as an indication of a city's status as an international business center. The loss of these types of headquarters is then interpreted as a decline in the city's status. In fact, using such headquarters' concentration as an index is an increasingly problematic measure, given the way in which corporations are classified, the locational options telecommunications offer corporations, and the analysis developed earlier about a trend toward outsourcing the functions of corporate headquarters.

A number of variables determine which headquarters concentrate in major international financial and business centers. First, how we measure or simply count headquarters makes a difference. Frequently, the key measure is the size of the firm in terms of employment and overall revenue. Using this measure, some of the largest firms in the world are still manufacturing firms, and many of these have their main headquarters in proximity to their major factory complex, which is unlikely to be in a large city because of space constraints. Such firms *are* likely, however, to have secondary headquarters for highly specialized functions in major cities. Furthermore, many manufacturing firms are oriented to the national market and do not need to be located in a city's national business center. Thus, the much-publicized departure of major headquarters from New York City in the 1960s and 1970s involved these types of firms, as did the large numbers of departures from Chicago in the 1990s. A quick look at the Fortune 500 list of the largest US firms shows that many have left large cities. If, however, instead of size, the measure is the share of total firm revenue coming from international sales, many firms that are not on the Fortune 500 list come into play. In the case of New York, for example, the results change dramatically: in 1990, 40% of US firms with half their revenue from international sales had their headquarters in New York City. Further, while moving away from major metropolitan areas has become the general trend for firms in a broad range of economic sectors, two of the largest components of producer services—the high-tech industry and financial services—continue to concentrate in large cities. "In this instance, profound deregulation has encouraged firm consolidation and market expansion. In response, the now-larger companies have chosen to locate their headquarters in larger metropolitan areas" (Klier and Testa 2002: 14). Klier and Testa's calculations regarding the headquarters of large US corporations (employing more than 2,500 worldwide) also show that in 2000, New York still was home to 14% of these companies, and the top five US metro areas combined accounted for 33% of such firms.

Second, the nature of the urban system in a country is a factor in the geographic distribution of headquarters. Sharp urban primacy tends to entail a disproportionate concentration of headquarters in the primate city no matter what measure one uses. Third, different economic histories and business traditions may combine to produce different results. Finally, headquarters concentration may be linked to a specific economic phase. For example, unlike New York's loss of top Fortune 500 headquarters, Tokyo has gained these types of headquarters. Osaka and Nagoya, the two other major economic centers in Japan, lost headquarters to Tokyo. This change seems to be linked to the combination of the increasing internationalization of the Japanese economy and the ongoing role of government regulation on cross-border transactions. Firms need easy access to government regulators. As a result, there was an increase in central headquarters command and servicing functions in Tokyo. In brief, understanding the meaning of headquarters concentration requires disaggregation across several variables. Although headquarters are still disproportionately concentrated in major cities, the patterns that became evident in the mid-1980s and continue today do represent a change (see Exhibits 4.1–4.5 and A.4.1–A.4.8).

The discussion about producer services, the producer-services complex, and the locational patterns of headquarters point to two significant developments since the 1980s. One is the growing service intensity in the organization of the economy; the other is the emergence of a producer-services complex that, although strongly geared toward the corporate sector, is far more likely to remain concentrated in urban centers than are the headquarters it serves.

The Servicing of Transnational Corporations

The territorial dispersal of multi-establishment firms, whether at the regional, national, or global level, has been one important factor in the sharp rise of producer services (see Exhibits A.4.7–A.4.8). Firms running multiple plants, offices, and service outlets must coordinate planning, internal administration, distribution, marketing, and other central headquarters activities. As large corporations move into the production and sale of final consumer services, a wide range of management functions previously performed by independently owned consumer-service firms are moved to the central headquarters of the new corporate chains. Regional, national, or global chains of motels, food outlets, and flower shops require vast centralized administrative and servicing structures. A parallel pattern of expansion of central high-level planning and control operations takes place in governments, brought about partly by the technical developments that make this expansion possible and partly by the growing complexity of regulatory and administrative tasks. Thus, governments are also buying more outside consulting services of all sorts and outsourcing what were once government jobs.

Formally, the development of the modern corporation and its massive participation in world markets and foreign countries have made planning, internal administration, product development, and research increasingly important and complex. Diversification of product lines, mergers, and transnationalization of economic activities all require highly specialized skills. A firm with several geographically dispersed manufacturing plants contributes to the development of new types of planning in production and distribution surrounding the firm. The development of multisite manufacturing, service, and banking has created an expanded demand for a wide range of specialized service activities to manage and control global networks of factories, service outlets, and branch offices. Although to some extent these activities can be carried out in-house, a large share is not. Together, headquarters and the producer services deliver the components of what might be called *global control capability*. High levels of specialization, the possibility of externalizing the production of some of these services, and the growing demand by large and small firms and increasingly also governments are all conditions that have both resulted from and made possible the development of a market for freestanding producer-services firms.

This, in turn, means that small firms can buy components of that global control capability, such as management consulting or international legal advice, as can firms and governments from anywhere in the world. This accessibility contributes to the formation of marketplaces for such services in major cities. Thus, although the large corporation is undoubtedly a key agent inducing the development of this capability and is its prime beneficiary, it is not the sole user.

A brief examination of the territorial dispersal entailed by transnational operations of large enterprises illustrates some of the points raised here. Exhibits A.4.7 and A.4.8 provide information about the operations of major corporations outside their home countries. Chapter 2 introduced data about the number of transnational corporations (TNCs) and their affiliates worldwide (see Exhibit 2.6) and provided indicative data about the distribution of financial and banking operations of major firms across the network of off-shore tax havens (Exhibit 2.7). These and other figures throughout this book point to a vast global operational space dispersed over a multiplicity of locations. These types of extensive operations feed the growth of central management, coordination, control, and servicing functions. Some of these functions are performed in the headquarters; others are bought or contracted for, thereby feeding the growth of the producer-services complex.

An Emerging Global Labor Market

The early 1990s saw the beginnings of a global labor market. Today, in 2011, the elements are in place. But as a labor market, it is not very open and not very global. It is a mix of markets, government programs that allow firms to hire foreign workers, and intermediaries such as global manpower firms and other employment placement services. Elementary as this global labor market is, its future would seem in doubt given the current economic recession, stronger government intervention in economies, growing sentiment against low-wage immigrant workers and foreign professionals, and more paperwork everywhere. And yet there are a number of trends that suggest we are entering a new era when it comes to the need and the advantages of having a global labor market from the perspective of firms. The advantages for the workers themselves and for the larger economy of a city or a country are a separate matter.

In what follows, the focus is on firms. I base our understanding on both existing data and our in-depth interviews with firms and experts from across the world. This includes such combinations as the manager of the China-based operations of a Singaporean firm or the US-based operation of a Mexican firm. The data we use come from specialized manpower reports and include trend data not usually used in analyses of the employment of foreign workers. Based on this information, I detect three trends that mark a new phase in the development of a global labor market that goes well beyond the familiar notion of the search for "talent." The key argument put forth by firms recruiting foreign professionals is the scarcity of talent in a country, with the best-known recent case the need for importing high-tech workers in the US, the UK, and Germany. The structural trends discussed here point to a vastly expanded need for a global labor market and a qualitative change in the parameters of that market. The reasons for these changes are the changing character of economic globalization, the growing segmentation of specialized labor markets, and the demographic turn. All three will take us well beyond the current understanding of the need for foreign workers, particularly foreign professionals.

Three Changes in the Role of Foreign Talent for Global Firms

The pattern that has dominated till quite recently was to bring home-country professionals to run a firm's overseas operations. This pattern is increasingly being recognized as insufficient. We can detect three changes feeding a tipping point in the global labor market.

First, the available evidence suggests that the importance of hiring foreign professional workers will only grow. This has to do with the fact that the global economy is not as flat as is often thought, and indeed is not about to become flatter anytime soon. Even in some of the most globally standardized industries, global firms encounter and need to engage the enduring particularities of national, regional, and even local political economies, as well as the distinctive economic cultures of countries. Employing local professionals is not only a good idea because of the talent aspect. It is also becoming necessary to maximize operational effectiveness and success because they can bridge between the foreign firm and a country's national economic culture.

Second, and partly due to the above, global firms will have to bring foreign professionals into the highest level of home headquarters to understand and learn from the specificity of the foreign location and its uses/ understandings of talent. This is in sharp contrast with the older and still prevalent modus operandi, which is to bring foreign professionals into a firm's home-country headquarters so as to teach them the firm's culture; this older pattern will continue, but it will increasingly become insufficient.

Third, the older pattern of bringing home-country professionals to run overseas operations will increasingly need to be actively accompanied by the hiring of local professionals, including for the highest posts, such as heading the overseas offices. Indeed, in our interviews, we also found indications that global firms are hiring local professionals to *run* their foreign offices, not only to *staff* their foreign offices.

My own research has led me to emphasize a very specific aspect that is often obscured by the more general analyses of the search for talent. It is the problem of "incomplete knowledge." Firms have always confronted incomplete knowledge in market economies. When such firms go global, this problem becomes acute. The corporate services for firms (accounting, law, finance, forecasting, credit rating, and kindred specialized corporate services) are, in my analysis, an "organizational commodity" that becomes more and more important the more a firm (or an economic sector) operates in globalized markets (Sassen 2001: chap. 5; 2010). This holds for global firms and markets, no matter what the sector—mining, agribusiness, finance, insurance, and so on. I go further. The proposition I developed to organize the many different conditions and needs is that the more digitized and the more globalized the operations of a firm, the more acute is its incomplete knowledge problem, partly because of the acceleration of operations and decisions in highly digitized sectors. Adding foreign professionals to a firm's staff is one key component to address this problem of incomplete knowledge. These foreign workers bring not only the basic skill or talent the firm knows it needs. They also bring a type of tacit or difficult-to-codify knowledge about the economic "culture" of their country of origin. Thus, bringing in foreign talent means, in part, addressing the problem of incomplete knowledge: foreign talent is not only brought to headquarters to learn the established culture of the firm but also to bring in new, country-specific understandings of what is a good investment, what is informal trust, and so on. And this is one of the key aspects of the changing role of foreign talent in a global economy.

This also works at the level of the city, particularly the seventy-five-plus global cities in today's world. The city's specificity in addressing the incomplete knowledge problem, especially for global actors, is that its diverse networks, information loops, and professionals coming from diverse parts of the world produce a particular type of knowledge capital. I refer to it as *"urban* knowledge capital." It is a kind of knowledge capital that is more than the sum of the "knowledges" of the professionals and the firms in a city. This, then, also explains why global capitalism produced a systemic demand for a growing number of global cities across the world as globalization expanded in the 1990s and onward. Each of these is a site for the production of urban knowledge capital, in good part specific to each city. Indeed, since the beginning, I have argued that this phase of globalization *needs* the specialized differences of cities: this specialized difference makes the urban knowledge capital of each global city specific. It is going to be different in Rome from what it is in Milano, different in New York from Chicago, in Hong Kong from Shanghai, and so on. And the fact of these specialized differences then also explains the growing importance of local talent in a global firm: local workers can bring that specific knowledge into the firm where they are employed.

The specifics of the current period are well captured in the findings from our in-depth interviews with global firms (Sassen with Nicol and

Walinska 2011). They bring to the fore the enormously variable conditions under which firms function. All of our interviewees pointed out the particular differences in each of the countries where they operate. And they made clear that they were learning that they had to address this fact and change old strategies. These differences hold not only for aspects such as extremely different political economies and management cultures across countries worldwide, with the United States and China probably the most familiar contrast. Nor is it only the global firms of the dominant economic cultures, notably the United States and Europe, that find these sharp differences. Also, global firms from less dominant countries, such as Mexico, India, and Malaysia, found these differences were important and that they had to recognize them.

Some of the interviews provided unexpected insights into how firms handle foreign professionals. Thus, in the case of today's two global powers, China and the United States, it is common to expect the United States to come across as more enlightened vis à vis foreign professionals than China, given its long immigration history and the many benefits that immigration has brought to the United States. Instead, we hear more critiques of the United States on this account and a view of China, a far less democratic and more closed system, as having a more enlightened position regarding foreign talent. One reason might be that the leadership in China knows it needs to bring in foreign professionals and firms, while the United States is perhaps less aware of its own needs and takes the presence of foreign professionals for granted. The second aspect that comes through is the sectoral difference: a global firm that specializes in manpower for other firms (recruiting the appropriate workers for global firms) has to deal with the law and policies of each of the countries involved—this is an ongoing part of a manpower firm's work. This is quite different from a firm whose business is to make products and deliver services rather than to recruit and hire foreign talent. Both types of firms are key actors in the development of a global labor market for professionals.

Finally, this is still a partial labor market that requires the ongoing participation of governments because foreign workers are involved. Much of the above is a question of systemic positioning—each country has its own specific way of being articulated with the global economy. But it also shows us the enormous variability and segmentations in the global labor market. To a good extent, the global labor market for professionals is, in fact, made up of multiple specialized labor markets rather than being one single market. It further underlines the fact that the differences among the seventy-plus global cities in the world today matter far more than is conveyed by notions that the global economy is flat.

Growing Segmentation in the Global Labor Market

Much of what is signaled by the structural trends discussed above for the case of top-level professionals actually concerns a broad range of types of jobs (see Exhibit 4.8). Manpower's 2008 survey of more than 28,000 employers across twenty-seven countries and territories that employ foreign workers found that the top ten jobs employers are filling with foreign workers in the surveyed firms are: laborers, engineers, production operators, technicians, IT staff, sales representatives, administrative assistants/PAs, customer service representatives, senior executives/board members, and accounting and finance staff (see Exhibit 4.9). High-skilled foreign workers are employed for various reasons, including, for instance, language abilities and knowledge of foreign markets (see Exhibit 4.10).

Exhibit 4.8   Percentage of Foreign High-skilled Workers by Sectors 2000

	Country			
Sector	Germany	France	United Kingdom	Netherlands
Chemical	4.83	2.19	4.14	10.33
Manufacturing	1.93	3.09	3.56	7.30
Financial	1.58	1.56	0.28	1.05
IT	4.54	2.60	3.41	4.49
R&D	10.88	10.68	8.84	9.58

Source: Bauer, Thomas K. and Kunze, Astrid, 2004. "The Demand for High-skilled Workers and Immigration Policy," IZA Discussion Papers 999, Institute for the Study of Labor (IZA). Data from the International Employer Survey 2000. Reported percentages are the ratio of the number of foreign high-skilled workers divided by the number of high-skilled workers.

This is, clearly, an enormously diverse range of occupations, from manual production workers to senior executives. Manpower's findings are also confirmed by the research commissioned by the BBC World Service in 2009 to the Migration Policy Institute (2009); it examines the employment of foreign workers worldwide and finds that the need for foreign workers concerns not only professional talent but also production workers. The

Exhibit 4.9   Top Ten Jobs Filled With Foreign Workers 2007

Rank	Occupation
1	Laborers
2	Engineers
3	Production operators
4	Technicians
5	IT staff
6	Sales representatives
7	Administrative assistants/PAs
8	Customer service representatives
9	Senior executives/board members
10	Accounting and finance staff

Source: Manpower Inc. 2008. *Borderless Workforce Survey Global Summary.* (http://files
.shareholder.com/downloads/MAN/1216175933x0x208357/41b8de87-062c-4840-9b0a-
ff48bd175b4/2008_Borderless%20Workforce%20Survey_Global%20Results_FINAL.pdf):
Manpower Inc.

Exhibit 4.10   Reasons for Hiring Foreign High-skilled Workers 2007

Factor ("We hire foreign employees because")	Agree (%)	Strongly Agree (%)
Overall they are the best candidates.	49.07	9.26
There is a lack of good domestic applicants.	55.45	10.91
They know foreign markets.	64.86	36.04
They speak foreign languages.	71.17	47.75
They speak English.	56.13	26.42
The type of knowledge required for these jobs is not produced by the domestic education system.	27.93	4.5
Their skills better fit our work tastes.	51.35	15.32

Note: Bauer, Thomas K. and Kunze, Astrid, 2004. "The Demand for High-skilled Workers and
Immigration Policy," IZA Discussion Papers 999, Institute for the Study of Labor (IZA). Results
reported using German subsample from IZA International Employer Survey 2000. Proportion
of firms responding that they agree (strongly agree) that a factor was a consideration in the
decision making process for hiring foreign employees with a university degree.

intensifying segmentation of the global labor market takes many forms. An expansive interpretation of the global labor market would lead us to say that the sources of segmentation include (1) a mix of specialized markets for talent and their specific recruitment channels; (2) the work of intermediaries, such as employment placement services and professional recruitment agencies; and (3) the multiplication of diverse government policies aimed at contracting foreign workers, some operating from the employers' side and others from the workers' side.

Foreign workers do have preferred destinations, and they do not always match with the places with the greatest need. The data for 2007 (see Exhibit 4.11) show considerable lack of correspondence between the top ten countries preferred by foreign workers and the top ten countries in most need of such workers. There is better overlap when we consider the top twenty on each side. Given a world where most migrations are not centrally planned, we cannot assume that eventually there will be a better match.

Exhibit 4.11   Comparison of Top Countries Preferred by Foreign Talent and Top Ten Source Countries for Foreign Talent

Top Countries Preferred by Foreign Talent		Top Source Countries for Foreign Talent	
Rank	Country	Rank	Country
1	United States	1	China
2	United Kingdom	2	United States
3	Spain	3	India
4	Canada	4	United Kingdom
5	Australia	5	Germany
6	United Arab Emirates	6	Japan
7	France	7	Spain
8	Italy	8	France
9	Germany	9	Canada
10	Argentina	10	Poland

Exhibit 4.12   Indicators Used to Determine a Country's Attractiveness to Migrants and Accessibility for Migrants

		Top Countries by Score in this Category	
Attractiveness to Migrants		*Rank*	*Country*
1.1	Nominal GDP	1	United States
1.2	Nominal GDP per head at PPP	2	United Kingdom
1.3	Historic/commercial links	3	Australia
1.4	Regional integration	4	Norway
1.5	Quality of health care	5	France
1.6	Quality of education	6	Canada
1.7	Meritocratic remuneration	7	Switzerland
1.8	Foreign direct investment	8	Sweden
1.9	Ability/ease of remitting money	9	Ireland
1.1	Access to financial services	10	Hong Kong
1.11	Access to capital		
1.12	Ease of starting a business		
1.13	Civil liberties		
1.14	Social unrest		

		Top Countries by Score in this Category	
Accessibility for Migrants		*Rank*	*Country*
2.1	Government policy toward migration	1	Australia
2.2	Ease of hiring foreign nationals	2	Canada
2.3	Licensing requirement for migrants	3	Singapore
2.4	Ease of family reunification	4	New Zealand

	Top Countries by Score in this Category	
Accessibility for Migrants	Rank	Country
2.5 Programs to integrate migrants	5	Israel
2.6 Openness of host country culture to migrants	6	Portugal
2.7 Power of trade unions	7	United States
2.8 De jure or de facto discrimination	8	Costa Rica
	9	Sweden
	10	Hong Kong

	Top Countries with Need for Migrants	
Need for Migrants	Rank	Country
1.1 Old age dependency ratio	1	Japan
1.2 Natural increase	2	Italy
1.3 Employment ratio	3	Portugal
1.4 Rigidity of employment	4	Finland
1.5 Labor productivity	5	Czech Republic
1.6 Unfunded pension and health care liabilities	6	Greece
1.7 Public spending on pensions	7	France
1.8 Unemployment benefits	8	Latvia
1.9 Internal labor mobility	9	Belgium
1.10 Labor force	10	Austria

Source: Global Migration Barometer. 2008. Methodology, *Results and Findings*. London: Economist Intelligence Unit.

The Global Migration Barometer uses a composite of two categories, Attractiveness to Migrants and Accessibility for Migrants, to measure a country's appeal to migrants and its attitudes toward migrants. Each category has a range of indicators. The survey uses the Need for Migrants category to assess a country's possible need for migrants to sustain economic growth. It uses a range of indicators.

One effort might be to understand why countries that most need foreign workers are less attractive (see Exhibit 4.12). From some of the data, we know that foreign employees value the strength of democracy, the rule of law, and the openness of the labor and entrepreneurial markets of a country (Global Migration Barometer 2008). The key actors in the global labor market—firms and foreign workers, whether professionals or manual workers—want more market and less government regulation. The data on professionals also show they respond to market conditions: one of the best-known examples is the return of 10,000 plus high-tech workers from Silicon Valley to their native India when the dot-com crisis in Silicon Valley closed many firms and, as it happens, India had become a major destination for high-tech firms and jobs.

The second issue that deserves further examination is the increasingly complex and diversified combination of regimes through which migrants move. The number of these regimes has grown sharply since the 1980s, and especially since the 1990s, when globalization expanded rapidly and incorporated most countries in the world. The diversity of national regimes through which this labor market functions becomes evident when we consider the top ten senders and receivers of foreign workers. According to the already mentioned Manpower (2008) survey of 28,000 employers across twenty-seven countries, the top ten countries from which they hire foreign workers are, in order of numbers: China, United States, India, United Kingdom, Germany, Japan, Spain, France, Canada, and Poland. From the perspective of the global labor market and the firms involved in the hiring and in the processing of the necessary paperwork, this is clearly an enormous mix of national visa regimes.

From the perspective of firms, the top ten foreign destinations to which they fear losing their national workers are China, United States, India, United Kingdom, Japan, Australia, Germany, Russia, Spain, and Brazil (see Exhibit 4.13). An issue that has always been important is the question of brain drain—seen from the countries that lose talent. Interesting here is Manpower's finding that the United States is no longer seen as the most threatening country in terms of the competition for foreign talent—it is China. After China and the United States is a mix of expected and unexpected countries: India, United Kingdom, Japan, Australia, Germany, Russia, Spain, and Brazil. We should add that some of the countries on this list reappear on the opposite list—the countries where Manpower found the most concerned employers about the loss of national talent to a foreign

Exhibit 4.13   Losing National Workers: Top Countries Seen as Threats

Rank	Country
1	China
2	United States
3	India
4	United Kingdom
5	Japan
6	Australia
7	Germany
8	Russia
9	Spain
10	Brazil

Source: Manpower Inc. 2008. Borderless Workforce Survey Global

Summary. (http://files.shareholder.com/downloads/MAN/1216175933x0x208357/41b8de87-062c-4840-9b0a-ff48bd175b4/2008_Borderless%20Workforce%20Survey_Global%20 Results_FINAL.pdf): Manpower Inc.

country included a great diversity of countries: Peru at 82%, Argentina at 66%, South Africa at 65%, but also India at 57%, Germany at 39%, and France at 38% (see Exhibit 4.14).

The existing labor market is not sufficiently developed to meet a finely grained demand. And the key intermediaries would have a hard time making hyper-segmented demand for specialized talent a profitable endeavor until better scale economies arise. Government programs would most likely be overwhelmed with bureaucratic obstacles if they had to develop dozens of new types of visas for highly specialized workers. Finally, a major contextual condition that heightens the urgency of developing a working global labor market is the demographic turn. It is generally accepted today that the demographics of highly developed societies are fast moving toward negative growth. Today's high unemployment and overall low economic growth make it difficult to imagine we might soon face shortages in particular sectors. Yet the immediate demographic future is already on its way—it is not a matter of forecasting but merely a matter of time.

Exhibit 4.14   Employers Concern About Brain Drain from Country

Most Concerned Employers			Least Concerned Employers		
Rank	Country	Percentage	Rank	Country	Percentage
1	Peru	82%	1	China	1%
2	Argentina	66%	2	Ireland	7%
3	South Africa	65%	3	Japan	12%
4	Taiwan	64%	4	Switzerland	12%
5	India	57%	5	Netherlands	13%
6	New Zealand	52%	6	United States	14%
7	Italy	42%	7	Belgium	17%
8	Spain	41%	8	Norway	17%
9	Germany	39%	9	United Kingdom	18%
10	France	38%	10	Canada	19%
11	Mexico	37%	11	Hong Kong	20%
12	Austria	31%	12	Singapore	22%

Source: Manpower Inc. 2008. *Borderless Workforce Survey Global* Summary:(http://files .shareholder.com/downloads/MAN/1216175933x0x208357/41b8de87-062c-4840-9b0a-ff48bd175b4/2008_Borderless%20Workforce%20Survey_Global%20Results_FINAL.pdf): Manpower Inc.

If we consider the new expanded ways in which foreign workers, especially professionals in innovative sectors, are being used, we can see that the demand for such workers will continue. One interesting factor here is that smaller or less powerful firms in need of foreign workers found the economic and financial crisis of 2008 actually made it easier to hire foreign workers because the larger firms were less aggressive in recruiting. Further, as globalization incorporates more and more countries into specific specialized economic circuits, both global cities and foreign workers will only take on more importance. Compared to the 1980s, our current global economy is far more diversified and complex. Countries that were passive recipients of foreign firms today have developed their own capabilities and notions of what are their priorities and preferences. One type of glue that keeps all these diverse sectors and geographies connected is the global circulation of professionals, and, in less visible ways, the circulation of manual skilled workers. A critical item on the agenda for firms that employ these workers and intermediaries such as global employment service firms is to ensure that proper protection and guarantees of contract are in place for both types of foreign workers.

Conclusion: Cities as Postindustrial Production Sites

A central concern in this chapter is cities as production sites for the leading service industries of our time and, hence, the recovery of the infrastructure of activities, firms, and jobs necessary for running the advanced corporate economy. Specialized services are usually understood in terms of specialized outputs rather than the production process involved. A focus on the production process allows us (1) to capture some of the locational characteristics of these service industries and (2) to examine the proposition that there is a producer-services complex with locational and production characteristics that differ from those of the corporations it serves. It is this producer-services complex more than headquarters generally that benefits from, and even needs, a city location. We see this dynamic for agglomeration operating at different levels of the urban hierarchy, from the global to the regional.

Major cities concentrate infrastructure and servicing, a key dynamic that produces a capability for global control. This capability is essential if geographic dispersal of economic activity—whether factories, offices, or financial markets—is to take place under continued concentration of ownership and profit appropriation. It cannot simply be subsumed under the structural aspects of the globalization of economic activity; it needs to be produced. It is insufficient to posit, or take for granted, the power of large corporations, no matter how vast this power is.

By focusing on the production of this capability, I add a neglected dimension to the familiar issue of the power of large corporations. The emphasis shifts to the *practice* of global control: the work of producing and reproducing the organization and management of a global production system and a global marketplace for finance, both under conditions of economic concentration. Power is essential in the organization of the world economy, but so is production: in this case, the production of those inputs that constitute the capability for global control and the infrastructure of jobs involved in this production. This allows us to focus on cities and on the urban social order associated with these activities.

Notes

1   The 2008 MasterCard Study of Centers of Global Commerce compiles one hundred factors that cover a very wide range of conditions, from macro-level factors such as political and legal frameworks to the particulars of how easy it is to execute an import or export operation or how many days it takes to open and to close a firm, as well as livability factors and a city's global recognition. The author is one of the experts on this project.

2   Mixed markets create measurement problems. These problems can be partly overcome by the fact that the consumer and business markets in these industries often involve very different sets of firms and different types of location patterns, and hence, they can be distinguished on this basis. Given the existence of mixed markets and the difficulty of distinguishing between markets in the organization of the pertinent data, it is helpful to group these services under the category of "mostly" producer services—that is, services produced mostly for firms rather than for individuals. It has become customary to refer to them, for convenience, as *producer services*.

3   Jobs were and remain far more concentrated in the central business district in New York City compared with other major cities in the United States. By the late 1980s, about 27% of all jobs in the consolidated statistical area were in Manhattan compared with 9% nationally (Drennan 1989). The 90% concentration ratio of finance was far above the norm.

4   The data on producer services are creating a certain amount of confusion in the United States. Faster growth at the national level and in medium-size cities is often interpreted as indicating a loss of share and declining position of leading centers such as New York or Chicago. Thus, one way of reading these data is as decentralization of producer services; that is, New York and Chicago are losing a share of all producer services in the United States—a zero-sum situation in which growth in a new location is construed ipso facto as a loss in an older location. Another way is to read it as growth everywhere. The evidence points to the second type of explanation: The growing service intensity in the economy nationwide is the main factor explaining growth in medium-size cities rather than the loss of producer services firms in major cities and their relocation to other cities.

Chapter 4 Appendix

Exhibit A.4.1a Financial Dimension and Selected Subindicators (Part 1 of 2)

Rank	Indicator 4: Financial Dimension	Total Value of Equities Trading	Total Number of Derivatives Contracts	Total Number of Commodities Contracts
1	London	New York	Seoul	New York
2	New York	London	Chicago	London
3	Frankfurt	Tokyo	Frankfurt	Chicago
4	Seoul	Frankfurt	London	Shanghai
5	Chicago	Shanghai	Philadelphia	Tokyo
6	Tokyo	Singapore	Mumbai	Mumbai
7	Mumbai	Paris	Sao Paulo	Osaka
8	Moscow	Milan	Johannesburg	Kuala Lumpur
9	Shanghai	Hong Kong	New York	Sao Paulo
10	Madrid	Shenzhen	Mexico City	Johannesburg
11	Singapore	Seoul	Amsterdam	Paris
12	Paris	Zurich	Boston	Dubai
13	Hong Kong	Toronto	Taipei	Sydney

(Continued)

Exhibit A.4.1a   (Continued)

Rank	Indicator 4: Financial Dimension	Total Value of Equities Trading	Total Number of Derivatives Contracts	Total Number of Commodities Contracts
14	Sydney	Amsterdam	Osaka	Buenos Aires
15	Milan	Sydney	Tel Aviv	Singapore
16	Sao Paulo	Moscow	Paris	Bangkok
17	Amsterdam	Mumbai	Sydney	Taipei
18	Copenhagen	Taipei	Hong Kong	Budapest
19	Taipei	Stockholm	Moscow	Jakarta
20	Zurich	Philadelphia	Buenos Aires	Hamburg
21	Toronto	Madrid	Copenhagen	Dusseldorf
22	Johannesburg	Riyadh	Stockholm	Moscow
23	Stockholm	Sao Paulo	Singapore	New Delhi
24	Bangkok	Johannesburg	Milan	St. Petersburg
25	Philadelphia	Istanbul	Tokyo	Hong Kong
26	Buenos Aires	Osaka	Montreal	Seoul
27	Dubai	Copenhagen	Madrid	Frankfurt
28	Kuala Lumpur	Brussels	Warsaw	Amsterdam
29	Mexico City	Dusseldorf	Athens	Madrid
30	Shenzhen	Barcelona	Budapest	Toronto

Note: Top ten cities from 2008 WCOC indicated.

Source: Exhibit prepared by Saskia Sassen, based on MasterCard. 2008. *2008 Worldwide Centers of Commerce Index*. Purchase, NY: MasterCard.

Exhibit A.4.1b Financial Dimension and Selected Subindicators (Part 2 of 2)

Rank	Indicator 4: Financial Dimension	Banking/Financial Services Companies	Insurance Companies	Investments/Securities Firms	Total Value of Bond Trading
1	London	London	London	New York	London
2	New York	New York	New York	London	Copenhagen
3	Frankfurt	Tokyo	Hong Kong	Tokyo	Madrid
4	Seoul	Hong Kong	Singapore	Hong Kong	Moscow
5	Chicago	Frankfurt	Paris	Singapore	Bogota
6	Tokyo	Singapore	Dublin	Chicago	Istanbul
7	Mumbai	Paris	Beijing	Paris	Seoul
8	Moscow	Shanghai	Shanghai	Seoul	Frankfurt
9	Shanghai	Milan	Milan	Frankfurt	Milan
10	Madrid	Madrid	Chicago	Madrid	Tel Aviv
11	Singapore	Amsterdam	Los Angeles	Sydney	Zurich
12	Paris	Sao Paulo	Boston	Toronto	Santiago
13	Hong Kong	Seoul	Toronto	Zurich	Barcelona
14	Sydney	Moscow	Tokyo	Los Angeles	Mumbai
15	Milan	Beijing	Madrid	Shanghai	Buenos Aires
16	Sao Paulo	Sydney	Sydney	Milan	Berlin

(Continued)

Exhibit A.4.1b (Continued)

Rank	Indicator 4: Financial Dimension	Banking/Financial Services Companies	Insurance Companies	Investments/ Securities Firms	Total Value of Bond Trading
17	Amsterdam	Zurich	Zurich	San Francisco	Dublin
18	Copenhagen	Chicago	Atlanta	Bangkok	Prague
19	Taipei	Mumbai	Houston	Beijing	Shanghai
20	Zurich	Kuala Lumpur	Bangkok	Sao Paulo	Singapore
21	Toronto	Mexico City	Melbourne	Miami	Amsterdam
22	Johannesburg	Jakarta	Santiago	Dubai	Paris
23	Stockholm	Brussels	Mumbai	Amsterdam	Toronto
24	Bangkok	Bangkok	Frankfurt	Boston	Cairo
25	Philadelphia	Geneva	Copenhagen	Atlanta	Shenzhen
26	Buenos Aires	Istanbul	Stockholm	Houston	Tokyo
27	Dubai	Munich	Vienna	Geneva	Stockholm
28	Kuala Lumpur	Warsaw	Montreal	Mumbai	Kuala Lumpur
29	Mexico City	Toronto	Mexico City	Mexico City	Sydney
30	Shenzhen	Los Angeles	Bogota	Buenos Aires	Budapest

Note: Top ten cities from 2008 WCOC indicated.

Source: Exhibit prepared by Saskia Sassen, based on MasterCard. 2008. *2008 Worldwide Centers of Commerce Index.* Purchase, NY: MasterCard.

Exhibit A.4.2 Business Center and Selected Subindicators

Rank	Indicator 5: Business Center	Air Passenger and Aircraft Traffic Through City Ports	Number of 5-Star Hotels	Volume of Commercial Real Estate Development	TEU Traffic Through City Ports	Air Cargo Traffic Through City Ports	International Air Passenger Traffic Through City Ports
1	Hong Kong	London	London	Hong Kong	Singapore	Hong Kong	London
2	London	Chicago	Dubai	New York	Shanghai	Tokyo	Paris
3	Singapore	Atlanta	Paris	Singapore	Hong Kong	Shanghai	Amsterdam
4	New York	Paris	Madrid	Sao Paulo	Shenzhen	Seoul	Frankfurt
5	Tokyo	Tokyo	Cairo	Toronto	Dubai	Frankfurt	Hong Kong
6	Los Angeles	Dallas	Singapore	Buenos Aires	Hamburg	Paris	Tokyo
7	Paris	New York	Bangkok	Vancouver	Los Angeles	Miami	Singapore
8	Chicago	Houston	Hong Kong	Dubai	New York	Singapore	Dubai
9	Amsterdam	Los Angeles	Shanghai	Milan	Tokyo	Los Angeles	Seoul
10	Shanghai	Frankfurt	Berlin	Rio de Janeiro	Jakarta	London	Bangkok
11	Seoul	Washington, DC	Seoul	Seoul	Manila	Dubai	Madrid
12	Frankfurt	Madrid	Mumbai	Tel Aviv	Barcelona	Amsterdam	Milan
13	Miami	Shanghai	Beijing	Tokyo	Vancouver	Taipei	Munich
14	Bangkok	Amsterdam	Sao Paulo	Miami	Taipei	New York	Rome
15	Toronto	Beijing	New York	Osaka	Melbourne	Chicago	New York

(Continued)

Exhibit A.4.2 (Continued)

Rank	Indicator 5: Business Center	Air Passenger and Aircraft Traffic Through City Ports	Number of 5-Star Hotels	Volume of Commercial Real Estate Development	TEU Traffic Through City Ports	Air Cargo Traffic Through City Ports	International Air Passenger Traffic Through City Ports
16	Dubai	Moscow	Sydney	Bangalore	Osaka	Bangkok	Moscow
17	Atlanta	Milan	Buenos Aires	Madrid	Sydney	Beijing	Dublin
18	Sydney	Toronto	Frankfurt	Caracas	Houston	Osaka	Taipei
19	Melbourne	Philadelphia	Milan	Istanbul	Bangkok	Brussels	Zurich
20	San Francisco	Rome	Tokyo	Moscow	Athens	Dallas	Copenhagen
21	Houston	Seoul	Atlanta	Shenzhen	Montreal	Atlanta	Vienna
22	Montreal	Hong Kong	Edinburgh	Kuala Lumpur	Buenos Aires	Kuala Lumpur	Barcelona
23	Madrid	Munich	Rome	Santiago	St. Petersburg	Milan	Brussels
24	Vancouver	Sao Paulo	Istanbul	St. Petersburg	Beirut	Sydney	Toronto
25	Washington, DC	San Francisco	Hamburg	Montreal	Miami	Shenzhen	Shanghai
26	Milan	Miami	Washington, DC	Amsterdam	Dublin	Bogota	Los Angeles
27	Brussels	Barcelona	New Delhi	Chicago	Amsterdam	San Francisco	Kuala Lumpur
28	Boston	Boston	San Francisco	London	Lisbon	Philadelphia	Miami
29	Dublin	Bangkok	Melbourne	San Francisco	Istanbul	Mumbai	Istanbul
30	Munich	Mexico City	Chicago	Shanghai	Rio de Janeiro	Sao Paulo	Dusseldorf

Note: Top ten cities from 2008 WCOC indicated.

Source: Exhibit prepared by Saskia Sassen, based on MasterCard. 2008. 2008 Worldwide Centers of Commerce Index. Purchase, NY: MasterCard.

Exhibit A.4.3   Cities Ranked by Assets of the World's Top 100 Largest Publicly Listed Financial Companies, 2003 (US$ millions)

Rank	City	Assets	Percentage of Top 100
	New York	6,503,764	15.53
	Tokyo	4,640,834	11.08
	Paris	3,799,065	9.07
	London	3,599,982	8.60
	Zurich	2,474,926	5.91
	Munich	2,238,616	5.35
	Frankfurt	1,997,733	4.77
	Amsterdam	1,686,464	4.03
	Edinburgh	1,544,645	3.69
	Brussels	1,383,624	3.30
	Toronto	1,082,111	2.58
	Washington, DC*	1,009,569	2.41
	Stockholm	821,879	1.96
	McLean, VA*	803,449	1.92
	Milan	627,724	1.50
	Osaka	514,090	1.23
	Rome	488,853	1.17
	Melbourne	445,715	1.06
	Madrid	443,010	1.06
	Winston-Salem, NC*	401,032	0.96
	Sydney	396,318	0.95
	San Francisco*	387,798	0.93
	Bilbao*	361,608	0.86

(Continued)

Exhibit A.4.3   (Continued)

Rank	City	Assets	Percentage of Top 100
	Antwerp*	326,951	0.7825
	Newark, NJ*	321,274	0.7726
	Ottawa*	310,551	0.7427
	Copenhagen*	308,456	0.7428
	The Hague*	294,646	0.7029
	Seoul	290,253	0.6930
	OTHERS	2,368,506	5.660
	TOTAL	41,873,446	100.00

Notes: Asterisk (*) denotes a city with only one headquarters of a top 100 company. Ranked by assets as determined by the *Wall Street Journal* Market Data Group and FactSet Research Systems, Inc. Figures are based on each company's fiscal 2003 results (2004 for Japanese firms).

Source: Based on "World Business" (2004).

Exhibit A.4.4   Cities Ranked by Assets of the World's Top 100 Largest Publicly Listed Financial Companies, 2003 (US$ millions)

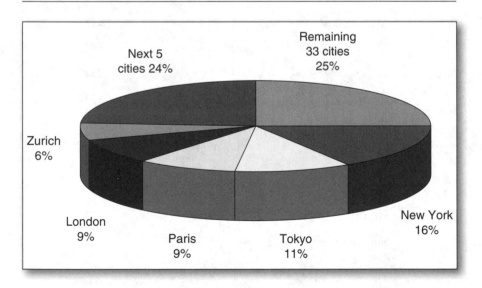

Notes: Ranked by assets as determined by the *Wall Street Journal* Market Data Group and FactSet Research Systems, Inc. Figures are based on each company's fiscal 2003 results (2004 for Japanese firms).

Source: Calculations based on "World Business" (2004).

Exhibit A.4.5   Cities Ranked by Assets of the World's Top Fifty Publicly Listed
Financial TNCs as Determined by Geographical Spread Index, 2008

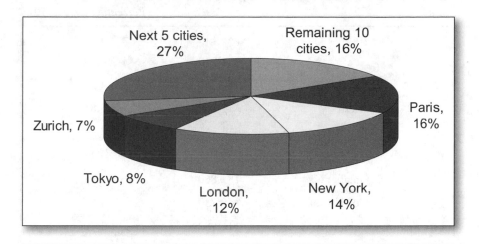

Notes: The Geographical Spread Index (GSI) is calculated as the square root of the Internationalization Index multiplied by the number of host countries.

Source: Calculations based on UNCTAD (2009b: 234).

Exhibit A.4.6a   Cities Ranked by Assets of the World's Fifty Largest Insurers, 2005

Rank	City	Assets	Percentage of Top 50
Total for Top 50	8,324,240	100.00	
Total for United States	2,760,140	33.16	
Top 20 Cities in the World (ranked by assets)			
1	Munich	1,374,460	16.51
2	New York	1,251,180	15.03
3	London	938,180	11.27
4	Paris	759,880	9.13
5	Zurich	553,280	6.64

(Continued)

Exhibit A.4.6a   (Continued)

Rank	City	Assets	Percentage of Top 50
6	Toronto	388,110	4.66
7	Newark, NJ	381,940	4.59
8	Tokyo	352,370	4.23
9	Trieste	317,660	3.81
10	The Hague	311,160	3.74
11	Hartford, CT	259,740	3.12
12	Omaha, NE	181,860	2.18
13	Northbrook, IL	149,730	1.80
14	Columbus, OH	116,880	1.40
15	Philadelphia, PA	110,380	1.33
16	St. Paul, MN	109,680	1.32
17	Hamilton, Bermuda	103,470	1.24
18	Taipei	68,840	0.83
19	Dorking	60,020	0.72
20	Sydney	55,400	0.67
Top 10 Cities in the United States			
1	New York	1,251,180	15.03
2	Newark, NJ	381,940	4.59
3	Hartford, CT	259,740	3.12
4	Omaha, NE	181,860	2.18
5	Northbrook, IL	149,730	1.80
6	Columbus, OH	116,880	1.40
7	Philadelphia, PA	110,380	1.33
8	St. Paul, MN	109,680	1.32
9	Columbus, GA	52,910	0.64
10	Warren, NJ	43,130	0.52

Note: Calculations based on "The Forbes Global 2000" (2005).

Exhibit A.4.6b   Cities Ranked by Assets of the World's Fifty Largest Insurers, 2009

Rank	City	Assets (US$ bn)	Percentage of Top 50
Total for Top 50		13,188.93	100.00
Total for United States		2,896.38	21.96
Top 20 Cities in the World (ranked by assets)			
1	Amsterdam	1,853.39	14.05
2	London	1,705.45	12.93
3	Munich	1,621.83	12.30
4	New York	1,431.96	10.86
5	Paris	1,311.53	9.94
6	Zurich	769.07	5.83
7	Trieste	546.50	4.14
8	Toronto	459.56	3.48
9	Tokyo	455.01	3.45
10	Newark, NJ	445.01	3.37
11	The Hague	399.80	3.03
12	Hartford, CT	287.58	2.18
13	Edinburgh	199.68	1.51
14	Taipei	169.07	1.28

(Continued)

Exhibit A.4.6b (Continued)

Rank	City	Assets (US$ bn)	Percentage of Top 50
15	Radnor, PA	163.14	1.24
16	Northbrook, IL	134.80	1.02
17	Beijing	127.83	0.97
18	St. Paul, MN	109.75	0.83
19	Richmond, VA	107.38	0.81
20	Dublin	100.38	0.76
Top 10 Cities in the United States			
1	New York	1,413.96	10.86
2	Newark, NJ	445.01	3.37
3	Hartford, CT	287.58	2.18
4	Radnor, PA	163.14	1.24
5	Northbrook, IL	134.8	1.02
6	St. Paul, MN	109.75	0.83
7	Richmond, VA	107.39	0.81
8	Columbus, GA	79.33	0.60
9	Chattanooga, TN	49.43	0.37
10	Warren, NJ	48.43	0.37

Note: Calculations based on "The Forbes Global 2000" (2005).

Exhibit A.4.7a The Twenty-Five Largest Nonfinancial Transnational Corporations, Ranked by Foreign Assets, 1990 (US$ billions and number of employees)

Rank	Corporation	Country	Industry[a]	Assets Foreign	Assets Total	Sales Foreign	Sales Total	Employment Foreign	Employment Total
1	Royal Dutch Shell	United Kingdom/ Netherlands	Petroleum refining	69.2b	106.4	47.1b	106.5	99,000	137,000
2	Ford	United States	Motor vehicles and parts	55.2	173.7	47.3	97.7	188,904	370,383
3	GM	United States	Motor vehicles and parts	52.6	180.2	37.3	122	251,130	767,200
4	Exxon	United States	Petroleum refining	51.6	87.7	90.5	115.8	65,000	104,000
5	IBM	United States	Computers	45.7	87.6	41.9	69	167,868	373,816
6	British Petroleum	United Kingdom	Petroleum refining	31.6	59.3	43.3	59.3	87,200	118,050
7	Asea Brown Boveri	Switzerland	Industrial and farm equipment	26.9	30.2	25.6d	26.7	200,177	215,154
8	Nestlé	Switzerland	Food	—c	28	35.8	36.5	192,070	199,021
9	Philips Electronics	Netherlands	Electronics	23.3	30.6	28.8d	30.8	217,149	272,800

(Continued)

Exhibit A.4.7a (Continued)

Rank	Corporation	Country	Industry[a]	Assets Foreign	Assets Total	Sales Foreign	Sales Total	Employment Foreign	Employment Total
10	Mobil	United States	Petroleum refining	22.3	41.7	44.3	57.8	27,593	67,300
11	Unilever	United Kingdom/ Netherlands	Food	—[c]	24.7	16.7b	39.6	261,000	304,000
12	Matsushita Electric	Japan	Electronics	—[c]	62	21	46.8	67,000	210,848
13	Fiat	Italy	Motor vehicles and parts	19.5	66.3	20.7[d]	47.5	66,712	303,238
14	Siemens	Germany	Electronics	—[c]	43.1	14.7[d]	39.2	143,000	373,000
15	Sony	Japan	Electronics	—[c]	32.6	12.7	20.9	62,100	112,900
16	Volkswagen	Germany	Motor vehiclesandparts	—[c]	42	25.5[d]	42.1	95,934	268,744
17	Elf Aquitaine	France	Petroleum refining	17	42.6	11.4[d]	32.4	33,957	90,000
18	Mitsubishi	Japan	Trading	16.7	73.8	45.5	129.3	—	32,417
19	GE	United States	Electronics	16.5	153.9	8.3	57.7	62,580	298,000
20	Du Pont	United States	Chemicals	16	38.9	17.5	37.8	36,400	124,900

Rank	Corporation	Country	Industry[a]	Assets		Sales		Employment	
				Foreign	Total	Foreign	Total	Foreign	Total
21	Alcatel Alsthom	France	Electronics	15.3	38.2	13	26.6	112,966	205,500
22	Mitsui	Japan	Trading	15	60.8	48.1	136.2	—	9,094
23	News Corporation	Australia	Publishing and printing	14.6	20.7	4.6	5.7	—	38,432
24	Bayer	Germany	Chemicals	14.2	25.4	20.3	25.9	80,000	171,000
25	B.A.T. Industries	United Kingdom	Tobacco	—[c]	48.1	16.5d	22.9	—	217,373

Notes:

a Industry classification of companies follows that in the Fortune Global 500 list in Fortune, July 29, 1991, and the Fortune Global Service 500 list in *Fortune*, August 26, 1991.

In the Fortune classification, companies are included in the industry or service that represents the greatest volume of their sales; industry groups are based on categories established by the US Office of Management and Budget. Several companies, however, are highly diversified.

b. Excludes other European countries.

c. Data for foreign assets not available; ranking is according to foreign assets estimated by the Transnational Corporations and Management Division on the basis of the ratio of foreign to total employment, foreign to total fixed assets, or other similar ratios.

d. Includes export sales, which are not separately reported.

Source: Based on UNCTAD, Programme on Transnational Corporations, company annual financial statements, Worldscope company accounts database, unpublished sources from companies, The Industrial Institute for Economic and Social Research (2005) in Stockholm, Sweden, and Stopford (1992). The Worldscope database uses standardized data definitions to adjust for differences in accounting terminology. Data for United States companies with fiscal year-end up to February 10, 1991, as well as for non-US companies with fiscal year-end until January 15, 1991, are classified as 1990 data.

Exhibit A.4.7b   The Twenty-Five Largest Nonfinancial Transnational Corporations Ranked by Foreign Assets, 2002 (US$ billions and number of employees)

Ranking by:

Assets	Index[a]	Corporation	Country	Industry[b]	Foreign	Foreign Total	Transnatl.	Assets	Sales Foreign	Employment Total
1	84	General Electric	United States	Electrical and electronic equipment	229.0	575.2	45.4	131.7	150,000	315,000
2	12	Vodafone Group Plc	United Kingdom	Telecommunications	207.6	232.9	33.6	42.3	56,667	66,667
3	67	Ford Motor Company	United States	Motor vehicles	165.0	295.2	54.5	163.4	188,453	350,321
4	16	British Petroleum Company Plc	United Kingdom	Petroleum expl./ref./dist.	126.1	159.1	146.0	180.2	97,400	116,300
5	95	General Motors	United States	Motor vehicles	107.9	370.8	48.0	186.8	101,000	350,000
6	45	Royal Dutch/Shell Group	United Kingdom/ Netherlands	Petroleum expl./ref./dist.	94.4	145.4	114.3	179.4	65,000	111,000
7	73	Toyota Motor Corporation	Japan	Motor vehicles	79.4	167.3	72.8	127.1	85,057	264,096
8	22	Total Fina Elf	France	Petroleum expl./ref./dist.	79.0	89.5	77.5	97.0	68,554	121,469

Assets	Index[a]	Corporation	Country	Industry[b]	Foreign	Foreign Total	Transnatl.	Assets	Sales Foreign	Employment Total
9	65	France Telecom	France	Telecommunications	73.5	111.7	18.2	44.1	102,016	243,573
10	41	ExxonMobil Corporation	United States	Petroleum expl./ref./dist.	60.8	94.9	141.3	200.9	56,000	92,000
11	53	Volkswagen Group	Germany	Motor vehicles	57.1	114.2	59.7	82.2	157,887	324,892
12	86	E.On	Germany	Electricity, gas, and water	52.3	118.5	13.1	35.1	42,063	107,856
13	78	RWE Group	Germany	Electricity, gas, and water	50.7	105.1	17.6	44.1	55,563	131,765
14	40	Vivendi Universal	France	Media	49.7	72.7	30.0	55.0	45,772	61,815
15	50	Chevron Texaco Corp	United States	Petroleum expl./ref./dist.	48.5	77.4	55.1	98.7	37,038	66,038
16	29	Hutchinson Whampoa Limited	Hong Kong, China	Diversified	48.0	63.3	8.1	14.2	124,942	154,813
17	—	Siemens AG	Germany	Electrical and electronic equipment	47.5	76.5	50.7	77.2	251,340	426,000

(Continued)

Assets	Index[a]	Corporation	Country	Industry[b]	Foreign	Foreign Total	Transnatl.	Assets	Sales Foreign	Employment Total
18	94	Électricité de France	France	Electricity, gas, and water	47.4	151.8	12.6	45.7	50,437	171,995
19	66	Fiat Spa	Italy	Motor vehicles	46.2	97.0	24.6	52.6	98,703	186,492
20	31	Honda Motor Co	Japan	Motor vehicles	43.6	63.8	49.2	65.4	42,885	63,310
21	9	News Corporation	Australia	Media	40.3	45.2	16.0	17.4	31,220	35,000
22	6	Roche Group	Switzerland	Pharmaceuticals	40.2	46.2	18.8	19.2	61,090	69,659
23	19	Suez	France	Electricity, gas, and water	38.7	44.8	34.2	43.6	138,200	198,750
24	58	BMW AG	Germany	Motor vehicles	37.6	58.2	30.2	40.0	20,120	96,263
25	64	Eni Group	Italy	Petroleum expl./ref./dist.	37.0	69.0	22.8	45.3	36,973	80,655

Notes:

a. The index of transnationality is calculated as the average of three ratios: foreign assets to total assets, foreign sales to total sales, and foreign employment to total employment.

b. Industry classification for companies follows the US Standard Industrial Classification as used by the US Securities and Exchange Commission.

c. Foreign sales are outside Europe whereas foreign employment is outside the United Kingdom and the Netherlands.

d. Data on foreign assets are either suppressed to avoid disclosure or they are not available. In case of nonavailability, they are estimated on the basis of the ratio of foreign to total assets or similar ratios.

Exhibit A.4.7c The Twenty-Five Largest Nonfinancial Transnational Corporations Ranked by Foreign Assets, 2007 (US$ billions and number of employees)

Ranking by:

Foreign Assets	Transnatl. Index[a]	Corporation	Country	Industry[b]	Assets Foreign	Assets Total	Sales Foreign	Sales Total	Employment Foreign	Employment Total
1	76	General Electric	United States	Electrical and electronic equipment	420.3	795.3	86.5	172.7	168,112	327,000
2	6	Vodafone Group Plc	United Kingdom	Telecommunications	230.6	254.9	60.3	71.1	62,008	72,375
3	35	Royal Dutch/ Shell Group	Netherlands/ United Kingdom	Petroleum expl./ref./distr	196.8	269.5	207.3	355.8	86,000	104,000
4	23	British Petroleum Company Plc	United Kingdom	Petroleum expl./ref./dist.	185.3	236.1	223.2	284.4	80,600	97,600
5	41	ExxonMobil	United States	Petroleum expl./ref./dist.	174.7	242.1	269.2	390.3	50,904	80,800
6	75	Toyota Motor Corporation	Japan	Motor vehicles	153.4	284.7	145.6	230.6	121,775	316,121
7	26	Total	France	Petroleum expl./ref./distr.	143.8	167.1	177.8	233.7	59,146	96,442

(Continued)

Exhibit A.4.7c (Continued)

Foreign Assets	Transnatl. Index[a]	Corporation	Country	Industry[b]	Assets Foreign	Assets Total	Sales Foreign	Sales Total	Employment Foreign	Employment Total
8	94	Electricité De France	France	Electricity, gas and water	129.0	274.0	40.3	87.8	16,971[c]	154,033
9	78	Ford Motor Company	United States	Motor vehicles	127.9	276.5	91.6	172.5	134,734	246,000
10	69	E.ON AG	Germany	Electricity, gas,	123.4	202.1	41.4	101.2	53,344	90,758
11	3	ArcelorMittal	Luxembourg	Metals and metal	119.5	133.6	105.2	105.2	244,872	311,000
12	38	Telefónica SA	Spain	Telecommunications	107.6	155.9	52.1	83.1	192,127	245,427
13	59	Volkswagen Group	Germany	Motor vehicles	104.4	214.0	120.8	160.3	153,388	328,594
14	90	ConocoPhillips	United States	Petroleum	103.5	177.8	56.0	187.4	14,591[c]	32,600
15	33	Siemens AG	Germany	Electrical and electronic equipment	103.1	134.8	76.0	106.7	272,000	398,000
16	63	Daimler Chrysler AG	Germany/United States	Motor vehicles	100.5	198.9	113.1	146.3	105,703	272,382
17	56	Chevron Corporation	United States	Petroleum	97.5	148.8	120.1	214.1	34,000	65,000
18	74	France Telecom	France	Telecommunications	97.0	149.0	37.0	78.0	81,159	187,331

Foreign Assets	Transnatl. Index[a]	Corporation	Country	Industry[b]	Assets Foreign	Assets Total	Sales Foreign	Sales Total	Employment Foreign	Employment Total
19	85	Deutsche Telekom AG	Germany	Telecommunications	96.0	177.6	46.8	92.0	92,488	241,426
20	39	Suez	France	Electricity, gas and water	90.7	116.5	52.3	69.9	82,070	149,131
21	61	BMW AG	Germany	Motor vehicles	84.4	131.0	64.9	82.5	27,376	107,539
22	13	Hutchinson Whampoa Ltd	Hong Kong	Diversified	83.4	102.4	33.3	39.6	190,428[c]	230,000
23	16	Honda Motor	Japan	Motor vehicles	83.2	110.7	87.3	105.3	158,962	178,960
24	68	Eni Group Co Ltd	Italy	Petroleum	78.3	149.3	73.5	128.5	39,319	75,862
25	29	Eads	Netherlands	Aircraft and parts	75.1	111.1	52.5	57.6	72,471	116,493

Notes:

a. The index of transnationality is calculated as the average of three ratios: foreign assets to total assets, foreign sales to total sales, and foreign employment to total employment.

b. Industry classification for companies follows the US Standard Industrial Classification as used by the US Securities and Exchange Commission (SEC).

c. Foreign employment data are calculated by applying the share of foreign employment in total employment of the previous year to total employment in 2007.

Source: UNCTAD (2009b: 225).

Exhibit A.4.8a   Geographical Concentration of TNCs by Foreign Assets, Foreign
Sales, Foreign Employment, and Number of Entries, 1996
(percentage of total and number)

Region/Economy	Foreign Assets	Foreign Sales	Foreign Employment	Number of Entities
European Union	37	38	46	39
France	9	8	9	11
Germany	12	11	12	9
Netherlands	8	8	10	3
United Kingdom	12	12	15	11
Japan	16	26	10	18
United States	33	27	20	30
Total value (US$ billions and number)	1,475	2,147.9	4,447,732	100

Source: UNCTAD (1997: 35).

Exhibit A.4.8b   Transnational Index[a] Values for the Top 100 TNCs Worldwide
in Selected Countries, 2006–2007

Region/Economy	Average TNI[a] 2006	Average TNI 2007	Number of Top TNCs 2007
Total for EU-27	64.2	66.4	57
France	63.8	63.6	14
Germany	54.8	56.5	13
United Kingdom	72.8	74.1	15
Japan	52.1	53.9	10
United States	57.8	57.1	20
World	61.6	62.4	100

Notes:

a. The Transnational Index, or TNI, is calculated as the average of the following three ratios: foreign assets to total assets, foreign sales to total sales, and foreign employment to total employment.

Source: UNCTAD (2009b: 19).

5

Issues and Case Studies in the New Urban Economy

S everal of the questions raised in Chapter 4 can be fruitfully addressed through a closer look at how individual cities developed global city functions. A first set of cities (Miami, Toronto, Sydney) helps us explore empirically one of the key organizing propositions of this chapter: the growing concentration and specialization of financial and service functions that lies at the heart of the new urban economy at a time when we might expect the development of global telecommunications to be pushing these sectors toward geographic dispersal. These specific case studies provide insights into how cities that were not quite global became global; this shift illuminates how globalization materializes in specific places. These cases also present, in somewhat schematic form, a logic for inquiry into these issues that can be replicated in studies of other cities. To illustrate these diverse issues, I chose cities that are neither in the absolute top tier nor as familiar as New York or London. These cases all function as natural experiments. A second set of cities (Hong Kong and Shanghai, the Gulf city-states, Istanbul) helps us explore empirically how cities navigate some of the major challenges and opportunities in the current decade.

I begin with an examination of the formation of global city functions. I chose Miami to illustrate this process because it captures the implantation of the growth dynamic described in Chapter 4. The question here is: Under what conditions do global city functions materialize? Miami brings an additional issue into the discussion: can a city lacking a history as a world trade and banking center become a global city? The second case study is Toronto, a city that partly rebuilt its financial district in the mid-1980s and hence could have opted for far more spatial dispersal than old financial centers could. This helps disentangle something that is not clear in older centers where spatial concentration of the financial center might be a function of an old, already-built environment inherited from an earlier economic era. The third city, Sydney, shows how these tendencies toward concentration operate in the case of a multipolar urban system and a vast, rich, continent-sized economy, as is Australia. Can we expect a similar multipolarity in the distribution of global city functions?

The second set of cities helps us explore three additional dynamics. The complex relation between Hong Kong and Shanghai, China's two leading financial and business centers, illuminates the shifting interaction between competition and specialized differentiation: they may have started as competitors, but they are increasingly strengthened through their specialized differences. I see a similar evolution for the case of Sydney and Melbourne, from competition in the 1980s to a more settled specialized differentiation in the current decade. More generally, I see this as a key aspect of the relationship among global cities: (1) competition is far less significant than is commonly asserted, and (2) the specialized differences of cities, which matter much more than is commonly understood (Xu and Yeh 2010: chap. 5). The case of the Gulf states helps us see a complex process of repositioning: from relying on oil exports, Gulf states are now in the process of developing a far more complex operational space, including Islamic finance, renewable energy, and culture. Finally, Istanbul shows us how a 3,000-year-old imperial capital becomes a strategic node in the new East–West axis that organizes today's world and overrides the older dominance of the North–South axis.

After examining these cities as laboratory cases, we turn to the general trend of sharp concentration of financial and top-level service functions at a time of advanced digital technologies. Is this a new trend? Is it likely to remain unchanged? We conclude with the question of urban form: have the new information technologies changed the spatial correlates of the center, the terrain where the international financial and business center and the producer-services complex materialize? Can the emerging megaregions incorporate two very different types of economic spaces—the "winners" (global cities) and the "losers" (de-industrializing cities)—in today's global economy, and can they do so in ways that benefit the "losers" in this brutal economic competition rather than merely further strengthening the winners, as seems to happen today?

The Development of Global City Functions: The Case of Miami

Each of today's global cities has a specific history that has contributed to its current status. Many of the world's major cities enjoyed a long history as banking and trading centers or as capitals of commercial empires.[1] This fact raises two immediate questions: What aspects of today's global cities are continuations of past functions? How can global city functions emerge in cities that lack a long history as international banking and trading centers?

Miami is a case in point. On the one hand, it is a city with a short history, one mostly lacking any significant international functions. On the other hand, its large Cuban immigration led to the development in the 1960s and 1970s of an international trading complex oriented to Latin America and the Caribbean and small-scale investments into real estate by individuals and firms from Latin America. The relative simplicity of Miami's history and international trading functions makes it relatively easy to disentangle two key processes: (1) the continuity of the Cuban-led trading complex and (2) the formation of a new business complex in the late 1980s that was not connected to the Cuban immigration but rather to the demands created by current processes of globalization.

The case of Miami thus helps us, first, to understand how a city that lacks a significant history as a world financial and business center can become a site for global city functions, and second, to disentangle the ways in which global city formation may or may not be related to an older internationalism.

The city already had a concentration of international trading operations in the 1970s, built and owned in good part by the prosperous resident Cuban elite (Portes and Stepick 1993). Since their arrival in the 1960s after the 1959 Castro revolution, the Cuban community has built an impressive international trading entrepôt, with a strong presence of firms and banks from Latin America and the Caribbean. Is the existence of the Cuban enclave, then, with its multiple trading operations for the Caribbean and Latin America, the base on which these new global city functions developed? Or is the latter a somewhat autonomous process that may benefit from the concentration of trading operations in Miami but that responds to a different logic? Does it represent a type of development that would have taken place anyway in the southern Atlantic region, although perhaps not in Miami without the Cuban enclave? In brief, what is the relationship between these two processes, one shaped by past events and the other by the current demands of economic globalization?

Some hypotheses in the research literature on global cities are of interest here, especially those that examine the spatial and organizational forms assumed by economic globalization today and the actual work of running transnational economic operations. Figures on the growth of Miami's foreign banks, foreign headquarters, prime office-space market, installation of major telecommunications facilities, high-income residential and commercial gentrification, and high-priced international tourism all point to developments that transcend both the Cuban enclave and the Caribbean import–export enterprises in its midst. They point to another dynamic, one at least partly rooted in the new forms of economic globalization, and suggest that the growth of Miami's new international corporate sector is part of this new dynamic rather than a mere expansion of the Cuban enclave's Latin American and Caribbean trading operations.

Overall, international business transactions with Latin America rose sharply over a short period of time, from the end of the 1980s to the 1990s (see also Chapter 2). Total foreign direct investment in the Latin American economies grew from an average of US$6.1 billion in 1984 to 1987 to $28.7 billion in 1994, nearly doubled to $56.1 billion in 1997, and reached more than US$95 billion in 1999; after this, it declined and stood at US$55 billion by 2004 (pp.18-22). Much of this capital was part of active entry by many foreign firms into several Latin American countries: they bought hotels, airlines, factories, and so forth. This, in turn, expanded the management and coordination work of these firms, which increasingly used Miami as a regional headquarters location. Privatization, deregulation of stock markets and other financial markets, and the new export-oriented development model in most of Latin America were major factors. These are all extremely complicated transactions that require vast specialized inputs—a far cry from the earlier type of trading that initiated the growth of Miami in the 1970s.

In the 1980s, a growing number of US, European, and Asian firms began to set up offices in Miami. Eastman Kodak moved its headquarters for Latin American operations from Rochester, New York, to Miami; Hewlett-Packard made a similar move from Mexico City to Miami; and GM relocated its headquarters for coordinating and managing Latin American operations from São Paulo, Brazil, to Miami. Firms and banks from Germany, France, Italy, South Korea, Hong Kong, and Japan, to name only a few, opened offices and brought in significant numbers of high-level personnel. Among these were major companies such as France's Aerospatiale, Italy's Rimoldi, and Japan's Mitsui, all of which opened operations in Miami. The city also received a significant inflow of secondary headquarters.

Large US firms reorganized and expanded their Miami offices to handle new trade with Latin America. For example, Texaco's Miami office increased its staff by 33% from the late 1980s to the early 1990s to handle new operations in Colombia and Venezuela. And so did Miami's AT&T headquarters, which at the time won 60% of a contract to upgrade Mexico's telecommunications infrastructure—no small job. The international shipping company DHL moved its headquarters near Miami, and Japan's Mitsubishi Power Systems chose the area for its American headquarters. By 2005, Southern Florida was home to 1,300 multinational corporations (Enterprise Florida 2005a; Nijman 2010; see Exhibit 5.1).

Exhibit 5.1   Miami Linkages 2002

Source: Miami: Mistress of the Americas by Jan Nijman, 2010. Reprinted with permission.

There is a significant international banking presence—from Latin America, the Caribbean, Europe, and Asia. By 1992, Miami had sixty-five foreign bank offices, a small number compared with 464 in New York and 133 in Los Angeles at the time, but close to Chicago's eighty. It made Miami the fourth US city in number of foreign bank offices, putting it ahead of San Francisco, Boston, and Atlanta. By 1998, Miami's number had grown to seventy-seven, and by 2005 it had about 100 international banking institutions (Enterprise Florida 2005b). This is not insignificant, considering that the ten top cities (including Miami) accounted for more than 90% of all foreign bank offices in the United States, with New York City accounting for almost half. Almost all Miami offices were bank agencies and representative offices, both of which are full banking offices. Today, Miami has the second largest concentration of foreign banks in the United States after New York (Nijman 2010).

Miami is also a key platform for the operations of Latin American firms in the United States and perhaps, eventually, even for operations with other Latin American countries. A specific role that Miami plays is as a bridge between cities and countries that are not particularly well articulated with the global economy. This is the case with many of Central America's banks. Nijman (2000) reports on a study that is worth elaborating on. In 2000, the twenty-two most important banks headquartered in Central America maintained ties with a cumulative total of 319 "correspondent banks" outside the region; such correspondent banks provide services to clients of Central American banks when these banks cannot provide them, for example, because they do not have their own branch where the service needs to be provided. Of these 319 links, 168 were with Miami. New York was second with only thirty-five links. Miami is a major factor in the external financial connections of Central America.

Finally, Miami is becoming a major telecommunications center for the region. For example, AT&T laid the first undersea fiber-optic cable to South America, connecting southern Florida to Puerto Rico, the Dominican Republic, Jamaica, and Colombia. The company worked with Italy, Spain, and Mexico to build another fiber-optic link connecting those countries with the Caribbean and Florida. Finally, there is the significant concentration of telecommunication facilities associated with the large regional CIA headquarters, which can benefit, often indirectly, commercial operations (Grosfoguel 1993), notably through established networks of highly specialized suppliers and a talent pool for servicing these often complex infrastructures.

These developments brought growth in financial and specialized services for business, which raised their share in the region's employment structure.

Employment in services generally grew by 46.3% from 1970 to 1990 and was 90% of all employment in Dade County by 2003 (Miami-Dade County, Florida 2003). Although this growth is partly a function of population growth and general economic restructuring, there also has been a marked recomposition in the components of services. In the recent past, the driving growth sectors had been domestic tourism and retail; by the late 1980s, they were finance and producer services, as well as new types of tourism—mostly international and high priced—and new types of retail—mostly upscale and catering to the expanded national and foreign corporate sector and design world. One critical factor in the newly emergent Miami-area economy was the growth of producer-services industries. Employment in these sectors almost doubled from 1970 to 1989 in Dade County, particularly in the Miami metropolitan area, reaching 20% of all private sector employment (Perez-Stable and Uriarte 1993). Employment in banking and in credit agencies almost tripled. Business services more than doubled, as did specialized services, from engineering to accounting. The sharpest increase was the quadrupling in legal services employment. (Although part of this increase may be a result of the growth of Miami's other major industries, drugs and guns, at least some of it is linked to the growth of international finance and service functions.) In the mid-1990s, employment in the leading sectors stabilized. By 2004, producer services were 42% of all private-sector employment; major components were financial- and credit-services employment, at 19.4% of private-sector employment, and business services, at 17.8% (Florida Agency for Workforce Innovation 2005).

Industrial services are also a factor in these developments. Miami is a great transportation hub, with ports and airports that are among the busiest in the United States. The city and its neighboring ports move more containerized cargo to Latin America than any other US port. In terms of turnover of foreign passengers and cargo, Miami International Airport is second only to New York City's John F. Kennedy Airport. In addition, the region now has a growing concentration of manufacturing firms aimed at the export market in the Caribbean and Latin America, as these areas become major buyers of US goods. Miami's Free Trade Zone is one of the largest in the country.

All of this activity around growth needs to be housed. By the end of the 1980s, Miami was in the top fifteen US metropolitan areas in terms of prime rental office-space supply. Although Miami's space of 44 million square feet were a fraction of top-listed New York City's 456.6 million square feet at the time, it was not insignificant. In addition, private investment in real estate, often for company housing by German, French, and Italian firms, grew sharply in the 1990s. By 1999, the Miami metropolitan area had 96.9 million square feet of office space compared with the New York metropolitan area's 688.4 million square feet (Lang 2000).

Why has this growth of a new international corporate sector taken place in Miami? One could argue that democratization and the opening of Latin American economies to foreign trade and investment should have made Miami less rather than more important. Yet Miami saw sharp growth in the concentration of top-level managerial and specialized service activities aimed at operations in Latin America. And, as described in Chapters 3 and 4, this is one type of evidence for cities that function as international business centers. This, in turn, raises a second question: Would these functions have been performed elsewhere had it not been for the Cuban enclave? The growth of the Cuban enclave supported the internationalization of the city by creating a pool of bilingual managers and entrepreneurs skilled in international business. This resource gave the city an edge in the competition for Latin American trade. But is it sufficient to explain the subsequent agglomeration of US, European, and Asian corporate headquarters and bank offices and the sharp expansion in financial services?

One angle into the role of the Cuban enclave in engendering these developments is offered by Nijman (2000), the leading researcher on Miami as a global city. He observes that while much attention has gone to the Cuban enclave, Miami actually has the highest international immigrant population of all major US cities and that it is unique in the sense that no other major US city has an absolute majority of recent immigrants. It is true that the size of this population is much smaller than that of Los Angeles and any other major US city, but the incidence is much higher: Miami has the highest proportion of foreign-born residents of any major city in the United States and the largest proportion of inhabitants who speak a language other than English. Finally, the socioeconomic status of a good share of its immigrant population is much higher than is typical in US cities. A relatively large number of immigrants in Miami are wealthy, educated, and in possession of considerable entrepreneurial skills and experience; this holds not only for the first waves of Cuban migration but also for more recent migration from other Caribbean and Latin American nations, as well as other parts of the world, including high-level professionals and managers and leading design and fashion people from Europe and Asia. Unlike what is common in major US cities, in Miami, many of the wealthiest people, entrepreneurs, politicians, and real estate owners are recent immigrants. "Miami's elite is a footloose cosmopolitan elite ... Los Angeles is the ultimate American place, made in America, with a mainstream American culture ... Miami, to most Americans, appears a 'foreign' place: hard to grasp and hard to say where it belongs. Perhaps that is because Miami is ahead of the curve, offering a glimpse of the urban future" (Nijman 2000: 135).

Putting these immigration facts alongside the scale of developments described earlier suggests that although it is not quite a global city of the first rank, Miami has emerged as a site for global city functions. Because Miami's media image was so strongly associated with immigration and drugs, it took time for the media to recognize the formation of a new international corporate sector. Miami did not erupt on the global media stage until the mid-1990s, when it also become a destination for major and minor figures in the international fashion and design worlds. But the actual processes had started a decade earlier. Today, Miami concentrates multiple transnational-level functions that used to be located in a variety of other areas. We can think of the Miami metropolitan area as a platform for international business and the long-distance coordination of the Latin American and Caribbean transactions of firms from any part of the world.

The development of global city functions in Miami is centered on the recent sharp growth in the absolute levels of international investment in Latin America, the growing complexity of the transactions involved, and the trend for firms all over the world to operate globally—all three discussed in preceding chapters. The Cuban enclave represents a significant set of resources, from the know-how to provide international servicing to Spanish-speaking personnel. But the particular forms of economic globalization evident during the last decade have implanted a growth dynamic in Miami that is distinct from the enclave, although benefiting from it. At the same time, although the new international corporate sector has made Miami a site for the transnational operations of firms from all over the world, these operations are still largely confined to Latin America and the Caribbean. In that sense, Miami is a site for global city functions, although not a global city in the way that Paris and London are.

Though driven in major part by immigrants and the legitimate international business experience that they brought to the city, Nijman (2010) argues that Miami's incredible transformation from the late 1960s to the mid-1980s is also due to the changes in banking laws that allowed the growth of international banking, banking revenue to be generated from massive amounts of money coming from cocaine profits, and construction and real estate development. But even after the crackdown on cocaine stopped the depositing of millions of dollars in the form of sacks of twenty-dollar bills at Miami banks, the banking sector continued to flourish, largely based on the reliable immigrant business community and the construction and real estate sectors that had developed during the cocaine years. And it continues to grow: the number of FDIC-insured institutions in

Miami and the number of deposits in those institutions have nearly doubled from 2000 to 2009 (Miami-Dade County, Florida 2010). Unlike many other major cities, Miami did not have the opportunity or need to develop a major manufacturing base, because by the time it was prepared to do so, the work was more cheaply obtained from neighboring Caribbean countries, making Miami instead a perfect services hub (Nijman 2010). With the multiple forms of connection to Latin America, by the early 1990s, Miami began to be seen by its former skeptics as the "Hong Kong of the Americas" because of its unique positioning as a well-managed financial capital with close proximity to and interconnectedness with a fast-developing region of the world (Booth and Long 1993). Miami has no stock market and few major corporate headquarters compared to cities like New York, London, and Tokyo, its strengths lie elsewhere—in the fact that it is highly connected, and that it is, in many cases, the network broker between the world's financial capitals and major South American capitals (Nijman 2010). For instance, in 2009, Miami ports imported US$37.9 billion in goods, $34.7 billion of which came from Latin America (92% of total), and exported US$21.8 billion in goods, $16.7 billion of which went to Latin America (77% of total; Miami-Dade County, Florida 2010). Miami's global importance, directly connected to its continued position as an important broker between north and south, may have plateaued, but additional growth and prominence may be possible due to the predicted economic growth of Latin America in the next several decades.

The case of Miami is not atypical. Global city capabilities are not ready made. They need to be developed over time. And globalizing tendencies are found in cities at various stages of development and in all parts of the world. Often, these tendencies begin at regional bridgeheads. The cases of Singapore and Dubai have received much attention in recent years. While Singapore has become more established as a global city than Dubai, both have promoted a growth strategy that aims at being global actors.

Singapore has become well established as a global city. By the early 1990s, Singapore had implemented a strategy for developing knowledge-intensive companies. The Singapore Science Park, for instance, was constructed under a 1980 government initiative to attract R&D investment. In May 1997, the Committee on Singapore's Competitiveness (CSC) was formed to promote Singapore's development of global city capacities. Singapore transferred resource-dependent production activities to developing areas while concentrating high-value-added activities in the center. The territory for this redeployment of activities was basically the growth triangle of Singapore, Malaysia, and Indonesia (Debrah et al. 2010). Singaporean government-linked companies (GLCs) are extending their reach into international markets by buying strategic positions in foreign firms (Parsa et. al 2003). For instance, Singapore Telecommunications acquired the second largest Australian telecommunications company, Optus, in 2001 (Singtel 2001). These strategies have made Singapore a regional hub and coordinating center.

Dubai has a more recent history of aggressive programs aimed at building global city capacities. The emirate has almost depleted its oil reserves and has therefore relied on expanding regional trade, business services, transportation services, and tourism. For instance, between 1980 and 2000, the critical period for Dubai's shift, the share of the service sector rose from 22% to 42% and manufacturing rose from 3.8% to 11.4% (Parsa et. al 2003). Increased integration into global markets also exposed Dubai to the 2008 global financial crisis, especially due to the internationalization of its real estate markets. This raised concerns about Dubai's solvency, and in February 2009, it launched a $20 billion bond program to meet its debt obligations, which was complemented by an additional $10 billion loan from the emirate of Abu Dhabi (CIA World Factbook 2010).

The Growing Density and Specialization of Functions in Financial Districts: Toronto

The leading financial districts in the world have all had rapid increases in the density of office buildings since the 1980s. There has also been a strong tendency toward growing specialization in the major activities housed in these buildings. It could be argued that one of the reasons for this continuing and growing concentration in a computer age is that these are mostly old districts that have inherited an infrastructure built in an earlier, pretelecommunications era and hence do not reflect a *necessary* built form for advanced financial and corporate services. In other words, the new growing density of city centers we see today, along with increased specialization, would be an imposed physical form from the past—they would not reflect the actual needs of advanced finance.

The case of Toronto is interesting because so much of the city's current financial district was built in the mid- to late 1980s, a time when finance was beginning to boom, the use of new technologies had become fairly established, and spatial dispersal was a real option. Toronto entered the 1980s with a far smaller and less prominent financial district than cities such as New York, London, or Amsterdam (City of Toronto 1990; Todd 1993, 1995), thus it was conceivably rather free to redevelop its financial center according to the most desirable spatial pattern. Toronto had not yet gained ascendance over Montreal as a financial and business center (Levine 1990). Furthermore, massive construction of state-of-the-art office buildings for corporate users in the 1980s was shifting from the city to the wider metropolitan region and included installation of all the most advanced communications facilities the 1980s offered. In terms of building and telecommunications technology, this might seem to be a case in which much of the office infrastructure of the financial sector could have been located outside the small confines of the downtown.

But that did not happen. According to Gunther Gad, a leading analyst of the spatial aspects of the office economy in Toronto, financial firms wanted a high-density office district. A survey aimed at these issues found that a fifteen-minute walk was seen as a "long walk" and was "resented" (Gad 1991: 206–207; see also Canadian Urban Institute 1993). The first trend that Toronto illustrates is that given the option of moving to a beautifully landscaped setting, surrounded by other major corporate headquarters, the financial sector insisted on a dense downtown location.

The second trend that Toronto illustrates sharply is the growing specialization of the downtown in financial and related specialized services. At one time, Toronto's downtown office district housed the headquarters of manufacturing and wholesaling firms, the printing plants of the two main newspapers, and a large number of insurance firms. Much space was also allocated to retail; at one time, there were street-level shops and eating places on most blocks, all of which were later put underground, further raising the actual and visual office density of the district. Until the 1950s, the present financial district was still the general office district of the metropolitan area, containing the headquarters of firms in all major industries. Beginning at that time and continuing into the subsequent two decades, firms in a broad range of industries—insurance, publishing, architecture, engineering—moved out. This is a pattern evident in other major cities, all of which saw the departure of the corporate headquarters of manufacturing firms, insurance companies, and other large offices. London lost many of its insurance headquarters; the downtowns of Frankfurt and Zurich became increasingly specialized financial districts; and in New York, a new midtown office district developed that accommodated growing industries such as advertising and legal services, leaving Wall Street to become an increasingly specialized financial district.

Between 1970 and 1989, office employment in Toronto's financial district doubled, and its share of all employment rose from 77.6% to 92.3%, with a corresponding fall in nonoffice jobs. But the composition of office jobs also changed from 1970 to 1989. Thus, the share of the insurance industry in all office activities fell from 14.6% to 9.8%, although it grew in absolute numbers; further, between 1996 and 1999, employment in Toronto's insurance industry fell by 11%, but professional jobs grew by 24% in 1996 to 1998. By 1989, well over half of all office employment was in finance, insurance, and real estate (FIRE), and 28% was in producer services. Banks, trust companies, investment services (including securities dealers), and real estate developers grew strongly in the 1980s (Gad 1991). So did other producer services: legal services, accounting, management consulting, and computer services. But some, such as architectural and engineering consulting, did not. Since the 1990s, most of the new employment has been in business and technical services, including accounting, legal, management, computer, and engineering firms, followed by sectors with longer-term growth, especially finance and real estate services. "The FIRE sector grew at a rate of 38% between 1981 and 1996, exceeding that of Boston, Chicago, and San Francisco but it was outpaced by growth in Atlanta, Dallas, Minneapolis, Philadelphia, and Seattle" (City of Toronto 2001); the financial services sector has consistently accounted for between 9% and 11% of Toronto's total employment in the 1990s and into 2000 and accounts for roughly 14% of Toronto's GDP today (City of Toronto 2010).

By the early 1990s, Toronto had the largest concentration of corporate offices in Canada. Fifty of Canada's largest financial institutions were head-quartered in Toronto, with thirty-nine of them in the financial district. They include the majority of Canada's banks, foreign banks, and trust companies. Canada's largest investment firms, several of the largest pension funds, and the various trade associations involved with finance and banking were also there by the early 1990s (Todd 1995). By 2010, Toronto was home to Canada's five largest banks and 90% of Canada's foreign banks, 85% of mutual funds, and more than half of Canada's venture capital firms (City of Toronto 2010). Many other financial institutions have Toronto head-office subsidiaries, and some insurance companies located elsewhere have investment departments in Toronto. Further, "65 per cent of Canada's pension fund managers are headquartered in Toronto and it accounts for 50 per cent of the pension assets under management" (City of Toronto 2005b). By 2010, Toronto's financial markets ranked third overall in North America and eighth in the world with a market capitalization of over US$2.1 trillion (TSFA 2010; TMX 2010).

A more detailed analysis of the banking industry shows yet other patterns. Until the 1970s, it was typical for a large bank in a major city of a developed country to consolidate all its operations in one building in a city's financial district. By the early 1980s, it had become common for such institutions to relocate back-office jobs and branch functions out of the main office in the financial district to other parts of a city's larger metropolitan region. The same pattern was evident in Toronto. Spatial dispersal of more routine operations also took place within other industries—again, a pattern fairly typical for all major business centers. These trends, together with the growth in the share of high-level professional and managerial jobs, led to an employment structure in Toronto's financial district that is highly bimodal, with 41% of all workers in top-level jobs by the end of the 1990s—up from 31.5% in 1980—and up to 52% by 2004 (TFSA 2010).

Generally, top-level functions and the most complex and innovative activities are carried out in the financial districts of major cities. Routine operations can be moved outside these financial districts. The more risk-laden, speculative activities, such as securities trading, have increased their share of activity in financial districts. The financial district in Toronto is the place where large, complex loans can be put together; where complicated mergers and acquisitions can be executed; and where large firms requiring massive investment capital for risky activities, such as real estate development or mining, can secure what they need, often combining several lenders and multiple lending strategies.

This is the specialized production process that takes place in the financial districts of today's major cities. The nature of these activities—the large amounts of capital, the complexity, the risk, and the multiplicity of firms involved in each transaction—also contributes to the high density. There is a built-in advantage in being located in a financial district where all the crucial players are located; the risk, complexity, and speculative character of much of this activity raises the importance of face-to-face interaction. The financial district offers multiple possibilities for face-to-face contact: breakfast meetings, lunches, inter- and intrafirm meetings, cocktail parties, and, most recently, health clubs. These are all opportunities for regularly meeting with many of the crucial individuals, for developing trust (of a specific sort) with potential partners in joint offerings, and for making innovative proposals in terms of mergers and acquisitions or joint ventures. Further, as developed in Chapter 4, there is a work process that benefits from intersecting with multiple specialized forms of knowledge, including knowledge about conditions in other countries. Telecommunications cannot replace these networks (Garcia 2002). The complexity, imperfect knowledge, high risk, and speculative character of many endeavors, as well as acceleration in the circulation of information and in the execution of transactions, heighten the importance of both personal contact and spatial concentration.

The growth and concentration of the financial district in Toronto continues to expand, often upward as well as outward to keep up with the demand for space in this desirable area (Hume 2010). The continuing necessity of face-to-face and real-time contact in the financial industry, even after physical trading floors are no longer necessary, was evident during the G-20 Summit in Toronto in June 2010. The district, in which 223,000 financial services employees work, was physically relocated to a secret suburban space; this involved the coordinated efforts of the Toronto Stock Exchange and several leading banks and brokerage houses (Pasternak 2010)—producing a sort of central planning episode in the financial sector. The fact itself that the exchanges, banks, and brokerage houses had to physically relocate employees to full-facility suburban locations points to the limits of advanced communications technologies—which in the case of Toronto represent the highest concentration of fiber-optic cables in North America (City of Toronto 2010). After the G-20 summit, they voted with their feet: despite having functioned relatively well at their suburban locations, exchanges and firms markets returned immediately to the concentrated financial district, where they evidently function best.

The case of Toronto suggests that the high density and specialization evident in all major financial districts is a response to the needs generated by current trends in the organization of the financial and related industries. Toronto could have built its financial sector on a more dispersed model, as did the headquarters of the major national and foreign firms that spread over Toronto's metropolitan area along hypermodern communications facilities. But it didn't, suggesting, first, that the density of Toronto's downtown financial district is not the result of an inherited, old-fashioned built infrastructure but a response to current economic requirements and second, that the locational patterns and constraints of the financial sector in a global city are different from those of corporate headquarters.

The Concentration of Functions and Geographic Scale: Sydney

The analysis of Toronto revealed two forms of concentration: The first, the main focus of the previous section, was the disproportionate concentration of financial functions in one small district in the city when there was the option of locating in a larger metropolitan area with state-of-the-art infrastructure and building. The second is the disproportionate concentration of all national financial and headquarters functions of Canada in a single city, Toronto. Is it unusual to have such sharp concentration of top-level economic functions in one city when the country is the size of a continent and has a history of multiple growth poles oriented toward world markets?

Here, I examine in some detail this second tendency by focusing on Australia. Along with Canada and the United States, Australia has an urban system characterized by considerable multipolarity. This effect has been strengthened in Australia by the fact that it is an island-continent, which has promoted a strong outward orientation in each of its major cities. We might expect, accordingly, to find strong tendencies toward the emergence of several highly internationalized financial and business centers. Or is Australia's space economy also characterized by a disproportionate concentration of international business and financial functions in one city? If both Canada and Australia have gone from multipolar to a strengthened dominance of one city, we can posit a systemic trend in current economic dynamics (see Chapter 4). During the period from World War II to the 1970s, Australia became a very rich country with thriving agricultural and manufacturing exports and low unemployment. In that period, Australia had several major urban areas and many growth poles. Melbourne, the old capital of the state of Victoria, had been and remained the traditional focus for commerce, banking, and headquarters and was generally the place of old wealth in Australia.

As did other developed economies, Australia experienced considerable restructuring beginning in the early 1970s: declines in manufacturing employment, growth in service employment, a shift to information-intensive industries, and a growing internationalization of production processes, services, and investment. In the mid-1980s, financial institutions were deregulated and integrated into global financial markets. There were massive increases in foreign direct investment, with a shift from agriculture, mining, and manufacturing to real estate and services and from European to Asian sources (Daly and Stimson 1992). Asian countries became and remain today the main source of foreign investment in all major industries, and generally there is a greater orientation of trading and investment toward the Pacific Rim. In the 1980s, producer services emerged as the major growth sector throughout all the metropolitan areas and (combined with wholesale and retail and community services) accounted for 48% of all employment nationwide in Australia by the end of the 1980s. The fastest-growing export sectors were producer services and tourism.

The shift in investment in the 1980s from manufacturing to finance, real estate, and services became particularly evident in metropolitan areas (Stimson 1993). Out of this conjunction, Sydney emerged as the major destination of investment in real estate and finance. From 1982 to 1983, investment in manufacturing in Sydney was A$1.15 billion, compared with A$1.32 billion in finance, real estate, and business services. By 1984, and also again in 1985, these levels of investment had changed, respectively, to A$0.82 billion and A$1.49 billion. At lower levels, these trends were evident in other major urban areas (Stimson 1993: 5). By 1986, however, the dispro-portionate concentration of finance and business services in Sydney increas-ingly outdistanced that of other major cities. A massive real estate boom from 1985 to 1988 made Sydney the dominant market in Australia, both in levels of investment and in prime office space.

Sydney became Australia's main international gateway city and its only "world city," according to Daly and Stimson (1992; see also Brotchie et al. 1995). By the late 1980s, Sydney had the largest concentration of interna-tional business and financial firms in Australia, surpassing Melbourne, once the main economic capital of the country (see Exhibit 5.2). By 2009, eighty-three (41.5%) of the country's top 200 firms were headquartered in Sydney, compared with Melbourne's forty-two (21.7%). Similar concentration exists in the banking sector. Sydney has also garnered a larger share of national employment in the major producer service sectors; it is home to 35% of the financial and insurance services sector, 27.6% of scientific and technical services, and 31.3% of the information, media, and telecommuni-cations sector (23.2%, 23.1%, and 23.5% in Melbourne, respectively). By 1990, Sydney's stock market ranked tenth in the world. Approximately two-thirds of multinational corporations that establish an Asia-Pacific regional headquarters in Australia do so in Sydney, and when focusing solely on the finance and insurance sector, that number rises to 80% (Fitzgerald 2005). Australia has also become an attractive location for sec-ondary headquarters of Asian firms, and Sydney, by far the country's most international city, became the preferred choice already in the 1980s (O'Connor 1990) and remained so for much well into the 2000s (Fitzgerald 2005; see Exhibit 5.2).

The 1980s are the critical period for understanding the character of the change. Australia had long been dependent on foreign investment to develop its manufacturing, mining, and agricultural sectors, but the share, composition, origins, and size of foreign investment in the 1980s point to a qualitative transformation and, in that sense, to a distinct process of eco-nomic internationalization. From 1983 through 1984 to 1988 through 1989, foreign direct investment in Australia grew at an average of 34% a year, from A$81.9 billion to A$222.9 billion. Foreign investment in manu-facturing also grew at a high rate, at 29% per year. But it grew at 83% a year in finance, real estate, and business services. This investment increas-ingly came from Japan and Asia, with declining shares coming from the United States and the United Kingdom, the two major investors in the past. Japan's share rose by 280%, reaching almost 15% of all foreign direct investment by 1989. In the 1990s, Singapore, Hong Kong, Taiwan, Canada, and Germany also became and remain significant investors. In the second half of the 1980s, particularly following the deregulation of

Exhibit 5.2 Corporate Concentration in Sydney and Melbourne, 2009

	Firms[a]	Banking Locations[b] Australian-Owned Banks	Foreign Subsidiary Banks	Branches of Foreign Banks	Share of National Employment[c] Financial & Insurance Services	Professional Scientific & Technical Service	Information, Media & Telecommunications
Sydney	83	6	8	34	35.0%	27.6%	31.3%
Melbourne	42	3	1	1	23.2%	23.1%	23.5%

Notes:

a. Top 200 Public Australian Companies.

b. The set of banks is limited to those with licenses to act as authorized deposit-taking institutions (ADIs) and, as such, does not include investment banks. Some foreign ADIs operate both subsidiary banks and branches in Australia.

c. "Share of National Employment" figures are from 2006, the latest available Australian Census year.

Sources:

a. Australia and New Zealand Banking Group Ltd (2009) and Forbes (2009).

b. New South Wales Department of State and Regional Development (2009).

c. Australian Bureau of Statistics (2006).

financial institutions, trading enterprises and banks were the major conduits through which capital entered the country. The real estate boom was directly linked to foreign investment, as was the real estate crisis of 1989 to 1990, when foreign investors ceased pouring money into these markets. More than 28% of all foreign direct investment in 1985 through 1986 went into real estate, rising to 46% by 1988 through 1989. Japanese investors accounted for more than one-third of this investment. The subsequent financial and real estate crisis brought these shares down sharply, but from 1996 to 2004, the share of foreign investment in real estate rose once again, going from 21.5% to 28.2%; the composition of countries investing has become much more internationalized, with Singapore being the largest single investor in 2004 at only 12%. Foreign investment in the 1980s, the decade that marks the sharp shift toward Sydney, was disproportionately concentrated in New South Wales and Queensland, with each typically absorbing around one-third of total investment, rather than in the older regions such as Victoria, home to Melbourne. Almost half of all investments in New South Wales (home to Sydney) were in commercial real estate.

The geography of these investments is even more specific than the regional dimensions discussed earlier. The bulk of these investments were in the central business districts (CBDs) of major cities, with Sydney the leading recipient. Between 1975 and 1984, foreign investors had financed about 10% of total investment in commercial real estate; between 1980 and 1984, there were actually declines, reflecting the fall in global foreign investment in the early 1980s. But they picked up shortly after that, and by 1984, about 15% of CBD offices in Sydney were foreign owned, compared to about 12.5% in Melbourne (Adrian 1984). In the second half of the 1980s, there were sharp increases in investments in all CBDs of major cities but especially in Sydney, Melbourne, and Brisbane. Stimson (1993) notes that by 1990, the value of land held by Japanese investors in Sydney's CBD was estimated at A$1.55 billion, all of which had been invested in the second half of the 1980s. At the height of the boom in 1988 to 1989, the officially estimated value of land in Sydney's CBD was put at $A17.4 billion, a tenth of which was owned by Japanese investors.

Melbourne's CBD was also the object of much foreign investment and acquisition, with record levels of construction in commercial real estate. In Brisbane, more than 40% of the total office floor space was built between 1983 and 1990. Since those boom years, levels of foreign investment have fallen equally sharply, leaving a depressed office market in CBDs, a situation evident in major business centers across the world at the time.

The 1990s and into the 2000s were years of great prosperity for Australia. But even so, Sydney captured a disproportionate share of that growth (Connell 2000; O'Neill and McGuirk 2002). Sydney now produces 25% of the country's GDP, is home to the regional headquarters of 500 global corporations operating in the Asia-Pacific area, and has further raised its concentration of financial and business services in Australia to approximately 65% of all of such activity in the country (City of Sydney 2011). Of foreign and domestic banks located in Australia, 82% are located in Sydney (City of Sydney 2011). The floor space in the city dedicated to property and business services has kept growing, as has that for financial services (Salmon 2006). Finance and insurance continues to be the fastest-growing industry in New South Wales, recording annual average growth of 3.6% annually in real terms between 1999 and 2009 (NSW 2010). The city continues to seek new businesses and investors by emphasizing the market time zone that bridges the New York and London markets, its multilingual culture, and its development of a large environmentally conscious business zone in its harbor area (NSW 2010).

It would seem, then, that even at the geographic scale and economic magnitude of a country like Australia, the ascendance of finance and services along with the internationalization of investment contributed to the disproportionate concentration of strategic functions and investment in one city. Several experts on the Australian economy have noted that its increasing internationalization and the formation of new linkages connecting regions, sectors, and cities to the global economy have been central elements in the economic restructuring of that country (Rimmer 1988; O'Connor 1990; Daly and Stimson 1992; Stimson 1993; Connell 2000; O'Neill and McGuirk 2002). Foreign investment patterns, international air passenger travel and tourism, and the location of activities and headquarters dependent on global networks all reflect this process of internationalization and concentration. But beneath these general trends lies the fact that Sydney has experienced much of this growth far more sharply than most other cities in Australia.

At the same time, as this global phase entered its third decade in 2010, it had become clear that it was precisely this differentiation that marked the current expanded phase of the global economy: Melbourne does not compete with Sydney for what Sydney has. It is its own specialized global city. We see this same pattern in the case of Shanghai and Hong Kong, discussed next.

Competition or Specialized Differences: The Financial Centers of Hong Kong and Shanghai

Despite the common perception that Hong Kong and Shanghai, the two leading financial and business centers in China, are in direct competition for business, the two cities compete far less with each other than is commonly thought. Globalization homogenizes standards and engenders global markets for standardized products, but in fact it may be the diversity of the functions and specialized capabilities performed by these cities that strengthens their role in the global economy.

Hong Kong, with its open economy and historical connection to international trade, has long been the financial leader in China. Historically, it developed as a global financial center in part because of skilled and internationally connected refugees arriving from regional communist regimes, especially from Shanghai—of all places! There are here some vague similarities with Miami in this regard (Nijman 2010). The city's free-market economy, complemented by few legal restrictions to enter its exchanges and its historical lack of a *hukou* (household registration) system, made it the choice for Chinese investors to enter the international market and the choice place for foreign investors to enter the Chinese market. With more than 1,200 listed companies and a flat tax rate of 15%, it remains a key global destination for investors (Richburg 2010). Hong Kong has also been the leader in complex financial activities like arbitrage and program trading, in part because of some of the inefficiencies remaining between itself and the mainland, and in the fall of 2010 for the first time surpassed Tokyo to lead Asia in short sales (Thomasson 2010). (See Exhibits 4.1 to 4.5; A.4.1 and A.4.2.)

Hong Kong remains primarily financial, with 88% of its economy in the financial sector, which some view as a major weakness given the fluctuations in the global economy (Fernando 2010). Further, some of the growth of Hong Kong's financial and services sector as a percentage of its GDP can be attributed to the movement of its manufacturing industry to the mainland and, in particular, nearby Shenzhen. Both Hong Kong and Shenzhen seek to benefit from their proximity to one another, in building a "Shen-Kong metropolis" in which Shenzhen functions as the backyard of Hong Kong, the region's financial hub (Chen 2009; Chen and de'Medici 2010). But Hong Kong is highly dependent on mainland China historically for natural resources, food, and raw materials. Increasing its dependence on the mainland since the transfer of sovereignty, it has been quickly integrated further into the Chinese system through financial, trade, and tourist links, and its connections with the mainland may have cushioned it from the global economic downturn of 2008 through 2009. About 40% of firms listed on the Hong Kong Stock Exchange are now from the mainland (CIA World Factbook 2010), and companies doing business in the mainland make up 58% of the city's market value, according to Charles Li, head of the city's bourse (Thomasson 2010).

Shanghai has a highly diversified economy and is more closely linked to the domestic economy, and it is largely a national financial center (Chen 2009; see Exhibits 4.1 to 4.5; A.4.1 and A.4.2). These are its strengths and these are what make it different from Hong Kong. At this point, there is far less competition than the experts foresaw in the late 1990s (Sassen 1999); there is, above all, a highly specialized division of financial functions. For several years following the reopening of the Shanghai stock exchange and other economic reforms of the early 1990s, the market remained largely controlled by state resources, and today it is still subject to extensive legal restrictions on foreign investors. All of the Shanghai Stock Exchange (SSE) A-share investments are restricted to mainland Chinese, and even B-share stocks remain 87% mainland Chinese and 8% Chinese overseas, leaving the remaining share of B-share stocks owned by all other countries and regions at about 5% (Shanghai Stock Exchange 2010). In my reading, this is not all bad; for one, it makes Shanghai far less subject to global financial crises.

Though it has a growing a stock exchange with nearly 900 companies listed, Shanghai continues to thrive through other sectors in its economy (Richburg 2010). Shanghai continues to be a major port city that connects foreign trade to the Yangtze River, the third-longest river in the world, and its surrounding region, which is home to one-third of China's population. This major artery to international trade carries passengers, mined resources such as coal, and manufacturing industry of all sorts to and from deep within China's interior. Shanghai's position as a critical player connecting China to the world cannot be underestimated, but even with a somewhat liberalized economic system by 2020, as planned, I have long thought that it may remain more comparable to Chicago, while Hong Kong remains more comparable to New York (*Urban Geography* 2002, 2008).

Additionally, an area in which Shanghai is, perhaps inadvertently, gaining the attention of foreign investors is "new town" development, which was initially a policy to expand suburban areas and de-densify the crowded city center. In part due to the lack of amenities, such as restaurants and transportation, "new towns" have instead developed more in the direction of weekend homes for elite urban residents or as property investments (Wang et al. 2010). Rather than being compared with Hong Kong, Shanghai is perhaps more comparable to Shenzhen, which has grown quickly as an "instant city" in part due to its proximity to Hong Kong (Chen and de'Medici 2010). Hong Kong and Shenzhen share many resources, including human resources through the commuters that travel between the two cities daily. Its sectoral diversity and massive material economy makes

Shanghai far less dependent on finance than other major global cities. This, along with its close economic ties to both the Chinese interior and the central government, significantly reduced the impact of the global economic downtown of 2008 through 2009 on the city compared to its impact on Hong Kong.

Making New Global Circuits in Energy and Finance: The Gulf States

The geopolitics of oil has been one major factor shaping the Gulf's global circuits. But so will the geopolitics of declining oil reserves. The Gulf states have acted on this changing history by diversifying their economic base.

Dubai is the most extreme version of this transformation: it has changed itself from an oil exporter and trade entrepots to a state-of-the art platform for firms and households whose business space extends far beyond the Gulf. Firms from a large number of foreign countries—Indian, American, British, and many more—have set up headquarters in Dubai. And so have professionals from many different nationalities. Over the last two decades, several gulf cities have become major actors in the global financial system—through participation in financial trading networks, creation of new financial exchanges, and formation of sovereign investment funds.[2] Several of the Gulf states are now also positioning themselves as centers for Islamic finance, a sector where Malaysia, Indonesia, and Singapore are the fastest-growing markets.[3] Some Gulf cities are aiming at becoming airport hubs for long-distance passengers who in the past might have changed in London, Amsterdam, or Frankfurt. Finally, entering the field of renewable energy is a strong option at least for some oil-based economies. The substantive projects we see in Abu Dhabi around renewable energy and eco cities, and in Sharja around educational and cultural circuits, are important alternatives to mere oil extraction.[4]

Here, I want to focus briefly on an intermediate step in such a switch, a step often overlooked and one that involves the *making of complex capabilities* well beyond the production of energy as such. These are, in turn, capabilities for the *making* of global markets and the global circuits through which those markets will function. It is a step that often gets eliminated from the discussion: thus, in the much-heard phrase "to replace oil with renewable energy," the word "replace" shifts the focus away from the work that needs to be done beyond the fact of choosing an alternative energy. Nor is it enough to develop "free-trade zones," an arrangement that gives special rights to foreign investors and firms. It seems to me that the status of "free-trade zone" is merely one element in such a project and that the project cannot simply be thought of as developing such a zone.

What it takes is the launching and maintaining of a range of necessary types of circuits—for the engineering and the science, for the financing and the setting up of new types of financial exchanges, for connecting with new buyers and new intermediaries, for the implementing of new kinds of shipping and piping, and so on.

The development of global markets for alternative renewable energy and the development of global markets for Islamic finance will both require specific complex capabilities. The new geopolitics of energy and finance generate a need for a more complex global space than that of conventional free-trade zones—that is, they are about more than merely facilitating the operations of foreign actors.[5] These new geopolitics will demand the type of complex global space that is the global city. Free-trade zones are not global cities. The global city is a space for the making of such complex capabilities (which can be used for good or not-so-good aims).[6] And it is this process of making that constitutes the space that is the global city.[7] As for renewable energy, Abu Dhabi's Masdar City is probably the most significant move toward a space for the making of these types of complex capabilities. Manama, Doha, Dubai, and Abu Dhabi are all developing global platforms for renewable energy, as is Saudi Arabia.

In brief, the Gulf cities have generated an alternative set of global circuits, most notably in energy and finance, but also in education and culture. The dominant image of the Gulf in the global imagination is that of Dubai, with its glamorous excess built on whole armies of low-wage immigrant workers. But the Gulf cities have kept moving toward different possible futures, perhaps none as much as Abu Dhabi and Sharja. To this should be added the educational and cultural developments that have grown in the region. There is an enormous potential for a radically diversified range of developments given the region's vast resources, the complex capabilities they have developed over the last decades, and the new ones that will have to be developed for their new plans. The outcome should be a vastly expanded range of global circuits that articulate Gulf cities with whole new sets of cities in the rest of the world.

An Old Imperial City in Today's New East–West Geopolitics: Istanbul

A 3,000-year-old city is emerging today as a key strategic node in the emerging geopolitics of East–West flows. Istanbul has long been the intersection of vast and diverse mobilities of people and goods across the East–West and the North–South axes of the world in its region. But the period of nation building in Turkey, as in other nation-states, was one of internal transformation and development of a national economy. Today, in a global age whose key axis is becoming the East–West rather than the North–South one that has dominated an older international colonial history, it is Istanbul's strategic location that is ascendant.

But location is not enough to explain Istanbul's ascendance. It is also the deep history of this city and the specialized capabilities it has generated. Out of this long history of intersections comes the *need* to develop specific capabilities for handling and enhancing network functions; it is not simply a question of location *at* intersections. It seems to me that developing such capabilities across diverse histories and geographies is a particularity of Istanbul's deep history. It is also one of growing importance in today's networked world. Several major trends make this visible. Here, I limit myself to three. A first trend concerns the flows of capital: Istanbul is at the center of a geography of capital flows that stretches both East and West. Even though the EU is Turkey's dominant trade and investment partner, current post–Cold War geopolitics make Asian countries increasingly important. The second trend concerns the in- and outflows of people, and here again we see a remarkable bimodality between Europe and Asia.

The diversity of people migrating to and through Istanbul raises a question about the specific forms of knowledge that arise out of these intersections, about the contents at the heart of networked flows at a time of growing worldwide articulation among diverse, complex cultures in the world. The answer, perhaps, is reflected in a third trend coming out of a study of the top sixty cities in the world in terms of political and cultural variables (A. T. Kearney 2010). Istanbul sits in the top thirty, specifically as a global policy nexus, and as a city for human capital and talent.

Next, I discuss these three trends in some detail.

In terms of capital flows, Turkey's dominant trade and investment partnership is with the EU. In 2007, trade between Turkey and the EU stood at US$12.4 billion, an astounding thirty-fold increase over the 1990 to 2000 annual average. Of all EU countries, the Netherlands' US$5.7 billion made it by far the largest single investor in Turkey, with a group of smaller EU countries together accounting for another US$4.9 billion. The long history of economic interactions with Europe since World War II and during the Cold War has fed this overwhelming dominance.

But Asia is rising fast. At the end of 2007, by far the two largest recipients of Turkish foreign direct investment (FDI) were the Netherlands and Azerbaijan, a striking juxtaposition that fully captures Turkey's geographic articulation of East and West. They were followed by Malta, Luxembourg, Germany, the United States, and Kazakhstan. As for the major sectors of this FDI, the construction and the real estate industries together account for 20% of the foreign firms operating in Turkey. Turkish construction companies work in a large number of foreign countries, too, with the most significant concentration of cumulative value from 1980 to 2009 in Italy (US$102 billion), Libya (US$50 billion), and Ukraine (US$21billion). A number of countries follow, with cumulative investments ranging between US$10 and $16 billion, including Switzerland, Luxembourg, Russia, and Sudan, once again highlighting Turkey's bridging of different historical geographies (Turkish Statistical Institute 2009).

Along with a trade orientation that spans its geopolitical region (see *Urban Age*, Istanbul Newsletter 2008: 38), there has been a dramatic increase in Turkey's total FDI stock abroad. By 2007, Turkey's FDI stood at US$12.2 billion, an eleven-fold increase compared to 1990 (US$1.1 billion) and three-and-a-half-fold increase compared to 2000 (US$3.7 billion). Similarly, while capital began flowing out of Turkey at exponential rates, by 2007, the inward flow of FDI stood at US$146 billion, a thirteen-fold increase over 1990 (US$11 billion) and seven-and-a-half-fold compared to 2000 (US$19.2 billion; see Exhibit 5.3) it is the combination of capital flowing into and out of, to, and through the region that marks the intersection of capital mobilities in Istanbul. Such a dramatic increase in capital relations across and within the region within two decades has led to the developing capacity of Istanbul's changing manufacturing, financial, and service industries, now a magnet for human capital and innovation.

Istanbul concentrates a disproportionate share of foreign firms operating in Turkey (Istanbul Metropolitan Municipality, Annual; Turkish Government's Statistical Records, Annual). Of the more than 19,000 foreign firms operating in Turkey, well over half are headquartered in Istanbul. About 10,700 are EU firms, including 3,100 from Germany and 1,800 from Britain. At the other end, 4,300 foreign firms are from Asia, including 910 from Iran, 450 from Azerbaijan, and 300 from China. While EU firms are still dominant, the rise of Asia and the changing geopolitics of its immediate region put Istanbul at the center of a vast space now characterized by the copresence of multiple and diverse firms and projects from all over the world. According to a study of the future of European cities, Istanbul is one of the key cities in what is considered to be emergent Europe, a geographic space that runs between Western Europe and West Asia (see Exhibit 5.4).

While capital flows are one way of identifying economic relations extending to and through the city, the flow of people brings skills, inventiveness, and cultures. These are all elements easily overlooked in debates about migration. The fine grain of cultures shaped by people on the move

Exhibit 5.3   FDI Flows and Foreign Firms Operating in Turkey (2007–2009)*

	International Firms Operating in Turkey in 2007	FDI into Turkey 2004–2008 (US$ millions)	FDI out of Turkey 1980–2009 (US$ millions)
European Union (27)	10,720	44,245	8,679
Germany	3,125	2,992	665
The Netherlands	1,419	13,043	4,266
United Kingdom	1,831	2,957	536
France	—	3,633	105
Italy	—	1,191	120
Other EU Countries	4,345	20,429	2,986
Other European Countries (Excluding EU)	1,691	2,401	1,016
Africa	309	111	426
USA	834	6,048	702
Canada	120	242	2
Central-South America and Caribbean	105	595	17
Near and Middle Eastern Countries	3,072	6,381	3,826
Azerbaijan	453	—	3,420
Iraq	511	—	7
Iran	910	—	162
Gulf Arabian Countries	—	5,722	56
China	300	—	26
South Korea	134	—	—
Japan	—	—	—
Other Asian countries	796	1,058	867

Note: *More than half of these international firms have their main offices in Istanbul.

Source: Turkish Government's Statistical Records. Annual Report. DIE (Turkish Government Statistical Institute) Report, Ankara, Annual; Turkish Statistical Institute (Turksta). Ankara. (http://www.turkstat.gov).

Exhibit 5.4   Top Ten Emerging European Cities 2009

Rank	City	Country
1	Budapest	Hungary
2	Warsaw	Poland
3	Moscow	Russia
4	Istanbul	Turkey
5	Sofia	Bulgaria
6	Bucharest	Romania
7	St. Petersburg	Russia
8	Ankara	Turkey
9	Kiev	Ukraine
10	Yekaterinburg	Russia

Source: Ernst and Young 2010. Reinventing European Growth: 2009 European Attractiveness Survey

and by the intersections of global and local get wired into cities and feed "citiness." All of this has affected Istanbul's unique geopolitics and cultures. As of 2006, Turkey's global emigration map was still dominated by one recipient country: Germany (see Exhibit 5.5). Whether we are counting the 1.7 million Turkish nationals, the 2.7 million born in Turkey though not necessarily holding Turkish nationality, or the even larger number of second- and third-generation Turkish-Germans who now, thanks to a recent change in Germany's naturalization law, no longer hold an ambiguous citizenship status, the Turkish presence in Germany is very strong. The next largest foreign resident Turkish populations are in France (229,000), the Netherlands (171,000), Austria (150,000), and Belgium (111,000), followed by a large number of countries with smaller numbers: from Sweden with just under 100,000 to Russia with 2,000.

The global geography of Turkish emigration is changing. Mirroring the flows of capital that move East and West, major destinations of people leaving Turkey continue to be European, but in addition we see growing, although still smaller, flows to Asia. Cumulative departures from 2000 to 2006 were 322,000 to Germany, 57,000 to France, and 55,700 to Austria,

Exhibit 5.5   Migration, Numbers by Country of Origin and Country of
Destination. Raw Figure of Short-term Foreign Trips to Turkey

	Cumulative Arrivals for Short-term Visits (Nationals and nonnationals) 2000–2006	*Cumulative Inflow of Migrants Into Turkey 2000–2006*	*Cumulative Outflow of Migrants 2000–2006*
Germany	23,933,415	48,400	322,000
Russian Federation	8,959,822	46,200	—
United Kingdom	8,724,427	32,300	—
Bulgaria	6,872,570	373,700	—
The Netherlands	6,335,209	—	30,900
Iran	4,089,853	41,500	—
France	3,869,890	—	56,900
Austria	2,809,797	—	55,700
USA	2,671,226	41,900	—
Greece	2,569,173	45,800	—
Belgium	2,552,993	—	23,100
Israel	2,270,623	—	—
Italy	2,104,938	—	—
Ukraine	1,931,396	—	—
Azerbaijan	1,836,595	73,300	—
Georgia	1,824,789	—	—
Sweden	1,774,612	—	7,200
Romania	1,429,198	—	—
Switzerland	1,331,262	—	18,400

Source: Turkish Government's Statistical Records. Annual report. DIE (Turkish Government Statistical Institute) Report, Ankara, Annual.

followed by smaller numbers to a variety of other countries. But the dominance of Turkey's relationship with the EU can mask the shifting geography of its migrations. In 2006, for example, departures for Germany numbered 30,000, followed by 20,000 to Saudi Arabia, 8,300 to France, and a number of smaller but significant flows to the post-Soviet Asian republics.

Migration into Turkey is small, with only 1.9% foreign-born among the total population, a figure that includes return migrants from Germany and elsewhere. But also, here we see new geographies of origin beyond the EU. In 2006, 191,000 foreigners moved into Turkey, mostly from Bulgaria and Azerbaijan. These two nationalities also dominated the cumulative inflow from 2000 to 2006, with 373,700 from Bulgaria and 73,000 from Azerbaijan, while only 48,400 migrated from Germany. These dominant inflows were followed by smaller but significant populations coming from Greece, Russia, the United States, Iran, Iraq, the United Kingdom, and elsewhere. The origins of migrations are shifting from West to East. Most of the inflow comes from Bulgaria and Azerbaijan, while most of the outflow goes to Germany and France.

Another important but more temporary intersection of work and national cultures occurs on short-term trips (Turkish Government's Statistical Records Annual). As is the case in most countries, migration figures are dwarfed by the numbers of foreigners entering Turkey for various short-term purposes as well as citizens coming for short-term visits. In 2006, the largest single purposes for coming were travel, entertainment, culture, and visits to family and friends. And yet people do travel to Turkey for work. In 2006, the largest single groups of foreigners were the 7 million managers and professionals and another 1.1 million in secondary service professions. Entries of foreigners reached 19.3 million in 2006, up from 13.7 million in 2004 and 11.3 million in 2001. Between 2001 and 2006, more than 23 million people visited Turkey from Germany, nearly 9 million from Russia and the United Kingdom each, 7 million from Bulgaria, and 4 million from Iran. These are far from insignificant numbers. They represent the incredibly diverse range of people moving into and out of the country, each carrying with them specific histories and cultures, feeding Istanbul's cosmopolitanism (Turkish Government's Statistical Records Annual).

Some of these emergent geographies of the flows of capital and of people feed into the two final variables I want to discuss. One is the significant role of Istanbul as a center for global policy exchange. Kearney's 2010 study of sixty cities along five variables (business activity, human capital, information exchange, culture, and policy engagement) finds Istanbul in the top ten cities worldwide on the policy engagement variable, along with Washington, Beijing, Paris, Cairo, London, and Brussels, among others (see Exhibit 5.6).

The study defines the policy engagement variable as "influence on global policy-making and political dialogue." The second, not unconnected, is the fact that the study finds Istanbul in the top fifteen cities on the human capital variable—defined as a city that "acts as a magnet for diverse groups of people and talent" (see Exhibit 5.7). Among the other cities in the top group are Tokyo, New York, Hong Kong, Chicago, Sydney, and London. In the case of Istanbul, the key factor feeding its high rank is the large number of international schools, which functions as an indicator for characteristics of the parents of these children.

It is worth noting that of the five factors measured, the most important one feeding the top-ranking cities is the presence of a foreign-born population: it is the single largest factor by far, feeding New York's top rank on the human capital variable, and one of the two largest factors in Hong Kong's fourth-place ranking. Istanbul is well positioned to gain ground here: even though it is still a country with a very small foreign-born population, it is clear that it has benefited from an enormous variety of origins among its immigrants. I see both of these prominent positions, in policy engagement and human capital, as having to do with Istanbul's strategic role at the intersection of diverse economic and geopolitical geographies. In an increasingly networked world, this role and the capabilities involved have taken on growing importance.

Cities have long been at the intersection of cross-border circuits—flows of capital, labor, goods, raw materials, merchants, travelers. Asia and Africa have seen some of the oldest and vastest of these flows, and Europe some of the densest. Cities are strategic spaces for the economies and cultures that arise from these flows, for making the capabilities needed to handle and govern these intersections, and for the housing of power—economic, political, and cultural. These circuits are multidirectional and criss-cross the world, feeding into intercity geographies. The formation of intercity geographies is today contributing a critical infrastructure for a new global political economy, new cultural spaces, and new types of politics. Some of these intercity geographies are thick and highly visible—the flows of professionals, tourists, artists, and migrants among specific groups of cities. Others are thin and barely visible—the highly specialized financial trading networks that connect particular cities, depending on the type of instrument involved, or the global commodity chains for diverse products that run from exporting hubs to importing hubs.

The vast expansion of the geographies of these flows in the current period has further brought out the importance of cities at these intersections. For some cities, such as Istanbul, this is an old history; for others, such as Miami, it is a new one. The ascendance of Asia on the world

Exhibit 5.6 Cities with Global Policy Influence

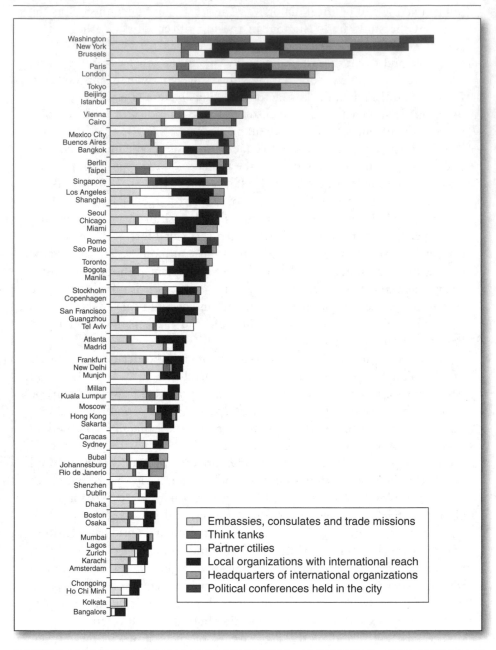

Exhibit 5.7   Cities with Human Capital

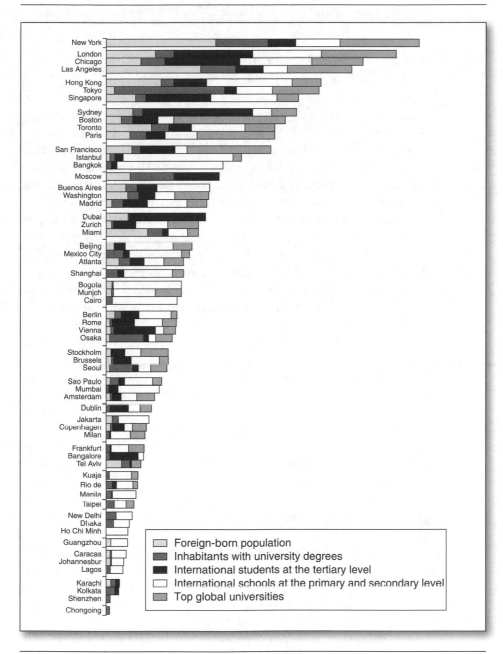

economic and geopolitical map has brought added strategic importance to some of these cities, among which Istanbul holds the most prominence.

Globalization and Concentration: The Case of Leading Financial Centers

The major economies in the developed world display a similar pattern of sharp concentration of financial activity and related producer services in one center: Paris in France, Milan in Italy, Zurich in Switzerland, Frankfurt in Germany, Toronto in Canada, Tokyo in Japan, Amsterdam in the Netherlands, and, as just shown, Sydney in Australia. The evidence also shows that the concentration of financial activity in such leading centers has actually generally increased starting in the late 1980s. Thus, Basel, formerly a very important financial center in Switzerland, in the 1980s began to be overshadowed by Zurich (Keil and Ronneberger 1992); and Montreal, certainly the other major center in Canada, was overtaken by Toronto in the late 1980s (Levine 1990). Similarly, Osaka was once a far more powerful competitor with Tokyo in the financial markets in Japan than it had become by the late 1980s (Sassen [1991] 2001: chaps. 6, 7). And London and New York lengthened the distance between them and the other major centers in their respective countries.

This growing concentration in top centers did not necessarily mean that a country's secondary centers declined. Mostly they also grew. So this is, to a large extent, a dynamic whereby overall growth produces growing concentration at the top—the leading centers grow faster than the rest, or, at the least, even high-growth secondary centers cannot close the gap. This is, in many ways, a disturbing and counterintuitive trend for a sector operating largely in electronic networks and dealing with a digitized product. One might have expected dispersal rather than concentration given the capacities of computer-centered networks and the high costs of operating in central cities.

Is this tendency toward concentration within each country a new development for financial centers? A broader historical view points to some interesting patterns. Since its earliest beginnings, financial work was spatially concentrated (Arrighi 1994). Financiers often operated in the context of empires, such as the British or Dutch empires, or quasi-empires, such as the United States with its superior economic and military power in the mid-twentieth century. Some of the first financial centers in Europe were medieval Italian cities; a good case is Florence, a city whose currency, the florin, was one of the most stable in the continent. But by the seventeenth century, a single financial center became dominant. It was Amsterdam, which introduced central banking and the stock market, probably reflecting its vast international merchant and trading operations, and the city's role as an unrivaled international center for trading and exchange. One hundred years later, London had emerged as the major international financial center and the major market for European government debt. London remained the financial capital of the world, clearly as a function of the British Empire, until well into the twentieth century. By 1914, New York, which had won its competition with Philadelphia and Boston for the banking business in the United States, emerged as a challenger to London. London, however, was also the strategic cog in the international financial system, a role that New York was not quite ready to assume. But after World War II, the immense economic might of the United States and the destruction of Britain and other European countries left New York as the world's financial center.

Yet the context for this trend toward a leading financial center had begun to change since World War I. Against the earlier pattern of empires, the formation of nation-states made possible a multiplicity of financial centers, typically the national capital in each country. Furthermore, the ascendance of mass manufacturing contributed to vast, typically regionally based fortunes and the formation of secondary financial centers in those regions: Chicago and Osaka are two examples. The Keynesian policies aimed at promoting a country's development of regional convergence became increasingly common across the world. By the 1960s, these various trends had contributed to a proliferation of financial centers inside countries (e.g., Italy had eleven financial centers and Germany had seven), highly regulated banking systems, and strict national protections. The dominance of mass manufacturing in much of the twentieth century meant that finance and banking were, to a large extent, shaped by the needs of manufacturing economies and mass consumption. Although New York may have been the leading international financial center since the early twentieth century, it was so as part of a national US government strategy seeking global dominance along patterns that were quite different from those that emerged in the 1980s (Sassen 2008a: chap. 4).

The developments that took off in the 1980s represented a sharp departure from this pattern of fairly closed and protected national financial systems centered on mass production and mass consumption. The opening of national economies to foreign investors and the explosion in financial innovations that raised the speculative character of finance and began to replace highly regulated national commercial banking as a source of capital strengthened the tendencies toward concentration in a limited number of financial centers. Although this is reminiscent of older imperial patterns, the actual conditions and processes involved are different. In the 1980s, there was massive growth in the absolute levels of financial activity worldwide. But this growth became more sharply concentrated in a limited number of countries and cities. International bank lending grew from US$1.89 trillion in 1980 to US$6.24 trillion in 1991—a three-fold increase in a decade—and to US$9.03 trillion in 1998 (author's calculations based on Bank for International Settlements [1992, 1999, 2004]); it has become increasingly problematic to track bank lending given that many of the largest banks, which account for a good share of these loans, also became financial services firms. The same seven countries accounted for almost two-thirds of this lending in 1980, then saw their share rise to three-fourths in 1998 and fall back to 1980 levels by 2004, according to data from the Bank for International Settlements (2004), the leading institution worldwide in charge of overseeing banking activity. Much of this lending activity was executed in the leading financial center of each of these countries or in specialized markets, such as Chicago, which dominated the world's trading in futures. By the late 1990s, five cities—New York, London, Tokyo, Paris, and Frankfurt—accounted for a disproportionate share of all financial activity. Strong patterns of concentration were also evident in stock market capitalization and in foreign-exchange markets (Exhibit 5.8); these also show the ongoing concentration in a limited number of financial centers.

Notice again that this unchanged level of concentration happened in the context of enormous absolute increases, deregulation, and globalization of the industry worldwide, which means that a growing number of countries had become integrated into the world markets. Furthermore, it happened at a time when financial services are more mobile than ever before: globalization, deregulation (an essential ingredient for globalization), and securitization have been the keys to this mobility—in the context of massive advances in telecommunications and electronic networks.[8] One result has been growing competition among centers for hypermobile financial activity. But there has been an overemphasis on competition in both general and specialized accounts of this subject. As I argued in Chapter 3, there is also a functional division of labor among various major financial centers. The shape of this global industry is more akin to a division of functions across multiple countries.

The hypermobility of financial capital puts added emphasis on the importance of technology. It is now possible to move money from one part of the world to another and make deals without ever leaving the computer terminal. Thanks to electronics, there are disembodied marketplaces—what we can think of as the cyberspace of international finance. NASDAQ (National Association of Securities Dealers Automated Quotations) and

Exhibit 5.8   Reported Foreign Exchange Turnover for Selected Countries, Selected Years 1992–2007 (percent share)

	1992	1995	1998	2001	2004	2007
United Kingdom	27.0	29.5	32.5	31.2	31.0	34.1
United States	15.5	15.5	17.9	15.7	19.2	16.6
Japan	11.2	10.2	6.9	9.1	8.2	6.0
Singapore	6.9	6.7	7.1	6.2	5.2	5.8
Germany	5.1	4.8	4.8	5.5	4.8	2.5
Hong Kong	5.6	5.7	4.0	4.1	4.2	4.4
Australia	2.7	2.5	2.4	3.2	4.2	4.3
France	3.1	3.7	3.7	3.0	2.6	3.0
Canada	2.0	1.9	1.9	2.6	2.2	1.5
Netherlands	1.9	1.7	2.1	1.9	2.0	0.6
Denmark	2.5	2.0	1.4	1.4	1.7	2.2
Sweden	2.0	1.3	0.8	1.5	1.3	1.1

Note: Turnover of spot, outright forward, and foreign exchange swaps. Adjusted for local double-counting ("net-gross").

Source: Bank for International Settlements (2005, 2007: 6–7).

some of the standardized foreign-exchange markets are examples of disembodied markets, unlike the older-style stock market with its trading floor.

Yet the trend toward concentration continues, albeit in an expanding network of leading centers: it is no longer the absolute dominance of New York, London, and Tokyo evident in the 1980s and into the 1990s (Sassen [1991] 2001). Further, the formation of a single European market and financial system is generating a European financial system that centralizes financial functions and capital in a limited number of major centers. These are partly taking over major financial functions from what were once the leading financial centers in each European country, as well as launching new types of collaborations among Europe's financial centers, mixing often leading and minor financial centers. Indeed, the consolidation of alliances, notably the one between Paris, Amsterdam, Brussels, and Lisbon (Euronext), is an emerging trend.

These tendencies toward concentration seem to be built into the nature of the financial system. Centers at the top are characterized by a multiplicity of financial institutions and markets, with significant shares of world activity in various specialized financial markets. They usually have a large number of banks and financial institutions that account for a significant share of international lending, foreign exchange trading, and fund management. They also have large or significant markets in tradable securities—whether bonds, stocks, or their derivatives. Among the large financial centers, some are dominated by international business and others by domestic business. Thus, London, with its enormous presence of foreign firms from all over the world and its strong Eurodollar and foreign-exchange markets, is extremely international, whereas New York and Tokyo, with their vast national economies, will inevitably have a very large number of domestic borrowers, lenders, and investors. Finally, the globalization of the industry has raised the level of complexity of transactions, and deregulation has promoted the invention of many new and increasingly speculative instruments. This change has contributed to the power of the leading centers, insofar as they are the only ones with the capability to produce authoritative innovations and to handle the levels of complexity in today's financial system.

In the next section, I examine these issues in greater detail with a particular focus on the networks that connect these centers and the impact of digitization on place.

Why Do Financial Centers Still Exist in the Global Digital Era?

The global financial system has reached levels of complexity that require the existence of a cross-border network of financial centers. This complexity is partly fed by the increasingly complicated financial services required by global firms. But they are also fed by an internal dynamic to finance: the development of more and more speculative financial instruments that seem to feed on each other, reaching either extreme accumulations of financial capital or catastrophic plunges (see Chapter 8). This network of financial centers differs sharply from earlier versions of the international financial system. In a world of largely closed national financial systems, each country duplicated most of the necessary functions for its economy; collaborations among different national financial markets were often no more than the execution of the same set of operations in both countries involved, as in clearing and settlement. With few exceptions, such as the offshore markets and some of the large banks, the international system consisted of a string of closed domestic systems and the limited, mostly routinized interactions among them (see Sassen 2008a: chap. 5; [1991] 2001: chap. 4).

The global integration of markets and deregulations that took off in the 1980s led to the elimination of various redundant systems, making collaboration a far more complex matter—it was no longer mere duplication of basic banking procedures in each country involved in a given transaction. Having something approaching one system embedded in all countries now linked to the global financial system has had the perhaps ironic effect of raising the importance of leading financial centers; they are also the centers that created many of the standards and rules that had to be adopted by all participating countries. Rather than a global system consisting of each country's center for global operations duplicating all key functions and specialized markets, there is now a more globally distributed system, with the twenty or so global leading centers having distinct specializations, besides the basic functions that all global financial centers need to have. Each of today's leading financial centers (see Exhibits 4.1–4.4) possesses distinctive strengths, as is well captured in the discussion of Hong Kong and Shanghai in this chapter. In this context, London and New York, with their enormous concentrations of resources and talent, continue to be the powerhouses in the global network for the most strategic and complex operations for the system as a whole, but they are increasingly dependent on the larger network of about twenty leading financial centers. They are the leading exporters of financial services and typically are part of any major international public offering, such as the privatization of British Telecom and France Telecom.

This dominance, on the one hand, does not preclude the fact that one of the ways in which the global financial system grows is by incorporating more and more *national* economies, a process that happens through the development of a state-of-the-art financial center in each country—which often evolves into a second- or third-tier global city. On the other hand, in the case of the European Union, the formation of a single-currency Eurozone is spelling the end of an era in which each country had its full-fledged financial center. A steep hierarchy is very likely, with Frankfurt and Paris at the top in the Eurozone and a crisscross of alliances centered in either of these major centers or among centers not included in those alliances.

The major financial centers of a growing number of countries worldwide are increasingly fulfilling gateway functions for the in-and-out circulation of national and foreign capital. Each of these centers is the nexus between that country's wealth and the global market and between foreign investors and that country's investment opportunities. The result is that the sources of and destinations for investment are growing. Gateway functions are their main mechanism for integration into the global financial market rather than, say, the production of innovations to package the capital flowing in and out; the production of innovations tends to remain concentrated in the leading twenty or so centers, as these have not only the specialized talents but also the clout to persuade investors to buy innovative instruments. Further, the complex operations in most second- and third-tier financial centers tend to be executed by foreign global investment, accounting, and legal services firms through affiliates, branches, or direct imports of those services.

These gateways for the global market are also gateways for the dynamics of financial crises: capital can flow out as easily and quickly as it flows in. And what was once thought of as *national* capital can now as easily join the exodus. For example, during Mexico's international financial crisis of December 1994, we now know that the first capitals to flee the Mexican markets were national, not foreign. In the financial crisis of 1997 to 1998, much of the capital flight out of Brazil of an estimated US$1 billion a day by early September 1998 was Brazilian, not foreign. More recently, the global financial crisis of 2008 to 2009 erupted with the US-based credit-default swap crisis and its global repercussions (see Chapter 8).

Because the globally integrated financial system is not just about competition among financial centers or among countries, specialized collaborative efforts are increasing across borders. This also has the effect of further strengthening the networked features of this system. The financial system would not really gain from the downfall of Tokyo or Hong Kong or, for that matter, Buenos Aires. The ongoing growth of London, New York, Paris, or Frankfurt is, in part, a function of a global network of financial centers. These same features that make it strong and powerful are also the conduits for spreading the effects of a crisis.

Finally, although electronic networks are growing in number and in scope, they are unlikely to eliminate the need for financial centers (Sassen 2008a: chap. 5 and 7; 2009). Rather, they are intensifying the networks connecting such centers in strategic or functional alliances among exchanges in different cities. These alliances may well evolve into the equivalent of the cross-border mergers and acquisitions of firms. Electronic trading is also contributing to a radically new pattern whereby one market—for example, Frankfurt's Deutsche Eurex—can operate on screens in many other markets around the world, or one brokerage firm, notably Cantor Fitzgerald, could (since September 1998) have its prices of Treasury futures listed on screens used by traders all around the United States. Further, electronic trading will not eliminate the need for financial centers because these combine multiple resources and talents necessary for executing complex operations and servicing global firms and markets. Finally, financial centers cannot be reduced to their exchanges. They are part of a far more complex architecture in the financial system, and they constitute far more complex structures within that architecture than the exchanges.

In the Digital Era: More Concentration than Dispersal

What stands out in this context of an expanding global financial industry with a growing number of leading centers where most countries in the world now have an international financial center is the disproportionate power of the twenty or so leading centers. One measure of this power is the disproportionate concentration of financial capital in a limited number of financial centers. This mix of a growth in the numbers of centers along with the consolidation of a few centers is also evident within countries. In the United States, for example, New York has the largest concentration of the leading investment banks with only one other major international financial center, Chicago. Boston is a strong financial center but has lost share to New York, as has Philadelphia. Several of the other financial centers have also lost share. We already examined how Sydney and Toronto took over functions and market share from what were once the major commercial centers in their respective countries. So have São Paulo and Mumbai, which gained share and functions from, respectively, Rio de Janeiro in Brazil and New Delhi and Calcutta in India. These are all enormous countries, and one might have thought that they could sustain multiple major financial centers. In France, Paris today holds larger shares of most financial sectors than it did in the 1970s, and once-important stock markets such as Lyon have become "provincial," even though Lyon is today the hub of a thriving economic region. Milan privatized its exchange in September 1997 and electronically merged Italy's ten regional markets. Frankfurt now lays claim to a larger share of the financial market in Germany than it did in the early 1980s, as does Zurich in Switzerland. Further, these processes of growing concentration moved fast. For example, by 1997, Frankfurt's market capitalization was five times greater than all other regional markets in Germany combined, whereas in 1992, it was only twice as large. This story holds true for many countries and it continues today. What stands out is that this pattern toward the consolidation of one or two leading financial centers in a county is a function of rapid growth in the sector, not necessarily of decay in the losing cities.

Note that there are both consolidation in fewer major centers across and within countries *and* a sharp growth in the number of centers that become part of the global network as countries deregulate their economies. São Paulo and Mumbai, for example, joined the global financial network after Brazil and India partly deregulated their financial systems in the early 1990s. This mode of incorporation into the global network is often at the cost of losing functions that they had when they were largely national centers; today, foreign financial, accounting, and legal services firms have entered their markets to handle the new cross-border operations. Incorporation of a country's financial center into the global network typically happens without a gain in the share of the global market that they can command even though their volume and value of operations will tend to grow sharply in absolute terms. In a globalized market, the owners or beneficiaries of the absolute growth in stock market value may well be foreign investors.

All of these trends bring up, once again, the question of why this rapid growth in the network of financial centers, overall volumes, and electronic networks has resulted in, or failed to reduce, the high concentration of market shares in the leading financial centers of the world. Both globalization and electronic trading are about expansion and dispersal beyond what had been the confined realm of national economies and floor trading. Indeed, given globalization and electronic trading, one might well ask why financial centers matter at all.

Agglomeration in the Digital Era

The continuing weight of major centers is, in a way, counterintuitive, as is the existence of an expanding network of financial centers. The rapid development of electronic exchanges and the growing digitization of much financial activity suggest that location should not matter. In fact, geographic dispersal would seem to be a good option given the high cost of operating in major financial centers, and digitization would seem to eliminate most reasons for having a geographic base. Further, the geographic mobility of financial experts and financial services firms has continued to increase and has resulted in a variety of new industries catering to the needs of the transnational professional and managerial classes, thereby enabling even more mobility.

There has been geographic decentralization of certain types of financial activities, aimed at securing business in the growing number of countries becoming integrated into the global economy. But this is merely a geographic decentralization of a firm's operations, with central headquarters keeping control and appropriation of profits. Many of the leading investment banks now have operations in more countries than they did in the early 1980s. The same can be said for the top accounting and legal services and other specialized corporate services, as well as some markets. For example, in the 1980s, all basic wholesale foreign-exchange operations were in London. Today, these operations are distributed between London and several other centers (even though the number of these centers is far smaller than the number of countries whose currency is being traded).

There are at least three reasons that explain the trend toward consolidation in a few centers rather than massive dispersal. I developed this analysis in *The Global City* (Sassen [1991] 2001), initially focusing on New York, London, and Tokyo in the 1980s, and since then on the larger network of financial centers. The reasons explaining the primacy of leading centers have become even clearer and sharper over the last few years, partly due to the rise in speculative finance and the fact that electronic markets have contributed to a new type of risk, one that might be called *market-risk*, whereby the so-called export of risk by a firm through the use of derivatives produces a boomerang effect for firms when electronic markets absorb the aggregate risk exported by all firms in such markets (Sassen 2008a: chap. 7). The 2008 financial crisis is an example of this. New financial instruments like credit default swaps (CDS) and new forms of collateralized debt obligations (CDOs) increased systemic risk, a subject I return to in Chapter 8.

1. *Social Connectivity.* First, and as already discussed in Chapter 1 for the case of firms, although the new telecommunications technologies do indeed facilitate geographic dispersal of financial activities without losing system integration, they have also had the effect of strengthening the importance of central coordination and control functions for financial firms and, even, markets. This is particularly so given the trend toward making financial exchanges into (publicly listed) corporations and, hence, the development of central management functions—something that does sound strange for an exchange but in fact is part of how these operate. Operating a widely dispersed network of branches and affiliates and operating in multiple markets has made central functions far more complicated for any firm. And now we can add financial exchanges, where it is perhaps even more complicated given the speed of transactions enabled by electronic networks. The execution of these central functions requires access to top talent and to innovative milieux—in technology, accounting, legal services, economic forecasting, and all sorts of other, many new, specialized corporate services. Financial centers have massive concentrations of state-of-the-art resources that allow them to maximize the benefits of telecommunications and, in the case of leading centers, to organize and govern the new conditions for

operating globally. Even electronic markets such as NASDAQ and E*Trade rely on traders and banks located somewhere, with at least some in a major financial center.

One fact that has become increasingly evident is that to maximize the benefits of the new information technologies, you need not only the infrastructure but also a complex mix of other resources. Most of the value that these technologies can produce for advanced service firms lies in the externalities. And this means the material and human resources—state-of-the-art office buildings, top talent, and the capacity for social networking that maximize the benefits of connectivity. Any town can have fiber-optic cables. But do they have the rest?

A second fact emerging with greater clarity concerns the meaning of *information*. There are two types of information in this internationalized world of transactions. One is the datum: At what level did Wall Street close? Did Argentina complete the public sector sale of its water utility? Has Japan declared such-and-such bank insolvent? But there is a far more difficult type of information, akin to a mix of interpretation, evaluation, and judgment. It entails negotiating a series of data and a series of interpretations of other data in the hope of producing a higher-order datum. Access to the first kind of information is now global and immediate, thanks to the digital revolution. You can be a broker in the Colorado Rockies and have access to this type of information. But the second type of information requires a complicated mixture of elements—the social infrastructure for global connectivity—and it is this that gives major financial centers a leading edge.

One can, in principle, reproduce the technical infrastructure anywhere. Singapore, for example, has technical connectivity matching Hong Kong's. But does it have Hong Kong's social connectivity? When the more complex forms of information needed to execute major international deals cannot be gotten from existing databases, no matter what a firm can pay, then that firm needs the social information loop with the associated interpretations and inferences that come with bouncing information among talented, informed people. The importance of this input has given a whole new weight to credit-rating agencies, for example. Part of the rating has to do with interpreting and inferring the quality of a firm's or government's resources. Credit-rating firms are in the business of producing *authoritative* interpretations and presenting them as information available to all (Sinclair 2004). But firms, especially global firms in finance, need more than what credit-ratings firms sell. They need to build this advanced type of interpretation into their daily work process, and this takes not only talent but also information-rich milieux (Sassen 2008a: chap. 7). Financial centers generally, and leading ones especially, are such milieux.

Risk management, for example, which has become increasingly important with globalization as a result of the growing complexity and uncertainty that comes with operating in multiple countries and markets, requires enormous fine-tuning of central operations. We now know that many, if not most, major trading losses during the decade of the 1990s have involved human error or fraud. The quality of risk management depends more heavily on the top people in a firm than simply on technical conditions, such as electronic surveillance. Consolidating risk-management operations in one site, usually a central one for the firm, is now seen generally as more effective. This is the case of several major banks: Chase and Morgan Stanley in the United States, Deutsche Bank and Credit Suisse in Europe.

In brief, financial centers provide the social connectivity that allows a firm or market to maximize the benefits of its technological connectivity and to handle the added pressures that speed brings to financial firms.

2. *Need for Enormous Resources.* Global players in the financial industry need enormous resources, a trend that is leading, first, to rapid mergers and acquisitions of firms and, second, to strategic alliances among financial exchanges in different countries. Both of these are happening on a scale and in combinations few had foreseen a decade ago. Examples from the late 1990s, when these trends took off, are the mergers of Citibank with Travelers Group (which few had predicted just two years earlier), Salomon Brothers with Smith Barney, Bankers Trust with Alex Brown, and so on. This wave of mergers was so sharp that, subsequently, when powerful firms such as Deutsche Bank and Dresdner Bank each decided to purchase a US security firm, they complained of a lack of suitable candidates. One common opinion among analysts emerging in the early 2000s is that midsize firms will find it difficult to survive in the global market given global megafirms such as Morgan Stanley and Goldman Sachs. Indeed, the late 2000s saw a whole new wave of mergers and acquisitions as the crisis erupted. Increasingly common are mergers among accounting firms, law firms, insurance brokers—in brief, firms that need to provide a global service. Analysts foresee a system dominated by a few global investment banks, about twenty-five large fund managers, and an increasingly consolidated set of specialized service firms. A similar trend is expected in the global telecommunications industry, which will have to consolidate to offer a state-of-the-art, globe-spanning service to its global clients, among which are the financial firms; indeed, the early last decade saw the demise of several large telecommunications firms and their partial absorption by some of the remaining firms.

Another kind of merger is the consolidation of electronic networks that connect a very select number of exchanges. Europe's more than thirty stock exchanges have been seeking to shape various alliances. Until recently, Euronext was Europe's largest stock exchange merger, an alliance among the Paris, Amsterdam, Lisbon, and Brussels bourses. Then came the merger of Euronext with the New York Exchange, and in 2011, the Deutsche Borse acquired 60% of NYSEEuronext. The London Stock Exchange has been the object of hostile takeover attempts since 2005. In the 1990s, the Tallinn Stock Exchange in Estonia and its Helsinki counterpart created an alliance, and a range of looser networks connecting exchanges were launched. For instance, NASDAQ, the second-largest US stock market after the New York Stock Exchange, set up NASDAQ Japan, NASDAQ Canada, and several other such alliances. This gave investors in Japan and Canada direct access to the market in the United States. The Toronto Stock Exchange joined an alliance with the New York Stock Exchange (NYSE) to create a separate global trading platform. The NYSE is a founding member of a global trading alliance, Global Equity Market (GEM), which includes ten exchanges, among them Tokyo and Euronext. This enormous organizational innovation contributed to a sharp rise in the total value of the world's financial stock (equity market capitalization and outstanding bonds and loans) which reached an all time high US$212 trillion at the end of 2010 (McKinsey 2011). (See generally Exhibits 5.9, 5.10, and 4.1–4.4.)

Does the fact of fewer global players affect the spread of such operations? Not necessarily, since the firms or exchanges can keep operations and alliances across the world. But it will strengthen the hierarchy in the global network. The value of institutionally managed assets stood at US$15 trillion by early 1999; by 2010 it stood at US$ 56.4 trillion according to Boston Consulting Group (2011). The worldwide distribution of equities under institutional management shows considerable spread among a large number of cities that have become integrated in the global equity market with deregulation of their economies and the whole notion of emerging markets as an attractive investment destination over the last few years. Thomson Financial (1999), for example, has estimated that at the end of 1998 (the last year for which Thomson Financial produced this information), twenty-five cities accounted for 83% of the world's equities under institutional management. (At the time, these twenty-five cities also accounted for roughly 48% of the total market capitalization of the world, which stood at US$22 trillion at the end of 1998.) However, this global market is characterized by a disproportionate concentration in the top six or seven cities. London, New York, and Tokyo together accounted for a third of the world's total equities under institutional management at the end of 1998.

These developments make clear a second important trend that in many ways characterizes the current global era. These various centers don't just

Exhibit 5.9   Largest Exchanges by Value of Share Trading in 2009 and 2008

Rank	Exchange	US$ bn 2009	US$ bn 2008	% Change in US$
1	NYSE Euronext US	17,521	27,651	–36.6%
2	NASDAQ OMX US	13,608	23,845	–42.9%
3	Shanghai Stock Exchange	5,056	2,584	95.7%
4	Tokyo Stock Exchange Group	3,704	5,243	–29.4%
5	Shenzhen Stock Exchange	2,772	1,242	123.2%
6	NYSE Euronext Europe	1,935	3,837	–49.6%
7	London Stock Exchange	1,772	3,844	–53.9%
8	Korea Exchange	1,570	1,435	9.4%
9	Deutsche Börse	1,516	3,148	–51.8%
10	Hong Kong Exchanges	1,416	1,562	–9.3%

Source: World Federation of Exchanges. First Half 2010 Market Highlights.

compete with each other: There is collaboration and division of labor. In the international system of the postwar decades, each country's financial center, in principle, covered the universe of necessary functions to service its national companies and markets. The world of finance was, of course, much simpler than it is today. In the initial stages of deregulation in the 1980s, there was a strong tendency to see the relations between the major centers as one of straight competition, especially among the leading centers—New York, London, and Tokyo. But in my research at the time, I had already found a division of labor among these three centers, along with competition in certain areas. What we are seeing now is yet a third pattern: strategic alliances not only between firms across borders but also between markets. There is competition, strategic collaboration, and hierarchy. But this can also generate massive failures and abuses when top management fails. This was the case in the highly publicized Enron case a decade ago and, more recently, in the Bernie Madoff fraud.

Exhibit 5.10   Top Five Performing Broad Market Indexes 2009, in Local Currency

Rank	Americas	% Change 2009/2008
1.	Buenos Aires Stock Exchange	103.6%
2.	Lima Stock Exchange	101.0%
3.	BM&FBOVESPA	82.7%
4.	Colombia Stock Exchange	53.5%
5.	Santiago Stock Exchange	46.9%
Rank	Asia/Pacific	% Change 2009/2008
1.	Colombo Stock Exchange	125.2%
2.	Shenzhen Stock Exchange	117.1%
3.	Bombay Stock Exchange	90.2%
4.	National Stock Exchange India	88.6%
5.	Indonesia Stock Exchange	87.0%
Rank	Europe/Africa/Middle East	% Change 2009/2008
1.	Istanbul Stock Exchange	96.6%
2.	Tel Aviv Stock Exchange	78.8%
3.	Oslo Bors	60.1%
4.	Luxembourg Stock Exchange	54.6%
5.	Warsaw Stock Exchange	46.9%

Source: World Federation of Exchanges. First Half 2010 Market Highlights.

In brief, the need for enormous resources to handle increasingly global operations and the growth of complex central functions produce both tendencies toward concentration among the top centers of finance along with an expanding number of financial centers.

3. *Denationalization of the Corporate Elite.* Finally, national attachments and identities are becoming weaker for these global players and their

customers. Thus, the major US and European investment banks have set up specialized offices in London to handle various aspects of their global business. Deregulation and privatization have further weakened the need for *national* financial centers. The nationality question simply plays differently in these sectors than it did as recently as the early 1980s. Global financial products are accessible in national markets, and national investors can operate in global markets. It is interesting to see that investment banks used to split up their analysts team by country to cover a national market; now they are more likely to do it by specialized sector.

In *Losing Control?* (Sassen 1996; see also 2008a: chap. 5), I described this process as the incipient denationalizing of certain institutional arenas, a necessary condition for economic globalization as we know it today. The sophistication of the global economy lies in the fact that its organizational side (as opposed to the consumer side) needs to involve only strategic institutional areas—most national systems can be left basically unaltered. China is a good example. It adopted international accounting rules already in 1993, as this was an advantage for a country with an accounting system that differed sharply from the prevalent Anglo-American standards generally being used in international transactions. But China did not have to go through a fundamental reorganization of its whole economy to do this: it only used those standards when transacting with foreign firms. Japanese firms operating overseas adopted such standards long before Japan's government considered requiring them. In this regard, the organizational side of globalization is quite different from the global mass-consumer markets, in which success necessitates altering national tastes at a mass level.

This process of denationalization in the realm of the economy has an instrumental and practical connotation, often with negative consequences for the national economy and national firms. For example, I argue that denationalization of key economic sectors in South Korea and Thailand was facilitated by the 1997 through 1998 Asian financial crisis because it enabled foreign firms to buy up large numbers of firms and property in these countries where once their national elites had been in full control. But this process also led to a vast number of failures by medium-sized national firms and multiple take-overs by foreign firms of healthy national firms serving largely national customers. In some ways, the Asian financial crisis partially functioned as a mechanism to denationalize control over key sectors of the South Korean and Thai economies; even as they allowed the massive entry of foreign investment, leading national firms had never fully relinquished control. This is another instance of growing concentration of control over capital through the geographic dispersal of a firm's operations. It is, in many ways, a highly problematic feature of today's global economy.

Major international business centers produce what can be thought of as a new subculture. In a witty insight, *The Economist,* in its coverage of the January 1997 World Economic Forum meeting held in Davos, titled one of its stories "From Chatham House Man to Davos Man," alluding to, respectively, the "national" and the "global" version of international relations. The resistance to mergers and acquisitions, especially hostile takeovers, in Europe in the 1980s and 1990s or to foreign ownership and control in East Asia points to national business cultures that are somewhat incompatible with the new global economic culture. I find that global cities and financial centers contribute to denationalizing the corporate elite. Whether this is good or bad is a separate issue; but it is, I believe, one of the conditions for setting in place the systems and subcultures necessary for a global economic system.

The Space Economy of Centrality

What are the spatial consequences of this new economic core of activities? What is the urban form that accommodates them?

Three distinct patterns are emerging in major cities and their regions in the developed countries and increasingly also in the rest of the world. First, beginning in the 1980s, there was an increase in the number of firms in the centers of major cities mostly explained by growth in leading sectors and ancillary industries. This type of economic growth in city centers also took place in some of the most dynamic cities in rapidly growing Global South countries, such as Seoul, Bangkok, Taipei, Mumbai, São Paulo, Mexico City, and Buenos Aires. Second, along with this central city growth came the formation of dense nodes of commercial development and business activity in a broader urban region, a pattern that is less evident in developing countries except in the export-oriented growth poles discussed earlier or in cities such as Johannesburg, which are undergoing major social transformation in their centers. These nodes assumed different forms: suburban office complexes, edge cities, exopoles, and urban agglomerations in peripheral areas. *Edge cities* are significant concentrations of offices and business activities alongside residential areas in peripheral areas that are completely connected to central locations via state-of-the-art electronic means. Until recently, these urban forms were only rarely evident in developing countries, where vast urban sprawl with a seemingly endless metropolitanization of the region around cities has been the norm. But by 2010, it had become clear that they are now present across the world (Ciccolella and Mignaqui 2002; Ren 2011). In developed countries, the revitalized urban center and the new regional nodes together constitute the spatial base for cities at the top of transnational hierarchies. The third pattern is the growing intensity in the *localness*, or marginality, of areas and sectors that operate outside that world market-oriented subsystem, and this includes an increase in poverty and disadvantage. A significant exception to this trend toward a peripheral localness is the emergence of what I call global slums—major slums in global cities that are positioning themselves as actors on a global stage (Sassen 2011b). The general dynamic that emerges from these three patterns operates in cities with very diverse economic, political, social, and cultural arrangements. There is by now a vast scholarship on these trends and spatial arrangements that took off in the 1980s and continued through the early 2000s (see, among others, Cobos 1984; Gans 1984; Hausserman and Siebel 1987; Henderson and Castells 1987; Cheshire and Hay 1989; Benko and Dunford 1991; Scott 2001; Krause and Petro 2003; Abrahamson 2004; Gugler 2004; Rutherford 2004; Amen, Archer, and Bosman 2006; Sassen 2008b).

A few questions spring to mind. One question is whether the type of spatial organization characterized by dense strategic nodes spread over the broader region might constitute a new form of organizing the territory of the center. This would contrast with the more conventional view that sees it as an instance of suburbanization or geographic dispersal. I argue that insofar as these various nodes are articulated through digital and other advanced communication systems, they represent the new geographic correlate of the most advanced type of center. The places that fall outside this new grid of digital highways are peripheralized. We might ask whether this is more so today than in earlier periods, when suburban and noncentral areas were integrated into the center because they were primarily geared *to* the center. If anything, today the pattern is for nodes in an urban region to develop transversal relations rather than only a radial format with the major city at the center.

Another question is whether this new terrain of centrality is differentiated. Basically, is the old central city, which is still the largest and densest of all the nodes, the most strategic and powerful node? Does it have a sort of gravitational power over the region that makes the new grid of nodes and digital highways cohere as a complex spatial agglomeration? From a larger transnational perspective, these are vastly expanded central regions. This reconstitution of the center is different from the agglomerations still prevalent in most cities that fall outside the global city dynamic and the accumulation regime it entails. The reconstitution of the center at a larger metropolitan scale points to a reorganization of space/time dimensions in the urban economy (Sassen [1991] 2001: chap. 5).

Such a rescaling can enable the traditional perimeter of the city, a kind of periphery, to develop its full industrial and structural growth potential. For example, commercial and office space development lead to a reconcentration of economic activity into a variety of nodes in the urban periphery (Kotkin 2005). This geographic shift has much to do with the locational decisions of transnational and national firms that make the urban peripheries the growth centers of the most dynamic industries. It is not the same as largely residential suburbanization or metropolitanization.

There are differences in the pattern of global city formation in parts of the United States and in parts of Western Europe (e.g., Fainstein 1993; Hitz et al. 1995; Graham and Marvin 1996; Allen, Massey, and Pryke 1999; Marcuse and Van Kempen 2000; Abrahamson 2004; Rutherford 2004; Kazepov 2005; Witlock et al. 2008; Derudder et al. 2010). In the United States, major cities such as New York and Chicago have large centers that have been rebuilt many times, given the brutal neglect suffered by much urban infrastructure and the imposed obsolescence so characteristic of US cities. This neglect and accelerated obsolescence produce vast spaces for rebuilding the center according to the requirements of whatever the prevalent regime of urban accumulation or pattern of spatial organization of the urban economy is at a given time.

In Europe, urban centers are far more protected, and they rarely contain significant stretches of abandoned space; the expansion of workplaces and the need for "intelligent" buildings necessarily will have to take place partly outside the old centers. One of the most extreme cases is the complex of La Defense, the massive, state-of-the-art office complex developed right outside Paris to avoid harming the built environment inside the city. This is an explicit instance of government policy and planning aimed at addressing the growing demand for central office space of prime quality. Yet another variant of this expansion of the center onto hitherto peripheral land can be seen in London's Docklands. This vast underutilized harbor area in London became the site of an expensive, state-of-the-art development project to accommodate the rapidly growing demand for office space, especially in the financial sector. The financial and real estate crisis of the early 1990s resulted in the collapse of the project. But by 1993, reorganization under a new consortium and a rapid demand by worldwide buyers brought full occupancy of the complex (Fainstein 2001). Similar projects for recentralizing peripheral areas were launched in several major cities in Europe, North America, and Japan during the late 1980s. What was seen in the 1980s as a derelict marginal area, Times Square in New York City, by the late 1990s had become a prime office, commercial, and entertainment area (Fainstein and Judd 1999). As with the Docklands and Times Square redevelopments, many of these did not succeed until the mid- or late 1990s, years after the crisis of 1990 to 1991. What was once the suburban fringe and urban perimeter in many of today's global and other cities has now been reconstituted as some variant of central city space.

Towards Novel Spatial Formats: Global Cities and Megaregions

The preceding sections signal the emergence of novel spatial formats due to major shifts in the scales, spaces, and contents of economic activity. Among the more prominent of these are global cities and megaregions, both of which are contributing to a whole series of old and new global intercity geographies. These shifts, in turn, call for shifts in our interpretations and policy frameworks to adjust to these novel spatial formats and maximize their benefits and distributive potential. There is by now a considerable scholarship on megaregions (e.g., Regional Planning Association 2007; Xu and Yeh 2010).

My concern here is different from the prevailing discussions, which tend to focus on geographies and on governance issues. While megaregions and global cities are different formats, elsewhere (Sassen 2007) I have argued that analytically, we can identify similar dynamics at work in each. Two such dynamics stand out. One is scaling and its consequences—in this case, megaregional scaling and global scaling. The other dynamic is the interaction between geographic dispersal and new kinds of agglomeration economies, which in this case are operating, respectively, within a megaregion and in global cities. Specifying a common analytic ground for these two very diverse spatial formats should enable us to develop a sharper approach to empirical research, and possibly, policy. These diverse spatial formats also should help in assessing the extent to which policy decisions can encourage greater economic integration between a country's more globalized city (or cities) and its other areas currently performing subordinate functions within the national territorial hierarchy. In other words, taking a megaregional scale might help in connecting the "winners" and the "laggards." Since I have already discussed global cities in this chapter, in what follows, I examine these questions through the lens of the megaregion.

The fact that the megaregion is a scale that includes both globalizing and provincial cities, as well as high- and low-development areas, presents us with an opportunity: connecting winning areas and lagging areas within a country's megaregions. One consequence of such connecting is that laggards can become part of a policy effort that now only focuses on winners, as is typical with the "targeting" of resources to enable the formation of world-class cities and silicon valleys. More precisely, laggards can be enabled to become dynamically interconnected with winners within a megaregion in ways that replicate current practices at the global scale, notably outsourcing to low-cost areas, and in novel ways made possible because the low-cost area is within a megaregion. The hope would be that rather than pursuing the usual economic policies focused on the most advanced sectors, this would make a strong case for concentrating on the poorer regions, not as charity but as a recognition that they are part of the advanced sectors; after all, when major firms outsource jobs to low-cost areas across the world, they are outsourcing some of *their* tasks. Many advanced economic sectors combine sufficiently diverse tasks that they have both a preference for lower-cost areas for some of these tasks and for dense high-cost areas for other tasks.

To mention just one of several examples, this type of framing would bring value to poorer areas within the most developed countries, as these might be developed to house activities that are now outsourced to low-wage countries. One key aim should be to avoid a race to the bottom in workplace and wage standards as happens when these activities are offshored, which might be simpler to ensure when both headquarters and low-wage activities are in the same country. A second aim should be to provide alternative or complementary development paths to what is today's prevalent path, that is, the policy preference for high-end economic activities, such as bio-tech parks and luxury office parks.

Parallel to this effort to incorporate laggards, or less successful areas, into policy frames that today target mostly successful areas is the effort to understand how cities in the middle range of urban hierarchies fit in today's global intercity geographies. In the case of the United States, for instance, many of these mid-range cities are also part of megaregions. The analytic bridge between megaregions and intercity geographies is the fact that the operational chains of a growing number of firms today are part of both these spatial formats (see Sassen 2008b; Derudder et al. 2010). This opens up a whole new research agenda about economic globalization and place, in addition to the existing global city scholarship. One component of this is whether a megaregion can seek to accommodate a larger range of the operations constituting a firm's value chain—from high-agglomeration sites to dispersal sites. Practically speaking, this points to the possibility of bringing into or back to a megaregion some of the services and goods-producing jobs and operations now offshored to get at lower wages and fewer regulations.

Can these be reinserted in the low-growth, low-cost areas of a megaregion? What type of planning would it take, and can it be done in ways that optimize the benefits for all involved, not only firms, but also workers and localities? This would expand the project of optimizing growth beyond office parks and science parks, the preferred options today, and move across far more diverse economic sectors. It would use the lever of the megaregional scale to provide diverse spaces catering to different types of activities, ranging from those subject to high- and those subject to low-agglomeration economies. And, finally, the megaregional scale would help in optimizing the growth effect arising from the interactions of some of these diverse economies. This growth effect would be optimized by re-regionalizing some of the low-cost operations of firms today spread across the country and/or the world.

This way of thinking about the megaregional scale raises the importance of planning and coordination to secure optimal outcomes for all parties involved, including the challenge of securing the benefits firms pursue when they disperse their operations to low-wage areas. This would work for some types of economic sectors and types of firms, but not for all. Some activities that have been outsourced to other countries have not worked out and have been repatriated—they range from airline sales agents to particular types of design work in industries as diverse as garments and high tech. But many of these outsourced activities are doing fine as far as the firms are concerned. Research and specific policies would be needed to establish the what, how, and where of the advantages for the pertinent firms of accessing low-wage workers within the United States. This includes understanding how location of these low-cost components in the megaregion where a given firm is headquartered could compensate for higher costs. It may require megaregional investment in developing low-cost areas for such jobs—a kind of rural enterprise zone.

There is possibly a positive macro-level effect from repatriating some of these jobs if a race to the bottom can be avoided and a certain level of consumption capacity secured in the low-income areas of a region by ensuring reasonable wages or certain kinds of indirect subsidies. This brings a specific positive effect for a megaregion's less developed areas insofar as lower-wage households tend to spend a much larger share of their income in their place of residence—they lack the investment capital of upper-income strata, who can wind up allocating most of their income on overseas investments. Finally, this is also one element in the larger challenge of securing more equitable outcomes (for an analysis of options see, e.g., Henderson 2005). It is important to ask about the distributive effects of the current configuration and of potentially optimized outcomes as described here. There is sufficient evidence about how extreme maldistribution of the benefits of economic growth is undesirable in the long run.

These ways of specifying the meaning of a megaregion (or a region) take us beyond uses of the term as a sort of conceptual "packaging" to a more dynamic concept of the megaregion. Besides urbanization advantages, a megaregion is of a sufficiently large scale to optimize the benefits of diverse and interacting low- and high-income areas. What the megaregion offers in this context is a bigger range of types of locations than a city or a metro area—it offers locations offering high-agglomeration economies all the way to locations where the advantage comes from dispersal. This would mean a direct growth effect between a megaregion's high- and low-agglomeration sites: the more the former grow, the more the latter will also grow. Then it becomes desirable for a megaregion to maximize the copresence of these two types of locations. It also means freeing the lower-income area from its policy designation as a hopeless economic laggard.

In practical terms there are, clearly, massive challenges for a megaregion to achieve this type of copresence—maximizing the extent to which a megaregion can contain both the agglomeration and dispersal segments of a firm's chain of operations. For one, it is a counterintuitive proposition. It is not easy to see why a megaregion's highly dynamic economic spaces (the central areas of its global cities and silicon valleys), anchored by the headquarters of global and national firms, might actually be partly fed and strengthened by developing the "dispersal locations" of those same firms. Thinking of developing such "dispersal locations" as one way of making the most of negative externalities might make it more acceptable to the skeptics—you might as well go for activities that benefit from geographically dispersed arrangements once you hit excess congestion disadvantages. But one option at this point is of course such items as golf courses and ex-urban oversized luxury housing. This is an argument that could be countered because megaregions tend to contain much land that is not optimal for such uses but that could be optimal for developing "dispersal locations." Further, and critical to some of my substantive concerns for disadvantaged areas, these areas could benefit from such development— if a race to the bottom is avoided. Finally, it also raises a question as to whether this connecting of winners and laggards within a country's megaregions can be extended to cross-border intercity networks by strengthening the connections between winners and laggards in the global political economy.

Notes

1   For two extraordinary and different types of accounts, see Braudel (1984) and King (1990).

2   Examples of these networks are Dubai's participation in the London Stock Exchange and other exchanges. Qatar Holding, the investment arm of Qatar Investment Authority, and NYSE Euronext established the Qatar Exchange. To this we should add the Gulf states' sovereign wealth funds, with Abu Dhabi's fund the largest in the world. It is estimated that the assets of the top ten Gulf states' sovereign funds (including Abu Dhabi, Kuwait, and Qatar) stand at US$2.2 trillion, half of which are placed in international securities.

3   Islamic finance will generate whole new sets of global circuits for Gulf cities. While Malaysia has been the hub of Islamic finance, Dubai gained much ground over the last few years, and Abu Dhabi's Islamic Bank is planning to develop Sharia wealth management opportunities in Asia.

4   For instance, Abu Dhabi's Masdar has invested in what might be the world's largest wind farm to be located in the Thames Estuary.

5   I would say the same about Dubai's use of the term for some—not all—of its "free zones," as these are about more than facilitating the operations of foreign actors as is the typical format worldwide.

6   See *The Global City* (Princeton University Press 2001; 1st ed. 1991).

7   An aspect that is often misunderstood is that the making of the space that is the global city includes key decisions, regulations, and authorizations of particular components of national governments, notably ministries of finance, central banks, and departments of commerce. The work of these government agencies is strategic for the development of the global city (see Sassen 2008a: chap. 5). This is different from free-trade zones, where the effort is to keep the state out. Thus, my analysis suggests that these new developments in the Gulf region are going to entail involvement by particular, specialized branches of their governments.

8   Securitization is the replacement of traditional bank finance with tradable debt; for example, a mortgage is bundled up along with thousands of others into a package that can be traded on specialized markets. This is one of the major innovations in the financial industry in the 1980s. Securitization made it possible to sell all kinds of (supposedly worthy) debt, thereby adding to the overall volume of transactions in the industry.

Chapter 5 Appendix

Exhibit A.5.1   Largest Exchanges by Investment Flows in 2009 and 2008

Rank	Exchange	US$ bn 2009	US$ bn 2008	% Change in US$
1	NYSE Euronext US	234.2	280.2	−16.4%
2	London Stock Exchange	122.3	124.6	−1.8%
3	Australian Securities Exchange	86.2	48.9	76.3%
4	Hong Kong Exchanges	81.4	55.0	48.0%
5	Shanghai Stock Exchange	47.7	27.6	72.8%
6	Tokyo Stock Exchange	44.2	13.8	220.3%
7	BM&FBOVESPA	41.7	28.8	44.8%
8	Borsa Italiana	25.9	11.1	133.3%
9	Shenzhen Stock Exchange	25.4	17.4	46.0%
10	BME Spanish Exchanges	21.6	32.2	−32.9%

Source: World Federation of Exchanges 2010. Market Highlights. First half of 2010. Paris: World Federation of Exchanges.

Exhibit A.5.2 Largest Exchanges by Total Value of Bonds Traded in 2009 in US$

Rank	Exchange	US$ bn 2009	US$ bn 2008	% Change in US$	% Change in Local Currency
1.	BME Spanish Exchanges	8,138	6,823	19.3%	24.5%
2.	London Stock Exchange	6,896	6,118	12.7%	22.8%
3.	NASDAQ OMX Nordic Exchange	2,419	2,942	–17.8%	–14.5%
4.	Colombia Stock Exchange	960	468	105.0%	123.5%
5.	Korea Exchange	403	348	15.9%	36.3%
6.	Istanbul Stock Exchange	402	406	–1.2%	21.2%
7.	Borsa Italiana	313	256	22.1%	26.9%
8.	Tel Aviv Stock Exchange	246	262	–6.4%	2.9%
9.	Oslo Bors	227	124	82.8%	95.8%
10.	Santiago Stock Exchange	188	167	12.6%	19.2%

Source: World Federation of Exchanges. First Half 2010 Market Highlights.

Exhibit A.5.3   Largest Growth by Total Value of Bond Trading in 2009 in %
Change in US$

Rank	Exchange	% Change 2009/2008
1.	Amman Stock Exchange	316.4%
2.	Irish Stock Exchange	252.2%
3.	Colombia Stock Exchange	105.0%
4.	Egyptian Exchange	98.0%
5.	Bombay Stock Exchange	86.6%
6.	Oslo Bors	82.8%
7.	Tokyo Stock Exchange	73.2%
8.	National Stock Exchange India	69.9%
9.	Shenzhen Stock Exchange	53.4%
10.	TMX Group	52.5%

Source: World Federation of Exchanges. First Half 2010 Market Highlights.

Exhibit A.5.4   Derivatives by Types of Market

Top Five Exchanges by Value of Securitized Derivatives Traded in US$

Rank	Exchange	US$ bn 2009	US$ bn 2008	% Change
1	Hong Kong Exchanges	429.7	574.5	–25.2%
2	Korea Exchange	174.1	85.7	103.2%
3	Deutsche Börse	87.9	165.3	–46.8%
4	SIX Swiss Exchange	34.6	55.9	–38.1%
5	Tel Aviv Stock Exchange	33.8	38.7	–12.7%

Top Five Exchanges by Number of Stock Options Contracts Traded in 2009

Rank	Exchange	Number of Contracts Traded in 2009	Number of Contracts Traded in 2008	% Change
1.	International Securities Exchange	946,693,771	989,525,443	–4.3%
2.	Chicago Board Options Exchange	911,976,695	933,855,344	–2.3%
3.	Philadelphia Stock Exchange	579,907,593	537,954,692	7.8%
4.	BM&FBOVESPA	546,317,664	350,063,629	56.1%
5.	Eurex	282,834,019	349,331,404	–19.0%

Top Five Exchanges by Number of Single Stock Futures Contracts Traded in 2009

Rank	Exchange	Number of Contracts Traded in 2009	Number of Contracts Traded in 2008	% Change
1.	NYSE Liffe Europe	165,796,059	124,468,809	33.2%
2.	National Stock Exchange India	161,053,345	225,777,205	–28.7%
3.	Eurex	113,751,549	130,210,348	–12.6%
4.	Johannesburg Stock Exchange	88,866,925	420,344,791	–78.8%
5.	BME Spanish Exchanges	37,509,467	46,237,747	–18.9%

(Continued)

Exhibit A.5.4   (Continued)

Top Five Exchanges by Number of Stock Index Options Contracts Traded in 2009

Rank	Exchange	Number of Contracts Traded in 2009	Number of Contracts Traded in 2008	% Change
1.	Korea Exchange	2,920,990,655	2,766,474,406	5.6%
2.	Eurex	364,953,360	514,894,678	–29.1%
3.	National Stock Exchange India	321,265,217	150,916,778	112.9%
4.	Chicago Board Options Exchange	222,781,717	259,496,193	–14.1%
5.	Taifex	76,177,097	98,122,308	–22.4%

Top Five Exchanges by Number of Stock Index Futures Contracts Traded in 2009

Rank	Exchange	Number of Contracts Traded in 2009	Number of Contracts Traded in 2008	% Change
1.	CME Group	703,072,175	882,432,628	–20.3%
2.	Eurex	367,546,179	511,748,879	–28.2%
3.	National Stock Exchange India	195,759,414	202,390,223	–3.3%
4.	Osaka Securities Exchange	130,107,633	131,028,334	–0.7%
5.	Korea Exchange	83,117,062	66,436,912	25.1%

Source: World Federation of Exchanges. First Half 2010 Market Highlights.

6

The New Inequalities
Within Cities

When manufacturing was the leading sector in market-based economies for much of the twentieth century, it created the conditions for the expansion of a vast middle class because (1) it facilitated unionization; (2) it was based in good part on household consumption, and hence wage levels mattered in that they created an effective demand; and (3) the relatively high wage levels and social benefits typical of the leading manufacturing sectors became a model for broader sectors of the economy. What is the impact of the ascendance of finance and producer services on the broader social and economic structure of major cities? And what are the consequences of the new urban economy for the earnings distribution of a city's workforce? It would seem that workers lacking the high levels of education required by today's advanced economic sectors in these major cities have become superfluous. The same might be said about the place of firms and sectors that appear to be backward or to lack the advanced technological and human capital base of the new leading sectors. Or are significant shares of such workers, firms, and sectors actually articulated to the economic core, but under conditions of severe segmentation in the social, economic, racial, and organizational traits of firms and workers? If so, to what extent is this segmentation produced or strengthened by the existence of ethnic or racial segmentation in combination with racism and discrimination?

Research covering the last two and even three decades shows sharp increases in socioeconomic and spatial inequalities within major cities of the developed world and now increasingly also in cities of the global South. These trends can be interpreted as merely a quantitative increase in the degree of inequality, one that is not associated with the emergence of new social forms or class realignments. But they can also be interpreted as social and economic restructuring. There is considerable evidence showing the emergence of new social forms: (1) the growth of an informal economy in large cities in highly developed countries, (2) high-income commercial and residential gentrification, and (3) the sharp rise in rich countries of a type of homelessness, for example, of families, that differs from older types, such as the proverbial hobo.

My concern in this chapter is to describe the general outlines of this transformation. The nature of the subject is such that a fully developed account would require introducing the specific conditions typical to each city, a task that falls outside the scope of this book (for a more detailed account, see Sassen [1991] 2001: chaps. 8–9; 2008b; 2010). For that reason, too, much of the empirical background shaping some of the specific statements made here comes from the case of the United States. Another reason for focusing particularly on the United States is that the trends under discussion are sharper. Most European countries have significant protections built into their social welfare systems that keep people from sinking below a certain threshold; thus, while these same structural changes are happening, the social outcomes are less extreme and hence, in a way, less visible. The first half of the chapter discusses the transformation in the organization of the labor process, particularly as it materializes in large cities. The second half focuses on the earnings distribution in a service-dominated economy. This discussion includes somewhat more detailed accounts of the informal economy and of the restructuring of urban consumption, two key processes that are part of the changed earnings distribution.

Transformations in the Organization of the Labor Process

The consolidation of a new economic core of professional and servicing activities needs to be viewed alongside the general move to a service economy and the decline of manufacturing. New economic sectors are reshaping the job supply. So too, however, are new ways of organizing work in both new and old sectors of the economy. The computer can now be used to do professional, clerical, and manufacturing work. Components of the work process that even fifteen years ago took place on the shop floor and were classified as production jobs today have been replaced by a combination of machine/service worker or worker/engineer. The machine in this case is typically computerized; for example, certain operations that once required a highly skilled craftsperson can now be done through computer-aided design and calibration. Activities that were once consolidated in a single-service retail establishment have now been divided between a service delivery outlet and central headquarters. Finally, much work that was once standardized mass production is today increasingly characterized by customization, flexible specialization, networks of subcontractors, and informalization—even, at times, including sweatshops and industrial homework. In brief, the changes in the job supply evident in major cities are a function of new sectors as well as of the reorganization of work in both the new and the old sectors.

The historical forms assumed by economic growth in the post–World War II era that contributed to the vast expansion of a middle class—notably, fixed-capital intensity, standardized production, and suburbanization-led growth—deterred and reduced systemic tendencies toward inequality by constituting an economic regime centered on mass production and mass consumption. Further, so did the cultural forms accompanying these processes, particularly through their shaping of the structures of everyday life: a large suburban middle class contributes to mass consumption and, thus, to standardization in production. These various trends led to greater levels of unionization and other forms of workers' empowerment helped by large scales of production and the centrality of mass production and mass consumption in national economic growth and profits. This form of economic growth, along with government programs, contributed to reduce poverty and expand the middle class in the United States and in most highly developed economies (see Exhibits 6.1, 6.2, and 6.3).

Of all the highly developed countries, it is the United States where these deep structural trends are most legible. National-level data for the United States show a sharp growth in inequality. For instance, economic growth from 2001 to 2005 was high but very unequally distributed. Most of it went to the upper 10% and, especially, the upper 1% of households. The rest, that is 90% of households, saw a 4.2% decline in their market-based incomes (Mishel 2007). If we disaggregate that 90%, the incidence of the loss grows as we descend the income ladder. Since the beginning of the so-called economic recovery in 2001, the income share of the top 1% grew 3.6 percentage points to 21.8% in 2005, gaining $268 billion of total US household income. In contrast, that of the lower 50% of US households fell by 1.4 percentage points to 16% in 2005, for a loss of $272 billion in income since 2001. Exhibit 6.1 traces a longer-term pattern from 1917 that shows clearly the return to extreme inequality after the decades of the

Exhibit 6.1   Top Decile Income Share, 1917–2005

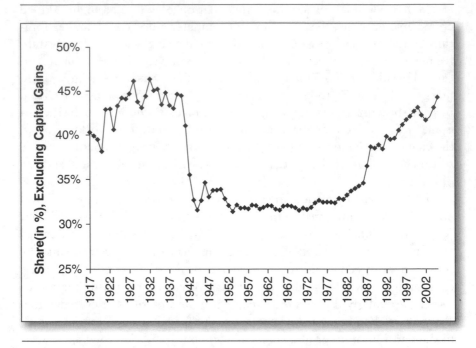

Note: Income is defined as market income but excludes capital gains.

Source: Mishel, L. 2004. "Unfettered markets, income inequality, and religious values." *Viewpoints*, 25 May. Washington, DC: Economic Policy Institute. Retrieved July 26, 2008 http://www.epi .org/publications/entry/webfeatures_viewpoints_moral_markets_presentation/. Reprinted with permission.

Keynesian period. Since the 1970s, the overall trend in the United States has been toward a growth in poverty, with frequent ups and downs.

It was also in that postwar period extending into the late 1960s and early 1970s that the incorporation of workers into formal labor-market relations reached its highest level in the most advanced economies. The formalization of the employment relation carries with it the implementation (albeit frequently precarious) of a set of regulations that have had the overall effect of protecting workers and securing the fruits of frequently violent labor struggles. But this formalization also entailed the exclusion of distinct segments of the workforce, such as women and minorities; this was particularly so in certain heavily unionized industries.

In part because of the formalization of the labor process, job growth in the 1960s occurred in all quality deciles for full-time workers, with somewhat more growth in the top deciles and somewhat less growth in the lowest deciles (see Exhibit 6.5). From a limited standpoint, much analysis

Exhibit 6.2   Income Ratio of Highest Earners to Bottom 90%

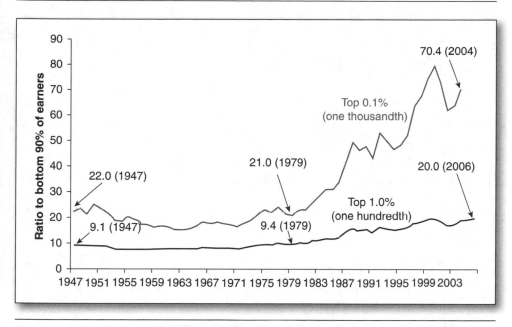

Source: Mishel, L. 2008. "Surging Wage Growth for Topmost Sliver." Economic Snapshots. June 18, 2008. Economic Policy Institute. Retrieved July 26, 2008. http://www.epi.org/content.cfm/webfeatures_snapshots_20080618. Reprinted with permission.

Exhibit 6.3   Percent Change in After-Tax Income USA 1979–2007

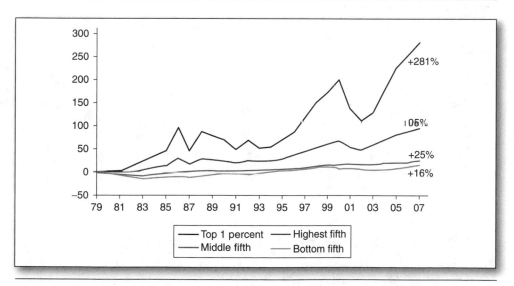

Source: Sherman, Arloc and Chad Stone. 2010. Income Gaps Between Very Rich and Everyone Else More than Tripled in Last Three Decades, New Data Show. June 25. Washington, DC: CBPP. p. 2. URL: http://www.cbpp.org/cms/index.cfm?fa=view&id=3220.

Exhibit 6.4   Poor People in the United States, 1970–2008 (in thousands)

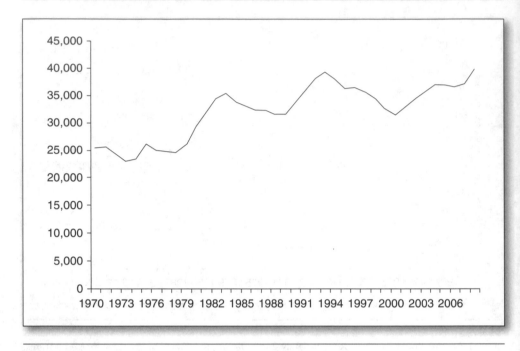

Source: Compiled from U.S. Bureau of the Census (2009a, Table B-1).

Exhibit 6.5   US Job Growth by Job Quality Decile, Full-Time Workers Ages 18–64, 1963–70

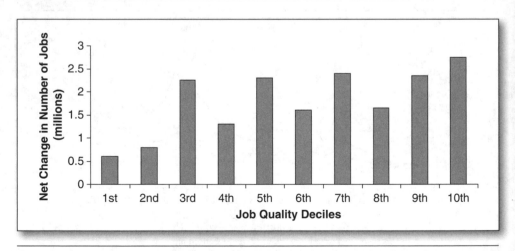

Source: Milkman, R. and Dwyer, R. 2002. "Growing Apart: The 'New Economy' and Job Polarization in California, 1992–2000." University of California Institute for Labor and Employment, Multi-Campus Research Unit, 2000; p. 12. Reprinted with permission.

of postindustrial society and advanced economies generally posits a massive growth in the need for highly educated workers, which suggests sharply reduced employment opportunities for workers with low educational levels generally and for immigrants in particular. Yet detailed empirical studies of major cities in highly developed countries show ongoing demand for low-wage workers and a significant supply of old and new jobs requiring little education and paying low wages. In the day-to-day work of the leading sectors in global cities, a large share of the jobs involved are lowly paid and manual, many held by immigrant women. Even the most advanced professionals will require clerical, cleaning, and repair workers for their state-of-the art offices, and they will require truckers to bring the software but also the toilet paper. Although these types of workers and jobs are never represented as part of the global economy, they are in fact part of the infrastructure of jobs involved in running and implementing the global economy, including such an advanced form of it as is international finance. Further, the similarly state-of-the-art lifestyles of the professionals in these sectors have created a whole new demand for a range of household workers, particularly maids and nannies. The presence of a highly dynamic sector with a polarized income distribution has its own impact on the creation of low-wage jobs through the sphere of consumption (or, more generally, social reproduction). This pattern of polarized income distribution is evident in the job growth of the 1990s, which was much more bimodal, with the most growth in the lowest quintile and the two highest quintiles (see Exhibit 6.6).

The economic and social transformations in the economy since the mid-1970s assume specific forms in urban labor markets. Changes in the functioning of urban labor markets have a number of possible origins. The most evident of these changes stem from the long-term shifts in the occupational and industrial balance of employment. Such shifts directly affect the mix of job characteristics, including earnings levels and employment stability, and the types of careers available to local workers. On the demand side, these developments include the new flexibility that employers have tended to seek under the pressure of international competition, unstable product markets, and a weakening of political support for public-sector programs. This new flexibility tends to mean more part-time and temporary jobs. On the supply side, a key factor has been the persistence of high unemployment in the 1970s and 1980s in many large cities, which notably altered the bargaining position of employers, and the insecurity or marginalization of the most disadvantaged groups in the labor market. Workers desperate for jobs in the 1980s became willing to take increasingly unattractive jobs. In combination, these major developments on both sides of the labor market, and especially strong in the

Exhibit 6.6   US Job Growth by Job Quality Decile, Full-Time Workers Ages
                 18–64 1992–2000

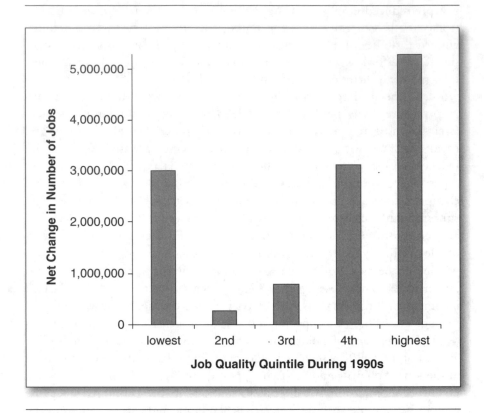

Source: Wright, E. O. and R. E. Dwyer. 2007. "The Patterns of Job Expansions in the USA: A Comparison of the 1960s and 1990s." Socio-Economic Review, Vol. 1, p. 302. Reprinted with permission.

urban core, seem likely to have induced, on the one hand, a growing destabilization of employment with increasing casualization and/or informalization of jobs and, on the other hand, an increasing polarization of employment opportunities with new types of social divisions.

Metropolitan labor markets tend to reflect a variety of background factors beyond particular restructuring effects. The most important include their sheer size and density, the particular industrial and occupational mix of their employment base, the overall state of tightness or slack in labor demand, and in many cities, the presence and characteristics of immigrant groups. Two traits of labor markets in major cities today, as in the past, are fluidity and openness; thus, the specific features of a given area can influence the types of activity prospering there and the labor-market experiences of residents. Labor markets in and around cities are *structured* by particular sets of jobs, with distinctive combinations of rewards, security, and conditions of access.

The labor market characteristics of key industries in major cities have long evinced tendencies toward shorter-term employment relationships than in other types of settings. A significant share of urban establishments operate in competitive and often highly unstable markets in sectors as diverse as the garment trade, private consumer services, building contractors, and speculative financial services. The evidence shows much higher turnover rates in these activities than in large establishments and in monopolistic, bureaucratized organizations. One key explanation for their higher incidence in urban economies is that cities provide these more unstable activities easy access to workforces that can be adjusted up and down depending on demand for their products and services.

High rates of turnover also have implications on the supply side, adding to the attractions of the city for migrants, particularly for minorities who have difficulty gaining access to more closed sectors of employment and for young, single workers for whom job security may be a lower priority. The availability of these particular labor supplies must then have further implications for employers' strategies. The actual structure of urban labor markets has been more complex and changeable than can be explained in terms of agglomeration economies and the "natural selection" of activities and groups of workers. The high unemployment levels in many European cities in the 1980s and continuing in the 1990s, albeit with some declines, capture the overall outcome of these various processes (see Exhibit 6.7). The European case is particularly interesting because it has a stronger tradition of government protection of workers.

The potential importance of the presence or absence of a large immigrant labor force extends to a range of issues, including the level of wages in the lower part of the labor market and its implications for the cost of living and the competitiveness of local activities, as well as for patterns of segmentation and opportunities of advancement for indigenous workers. Furthermore, given the typical concentration of new migrants in central cities, immigration contributes to changes in spatial patterns in labor supply. The marked decentralization of the white population into the outer rings of metropolitan regions, again, especially in the United States where it has often taken the form of white flight to the suburbs, was counterbalanced by mostly third-world immigration into urban centers from the mid-1970s on. Beginning in the 1980s, there was a positive influx of young, highly educated whites

Exhibit 6.7   Unemployment in Select European Cities, 1980, 1990, 2001, and 2004 (percentage)

Unemployment				
City	1980	1990	2001	2004
Amsterdam	8.2	19.5 (1988)	4.3	7.3
Barcelona	15.5 (1981)	14.6 (1988)	10.4	12.0
Birmingham	15	10.3	9.5	8.5
Brussels	6	16.7 (1989)	18.3	21.2
Copenhagen	7.8	11.3 (1988)	4.5	5.2
Dortmund	5.7	11.9	13.5	15
Dublin	9.9	18.4 (1987)	6.7	5.4
Glasgow	8	15	10.8	7.8
Hamburg	3.2	11.2	7.6	10.7
Liverpool	16	20	11.1	8.0
Lyon	6.1	8.3	11.5	11.3
Madrid	12	12.5	12.4	6.6
Marseilles	12.2	18.1	20.3	16.9
Montpellier	6.8	10.3	18	NA
Paris	7	8.4	11.7	11.3
Rennes	8.1	10.1	9	NA
Rotterdam	8.8	17.1 (1988)	5.9	9.7
Seville	18.7	25.2	22.8	14.3
Valencia	9.9	17.5	14.2	7.4

Sources: 1980–1990 data based on European Institute of Urban Affairs (1992: 83–87). 2001 and 2004 data based on EUROSTAT (2005, 2010). The Urban Audit. Data accessible online at http://www.urbanaudit.org.

into central cities, and most recently, there has been significant growth in suburban immigrant settlement, especially in the United States. Today, major US cities tend to have higher shares of immigrants and highly educated high-income professionals than was the case in the 1960s and 1970s.

A sharp representation of these distributions emerges out of the urban moment of these polarization dynamics. Minoritized workers and house-holds are disproportionately concentrated in large cities. Thus, the official poverty rate for the United States is about 18%. While this is very high for a rich country, it is far higher in many US cities. This also holds for cities that are not considered poor: thus, the poverty rate is 38% in Miami, 25% in New York, Chicago, and Minneapolis, and 23% in Houston, Los Angeles, and Washington, DC These same cities have far more high-income households than the average for the United States: more than 30% in San Francisco, 26% in Washington, DC, 20% in New York and Boston, 19% in Los Angeles, and 17% in Chicago. Upper-middle-income households are between 19 and 21% in New York, San Francisco, Los Angeles, and Washington, DC and fall to 15% in Atlanta and 11% in Miami. Together, the upper- and upper-middle-income groups are about half of these cities' residents, a far larger proportion than in the postwar era up to the 1980s, when half of their populations were more likely to be in the middle sector. In 2006, the middle sector was between 18% and 25%. Exhibit 6.8 is an overview that brings out these segmentations in some of the most powerful and rich cities in the United States today.

One key growth trend that lies behind the expansion of a very high-income 10% of the population, which in major cities easily becomes 20%, is the expansion and consolidation of high-level services, mostly for firms. While these services are also bought by governments and households, it is above all the new requirements of doing business, running exchanges, and running complex organizations (whether hospitals, mines, financial services firms, or exchanges) that feeds the most advanced components of this sector and has made it into the economic core of major cities in highly developed countries. While this sector may not account for the majority of jobs, it establishes a new regime of economic activity and the associated spatial and social transformations particularly evident in major cities.[1]

A second key growth trend is that as the worldwide network of global cities has grown, it has brought with it an influx of high-income transna-tional professionals and managers. It has also meant a growth in white residents in some of our major cities.[2] Exhibits 6.8 and 6.9 show data for some of the major and minor global cities in the United States in the last decade. (See also 4.1–4.4.) Thus, Atlanta—which, according to a major global cities study, has now entered the top echelons of US global cities—has seen its white population grow by 20% from 2000 to 2005. And Washington, which has established itself as a key economic center over the last few years, has seen its white population grow by 15%. In comparison,

Exhibit 6.8   Economic Inequality in Major US Cities by Race, 2006

City	White Median Income	Black Median Income	Latino Median Income	Asian Median Income	White Poverty Rate (%)	Black Poverty Rate (%)	Latino Poverty Rate (%)
Atlanta	77,236	25,674	37,673	44,102	7.2	32.8	—
Boston	60,521	31,915	28,276	37,044	12.9	26.8	27.0
Chicago	60,166	28,607	39,526	51,677	9.7	32.0	21.6
Dallas	60,191	28,200	31,466	46,779	7.6	28.2	29.0
Houston	61,124	29,772	32,367	42,455	8.9	29.9	25.5
Los Angeles	62,634	31,051	35,496	49,920	10.0	26.3	24.9
Miami	63,723	18,710	25,673	36,541	14.7	41.0	24.8
New York	62,931	36,589	32,791	48,951	11.1	22.7	27.9
Philadelphia	43,580	26,728	23,469	36,221	13.8	31.6	39.2
San Francisco	82,177	31,080	49,561	55,072	9.1	31.1	15.2
Washington, DC	91,631	34,484	43,547	67,137	8.1	26.8	18.4
Average	65,992	29,346	34,531	46,900	10.3	29.9	25.2

Source: Based on Brookings Institute. "Living Cities Census Series" [Data file]. Retrieved May 2008 http://www.brookings.edu/projects/Living-Cities.aspx.

New York which has long been a global city, only had a 1.9% growth in this period; the equivalent periods for New York were the 1980s and early 1990s, when its only growing population segments, amid overall population decline, were highly educated young whites and immigrants. In the rest of the twenty-five cities in the Brookings sample, the white population had negative growth rates, ranking from small changes of between –2% and –5% for Denver, San Francisco, and Houston to –7% for Chicago and –14% for Miami. In this second group, Chicago is the only global city; its global power has grown sharply in the last decade, and its white resident population has actually grown considerably if we take the center of the city, rather than Cook County, the larger unit usually measured.[3]

The foreign-born population has also grown significantly—in a pattern reminiscent of New York in the 1980s, Atlanta also leads here. The share of the foreign population who have entered the United States since 2000 was 48% of Atlanta's foreign population, 33% of Washington's foreign population, 32% of Houston's, 24% of Miami's, 23% of Chicago's, and about 20% each of New York's, San Francisco's, and Los Angeles's. Thus, the older immigration cities have a relative decline in their increase in post-2000 foreign entries. Trends toward concentration of immigrants and ethnic populations in the center are also evident in other major cities in the developed world, from the well-known case of London to the little-known one of Tokyo.

The expansion of low-wage jobs as a function of growth trends implies a reorganization of the capital–labor relation. To see this effect clearly, we must distinguish the *characteristics* of jobs from their sectoral

Exhibit 6.9   Major US Cities: Foreign-born Population Entering US Since 2000, 2006

City	Foreign-born Population	Entering US Since 2000	Share (%)
Atlanta	34,682	16,563	47.8
Boston	156,591	45,030	28.8
Chicago	599,802	140,332	23.4
Dallas	321,253	98,043	30.5
Houston	576,035	177,772	30.9
Los Angeles	1,507,032	308,462	20.5
Miami	206,485	49,499	24.0
New York	3,038,139	628,944	20.7
Philadelphia	157,661	54,095	34.3
San Francisco	270,357	51,923	19.2
Washington, DC	73,820	24,189	32.8

Source: Brookings Institute. "Living Cities Census Series" [Data file]. Retrieved May 2008 http://www.brookings.edu/projects/Living-Cities.aspx.

location. That is, highly dynamic, technologically advanced growth sectors may well contain low-wage, dead-end jobs. Furthermore, the distinction between sectoral characteristics and sectoral growth patterns is crucial: backward sectors such as downgraded manufacturing or low-wage service occupations can be part of major growth trends in a highly developed economy. It is often assumed that backward sectors express decline trends. Similarly, there is a tendency to assume that advanced industries, such as finance, have mostly good, white-collar jobs, when in fact they also have a significant share of low-paying jobs, from cleaners to stock clerks.

It is easy to think of finance and specialized services as a matter of expertise rather than of production. High-level business services, from accounting to decision-making expertise, are not usually analyzed in terms of their production processes. Insufficient attention has gone to the actual array of jobs, from high-paying to low-paying, involved in the production of these services. The production process itself, moreover, includes a variety of workers and firms not usually thought of as part of the information economy—notably, secretaries, maintenance workers, and truckers. These jobs are also key components of the service economy. No matter how high a place a city occupies in the new transnational hierarchies, it will have a significant share of low-wage jobs, often viewed as irrelevant in an advanced information economy when they are actually an integral component.

There have been transformations in the forms of organizing manufacturing, with a growing presence of small-batch production, high product differentiation, and rapid changes in output. These elements have promoted subcontracting and the use of flexible ways of organizing production, both of which can be found in advanced or in backward industries. Such ways of organizing production assume distinct forms in the labor market, in the components of labor demand, and in the conditions under which labor is employed. Indications of these changes are the decline of unions in manufacturing, the loss of various contractual protections, and the increase of involuntary part-time and temporary work and other forms of contingent labor. An extreme indication of this downgrading is the growth of sweatshops and industrial homework. The expansion of a downgraded manufacturing sector partly involves the same industries that used to have largely organized plants and reasonably well-paid jobs, but it replaces these with different forms of production and organization of the work process, such as piecework and industrial homework. But it also involves new kinds of activity associated with the new major growth trends. The possibility for manufacturers to develop alternatives to the organized factory becomes particularly significant in growth sectors. The consolidation of a downgraded manufacturing sector—whether through social or technical transformation—can be seen as a politico-economic response to the growing average wages and militancy in the 1960s and early 1970s in a growing number of countries.

New types of labor market segmentation began to emerge in the 1980s. Two characteristics stand out. One is a shift of some labor market functions and costs to households and communities. The second is the weaker role of the firm in structuring the employment relation; more is now left to the market. The first is particularly evident in the immigrant community. But it is part, possibly, of a more generalized pattern that deserves further research (see Sassen 1995). There is a large body of evidence showing that once one or a few immigrant workers are hired in a given workplace, they will bring in other members from their communities as job openings arise. There is also evidence showing great willingness on the part of immigrant workers to help those they bring in with some training on the job, teaching the language, and just generally socializing them into the job and workplace. This amounts to a displacement of traditional labor market functions such as recruitment, screening, and training from the labor market and the firm to the community or household. This displacement of labor market functions to the community or household raises the responsibility and the costs for workers of participating in the labor force, even if these costs are often not monetized.[4] These are all subjects that require new research given the transitions we are living through.

As for the weaker role of the firm in organizing the employment relation, it takes on many different forms. One is the declining weight of internal labor markets in structuring employment. This corresponds both to the shrinking weight of vertically integrated firms and the restructuring of labor demand in many firms toward bipolarity—a demand for highly specialized and educated workers alongside a demand for basically unskilled workers whether for clerical work, services, industrial services, or production jobs. The shrinking demand for intermediate levels of skill and training has, in turn, reduced the need and advantages for firms of having internal labor markets with long promotion lines that function as training-on-the-job mechanisms. The decentralization of the large, vertically integrated manufacturing firms, including the offshoring of parts of the production process, has contributed to the decline in the share of unionized shops, the deterioration of wages, and the expansion of sweatshops and industrial homework. This process includes the downgrading of jobs within existing industries and the job-supply patterns of some of the new industries, notably electronics assembly.

The recomposition in household consumption patterns particularly evident in large cities contributes to a different organization of work from that prevalent in large, standardized establishments. This difference in the organization of work is evident in both the retail and the production phases. High-income gentrification generates a demand for goods and services that are frequently not mass produced or sold through mass outlets. Customized production, small runs, specialty items, and fine food dishes are generally produced through labor-intensive methods and sold through small, full-service outlets. Subcontracting part of this production to low-cost operations, as well as sweatshops or households, is common. The overall outcome for the job supply and the range of firms involved in this production and delivery are rather different from those characterizing the large department stores and supermarkets where standardized products and services are prevalent, and hence acquisition from large, standardized factories located outside the city or the region is the norm. Proximity to stores is of far greater importance with customized producers. Furthermore, unlike customized production and delivery, mass production and mass distribution outlets facilitate unionizing.

The observed changes in the occupational and earnings distributions are outcomes not only of industrial shifts but also of changes in the organization of firms and of labor markets. There has been a strengthening of differences within major sectors, notably within services. One set of service industries tends toward growing capital–labor ratios, growing productivity, and intensive use of the most advanced technologies and the other toward continued labor intensity and low wages. Median earnings and median educational levels are also increasingly divergent for each of these subsectors. These characteristics in each set of industries contribute to a type of cumulative causation within each set: the first group of industries experiences pressures toward even higher capital–labor ratios and productivity levels, given high wages, while in the second group of industries, low wages are a deterrent toward greater use of capital-intensive technologies, and low productivity leads to even more demand for very-low-wage workers. These conditions, in turn, contribute to reproduce the difference in profit-making capacities embedded in each of these subsectors.

What we might call "urban manufacturing" (see Mitchell and Sassen 1996) remains a crucial economic sector in all of these economies, even when more traditional forms of manufacturing may have ceased to be so in some of these cities. Manufacturing in a city like New York ranges from apparel production for the fashion industry to woodwork and metal making for architects, furniture designers, and other design industries. For instance, such leading cultural industries as theater and opera demand significant inputs from manufacturing for costumes and stage sets. I define urban manufacturing as a kind of manufacturing that (1) inverts the traditional relationship of manufacturing and services, in that this is manufacturing that services service industries, and (2) needs an urban location because (a) that is where its demand is located, (b) its production process is deeply networked in terms of suppliers and subcontractors, and (c) it typically requires rather fast turnover times and much detailed consulting and checking with the customer. At the level of policy, urban manufacturing is typically not receiving the kind of support and recognition it needs in order to survive in today's urban economies dominated by high-profit-making firms. In fact, urban manufacturing to some extent takes place in sweatshops. Yet a strong urban manufacturing sector is necessary for many of today's key service industries.

Two rather contrasting components of advanced service-based urban economies that characterize all global cities are the so-called cultural sector and a new type of informal economy. Beginning in the 1980s and taking off in the late 1990s, the so-called cultural industries saw rapid growth (Clark 2003; Florida 2004, 2006; Lloyd 2005). Although these have long played critical roles in major cities around the world, what happened during the last decade is a sort of industrializing of culture and an expansion of the designation of the economics involved. The development of conference and entertainment complexes is one case in point. Festivals of all kinds are another growth sector. Even street performers are now seen as value-adding and licensed in a growing number of cities. The notion of creative cities is the latest addition: it encompasses not only this mix of cultural and entertainment industries but also the fact that the growing specialized service industries employ increasingly talented creative people who, in turn, want culturally developed cities to live and work in. There is today a vast literature on these issues, among which the volume by Zukin (2005) stands out (but see also Florida 2006). The best work in this field, combining the notion of "creative industries" with a critical political economy, is Lloyd's book on neo-bohemias (2005). Two features of this cultural turning of cities are the emergence of cities as tourism destinations (Fainstein and Judd 1999) and as informal spaces for cultural work (Lloyd 2005). As more and more people live in suburbs and in small towns, large complex cities become a form of exotic landscape. A growing number of tourists want to go to a city not simply for its museums or antiquities but also to experience what might be called *urban exotica*—the punk scene, the mix of people from all over the world, the latest brand-name architecture, and street performers, to name just a few. The current vigor of informal cultural work in cities—parades, street performance, and the theatricalization of politics—is a whole subject unto itself. What matters for the purposes of this book is that these transformations in the world of the political also contribute to the experience of a renaissance in cities.

The Informal Economy

A good part of the downgraded manufacturing sector is an instance of the informalization of a growing range of economic activities in today's large cities. Although such informal sectors are thought to emerge only in global South cities, in the 1980s, rapid growth of informal work began to develop in most major global North cities, from New York and Los Angeles to Paris and Amsterdam. This became a controversial subject at the time given the lack of definitive data, but above all, because it went against the trend of increased regulation of the economy that began in the early 1900s. This trend also fed theoretical models that posit a progressive modernization of economies with no room for informalization, which in this context represented a move back, an undoing of a century-long pattern. But to some of us, there was no doubt this was happening; our fieldwork made it irrefutable (Portes, Castells, and Benton 1989; Sassen-Koob 1982, 1984; Sassen 1998: chap. 8; Renooy 1984; WIACT 1993; Komlosy et al. 1997). The issue was not the existence of informalization, but how to interpret it. Several detailed field studies in major cities of developed countries in the 1990s provided further important insights into the scale and dynamics of the informal economy. See the studies by Lazzarato (1997), Peraldi and Perrin (1996), Komlosy et al. (1997), Tabak and Chrichlow (2000), Martin (1997), Russell and Rath (2002), to name but a few that have detailed field studies on the informal economy in advanced economies.

Two spheres need to be distinguished for the circulation of goods and services produced in the informal economy. One sphere circulates internally and mostly meets the demands of its members, such as small immigrant-owned shops in the immigrant community; the other circulates through the "formal" sector of the economy. In this second sphere, informalization represents a direct profit-maximizing strategy, one that can operate through subcontracting, the use of sweatshops and homework, or direct acquisition of goods or services. All these options also raise the flexibility for contractors. Informalization tends to downgrade manufacturing work and, perhaps increasingly, also to downgrade mass-consumer services, whether public or private. But it also contributes to lowering the costs of high-priced goods and services for non-mass-consumer markets.

The combination of several trends particularly evident in major cities provides inducements to informalization: (1) the increased demand for high-priced, customized services and products by the expanding high-income population; (2) the increased demand for extremely low-cost services and products by the expanding low-income population; (3) the demand for customized services and goods or limited runs from firms that are either final or intermediate buyers, a trend that also leads to the growth of subcontracting; (4) the increasing inequality in the bidding power of different types of firms in a context of acute pressures on land because of the rapid growth and strong agglomeration patterns of the leading industries; and (5) the continuing demand by various firms and sectors of the population—including demand from leading industries and high-income workers—for goods and services typically produced in firms with low profit rates that find it increasingly difficult to survive above ground, given rising rents and production costs and multiple regulations.

The transformation of final and intermediate consumption and the growing inequality in the bidding power of firms and households create inducements for informalization in a broad range of activities and spheres of the economy. The existence of an informal economy, in turn, emerges as a mechanism for reducing costs, even in the case of firms and households that do not need it for survival, and for providing flexibility in instances where this is essential or advantageous (Sassen 1998: chap. 8).

The Earnings Distribution in a Service-Dominated Economy

What are the impacts of these various shifts on the earnings distribution and income structure in a service-dominated economy? By the 1990s, it had become clear that something was changing sharply. A growing body of studies on the occupational and earnings distribution in service industries in the 1990s found that services produce a larger share of low-wage jobs than does manufacturing, although the latter may increasingly be approaching parity with services. Moreover, several major service industries also were found to produce a larger share of jobs in the highest-paid occupations (Stanback and Noyelle 1982; Silver 1984; Nelson and Lorence 1985; Sheets, Nord, and Phelps 1987; Harrison and Bluestone 1988; Goldsmith and Blakely 1992; Munger 2002; Economic Policy Institute 2005b).

Much scholarly attention focused on the importance of manufacturing in reducing income inequality in the 1950s and 1960s (Blumberg 1981; Stanback et al. 1981). Central reasons typically identified for this effect are the greater productivity and higher levels of unionization found in manufacturing. Clearly, however, these studies tend to cover a period largely characterized by such conditions. Since the 1970s, the organization of jobs in manufacturing has undergone pronounced transformation. In what was at the time a major breakthrough and the most detailed analysis of occupational and industry data, Harrison and Bluestone (1988) found that earnings in manufacturing in the 1980s were lower than in the preceding two decades in many industries and occupations. This type of analysis has not been replicated with more updated data sets. Glickman and Glasmeier (1989) found that a majority of manufacturing jobs in the Sunbelt during the high-growth years of the 1970s and 1980s were low wage, and Fernandez-Kelly and Sassen (1992) found growth of sweatshops and homework and declining wages in several industry branches in New York and Los Angeles in the late 1980s.

A considerable number of studies with a strong theoretical bent (Sassen-Koob 1982, 1988; Massey 1984; Scott and Storper 1986; Lipietz 1988; Hill 1989) argued that the declining centrality of mass production in national growth and the shift to services as the leading economic sector contributed to the demise of a broader set of arrangements. In the post–World War II period, the economy functioned according to a dynamic that transmitted the benefits accruing to the core manufacturing industries onto more peripheral sectors of the economy. The benefits of price and market stability and increases in productivity could be transferred to a secondary set of firms, including suppliers and subcontractors, but also to less directly related industries, for example, through the consumption of high-wage factory workers. Although there was still a vast array of firms and workers that did not benefit from this shadow effect, their number was probably at a minimum in the postwar period. By the early 1980s, the wage-setting power of leading manufacturing industries had fallen sharply, as is evident in Exhibit 6.10. The rise in hourly production wages that begins in the 1990s is in good part due to the explosive growth of the high-tech manufacturing sector and of biotechnology (see generally Exhibits 6.9 and 6.10).

Scholarship on the impact of services on the income structure of cities, always a challenge compared to national income data, began to emerge in the 1980s for most countries. Several detailed analyses of the social impact of service growth in major metropolitan areas in the United States for the period of the shift of concern here are worth discussing (Stanback and Noyelle 1982; Ross and Trachte 1983; Nelson and Lorence 1985; Sheets et al. 1987; Fainstein et al. 1992). Sheets et al. (1987) found that from 1970 to 1980, several service industries had a significant effect on the growth of underemployment, which they define as employment paying below poverty-level wages in the 199 largest metropolitan areas. The strongest effect was associated with the growth of producer services and retail trade. The highest relative contribution resulted from what the authors call "corporate services" (FIRE [finance, insurance, and real estate], business services, legal services, membership organizations, and professional services), such that a 1% increase in employment in these services was found to result in a 0.37% increase in full-time, year-round, low-wage jobs. Furthermore, a 1% increase in distributive services resulted in a 0.32% increase in full-time, year-round, low-wage jobs. In contrast, a 1% increase in personal services was found to result in a 0.13% increase in such full-time jobs and a higher share of part-time, low-wage jobs. The retail industry had the highest effect on the creation of part-time, year-round, low-wage jobs, such that a 1% increase in retail employment was found to result in a 0.88% increase in such jobs. These changing features of the job supply contribute to explain the changes in the quality of jobs between the 1960s and the 1990s (see Exhibits 6.5 and 6.6).

The changing income ratio of the highest earners to the bottom 90% reveals the vast inequalities between these segments of the working population. As already discussed, in the last three decades, the income ratio between the top 1.0% and the bottom 90% changed from 9.4 to 20.0 in 1979 to 2007, and the income ratio between the top 0.1% and the bottom 90% changed from 21.0 to 70.4 between 1979 and 2004 (see Exhibit 6.2). Further, from 1970 to 2007, the real average hourly earnings of the least educated workers, those with less than a high school degree, has gradually decreased, while the wage for the most educated workers, those with college and advanced degrees, has increased (see Exhibit 6.10). Meanwhile, however, the weekly and hourly earnings of production and nonsupervisory workers in the United States, which comprises 80% of the workforce, has varied (see Exhibit 6.11). Though wages fell briefly in the early 1970s and recovered within a few years, they took a major plunge in the late 1970s and did not begin to recover until the early 1990s.

But what was the impact of services on the expansion of high-income jobs throughout this period? Nelson and Lorence (1985) examined this question using census data on the 125 largest urban areas. To establish why male earnings are more unequal in metropolises with high levels of service-sector employment, they measured the ratio of median earnings over the fifth percentile to identify the difference in earnings between the least affluent and the median metropolitan male earners; and they measured the ratio at the ninety-fifth percentile to establish the gap between median and affluent earners. Overall, they found that inequality in the 125 areas appeared to be the result of greater earnings disparity between the highest and the median earners than between the median and the lowest earners (Nelson

Exhibit 6.10   Average Real Hourly Wages of All Workers by Education in the
United States, 1973–2007 (2007 US$)

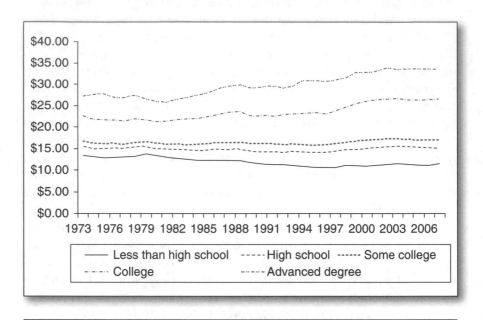

Note: Analysis of US Bureau of the Census Current Population Survey data described in Appendix B of the source publication.

Source: Compiled from Economic Policy Institute (2008b).

and Lorence 1985: 115). Furthermore, they found that the strongest effect came from the producer services and that the next strongest was far weaker (social services in 1970 and personal services in 1980). What had been only dimly perceived and discarded by many as measurement quirks became a full-blown reality in the 1990s. By 2008, these trends were still continuing. The growth in the share of income going to the top fifth of families in the United States grew, while every other sector of the population lost share (see Exhibit 6.12); average hourly wages of workers with top levels of education grew while those of workers with lower levels fell (see Exhibits 6.10 and 6.11); and income grew increasingly unequal (see Exhibit 6.2).

The share of income going to the top fifth of families has continued to grow for nearly four decades. Though the numbers were stark in 1970 and 1990 between the top earners and everyone else, the situation has continued to worsen. By 2008, the top fifth of families received 47.8% of the country's aggregate income—nearly half. In comparison, the bottom

Exhibit 6.11   Real Average Weekly and Hourly Earnings of Production and
Nonsupervisory Workers in the United States, 1970–2007 (2007 US$)

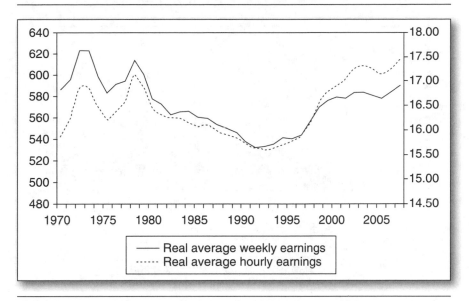

Notes: Analysis of US Bureau of the Census Current Population Survey data described in Appendix B of the source publication.

Production and nonsupervisory workers account for more than 80% of wage and salary employment.

Source: Compiled from Economic Policy Institute (2008a).

fifth of families received only 4% of aggregate income. And the top 5% of families now have 20.5% of the country's aggregate income—more than four times that of the bottom 20% (see Exhibit 6.12). Families may have several earners; hence, the figures can show lower degrees of inequality than among individual earners.

These trends also emerged in this period to variable extents for other major cities. For example, the occupational composition of residents in central Tokyo underwent considerable change with the shift to the new economy in the 1980s. There was a tendency for growing numbers of upper-level professional workers and low-wage workers to live in central cities: Sonobe (1993) found that the share of the former grew from 20% of all workers in 1975 to more than 23% in 1985, and (although difficult to measure) the numbers of low-wage legal and undocumented immigrants also grew and have grown sharply since then. The share of middle-level workers, however, fell: for example, the share of skilled workers fell from

Exhibit 6.12   Share of Aggregate Income Received by Each Fifth and Top 5% of
Families in the United States, 1970, 1990, and 2008 (percentage)

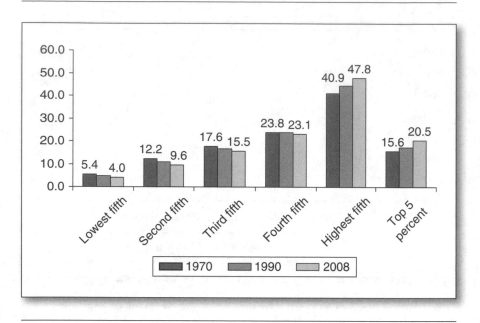

Source: Compiled from US Bureau of the Census (2009b).

16% in 1975 to 12% in 1985. Similar patterns hold for other areas of the city (Sonobe 1993). The total size of the resident workforce stayed the same, at about 4.3 million in 1975 and in 1985. The growth of high-income professional and managerial jobs in the second half of the 1980s and again in the late 1990s further reinforced this trend.

Gottschalk and Smeeding (1997) reviewed the research on earnings trends taking off in the 1980s across developed countries and found four trends: (1) Almost all industrial economies experienced some increase in wage inequality among prime-aged men in the 1980s, with Germany and Italy the exceptions; (2) there are large differences across countries, with the United States and the United Kingdom showing the sharpest inequality in earnings and Europe's Nordic countries the least; (3) the increasing demand for more skilled workers, coupled with the differences across countries in the growth in the supply of skilled workers, explains a large part of differences in trends and returns to education and experience, but it does not explain the whole difference; and (4) institutional constraints on wages also seem to matter. The fact that there was not a relative increase in unemployment among the least skilled in countries with centralized wage-setting institutions suggests that these institutions helped to limit the rise of inequality. In the 1990s, the United States and the United Kingdom stand out among all developed countries as showing the most pronounced increase in inequality (OECD 1996: 63).

What we are seeing are diverse outcomes, but they are all going in the same general direction of growing earnings inequality. A second group showed substantial increases but not as sharp as those in the United States: Canada, Australia, and Israel. Small changes over the period were evident in Japan, France, the Netherlands, Sweden, and Finland, though inequality began rising more sharply toward the end of the 1980s. Many of the Nordic countries started from a very low level of inequality, thus making its increase far less evident than in the United States. While the absolute decline at the bottom of the earnings distribution holds almost exclusively for the United States, even where no absolute declines are evident, there were relative declines in some countries, notably Japan and the United Kingdom (OECD 1993: Table 5.2). A recent study of twenty-five developed and developing nations showed all but one country rising in equality from the late 1980s to the late 1990s. Furthermore, in fifteen of the twenty-five, inequality rose by more than 7% through those years, with two of those fifteen rising by more than 15% (New Zealand and the Czech Republic). This same study reveals that while average incomes were generally rising across these nations, since 1973, the incomes of the top fifth percentile have risen by nearly 50%, while the bottom fifth's have declined by approximately 4% (Smeeding 2002).

In many OECD (Organization for Economic Cooperation and Development) countries, large shares of workers are covered by collective bargaining and the centralization of wage setting. This explains part of the difference in the degree of increases in inequality. The lower-income segments are especially likely not to be allowed to fall through some basic safety net level, unlike what is the case in the United States. This means that in the United States, the bottom 10% actually wind up with lower living standards than the bottom 10% in the other fourteen developed countries, even though the latter have a lower median than that of the United States. Even countries whose median is only about 70% of the US median have a better standard of living in the bottom percentile than the United States.

The growth in earnings inequality evident at the national level in the United States is fully evident in the New York area. From 1979 to 1996, earnings inequality in the New York–New Jersey region grew by more than 50%, notwithstanding the strong growth of the second half of the 1990s

(Brauer, Khan, and Miranda 1998), a figure we arrive at by using the top and bottom percentiles for year-round, full-time workers, both men and women. Full-time, year-round male workers ages 25 to 64 in the ninetieth percentile saw a 26% increase in real earnings from 1979 to 1996 (from $63,700 to $80,000), while earnings of those at the tenth percentile fell by 21% (from $19,000 to $15,000). The trend was similar for women with a gain from $39,300 to $54,000 at the top and a loss from $13,200 to $12,300 at the bottom. These gains at the ninetieth percentile were sharper than the 10% gain for the country. Between 1989 and 1996, total declines in earnings for full-time male workers at the tenth percentile were nearly double the nation's, while those at the top rose much faster than the nation's. The higher degree of inequality in the New York City (NYC) area is due largely to the financial-services industry. It pushed earnings in the top percentile higher. From 1989 to 1996, earnings at the ninetieth percentile grew by 8%, compared with 0.6% in the country as a whole. In that same period, earnings at the tenth percentile fell by 27% in the NYC region, compared with 7.8% for the country as a whole. Recent data show 34% of NYC families having annual incomes under $12,000, compared with the national average of only 16%. Manhattan also has the highest income disparity of all 3,200 counties in the United States (see Brauer et al. 1998; Orr and Rosen 2000; Nepomnyaschy and Garfinkel 2002; Beveridge 2003).

In the United States, much of the decline in the relative economic well-being of the least skilled has taken the form of collapsing real wages. Gottschalk and Smeeding (1997) describe who lost and who gained from 1973 to 1994: 78% of male workers in 1994 earned less than their counterparts in 1973. The growth in inequality in this period was driven in large part by this decline in real earnings of workers with the least education. The real weekly earnings of college graduates increased by 5%, while that of high school grads declined by 20%. Robert Topel (1997: 57) offers another angle: Indexed to 1969, real wages at the ninetieth percentile (high-wage workers) rose slightly, but they fell substantially at the fiftieth percentile and collapsed at the bottom of the distribution—the bottom tenth percentile. "As a measure of inequality, then, the 90–10 wage differential among American men expanded by a startling 49 percent in 26 years, with over two-thirds of this gap attributable to a decline in real wages among those in the 10th percentile." Several studies estimate that the decline in the real minimum wage accounts for 30% of the increase in earning inequality (Fortin and Lemieux 1997). According to Gordon (1996: 206), the most important factor has to do with management's decisions and practices. Estimates of the impact of unions put their decline at 20% of the increase in male earnings inequality, but for little in that of women (Freeman 1994;

Fortin and Lemieux 1997). Economic growth since the mid-1990s has helped raise real wages for all quintiles back above their 1970s levels, but this recovery has not been a balanced one. According to the US Bureau of the Census, from 1970 to 2003, the aggregate national income share of the top 5% in the United States went from 16% to 21% and for the top 20% from 41% to 48%. All these figures will tend to underestimate inequality insofar as the top earners also have nonsalary-based gains in wealth, and the bottom fifth measure will tend to exclude many of the poor who lack any source of income and are dependent on friends and family or become home- less and dependent on charities. In a 2005 report, the EPI stated: "These more aggregate statistics have also been suggestive of increasing inequality, as a larger-than-usual share of national income took the form of non-labor income (e.g., investment income and profits) that tend to accrue to those at the upper end of the wealth scale" (Economic Policy Institute 2005a).

The Birth of Global Slums

Increasing inequality on the global scale has also had a clearly urban dimension that can be seen in the formation of megaslums. The global eco- nomic restructuring that brought about the appearance of global cities has also promoted the formation of slums on an unprecedented scale. In *Planet of Slums*, Mike Davis shows how this global economic restructuring has made living in the countryside untenable for many of the world's poorest (Davis 2006). Privatization of public utilities, elimination of agricultural subsidies, reduction of tariffs on foreign imports, cuts in public spending— these same policies that opened international markets and produced unprecedented profit-making opportunities for the rich also destroyed rural livelihoods. In Davis's account, slum dwellers are drawn to cities not because of employment opportunities but because of the untenability of rural life. This produces urban population growth that is dissociated from economic growth.

Megaslums have emerged as products of global economic restructuring, but they are also increasingly integrated into global circuits (http://blogs .forbes.com/megacities/2011/03/22/the-global-city-and-the-global- slum/#more-33; http://blogs.forbes.com/megacities/2011/03/28/la-salada- the-largest-informal-market-in-south-america/). Communications technologies and a critical density have produced the emergence of slum dweller activist organizations that are active on an international scale. For instance, Slum Dwellers International is a transnational network of local slum dweller organizations that involves a credit and savings program, women's advo- cacy, information and strategy exchanges, and efforts to prevent eviction as well as various other development strategies (www.sdinet.org). This reflects the emergence of a new globally articulated subjectivity within slums. It is in this sense that we are witnessing the emergence of global slums.

The Restructuring of Urban Consumption

The rapid growth of industries with a strong concentration of high- and low-income jobs has assumed distinct forms in the consumption structure, which in turn has a feedback effect on the organization of work and the types of jobs being created. In the United States, the expansion of the high-income workforce in conjunction with the emergence of new cultural forms has led to a process of high-income gentrification that rests, in the last analysis, on the availability of a vast supply of low-wage workers. High-income gentrification is labor intensive, in contrast to the typical middle-class suburb that represents a capital-intensive process: tract housing, road and highway construction, dependence on private automobiles or commuter trains, marked reliance on appliances and household equipment of all sorts, and large shopping malls. Directly and indirectly, high-income gentrification replaces much of this capital intensity with workers. Similarly, high-income residents in the city depend to a much larger extent on hired maintenance staff than does the middle-class suburban home, with its concentrated input of family labor and machinery.

Although far less dramatic than in large cities in the United States, the elements of these patterns are also evident in major Western European cities, Latin American cities, and, increasingly, Asian cities (e.g., Roulleau-Berger 1999; Parnreiter 2002; Schiffer 2002). The growth of the high-income population in the resident and commuting workforce has contributed to changes in the organization of the production and delivery of consumer goods and services. Behind the delicatessens and specialty boutiques that have replaced many self-service supermarkets and department stores lies a very different organization of work from that prevalent in large, standardized establishments. This difference in the organization of work is evident in both the retail and the production phases (Gershuny and Miles 1983; Sassen 1998: chaps. 7, 8). High-income gentrification generates a demand for goods and services that are frequently not mass produced or sold through mass outlets. Customized production, small runs, specialty items, and fine food dishes are generally produced through labor-intensive methods and sold through small, full-service outlets. Subcontracting part of this production to low-cost operations and to sweatshops or households is common. The overall outcome for the job supply and the range of firms involved in this production and delivery differ from that characterizing the large department stores and supermarkets—though Wal-Mart has launched a new phase combining mass production, large standardized factories located outside of the region, and no unionization of workers. The niche markets of customized producers are not easy to unionize. By contrast, historically mass-production and mass-distribution outlets have facilitated unionizing (see Sayer and Walker 1992; Munger 2002).

The pronounced expansion of the high-income workers' stratum in major cities and their high levels of spending contribute to this outcome. All major cities have long had a core of wealthy residents or commuters. By itself, however, this core of wealthy people could not have created the large-scale residential and commercial gentrification in the city. As a stratum, the new high-income workers are to be distinguished from this core of wealthy residents. Their disposable income is generally not enough to make them into major investors. It is, however, sufficient for a significant expansion in the demand for highly priced goods and services—that is, to create a sufficiently large demand so as to ensure economic viability for the producers and providers of such goods and services. Furthermore, the level of disposable income is also a function of lifestyle and demographic patterns, such as postponing having children and larger numbers of two-earner households.

The expansion in the low income population has also contributed to the proliferation of small operations and the move away from large-scale standardized factories and large chain stores for low-price goods. In good part, the consumption needs of the low-income population are met by manufacturing and retail establishments that are small, rely on family labor, and often fall below minimum safety and health standards. Cheap, locally produced sweatshop garments, for example, can compete with low-cost Asian imports. A growing number of products and services ranging from low-cost furniture made in basements to "gypsy cabs" and family day care are available to meet the demand for the growing low-income population (see Komlosy et al. 1997; Sassen 1998: chap. 8; Russell and Rath 2002).

At the extreme, the expansion of production for the low-income population is evident in global slums. In large slums, an informal economy has expanded to meet the needs of a rapidly growing population. For instance, Arjun Appadurai has described the heterogeneous housing market that has emerged alongside this "explosive growth in small-scale hucksters, vendors, and retailers that have flooded Mumbai's pavements" (Appadurai 2000: 642). In Bombay, housing always comes at a price. "Pavements shade into *jopadpattis* (complexes of shacks with few amenities), which shade into semipermanent illegal structures. Another continuum links these structures to *chawls* (tenement housing originally built for mill workers in Central Bombay) and to other forms of substandard housing" (Appadurai 2000: 637). Urban consumption is being dramatically restructured in both extreme zones: global cities and global slums.

There are many instances of how the increased inequality in earnings reshapes the consumption structure and how this reshaping, in turn, has feedback effects on the organization of work. Some examples are the creation of a special taxi line for Wall Street that services only the financial district and an increase of gypsy cabs in low-income neighborhoods not serviced by regular cabs; the increase in highly customized woodwork in gentrified areas and low-cost informal rehabilitation in poor neighborhoods; the increase of homeworkers and sweatshops making either very expensive designer items for boutiques or very cheap products.

Conclusion: A Widening Gap

Developments in cities cannot be understood in isolation from fundamental changes in the larger organization of advanced economies. The combination of economic, political, and technical forces that has contributed to the decline of mass production as the central driving element in the economy brought about a decline in a broader institutional framework that shaped the employment relation. The group of service industries that were one of the driving economic forces beginning in the 1980s and continue as such today is characterized by greater earnings and occupational dispersion, weak unions, and a growing share of casualized low-wage jobs along with a growing share of high-income jobs. The associated institutional framework shaping the employment relation diverges from that of the growth period of mass manufacturing: today, there are more part-time and temporary jobs and generally fewer protections and fringe benefits for growing portions of the workforce. These changes in the employment relation have contributed to reshaping the sphere of social reproduction and consumption, which, in turn, has a feedback effect on economic organization and earnings. Whereas in the earlier period, this feedback effect contributed to expanding and reproducing the middle class, currently it reproduces growing earnings disparity, labor market casualization, and consumption restructuring along high- and low-end markets. A good fifth of the residents in major cities are part of a new high-income professional stratum that contributes to high-income consumption and customized production and services.

The greater intensity of these diverse trends in major cities than in medium-size towns results from at least three conditions. First is the concentration

of major growth sectors with either sharp earnings dispersion or disproportionate concentration of either low- or high-paying jobs in major cities.
Second is the proliferation of small, low-cost service operations made possible by the massive concentration of people in such cities in addition to a
large daily inflow of nonresident workers and tourists. The ratio between
the number of these service operations and the resident population is probably significantly higher in a very large city than in an average-size city.
Further, the large concentration of people in major cities tends to create
intense inducements to open up such operations as well as intense competition and very marginal returns. Under such conditions, the cost of labor is
crucial, and hence the likelihood of a high concentration of low-wage jobs
increases. Third, for these same reasons together with other components of
demand, the relative size of the downgraded manufacturing sector and the
informal economy tends to be larger in big cities such as New York or Los
Angeles than in average-size cities.

The overall result is a tendency toward increased economic polarization.
Looking at polarization in the use of land, the organization of labor markets, the housing market, and the consumption structure, I do not necessarily mean that the middle class is disappearing. I am, rather, referring to a
dynamic whereby growth contributes to inequality rather than to expansion of the middle class, as was the case in the middle of the century and
into the 1970s in the United States and even into the 1980s in several of the
developed countries. In many of these cities, the middle class represents a
significant share of the population and hence represents an important channel through which income and lifestyle coalesce into a social form. But as
the growth dynamics of new or newly reorganized economic sectors become
more and more prevalent, the core of the middle class will continue to thin
out as the sectors that ensure its reproduction are a smaller part of developed economies.

The middle class in the United States is a very broad category. It contains
prosperous segments of various recent immigrant populations as well as
established ethnic communities in large cities. Beginning in the 1980s, certain segments of the middle class gained income and earnings, thus becoming wealthier, while others became poorer. In the 1990s, these trends also
became evident in major cities of the global South—whether São Paulo,
Mumbai, or Shanghai. In brief, the middle class has become segmented in
a way that has a sharper upward and downward slant than has been the
case in other periods. The argument put forth here is that while the middle
strata still constitute the majority, the conditions that contributed to their
expansion and politico-economic power—the centrality of mass production
and mass consumption in economic growth and profit realization—have

been displaced by new sources of growth. This is not simply a quantitative transformation; here are the elements for a new economic regime.

The growth of service employment in cities, including advanced services, and the evidence of the associated growth of inequality raise questions about how fundamental a change this shift entails. Several of these questions concern the nature of service-based urban economies. The observed changes in the occupational and earnings distribution are outcomes not only of industrial shifts but also of changes in the organization of firms and of labor markets in both old and new sectors. There is considerable articulation of firms, sectors, and workers that may appear to have little connection to an urban economy dominated by finance and specialized services but in fact fulfill a series of functions that are an integral part of advanced service-based urban economies. They do so, however, under conditions of sharp social, earnings, and often racial or ethnic segmentation.

Notes

1   Metropolitan labor markets will tend to reflect a variety of background factors beyond particular restructuring effects. The most important include their sheer size and density, the particular industrial and occupational mix of their employment base, the overall state of tightness or slack in labor demand, and, in the case of some cities, the weight and characteristics of immigrant groups. Two key characteristics of the labor markets in major cities, today as well as a century ago, are the fluidity and openness that influence the types of activity prospering there, as well as the labor market experiences of their residents.

2   Brookings Institute. "Living Cities Census Series" [Data file]. Retrieved May 2008 http://www.brookings.edu/projects/Living-Cities.aspx.

3   Greene, R. P., et al., eds. 2006. *Chicago's Geographies: Metropolis for the 21st Century*. Washington, DC: Association of American Geographers.

4   There is an interesting parallel here with the earlier analysis in Gershuny and Miles (1983) showing that one of the components of the service economy is the shift of tasks traditionally performed by the firm onto the household: for example, furniture and even appliances sold unassembled to be put together by the buyer.

7

Global Cities and Global Survival Circuits

Although this entire book is an effort to recover the meaning of place and of multiple diverse social groups in constituting globalization, it is important to emphasize that this is not the usual focus in accounts about the global economy. Key concepts in the dominant account—global information economy, instant communication, Thomas Friedman's well known adage "the world is flat"—all suggest that place no longer matters and that the only type of worker that matters is the highly educated professional. This understanding of the global economy privileges the capability for global transmission over the material structures and work processes necessary for such transmission. In this type of account, immigrant workers belong to older, backward economic histories, not to the present; it cannot even incorporate the global migration of maids and nannies, so clearly connected to the new high-income professionals in global cities. From the dominant perspective, this migration of maids and nannies has little to do with global cities: these are just women deciding to take a go at it. Supposedly, then, their migrations and the jobs they do once they arrive tell us little about and give us no new insights into economic globalization. This notion that immigrant female domestic workers are unconnected to current global restructuring processes is further strengthened by the fact that women have been migrating for centuries to cities in their own and in foreign countries. But this does not mean that today's migrations are the same

273

as those older flows. Migrations take place within systems and reflect the features of the larger systems within which they take place (Sassen 1988).

This chapter contests several aspects of this common account. It examines the possible links between particular features of globalization and particular components of international migration that are especially evident in global cities. It asks whether the conditions and dynamics brought on by globalization are altering or re-inscribing old migration flows as well as generating new ones; thus, migrations of a given nationality may actually contain very diverse phases across the decades, as is evident in the new migrations of Chinese professionals, clearly a very different migration form that of an older flow.

We can distinguish two processes. One is whether globalization has enabled older processes that used to be national or regional to become global. The other is whether it has produced new conditions and dynamics. Given the enormous variety of migrations and the places where they wind up, the chapter will focus on one specific issue as a way of understanding the intersection of migration and globalization in cities: the global migration and trafficking of maids, nannies, nurses, and sex workers that has risen sharply since the 1990s and has vastly expanded its geography. Ehrenreich and Hochschild (2003) have given us a sharp formulation of this process: the current migration and trafficking of third-world women for jobs that used to be part of the first-world woman's domestic role.

But this focus is also a window into a far larger range of conditions. Migrations and trafficking networks are made, and they are made in response to larger economic constraints and opportunities (Sassen 2007: chap. 5). These include the destruction of traditional economies in the global South in good part due to IMF and World Bank restructuring programs aimed at modernizing and opening these economies to foreign firms and investors. Wealth for some and emergent middle classes were one outcome; but the newfound prosperity was accompanied by the disintegration of small-scale entrepreneurship and farming. This effect is further bolstered by new types of labor demand from the sharply expanded stratum of high-income households and the new spaces of consumption. As discussed in Chapters 4 to 6, immigrants meet labor demand from a range of employment sectors in global cities.

Women in the Global Economy

Analytically, we can anchor the current global migration of women for largely female-typed activities in two specific sets of dynamic configurations. One of these is the global city and the other a set of survival circuits emerging as a response to growing poverty of governments and whole economies in the global South. Global cities are key sites for not only the specialized servicing, financing, and management of global economic processes but also the incorporation of large numbers of immigrants in activities that service the strategic sectors. This incorporation happens directly through the demand for mostly low-paid clerical and blue-collar service workers, such as janitors and repair workers. And it happens indirectly through the consumption practices of high-income professionals, practices that foster the demand for maids and nannies as well as low-wage workers in expensive restaurants and shops. Low-wage workers get incorporated into the leading sectors. But it is a mode of incorporation that renders these workers invisible, therewith breaking the nexus between being workers in leading industries and the opportunity to become—as had been historically the case in industrialized economies—an empowered sector of the organized working class. In this sense, "women and immigrants" emerge as the systemic equivalent of the off-shore proletariat being produced via outsourcing (Sassen 2008c).

The global migration of maids and nannies also helps make visible the demands placed on the top-level professional and managerial workforce in global cities: the usual modes of handling household tasks and lifestyle issues do not apply in this case. This is a type of household that could be described as the *professional household without a "wife,"* regardless of whether it is a single man or woman or a couple composed of man and woman, or man and man, or woman and woman, so long as both partners are in demanding jobs and neither of the two has time to do the housework. This has brought with it the return of the so-called "serving classes" in all the global cities around the world, made up largely of immigrant and migrant women, including minority citizens (Sassen [1991] 2001: chap. 9; Parrenas 2001, Hondagneu-Sotelo 2003; Vecchio 2007; Hyatt 2008). Put this way, the new transnational corporate culture is revealed to be partly anchored in a world of work to which it seems unconnected: the immigrant cultures within which many of the other jobs of the advanced global "information" economy take place. (See also Aguiar and Herod 2005 on janitors in the corporate sector.)

As for the second site, in the 1990s and onward, there has been a proliferation of new or renewed survival circuits built on the backs of women— as trafficked workers for low-wage jobs and the sex industry and as migrant workers who send remittances back home. Beyond helping their families back home, their work and remittances also enhance the government revenue of deeply indebted countries. Their migration and remittances also offer new profit-making possibilities to quasi-entrepreneurs who have seen other opportunities vanish when global firms enter their countries and to longtime criminals who can now operate their illegal trades globally. These survival circuits are often complex, involving multiple locations and sets of actors, constituting increasingly global chains of traders and workers.

Both in the global city and in these survival circuits, women emerge as crucial actors for new and expanding types of economies. It is through these supposedly rather valueless economic actors that key components of these new economies have been built. Globalization plays a specific role here in a double sense, first, contributing to the formation of links between sending and receiving countries and, second, enabling local and regional practices to become global in scale. On the one hand, the particular dynamics that come together in the global city produce a strong demand for these types of workers, while the dynamics that mobilize women into these survival circuits produce an expanding supply of workers who can be pushed, or are sold, into those types of jobs. On the other hand, the technical infrastructure and transnationalism that underlie some of the key globalized industries are also making it possible for other types of actors to deploy their activities at global scales, whether money laundering or trafficking.[1]

Localizing the Global

Throughout this book, I have argued that economic globalization entails multiple localizations, many of which do not generally get coded as having anything to do with the global economy. The global city is one of the key places for many of these localizations. Cities serve as nexuses where many of the new organizational tendencies of economies and societies come together in specific localized configurations. They are also the sites for a disproportionate concentration of all immigrants in the global North and in the global South.

One of the localizations of the dynamics of globalization is the process of economic restructuring in global cities, which has generated a large growth in the demand for low-wage workers and jobs that offer few advancement possibilities (Chapter 6). This, amid an explosion in the wealth and power concentrated in these cities—in conditions where there is also a visible expansion in high-income jobs and high-priced urban space. *Women and immigrants* emerge as the labor supply that facilitates the imposition of low wages and few benefits, even when there is high demand for these workers and these jobs are in high-growth sectors. Access to women and immigrants breaks the historic nexus that would have led to empowering workers under these conditions, and, further, it legitimates this break culturally. The demographic transition evident in such cities, where a majority of resident workers today tend to be women—often women of color, both native and immigrant—can be understood as mediating between the new kinds of economic organization (as discussed in preceding chapters) and the chipping away of hard-earned higher wages and benefits among global North workers. For instance, if these jobs were held by native white men in the United States and in Europe, there might be far more pressure to upgrade these jobs.

Another localization that is rarely associated with globalization is the growing informalization of an expanding range of activities briefly discussed in Chapter 6. Some of the components of informalization make the community and the household once again important economic spaces in cities. In this setting, I see informalization as the low-cost (and often feminized) equivalent of deregulation at the top of the system (see Chapter 4). As with deregulation (e.g., as in financial deregulation), informalization introduces flexibility, reduces the so-called burdens of regulation, and lowers costs, in this case especially of labor. Informalization in the cities of the global North—whether New York, London, Paris, or Berlin—can be seen as a downgrading of a variety of activities for which there is an effective and often growing demand located inside these cities. Immigrant women and men are important actors in the new informal economies of these cities. They absorb the costs of in-formalizing these activities.

Yet another important localization of the dynamics of globalization is that of the new stratum of professional women. Elsewhere, I have examined the impact of the growth of top-level professional women in high-income gentrification in these cities—both residential and commercial—as well as in the reurbanization of middle-class family life (see Sassen [1991] 2001: chap. 9). The vast expansion in the demand for high-level professionals has brought with it a sharp increase in the employment of women in corporate professional jobs.[2] The complex and strategic character of these jobs requires long work hours and intense engagement with their jobs and work lives. This places heavy demands on their time. Urban residence is far more desirable than living in the suburbs, especially for single professionals or two professional career households. As a result, high-income residential areas in global cities have expanded, creating a reurbanization of family life, insofar as these professionals want it all, including dogs and children, even if they may not have the time for either. Given demanding and time-absorbing jobs, the usual modes of handling household tasks and lifestyle are inadequate. This is the type of household that I describe as the *professional household without a "wife,"* alluded to earlier. Growing shares of household tasks are relocated to the market; they are bought directly as goods and services or indirectly through hired labor. Here is a dynamic akin to a double movement: functions that used to be part of household work shift to the labor market in the case of high-income professional households, and at the same time, labor-market functions that used to take place in standardized workplaces shift to the immigrant household and community.[3]

This reconfiguration of economic spaces associated with globalization in cities has had different impacts on women and men, on male-typed and female-typed work cultures, on male- and female-centered forms of power and empowerment. Some of these transformations contain possibilities, even if limited, for women's autonomy and empowerment. For example, we might ask whether the growth of informalization in advanced urban economies reconfigures some types of economic relations between men and women. From the perspective of the immigrant woman, informalization makes the neighborhood and the household—including both the immigrant and the high-level professional household—sites for paid economic activity. This condition has its own dynamic possibilities for women. Economic downgrading through informalization creates so-called opportunities for low-income women and thus reconfigures some of the work and household hierarchies that women find themselves in. This becomes particularly clear in the case of immigrant women who come from countries with rather traditional male-centered cultures and/or from poor households that are sites of production for survival, as opposed to the middle class household, which becomes a site for consumption—more and more needed goods and services are bought rather than made in the home.

There is a large literature showing that immigrant women's regular wage work and improved access to other public realms has an impact on their gender relations, as it allows them to gain greater personal autonomy and independence. There are two arenas where immigrant women are active: institutions for public and private assistance and the immigrant/ethnic community. Immigrant women come to assume more active public and social roles, which further reinforces their status in the household and the settlement process (Hondagneu-Sotelo 1994; Mahler 1995). Women are more active in community building and community activism, and they are positioned differently from men regarding the broader economy and the state. They are the ones that are likely to have to handle the legal vulnerability of their families in the process of seeking public and social services. This allows them to gain more control over budgeting and other domestic decisions and greater leverage in requesting help from men in domestic chores. Their access to public services and other public resources gives them a chance to become incorporated in the mainstream society—and they are often the ones in the household who mediate in this process. It is likely that some women benefit more than others from these circumstances; more research is needed to establish the impact of class, education, and income on such gendered outcomes.

In short, besides the relatively greater empowerment of women in the household associated with waged employment, there is a second important outcome: their greater participation in the public sphere and their possible emergence as public actors. This greater participation by women suggests the possibility that they may emerge as more forceful and visible actors and make their role in the labor market more visible as well. Working-class immigrant men, on the other hand, function in a more confined sociopolitical space. They often work in warehouses, small industrial service operations, or factories, becoming a more invisible subject than the women in the regular weekly routines of these neighborhoods.

Here is, to some extent, a joining of two different dynamics in the condition of immigrant women in global cities described earlier. On the one hand, they are constituted as an invisible and disempowered class of workers in the service of the strategic sectors constituting the global economy. This invisibility keeps them from emerging as whatever would be the contemporary equivalent of the strong proletariat of earlier forms of economic organization, when workers' positions in leading sectors had the effect of empowering them. On the other hand, the access to wages and salaries (even if low) and the growing feminization of the job supply and business opportunities brought about with informalization do alter the gender hierarchies in their own communities.

The Other Workers in the Advanced Corporate Economy

In the day-to-day work of the leading sectors in global cities, a large share of the jobs involved are low paid and manual, many held by immigrant women. Even the most advanced professionals will require clerical, cleaning, and repair workers for their state-of-the-art offices, and they will require truckers to bring not only the software but also the light bulbs. Although these types of workers and jobs are never represented as part of the global economy, they are in fact part of the infrastructure of jobs involved in running and implementing the global economic system, including such an advanced form of it as international finance.

As already discussed in this book, high-level corporate services, from accounting to decision-making expertise, are not usually analyzed in terms of their work process. Such services are usually seen as a type of output, that is, high-level technical knowledge. Thus, insufficient attention has gone to the actual array of jobs, from high-paying to low-paying, involved in the production of these services. A focus on the work process brings to the fore the labor question. Information outputs need to be produced, and the buildings that hold the workers need to be built and cleaned. The rapid growth of the financial industry and highly specialized services generates not only high-level technical and administrative jobs but also low-wage unskilled jobs. In my research on New York and other cities, I found that between 30% and 50% of the workers in the leading sectors are actually low-wage workers (Sassen [1991] 2001: chaps. 8, 9; 2008c).

Further, the similarly state-of-the-art lifestyles of the professionals in these sectors have created a whole new demand for a range of household workers, particularly maids and nannies. As discussed earlier, the presence of a highly dynamic sector with a polarized income distribution has its own impact on the creation of low-wage jobs through the sphere of consumption (or, more generally, social reproduction). The rapid growth of industries with strong concentrations of high- and low-income jobs has assumed distinct forms in the consumption structure, which in turn has a feedback effect on the organization of work and the types of jobs being created. The expansion of the high-income workforce in conjunction with the emergence of new lifestyles has led to a process of high-income gentrification that rests, in the last analysis, on the availability of a vast supply of low-wage workers. High-price restaurants, luxury housing, luxury hotels, gourmet shops, boutiques, French hand laundries, and special cleaning services are all more labor intensive than their lower-price equivalents. This has reintroduced—to an extent not seen in a very long time—the whole notion of the serving classes in contemporary high-income households.[4] The immigrant woman serving the white middle-class professional woman has replaced the traditional image of the black female servant serving the white master. These trends give cities an increasingly sharp tendency toward social polarization.

The consumption needs of the growing low-income population in large cities are also increasingly met through labor-intensive rather than standardized and unionized forms of producing goods and services: manufacturing and retail establishments that are small, rely on family labor, and often fall below minimum safety and health standards. Cheap, locally produced sweatshop garments and bedding, for example, can compete with low-cost Asian imports. A growing range of products and services, from low-cost furniture made in basements to "gypsy cabs" and family day care, are available to meet the needs of the growing low-income population. There are numerous instances of how the increased inequality in earnings reshapes the consumption structure and how this, in turn, has feedback effects on the organization of work, both in the formal and in the informal economy.

This disparity between the high- and low-income classes has resulted in the formation of global labor markets at the top and at the bottom of the economic system. At the bottom, much of the staffing occurs through the efforts of individuals, largely immigrants, though an expanding network of organizations is getting involved (as well as illegal traffickers, as I discuss in the second half of this chapter). For example, Kelly Services, a Fortune 500 services company in global staffing, which operates offices in twenty-five countries, now has added a homecare division, which provides a full range of help. It is particularly geared to people who need assistance with daily living activities but also for those who lack the time to take care of the needs of household members who in the past would have been taken care of by the mother/wife figure in the household.[5]

More directly pertinent to the professional households under discussion here are a growing range of global staffing organizations whose advertised services cover various aspects of day care, including dropping off and picking up, as well as in-house tasks, from child minding to cleaning and cooking.[6] One international agency for nannies and au pairs (EF Au Pair Corporate Program) advertises directly to corporations, urging them to offer potential employees a full household and child care service as part of their employment package. Increasingly, the pattern is that the transnational professional class can access these services in the expanding network of global cities among which they are likely to circulate; further, they are standardized across these cities to maximize the comforts of the transnational professional class. (See Sassen [1991] 2001: chap. 7.)

At the top of the system, several major Fortune 500 global staffing companies provide firms with experts and talent for high-level professional and technical jobs. In 2001, the largest of these was the Swiss multinational Adecco, with offices in fifty-eight countries; in 2000, it provided firms worldwide with three million workers. Manpower, with offices in fifty-nine different countries, provided two million workers. Manpower has continued to grow and has outpaced Adecco. As of 2010, Manpower had three million associates, temporary, contract, and also permanent positions. It also had 400,000 clients and had operations in eighty-two countries (www.manpower .com/about/about.cfm). Kelly Services, mentioned earlier, provided 750,000 employees in 2000. As of 2009, Kelly Services provided employment to 480,000 employees annually and its revenue in 2009 was $4.3 billion (www .kellyservices.com/web/global/services/en/pages/about_us.html).

Note that it is at the top of the professional ladder and bottom of the occupational distribution that this internationalization in the supply of workers is happening; mid-level occupations, although increasingly handled through temporary employment agencies, have not internationalized their supply, and the highest ranks of strategic talent are recruited through headhunters and informal networks. The types of occupations involved at both the top and bottom are, in very different yet parallel ways, sensitive. Firms need reliable and, ideally, somewhat talented professionals; further, they need them specialized but standardized so they can use them globally. And professionals want the same in the workers they employ in their homes. The move of staffing organizations into the provision of domestic services signals both the emergence of a global labor market and efforts to standardize the service delivered by maids, nannies, and homecare nurses.

In brief, the top end of the corporate economy—the high-paid professionals and the corporate towers that project engineering expertise, precision, "techne"—is far easier to recognize as necessary for an advanced economic system than are truckers, industrial service workers, maids, nannies, and informal economies and immigrant communities. Yet they are all necessary ingredients. Firms, sectors, and workers that may appear as though they have little connection to an urban economy dominated by finance and specialized services can, in fact, be an integral part of that economy. They do so, however, under conditions of sharp social, earnings, and often gender, racial, or ethnic segmentation. They become part of an increasingly dynamic and multifaceted lower circuit of global capital that partially parallels the upper circuit of professionals—the lawyers, accountants, and telecommunications experts that service global capital.

Producing a Global Supply of the New Caretakers: The Feminization of Survival

The immigrant women described in the first half of this chapter enter the migration process in many different ways (Pessar and Mahler 2003). For some, it is family reunion; others come on their own. Many features of these migration processes have little to do with globalization. Here, I am concerned with one specific set of processes that I see as deeply linked to certain features of economic globalization today. These are migrations largely organized by third parties, typically governments or illegal traffickers. These women wind up in work situations that involve a far broader range of worlds than the ones I focus on in this chapter.

The last decade has seen a growing presence of women in a variety of cross-border circuits. These circuits are enormously diverse but share one feature: they are profit- or revenue-making circuits developed on the backs of the truly disadvantaged. They include the illegal trafficking in people for the sex industry and for various types of formal and informal labor markets. And they include cross-border migrations, both documented and not, that generate remittances that have become an important source of hard currency for governments in home countries. The formation and strengthening of these circuits is, in good part, a consequence of broader structural conditions. Among the key actors emerging out of these broader conditions to give shape to these particular circuits are the women themselves in search of work, but also, and increasingly so, illegal traffickers and contractors as well as governments of home countries.

I conceptualize these circuits as counter-geographies of globalization. They are deeply imbricated with some of the major dynamics constitutive of globalization: the formation of global markets, the intensifying of transnational and translocal networks, and the development of communication technologies that easily escape conventional surveillance practices. The strengthening and, in some of these cases, the formation of new global circuits is embedded or made possible by the existence of a global economic system and its associated development of various institutional supports for cross-border money flows and markets.[7] These counter-geographies are dynamic and changing in their locational features. They are partially in the shadow economy yet also use some of the institutional infrastructure of the regular, even corporate economy.

Crucial to the formation of a global supply of caretakers in demand in global cities are the systemic links between the growth of these alternative circuits for survival, for profit making, and for hard-currency earning on the one hand, and major conditions in developing countries that are associated with economic globalization on the other. Among these conditions are a growth in unemployment, the closure of a large number of typically small and medium-size enterprises oriented to national rather than export markets, and large, often increasing government debt. Although these economies are frequently grouped under the label *developing,* they are in some cases struggling or stagnant and even shrinking. (For the sake of briefness, I will use *developing* as shorthand for this variety of situations.) Many of these developments have produced additional responsibilities for women toward their households, as men have lost earnings opportunities and governments have cut back on social services that supported women and their family responsibilities.[8]

One way of articulating this in substantive terms is to posit that (1) the shrinking opportunities for male employment in many of these countries, (2) the shrinking opportunities for more traditional forms of profit making in these same countries as they increasingly accept foreign firms in a widening range of economic sectors and are pressured to develop export industries, and (3) the fall in revenues for the governments in many of these countries, partially linked to these conditions and to the burden of debt servicing, have (4) all contributed to raising the importance of alternative ways of making a living, making a profit, and securing government revenue.[9]

The variety of global circuits that are incorporating growing numbers of women have strengthened at a time when major dynamics linked to economic globalization have had significant impacts on developing economies, including the so-called middle-income countries of the global South. These countries have had to implement a bundle of new policies and accommodate new conditions associated with globalization: structural adjustment programs, the opening of these economies to foreign firms, the elimination of multiple state subsidies, and, it would seem almost inevitably, financial crises and the prevailing types of programmatic solutions put forth by the International Monetary Fund (IMF). It is now clear that in most of the countries involved, whether Mexico or Ukraine, Ghana or Thailand, these conditions have created enormous costs for certain sectors of the economy and of the population. Further, after twenty years of these programs, it is clear that in several of these countries, these conditions have not fundamentally reduced government debt. (See Exhibits 7.1 and A.7.1.)

As seen in Exhibit 7.1, many of the countries with large exports of female workers to the service industries of highly developed nations hold large amounts of external debt. For example, the Philippines, a prominent exporter of domestic help and other caregivers to such countries as both United Arab Emirates (Dubai) as well as the United States, owes $61.5 billion, while the Ukraine, another large exporter of domestic labor to the United States, holds $33.3 billion in external debt.

These conditions also play a substantial role in the lives of a growing number of women from developing or struggling economies, even when the articulations are often not self-evident or visible—a fact that has marked much of the difficulty of understanding the role of women in development generally. These are, in many ways, old conditions. What is different today is their rapid internationalization and considerable institutionalization.

One effort analytically here—paralleling the analysis on the significance of women and immigrants in the global city—is to uncover the systemic connections between, on the one hand, what are considered poor, low-earning, and low-value-added individuals, often represented as a burden

Exhibit 7.1 Total Government Health Spending Versus Debt Service Payments, Select Countries (2007–2009)

Country	Total External Debt	Total External Debt Payment	Total Health Spending	Total Spending on Debt Service Payments
Angola	$15.1 bn	$1.6 bn every year	1.5% of GDP (2005)	6.8% of GDP
Ecuador	$17.1 bn	$4.1 bn every year	2.2% of GDP (2004)	11.4% of GDP
Egypt	$34.4 bn	$2.5 bn every year	2.4% of GDP (2003)	2.8% of GDP
Georgia	$1.9 bn	$187 mn every year	2.4% of GDP (2003)	2.9% of GDP
Jamaica	$6.5 bn	$969 mn every year	2.4% of GDP (2003)	10.1% of GDP
Lebanon	$23.3 bn	$3.5 bn every year	2.4% of GDP (2003)	16.1% of GDP
Lesotho	$689.7 mn	$54.2 mn every year	2.4% of GDP (2003)	3.7% of GDP
Moldova	$2 bn	$250 mn	4.2% of GDP (2005)	8.62% of GDP
Morocco	$16.4 bn	$2.7 bn	1.7% of GDP (2004)	5.27% of GDP
Pakistan	$33.7 bn	$2.4 bn	0.4% of GDP (2004)	2.21% of GDP
Panama	$9.8 bn	$2 bn	5.2% of GDP (2004)	13.42% of GDP
Papua New Guinea	$1.85 bn	$388 mn	3% of GDP (2004)	6.7% of GDP
Paraguay	$3.1 bn	$489 mn	2.6% of GDP (2004)	6.7% of GDP
Philippines	$61.5 bn	$9.9 bn every year	1.4% of GDP (2003)	10% of GDP
Ukraine	$33.3 bn	$5.9 bn	3.7 of GDP (2004)	6.6% of GDP

Source: The Jubilee Debt Campaign UK website (http://www.jubileedebtcampaign.org.uk/), which cites figures from World Bank and the United Nations Human Development Report.

rather than a resource, and, on the other hand, what are emerging as significant sources for profit making, especially in the shadow economy, and for government revenue enhancement. Prostitution and labor migration are growing in importance as ways of making a living; illegal trafficking in women and children for the sex industry and in laborers is growing in importance as a way of making a profit; and the remittances sent by emigrants, as well as the organized export of workers, are increasingly important sources of revenues for some of these governments. Women make up by far the majority in prostitution and trafficking for the sex industry, and they are becoming a majority group in migration for labor. The employment and/or use of foreign-born women covers an increasingly broad range of economic sectors, some illegal and illicit (e.g., prostitution) and some in highly regulated industries (e.g., nursing). (See generally Chant and Craske 2002; Chant and Richey 2010.)

These circuits can be thought of as indicating the (albeit partial) feminization of survival, because it is increasingly on the backs of women that these forms of making a living, making a profit, and securing government revenue are realized. Thus, in using the notion of feminization of survival, I mean not only that households and indeed whole communities are increasingly dependent on women for their survival but also that governments are dependent on women's earnings in these various circuits, and so are types of enterprises whose ways of profit making exist at the margins of the licit economy. Finally, by using the term *circuits*, I want to underline the fact that there is a degree of institutionalization in these dynamics—they are not simply aggregates of individual actions.

Alternative Survival Circuits

It is in this context that alternative circuits of survival emerge and can be seen as articulated with more general conditions of economic decline and deeply indebted governments in the less developed world, which have been forced to make major cuts in general expenditures on health, education, and development. This is a context marked by a systemic condition characterized by high unemployment, poverty, bankruptcies of large numbers of firms, and shrinking resources in the state to meet social needs. Here, I want to focus briefly on some of the issues in the trafficking of women for sex industries and for work, the growing weight of this trafficking as a profit-making option, and the growing weight of emigrants' remittances in the account balance of many of the sending states.

Immigrants enter the macro level of development strategies through the remittances they send back home. These represent a major source of foreign

exchange reserves for the government in a good number of countries. Although the flows of remittances may be minor compared with the massive daily capital flows in global financial markets, they can matter enormously to developing or struggling economies. The World Bank estimates that remittances worldwide reached $318 billion in 2007, up from $230 billion in 2005 and $70 billion in 1998; of this total amount, $240 billion went to developing countries, up from $168 billion in 2005 and up 73% over 2001 (Migrant Remittances, 2008: 2). The next two exhibits provide summary information about remittances. Exhibit 7.2 shows the top receivers of remittances and also what proportion of each nation's GDP is derived from such remittances. Notably, among the top of nations that rely the most on remittances are small nations with little or no infrastructure and a failing economy. For example, 49% of Tajikistan's GDP comes from remittances, and 37% of Tonga's GDP is also received from its expatriate citizens. Honduras, Haiti, El Salvador, Jamaica, and the Philippines, countries with large diasporic populations, also rely heavily on remittances to make up their GDPs. Exhibit 7.3 shows the other side of this coin, that is, it reveals the main remittance senders, with the United States long at the top and the Russian Federation's extraordinary rise as a key host of remittance senders, going from $3.2 billion in 2003 to $27 billion by 2008. (See Exhibits 7.2 and 7.3.)

Trafficking involves the forced recruitment and/or transportation of people within and across states for work or services through a variety of forms, all involving coercion. Trafficking is a violation of several distinct types of rights: human, civil, political. Trafficking in people appears to be mainly related to the sex market, labor markets, and illegal migration. Much legislative work has been done to address trafficking: international treaties and charters, United Nations resolutions, and various bodies and commissions.[10] Nongovernmental organizations (NGOs) are also playing an increasingly important role.[11]

As tourism has grown sharply over the last decade and become a major development strategy for cities, regions, and whole countries, the entertainment sector has seen a parallel growth and recognition as a key development strategy (Fainstein and Judd 1999; Wonders and Michalowski 2001). In many places, the sex trade is part of the entertainment industry and has grown alongside the latter. At some point, the sex trade itself has become a development strategy in areas with high unemployment and poverty and governments desperate for revenue and foreign exchange reserves. When local manufacturing and agriculture can no longer function as sources of employment, profits, and government revenue, what was once a marginal source of earnings, profits, and revenues now becomes a far more important

Exhibit 7.2   Top Recipient Countries of Migrant Remittances as % of GDP, 2006–2009

Country	Workers' Remittances, Compensation of Employees, and Migrant Transfers, Debit (US$ million)				Remittances as a Share of GDP, 2008 (%)
	2006	2007	2008	2009	
Tajikistan	1,019	1,691	2,544	1,815	49.6%
Tonga	72	100	100	96	37.7%
Moldova	1,182	1,498	1,897	1,491	31.4%
Kyrgyz Republic	481	715	1,232	1,011	27.9%
Lesotho	361	443	443	496	27.3%
Samoa	108	120	135	131	25.8%
Lebanon	5,202	5,769	7,180	7,000	25.1%
Guyana	218	283	278	266	24.0%
Nepal	1,453	1,734	2,727	3,010	21.6%
Honduras	2,391	2,625	2,824	2,525	20.1%
Jordan	2,883	3,434	2,794	3,650	19.0%
Haiti	1,063	1,222	1,300	1,220	18.7%
El Salvador	3,485	3,711	2,804	3,460	17.2%
Bosnia and Herzegovina	2,157	2,700	2,735	2,627	14.8%
Jamaica	1,946	2,144	2,180	1,921	14.5%
Nicaragua	698	740	818	784	12.4%
Albania	1,359	1,468	1,495	1,495	12.2%
Guatemala	3,700	4,236	4,451	4,065	11.4%
Bangladesh	5,428	6,562	8,995	10,431	11.4%
Philippines	15,251	16,302	18,643	19,411	11.3%

Source: Ratha et al. (2009: 3).

Exhibit 7.3 Top Sending Countries of Migrant Remittances, 2003–2008

Country	Workers' Remittances, Compensation of Employees, and Migrant Transfers, Debit (US$ million)					
	2003	2004	2005	2006	2007	2008
United States	36,545	39,347	40,635	43,922	45,643	47,182
Russian Federation	3,233	5,188	7,008	11,467	17,763	26,145
Switzerland	11,411	12,921	13,324	14,377	16,273	18,954
Saudi Arabia	14,783	13,555	13,996	15,611	16,068	16,068
Germany	11,190	12,069	12,499	12,454	13,689	14,976
Spain	5,140	6,977	8,136	11,326	15,183	14,656
Italy	4,368	5,512	7,620	8,437	11,287	12,718
Luxembourg	5,077	6,000	6,627	7,561	9,280	10,922
Netherlands	4,236	5,032	5,928	6,831	7,830	8,431
Malaysia	3,464	5,064	5,679	5,569	6,385	6,385
China	1,645	2,067	2,603	3,025	4,372	5,737
Oman	1,672	1,826	2,257	2,788	3,670	5,181
United Kingdom	2,624	2,957	3,877	4,560	5,048	5,048
Norway	1,430	1,749	2,174	2,620	3,642	4,776
Japan	1,773	1,411	1,281	3,476	4,037	4,743
France	4,388	4,262	4,182	4,217	4,380	4,541
Czech Republic	1,102	1,431	1,677	2,030	2,625	3,826
Kuwait	2,144	2,403	2,648	3,183	2,824	3,824
Belgium	2,329	2,617	2,754	2,698	3,161	3,689
Kazakhstan	802	1,354	2,000	3,033	4,304	3,559

Source: Ratha et al. (2009: 3).

one. The increased importance of these sectors in development generates growing tie-ins. For example, when the IMF and the World Bank see tourism as a solution to some of the growth challenges in many poor countries and provide loans for its development or expansion, they may well be contributing to develop a broader institutional setting for the expansion of the entertainment industry and, indirectly, of the sex trade. This tie-in with development strategies signals that there may be a sharp expansion in the trafficking in women.

The 2010 Trafficking in Persons (TIP) Report, compiled by the US Department of State, marked the tenth anniversary of the United States Department of Security's fight against human trafficking. As President Obama has noted: "The victims of modern slavery have many faces. They are men and women, adults and children. Yet, all are denied basic human dignity and freedom. . . . All too often suffering from horrible physical and sexual abuse, it is hard for them to imagine that there might be a place of refuge."[3] (US Department of State 1010b: 1).The 2010 United States Department of State Bureau of Public Affairs report reflected on the fact that it has been ten years since the United States enacted the Trafficking Victims Protection Act (TVPA) and since the United Nations adopted the Palermo Protocol, which seeks to "prevent, suppress, and punish trafficking in persons, especially, women and children" (US Department of State 2010b: 1).

In 2000, the United States enacted the Trafficking Victims Protection Act (TVPA), and the United Nations adopted the Protocol to Prevent, Suppress, and Punish Trafficking in Persons, Especially Women and Children—also known as the Palermo Protocol. The US Department Fact Sheet further revealed that "more people are trafficked for forced labor than for commercial sex." Further, it noted that "the crime is less about duping and kidnapping people than it is about coercion of people who entered a form of service voluntarily or migrated willingly." The report also acknowledged that "men comprise a significant number of trafficking victims." Women are revealed to be the most vulnerable victims, however, as "traffickers often use sexual violence as a weapon against women to keep them in compelled service, whether in a field, a factory, a brothel, a home, or a war zone" (US Department of State, 2010b: 1).

In total, the TIP report projected that trafficking in human beings presents a $32 billion annual trade for traffickers. It also estimated that "12.3 million adults and children are in forced labor, bonded labor, and forced prostitution around the world" (US Department of State 2010b: 1). Of that

---

[3]US Department of State 2010b, http://www.state.gov/r/pa/scp/fs/2010/143115.htm.

number, 56% are calculated to be women and girls. The report also found a 59% increase in trafficking cases between 2008 and 2009 but also noted that there were 4,166 successful trafficking prosecutions in 2009, a 40% increase over 2008. Trafficking remains a problem with an alarming frequency of occurrence. The report found the prevalence of trafficking victims in the world was 1.8 per 1,000 inhabitants. And the problem is even more exacerbated in Asia and the Pacific, where the trafficking rate is 3 per 1,000 inhabitants. (US Department of State 2010).

The entry of organized crime into the sex trades, the formation of cross-border ethnic networks, and the growing transnationalization in so many aspects of tourism suggest that further development of a global sex industry is likely. This could mean greater attempts to enter into more and more markets and a general expansion of the industry. It is a worrisome possibility, especially in the context of growing numbers of women with few if any employment options. And such growing numbers are to be expected given high unemployment and poverty, the shrinking of a world of work opportunities that were embedded in the more traditional sectors of these economies, and the growing debt burden of governments, rendering them incapable of providing social services and support to the poor.

In short, the growing dire financial straits of governments and economies in the global South launches a new phase of global migration and people trafficking, strategies that function as both survival mechanisms and profit-making activities. To some extent, these are older processes that used to be national or regional and today operate on global scales. The same infrastructure that facilitates cross-border flows of capital, information, and trade is also making possible a range of cross-border flows not intended by the framers and designers of the current corporate globalization of economies. Women in the sex industry become—in certain kinds of economies—a crucial link supporting the expansion of the entertainment industry and therefore of tourism as a development strategy, which in turn becomes a source of government revenue. These tie-ins are structural, not a function of conspiracies. Their weight in an economy will be raised by the absence or limitations of other sources for securing a livelihood, profits, and revenues for, respectively, workers, enterprises, and governments.

Conclusion

The global migration and trafficking of women is anchored in particular features of the current globalization of economies in both the North and the South. To understand how globalization actually relates to the globalized extraction of services that used to be part of the first-world woman's domestic role requires that we look at globalization in ways that are different from the mainstream view. Rather than confining the description of globalization to the hypermobility of capital and to the ascendance of information economies, this book has sought to recover the fact that specific types of places and work processes are also part of economic globalization. This chapter focused on two such concrete conditions. One is the globalizing of often older survival and profit-making activities that contribute today to producing a global supply of low-wage women workers. The other, the growing demand for migrant nannies, maids, nurses, and sex workers in the global North, amounts to a sharp reorganization of labor demand. These dynamics are particularly visible in global cities, also strategic sites for global corporate capital.

The growing fiscal decline of governments and whole economies in the global South has promoted and enabled the proliferation of survival and profit-making activities that involve the migration and trafficking of women. To some extent, these are older processes that used to be national or regional and can today operate at global levels. The same infrastructure that facilitates cross-border flows of capital, information, and trade is also making possible a whole range of cross-border flows not intended by the framers and designers of the current globalization of economies. Growing numbers of traffickers and smugglers are making money off the backs of women, and many governments are increasingly dependent on their remittances. A key aspect here is that through their work and remittances, women enhance the government revenue of deeply indebted countries and offer new profit-making possibilities to so-called entrepreneurs who have seen other opportunities vanish as a consequence of global firms and markets entering their countries or to longtime criminals who can now operate their illegal trades globally. These survival circuits are often complex, involving multiple locations and sets of actors constituting increasingly global chains of traders and workers.

But globalization has also produced new conditions and dynamics. Strategic among these both for global corporate capital and some of the new labor demand dynamics that involve women from the global South are global cities. These are places that concentrate some of the key functions and resources for the management and coordination of global economic processes. The growth of these activities has, in turn, produced a sharp growth in the demand for highly paid professionals. Both the firms and the lifestyles of their professionals generate a demand for low-paid service workers. In this way, global cities are also sites for the incorporation of large numbers of low-paid women and immigrants into strategic economic sectors. This incorporation happens directly through the demand for mostly low-paid clerical and blue-collar service workers, such as janitors and repair workers. And it happens indirectly through the consumption practices of high-income professionals, which, in turn, generates a demand for maids and nannies as well as low-wage workers in expensive restaurants and shops. Low-wage workers get incorporated into the leading sectors, but they do so under conditions that render them invisible, therewith undermining what had historically functioned as a source of workers' empowerment—being employed in growth sectors.

Both in the global city and in these survival circuits, women emerge as crucial actors for new and expanding types of economies. It is through these supposedly rather valueless economic actors that key components of these new economies have been built. Globalization plays specific roles here. First, it contributes to the formation of links between sending and receiving countries. The technical infrastructure and transnationalism that underlie some of the key globalized industries are also making it possible for other types of actors to deploy their activities at global scales, whether money laundering or trafficking. Second, it enables local and regional practices to become global in scale. Third, it promotes dynamics that come together in global cities (and in tourism enclaves) to produce a strong demand for these types of workers; on the other hand, globalization also promotes dynamics that mobilize women into these survival circuits, thereby producing an expanding supply of workers who can be pushed, or are sold, into those types of jobs.

Notes

1   In my larger research project, I also focus on a range of what we could call liberating activities and practices that are enabled by globalization, for example, specific aspects of the human rights and environmental movements as well as particular activities of the antiglobalization network. One way of thinking about this is to posit that globalization enables the production of both exploitative and emancipatory countergeographies.

2   Indeed, women represent a specific type of resource in many of these settings because they are seen—whether rightly or not—as better cultural brokers, a significant issue for firms with global operations. Further, women are also seen as crucial in the interface with consumers in the financial services industry in that they are seen as inspiring more trust and thereby making it easier for individual investors to put their money in what are often known to be highly speculative endeavors (Fisher 2004).

3   I have developed this at length in Sassen (1995).

4   Some of these issues are well illustrated in the emergent research literature on domestic service (see, among others, Parrenas 2001; Ehrenreich and Hochschild

2003; Ribas-Mateos 2005) and in the rapid growth of international organizations catering to various household tasks discussed here.

5   Homecare services include assistance with bathing and dressing, food preparation, walking and getting in and out of bed, medication reminders, transportation, housekeeping, conversation, and companionship. Although less directly related to the needs of high-income professional households, many of these tasks used to be in the care of the typical housewife of the global North.

6   Very prominent in this market are the International Nanny and Au Pair Agency, headquartered in Britain, Nannies Incorporated, based in London and Paris, and the International Au Pair Association (IAPA), based in Canada.

7   I have argued this for the case of international labor migrations (e.g., Bonilla et al. 1998; Sassen 1998: chaps. 2–4; 1999; 2007: ch 5; see also, e.g., Castro 1999).

8   There is, also, an older literature on women and the debt, focused on the implementation of the first generation of structural adjustment programs in several developing countries linked to the growing debt of governments in the 1980s; this literature has documented the disproportionate burden these programs put on women. It is a large literature in many languages; it also includes a vast number of limited-circulation items produced by various activist and support organizations. For overviews, see, for example, Ward (1991); Ward and Pyle (1995); Bose and Acosta-Belen (1995); Beneria and Feldman (1992); Bradshaw et al. (1993); Tinker (1990); Moser (1989). And now there is a new literature on the second generation of such programs, one more directly linked to the implementation of the global economy in the 1990s (Chang and Abramovitz 2000; Chant and Craske 2002). In the context of crisis, trafficking becomes a significant source of revenue. In 2005, global remittances sent by immigrants to their home countries reached more than US$230 billion (World Bank 2006). The illegal trafficking of migrants generates estimated revenues of US$9.5 billion annually for organized crime associations and is ranked as their third most profitable operation after narcotics and arms dealing (US Department of State 2004).

9   Among the components under (1) and (2) are the closure of a large number of firms in often fairly traditional sectors oriented to the local or national market and the promotion of export-oriented cash crops that have increasingly replaced survival agriculture and food production for local or national markets.

10   See, for example, Chuang (1998). Trafficking has become sufficiently recognized as an issue that it was also addressed in the G8 meeting in Birmingham in May 1998 (International Organization for Migration 1998). The heads of the eight major industrialized countries stressed the importance of cooperation against international organized crime and trafficking in persons. The US president issued a set of directives to his administration to strengthen and increase efforts against trafficking in women and girls. This, in turn, generated the legislation initiative by Senator Paul Wellstone; Bill S. 600 was introduced in the US Senate in 1999.

11   The Coalition Against Trafficking in Women has centers and representatives in Australia, Bangladesh, Europe, Latin America, North America, Africa, and Asia Pacific. The Women's Rights Advocacy Program has established the Initiative Against Trafficking in Persons to combat the global trade in persons. Other organizations are referred to throughout this book.

Chapter 7 Appendix

Exhibit A.7.1   Highly Indebted Poor Countries: Exports, Foreign Investment, and Debt Service as Share of GDP, 1995–2006

Country	Trade Export of Goods and Services (% of GDP)				Foreign Direct Investment (% of GDP)			Debt Service Total (% of GDP)			
Year	1995	2003–2004	2005	2006	1995	2003	2006	1995	2003	2005	2006
1. Benin	20.2	13.7	13	/	0.4	1.4	0.5	6.8	6.9	7.4	—
2. Bolivia	/	/	36	42	/	/	-3	/	/	14.3	8.5
3. Burkina Faso	12.4	8.6	10	11	0.4	0.3	0.4	12.2	11.2	—	—
4. Ethiopia	13.6	16.9	16	16	0.2	0.9	2.4	18.4	6.8	4.1	6.8
5. Ghana	/	/	36	39	/	/	1	/	/	7	4.9
6. Guyana	/	/			/	/	9.8	/	/	88	—
7. Honduras	/	/	88	—	/	/	5.6	/	/	3.8	3.4
8. Madagascar	24.1	28.4	27	30	0.3	0.2	0.6	14.9[a]	6.1	5.7	...
9. Mali	21.2	26.4	27	30	4.5	3	3	13.4	5.8	5.7	—

(Continued)

Country	Trade Export of Goods and Services (% of GDP)				Foreign Direct Investment (% of GDP)			Debt Service Total (% of GDP)			
Year	1995	2003–2004	2005	2006	1995	2003	2006	1995	2003	2005	2006
10. Mauritania	49.1	40.2	36	55	0.7	18.1	6.2	22.9	27.7[b]	—	—
11. Mozambique	15.2	22.8	33	41	1.9	7.8	1.6	34.5	6.9	3.8	1.9
12. Nicaragua	/	/	29	31	/	/	4.9	/	/	6.7	4.1
13. Niger	17.2	15.5	15	—	0.4	1.1	0.4	16.7	—	5.9	—
14. Rwanda	5.2	8.6	11	12	0.2	0.3	0.4	20.4	14.6	8.1	9.6
15. Senegal	34.5	27.8	27	26	0.7	1.2	0.7	16.8	8.7	—	—
16. Tanzania	/	/	24	24	/	/	3.9	/	/	4.3	3.4
17. Uganda	—	—	13	15	2.1	3.1	2.9	19.8	7.1	9.3	4.8
18. Zambia	36	20.9	34	38	2.8	2.3	3.6	47.0[c]	29.6	10.9	3.6

Sources: United Nations Development Programme Annual Report 2005, "A Time For Bold Ambition: Together We Can Cut Poverty in Half"; United Nations Development Programme, "Human Development Report 2007–2008," 2008; World Bank, "Global Economic Prospects 2005: Trade, Regionalism and Development" (Washington, DC: World Bank, 2005): World Bank, "Increasing Aid and Its Effectiveness," in *Global Monitoring Report: Millennium Development Goals: From Consensus to Momentum.* 151–87 (Washington, DC: World Bank, 2005); http://hdrstats.undp.org/indicators/174.html.

Notes: An additional twenty countries are eligible for the HIPC program but have not yet met the necessary conditions.

[a] 1995–97; [b] 1998; [c] 1997

/ = Countries eligible for HIPC but not listed by World Bank and UNDP as Less Developed Countries (LDCs).

8

The Urbanizing of Global Governance Challenges

Many of today's major global governance challenges become tangible, urgent, and practical in cities worldwide. In this regard, we can speak of an urbanizing of such global challenges. Among such global governance challenges are those concerning the environment; human insecurity, including the spread of violence against people of all ages and a proliferation of racisms; the urbanizing of war that comes about with asymmetric war; and the sharp rise in economic forms of violence. But cities are also sites where these challenges can be studied empirically and where policy design and implementation often are more feasible than at the national level. Urban leaders and activists have had to deal with many of these issues long before national governments and interstate treaties did. Cities constitute a frontier space for new types of environmentally sustainable energy sources, construction processes, and infrastructures. Finally, cities are critical for emerging intercity networks that involve a broad range of actors (NGOs, formal urban governments, informal activists, global firms, and immigrants) that potentially could function as a political infrastructure with which to address some of these global governance challenges.

Here, I will focus especially on the environmental and financial challenges confronting cities. I will also briefly address asymmetric war.

Cities as Frontier Spaces for Global Governance

We can organize the urbanizing of these various challenges along three vectors. These do not capture everything, but they do point to three very diverse sets of challenges. I do not include financial crises here because they belong to a different realm of challenges.

(a) *New military asymmetries*. When national states go to war in the name of national security, nowadays major cities are likely to become key frontline spaces. In older wars, large armies needed large open fields or oceans in which to meet and fight, and these were the frontline spaces. The search for national security is, today, a source for urban insecurity. We can see this with the so-called War on Terror, whereby the invasion of Iraq became an urban war theater. But we also see the negative impacts of this war in the case of cities that are not even part of the immediate war theater—the bombings in Madrid, London, Casablanca, Bali, Mumbai, Lahore, and so many others. The traditional security paradigm based on national state security fails to accommodate this triangulation. What may be good for the protection of the national state apparatus may go at a high (increasingly high) price to major cities and their people.

(b) *Global warming, energy and water insecurity*. These and other environmental challenges are going to make cities frontline spaces. These challenges will tend to remain more diffuse for nation-states and for the state itself. One key reason is the more acute and direct dependence of everyday life in cities on massive infrastructures and on institutional-level supports for most people—apartment buildings, hospitals, vast sewage systems, water purification systems, vast underground transport systems, and whole electric grids dependent on computerized management vulnerable to breakdowns. We already know that a rise in water levels will flood some of the most densely populated cities in the world. Major disasters are becoming more acute and destructive than they may have been in the last few decades—for example, the floods in Pakistan in 2010 and in Austrialia in 2011 and the unusually strong 2011 earthquake and ensuing tsunami in Japan, a country long subject to such events, but never of such magnitude in modern times.

The urgency of some of these challenges goes well beyond lengthy negotiations and multiple international meetings, still the most common form of engagement at the level of national politics and especially international politics. When global warming hits cities, it will hit hard, and preparedness becomes critical. The new kinds of crises and the ensuing violence will be particularly felt in cities. A major simulation by NASA found that by the fifth day of a breakdown in the computerized systems that manage the electric grid, a major city like New York would be in an extreme condition and basically unmanageable through conventional instruments.

These challenges are emergent, but before we know it, they will become concrete and threatening in cities. This contrasts with possibly slower trajectories at the national level. In this sense, cities are the front line and will have to act on global warming whether national states sign on to international treaties or not. Because of this, many cities have had to develop capabilities to handle these challenges. The air-quality emergency in cities such as Tokyo and Los Angeles as long ago as the 1980s is one instance: these cities could not wait until an agreement such as Kyoto might appear, nor could they wait till national governments passed mandatory laws (e.g., for car fuel efficiency and zero emissions). With or without a treaty or law, they had to address air quality urgently. And they did.

(c) *Urban Violence*. Cities also enter the domain of global governance challenges as a site for the enactment of new forms of violence resulting from these various crises. We can foresee a variety of forms of violence that are likely to escape the macro-level normative propositions of good governance. For instance, São Paulo and Rio in Brazil and Ciudad Juarez and Tijuana in Mexico, to mention just some, have seen forms of gang and police violence in the last few years that point to a much larger breakdown than the typically invoked fact of inadequate policing. So do the failures of the powerful US army in Baghdad; to call this anarchy simply won't do. In terms of global governance questions, one challenge is to push macro-level frames to account for and factor in the types of stress that arise out of everyday life violence and insecurity in dense spaces. Some of these may eventually feed militarized responses, and this may well be inadequate or escalate the conflict.

Bridging the Ecologies of Cities and of the Biosphere

The massive processes of urbanization underway today are inevitably at the center of our environmental future. It is in cities and vast urban agglomerations that humankind is increasingly present on the planet and through cities that people mediate their relation to the various stocks and flows of environmental capital. The urban hinterland, once a mostly confined geographic zone, is today a global hinterland. With the expansion of the global economy, we have raised our capacity to annex larger portions of the planet to support a limited number of industries and places.

Here, I address the multiscalar character of cities: the diverse terrains and domains, many nonurban, onto which they project their effects and from which they meet their needs. I address cities' ecological features: the multiple mechanisms and feedback loops that articulate urban processes and their consequences. Furthermore, I examine the emergent articulations between these urban ecologies and nature's ecologies. The multiscalar and ecological features of key city processes need to become part of urban governance so that the process of governing cities becomes part of the process for developing a more environmentally sustainable and ecologically efficient society.

Urbanization and industrialization have made humankind the biggest consumer and destroyer of all significant ecosystems. Urbanization is an enormously distinctive presence that is contributing to changing a growing range of nature's ecologies both directly and indirectly, from the climate to species diversity and ocean purity. It is also leading to the formation of new, negative environmental conditions, such as heat islands, ozone holes, desertification, and water pollution, the result of which is a set of global ecological conditions never seen before. We can think of this as a shift from the long history of the planet dominated by the geological—the geocene— to an emergent epoch dominated by humans—the anthropocene.

Major cities have become distinct socio-ecological systems with planetary reach. The needs of cities and their growing populations and the profit motives of agribusiness have altered traditional rural economies and their long-standing cultural adaptation to biological diversity. Increasingly, rural populations have become consumers of goods, including even food, produced in the industrial economy, which is much less sensitive to biological diversity. The rural condition—the physical as well as cultural and mental aspects of rural life—has evolved into a new system of social relations, one that does not support biodiversity. These developments all signal that the urban condition—the built environment along with urban cultures and living styles—is a major factor in any environmental future and amounts to a radical transformation in the relationship between humankind and the rest of the planet.

But is it urbanization *per se* that creates environmental problems, or is it the particular types of urban systems and industrial processes we have implemented? Are negative global ecological conditions the result of urban agglomeration and density, that is, the urban format? Or are they the result of the specific types of urban systems we have developed: the urban content, meaning the transportation, waste disposal, building, heating and cooling, food provision, and industrial processes through which we extract, grow, make, package, distribute, and dispose of all the foods, services, and materials we use? It is, doubtless, the latter—the specific urban systems we have made: systems and processes we have created collectively and historically, partly through path-dependence dynamics that kept eliminating options as we proceeded and partly because of corporate profit motives.

That it is not urbanization *per se* that is damaging but the mode of urbanization is also signaled by the adoption of environmentally harmful production processes in rural societies. Until recently, these had environmentally sustainable economic practices such as crop rotation and foregoing the use of chemicals to fertilize and control insects. Further, our extreme capitalism has made the rural poor, especially in the global South, so poor that for the first time, many now are also engaging in environmentally destructive practices, notably practices that lead to desertification.

When we examine a range of major cities today, one outstanding feature is the sharp differences in their environmental sustainability. These differences result from diverse government and industrial policies, economic bases, cultures, community norms, and lifestyles.[1] There follow two very modest examples from the United States, but with the potential to be replicated throughout the country. They demonstrate that urban leadership and informed individuals can make a difference in a country often thought to be deeply antiregulation and generally opposed to government-run programs. Later on, I briefly describe two other examples that are more complex but that could also be replicated throughout.

The first case concerns energy systems and a city in Texas, a state best known for its devotion to oil, and shows how the determination to "green" a city can be developed and implemented even when the larger political landscape is not supportive. In 2000, Austin began to implement a Green Buildings Program that has been recognized internationally as a model program. It is transforming the local construction market by providing education, marketing, and monetary incentives to develop both the demand side (the buying public) and the supply side (building professionals). The program is primarily funded and managed by the city's community-owned utility, Austin Energy. This municipal utility also develops renewable energy sources for the city, including fifty-nine local wind turbines, four landfill methane gas recovery projects, and three solar energy sites providing more than 153 kilowatts of energy. Austin happens to be the only city in Texas run by a Democratic mayor; Texas is often thought to be one of the most Republican, free-market, antigovernment, antiregulation states in the United States. It shows how a well-designed effort and determination can succeed even in inhospitable situations.

The second case concerns Chicago, which has an economic history of heavy manufacturing, steel mills, agribusiness, and the most important heavy-haul transportation center in the country. Today, Chicago is determined to establish itself as a premier environmental city, with the goal of getting 20% of its energy from renewable sources by 2015. This includes solar, wind, biomass, small hydropower, and tapping landfill gas. Chicago has planted hundreds of thousands of trees beginning in the 1990s and continuing into the future, created more than 100 miles of bike paths in the city, installed solar panels on city museums, and built a rooftop garden on City Hall. The city government has also passed legislation to reduce urban "heat island" effects by allowing only reflective roofs or living roofs covered with vegetation.

These examples demonstrate that policy and proactive engagement are critical dimensions for environmental sustainability, whether they involve asking people to change their energy-consumption habits, insisting governments pass sustainability-oriented legislation, or demanding accountability from local and global corporations known to have environmentally damaging production processes.

But these types of interventions are not enough, even though they are necessary. We need to go much further. A few foundational elements that dominate our way of doing things and that are at the heart of what we need to address are shared across different cities. One is the fact that the energy and material that flow through our human economy return in altered form as pollution and waste to the ecosphere. The crux of the matter is that this set of flows is *made* and can be *unmade*, as is signaled by the two examples above from a country that has been particularly behind on environmental standards compared to other highly developed countries. This rupture is present in just about all economic sectors, from urban to rural.

It is against this backdrop that it is necessary to *delegate back to nature*.

Delegating Back to Nature

Our understanding of delegating back to nature is based on a recognition that cities and the biosphere each have multiple ecologies and multiple scales and that we need to build bridges between them (Sassen 2005, 2010; Sassen and Dotan 2011). This is a way of using the capacities of the biosphere and some of the innovations we humans have made—for instance, to allow algae to clean polluted water, we need bioreactors.

A simple return to nature will *not* do. What is necessary is to activate that in-between space between cities and the biosphere—with multiple biosphere capacities and multiple human-made technical and knowledge innovations and instruments. Nor can we simply posit the need for consuming less energy. Rather, the point is to consume differently, both as process and as content. We can illuminate this argument through Bettencourt et al.'s (2007) finding that large cities today consume energy and resources in a nonbiological manner—that is to say, in an unsustainable manner.

With an astonishing degree of regularity, biological processes exhibit economies of scale—material and energy flows tend to proportionally diminish with increasing size. For instance, an elephant requires less energy per pound than a mouse. But large cities today exhibit the opposite behavior—costs, wages, income, employment, resource consumption, rates of invention, and so forth all *accelerate* with increasing urban size. From the perspective of the biosphere, this is unsustainable. One way of conceptualizing what we need to do is precisely this notion of delegating back to nature to have a more balanced way of meeting our needs. This not the same as returning to nature, living like our ancestors did tens of thousands of years ago. The significance of delegating back to nature, at least partly, is that we need knowledge—scientific research but also the deep knowledge of older cultures for growing food, for instance. At its most extreme and therefore clearest, this means that particular kinds of socio-ecological processes delegated back to nature *must* be managed or accelerated in such a way as to keep pace with the urban material and energy flows in their lack of harmony with the biosphere.

Let me give two simple examples involving two different technologies and types of biological and technological knowledge (for more examples, see Sassen 2005; Sassen and Dotan 2011).

Self-Healing Concrete. One dramatic technology being developed is self-healing bacterial concrete. In this technology, bacteria residing within concrete structures seal cracks on concrete surfaces by depositing dense layers of calcium carbonate and other minerals. This sealing reduces the emissions of CO_2 from buildings, a significant fact in that buildings are the largest single source of greenhouse gases. Several groups have demonstrated the feasibility of this approach,[2] and early tests show positive results in reducing greenhouse gases. Human-made structures would thus more closely model the self-sustaining homeostatic physical structures found in nature.[3]

Bioreactor Landfill. The problems of concentrated capture and recycling are strongly felt in cities as a result of the extremely high population densities found in many cities. Landfill waste generated by human activity becomes a dangerous pollutant, source of greenhouse emissions, and terminal break in many natural cycles. The development of landfill bioreactors helps overcome this. Landfill bioreactors seek to accelerate waste decomposition by improving conditions for aerobic or anaerobic biological processes.

This is paired with the capture of by-products released from these processes, most notably carbon dioxide and methane, which is used as fuel known as "landfill gas" (LFG).[4] This both reduces the uncontrolled diffusion of greenhouse gases and provides a concentrated source of fuel as well as carbon dioxide for use in carbon sequestration and fuel generation. As of December 2008, the US Environmental Protection Agency reported that approximately 480 LFG energy projects were operating in the United States, generating approximately twelve billion kilowatt-hours of electricity per year and 255 million cubic feet of LFG for direct use.

The applications of scientific knowledge described above are a strategic first step. But cities are not merely about scientific knowledge. They are complex multiscalar and ecological systems, and they are systems of power and of social relations. It is at this point that forms of knowledge about the social and the political become critical inputs for succeeding in the larger process of delegating back to nature, issues addressed next.

Multiscalar Bridging

The multiscalar and ecological properties of cities help to make legible the variable ways in which cities are articulated with the biosphere and to put on the research and policy agenda the work of understanding how these articulations can be changed to a positive valence. Today's mostly negative interactions and the diversity of domains they cover are themselves an emergent socio-biospheric system that belongs to both the city and the biosphere and that bridges between them (Sassen 2005, 2010). Extreme examples are heat islands, ozone holes, and acid rain. The challenge is to turn what are today negative into positive bridges between cities and the biosphere.

Cities do not fit easily in existing theories about environmental sustainability and global environmental governance. The practical aim should be to work with what is there but at its most variable and complex. That is to say, to go beyond the two extremes that dominate discussion: (1) the only way for cities to contribute to sustainability is mitigation and adaptation, or (2) to start from scratch. Mitigation and adaptation are not enough to address environmental damage. And most cities cannot start from scratch. Thus, for most countries, Abu Dhabi's Mazdar project of a fully self-sustained city is not a model because it is far too expensive; it should be seen as a laboratory experiment. It becomes urgent to recognize that one path into making cities part of the solution is to work from what is there but with the aim of changing the negative valence of current articulations with the biosphere.

Delegating back implies management and human intervention in the formation of *novel* socio-ecological bridges with positive valence. For instance, the rate of waste production accelerates with urban scale whereas natural processes for waste removal would tend to decelerate with scale. So delegating waste management back to nature must involve novel socio-ecological formations that incorporate natural methods in novel ways; for instance, using algae rather than chemicals to process wastewater—it is the same process as in nature, but accelerated. In this sense, these processes are "wrapped" in technology at the moment they are delegated back to nature.

Two decades ago, there was a body of critical analysis of the "return to nature" as a viable option. Thus, Harvey (1996) notes that at best, traditional environmental ecologists can offer some return to an earlier form of urbanization regulated by the metabolic constraints of a bioregional world as it supposedly existed in the past, a world that, for Harvey, never really existed. At that time, and perhaps still in much of the world, much of what passed as ecological among social scientists studying cities actually dealt with quality-of-life issues for middle- and high-income people and neglected the needs of the poor (Satterthwaite 1999).

Though less so today than in the past, the range of issues posed by urbanization goes beyond those typically addressed by environmentalists. For many, the whole notion of sustainable cities is faulty in that it fails to name what are the actual dynamics and causalities that are at issue, that is, the actual processes that cause environmental damage. The articulation of environmental and urban research has long lacked a clear definition of key categories such as environment and sustainability. One difficulty is that environment has many different meanings, depending on ideology, politics, situation, positionality, and economic and political capacities; to this we can add the sort of theoretical issues discussed in the prior section. Nonetheless, there is a whole range of ecological issues central to how we should be thinking about our rapidly urbanizing world. How we respond to some of the large global-scale issues (warming, ozone, emissions) will have profound implications for urbanization processes (Girardet 2008). But these may not be the issues of concern to most people in cities in the South, a difference that goes back decades (e.g. Safi 1998; Pathak 1999; Mol and Sonnenfeld 2000).

With all these ambiguities and differences in the analytical categories and in the position of diverse social strata, we can nonetheless posit that the foundational condition cities share is that the entire energy and material flux coursing through the human economy returns in altered form as pollution and waste to the ecosphere. This is the radical difference between cities and the biosphere: multiscalar dynamics and horizontal eco-shifts enable the biosphere to avoid that rupture and thereby avoid producing "waste" and "pollution." The rupture at the heart of this set of flows in our cities is *made* and can, thus, be unmade.

Addressing this rupture will require instruments and changes that go beyond adaptation and mitigation. This rupture is present in just about all economic sectors, from urban to nonurban. Cities are, today, a source of much of the direct and indirect environmental damage and some of the most intractable conditions that feed the damage. Nevertheless, it is also the complexity of cities that is part of the solution. Thus, it is in cities where environmental damage has its most complex interactions and cumulative effects. We need to use and build upon those features of cities that can transform what are now negative interactions with the biosphere into positive interactions.

The Complexity and Global Projection of Cities

The complexity and diversity of cities can help us engage the legal systems and profit motives that underlie and enable many of the environmentally damaging aspects of our societies. The question of urban sustainability cannot be reduced to modest interventions that leave major systems, such as transportation, energy, and food production untouched. Furthermore, the actual features of these systems vary across countries and across cities within countries. While for some environmental issues, such as protecting the habitat of an endangered species, we can make considerable advances by acting simply on scientific knowledge, such is not the case when dealing with cities or with society at large. Nonscientific elements are a crucial part of the picture: questions of power, poverty and inequality, ideology and cultural preferences are all part of the question and the answer.

The spaces where environmental damage takes place often differ from the sites where responsibility for the damage lies, such as the headquarters of mining corporations, and where accountability should be demanded. A crucial issue is the massive investment around the world promoting large projects that damage the environment. Deforestation, mining, and construction of large dams are perhaps among the best-known cases. The scale and the increasingly global and private- rather than public-sector character of these investments suggest that citizens, governments, and nongovernmental organizations all lack the power to alter these investment patterns or influence their implementations.

However, global cities should actually be seen as structural platforms for acting on and contesting irresponsible and powerful corporate actors (Sassen 2001, 2005). This is because the geography of economic globalization is strategic, as I discussed at length in Chapters 2, 4, and 5. There are sites—the network of global cities—in this strategic geography where the density of economic transactions and top-level management functions come together and constitute a concentrated geography of global decision making. We can also see it as a strategic geography for demanding accountability from major corporate headquarters about environmental damage. For instance, a firm may have hundreds of mines across the world, but its headquarters might be in one or perhaps a few global cities.

It is precisely because the global economic system is characterized by enormous concentration of power in a limited number of large multinational corporations and global financial markets that makes for concentrated rather than widely dispersed sites where accountability and the changing of investment criteria can be demanded. Engaging a company's headquarters is actually easier than engaging the thousands of mines and factories in often remote sites protected by private militias or the millions of service outlets of such global firms. Direct engagement with the headquarters of global firms is facilitated by the recognition among consumers, politicians, and the media of an environmental crisis. For sure, dealing with the headquarters of large firms leaves out millions of independent small local firms responsible for much environmental damage, but these are more likely to be controllable through national regulations and local activism.

A second set of features concerns scaling, present both in the biosphere and in cities. Importantly, cities incorporate a range of scales at which a given ecological condition functions, and in that sense cities make legible the notion of scaling. For instance, one asphalted street in a village and a few buildings with air conditioners produce some heat emissions; thousands of such streets and buildings in a city produce a new socio-ecological condition—heat islands. This, in turn, implies that cities make the multiscalar aspect of ecological systems legible to residents of cities. The urban environment's capacity to make legible should be developed and strengthened because such legibility will become increasingly critical for policy matters concerning cities as well as regions beyond urban areas.

Scaling is one way of handling what are now often seen as either/or conditions: local versus global, markets versus nonmarket mechanisms, green versus brown environmentalism. I have found some of the analytic work on scaling being done among ecologists very illuminating in my efforts to conceptualize the city in this context (e.g., Dietz et al. 2009). Of particular relevance is the notion that complex systems are multiscalar systems as opposed to multilevel systems and that the complexity resides precisely in the relations across scales. The ecological literature finds that tension among scales is a feature of complex ecological systems, a condition that would certainly seem to hold for cities. Let me illustrate by developing on the earlier-mentioned case of how a few air-conditioned high-rise buildings merely add some harmful emissions, whereas a city's downtown creates new ecological systems, such as heat islands, which then feed ozone holes at the planetary scale. Providing an air-conditioned hospital is likely to be experienced as a positive element in a neighborhood of a large city or in a small town: it would be difficult to see the negatives for the average resident. But the fact that at the level of the city, it contributes to heat islands produces a tension between the advantage for that neighborhood and the damage to the larger environment, further accentuated by growing ozone holes. This tension among the different scales forces the issue of environmental damage and the need to find and develop solutions at all levels. In brief, understanding the tensions among the multiple scales of a city (in the example above, neighborhood versus city) enhances the analysis of environmental damages associated with urbanization. And it enhances our understanding of the ways in which cities are the source for solutions to such damages.

We begin to see the city not as a closed system but as a multiscalar system through which flow multiple specific socio-ecological circuits: "damage" circuits, "restoration" circuits, policy circuits, and so on. This also helps us avoid the fallacy of holding "the city" guilty of environmental damage. Eliminating cities would not necessarily solve the environmental crisis. We need to understand the functioning of and the possibilities for changing specific city-related systems: energy systems, economic systems, transportation systems, and the like, which entail modes of resource use that are environmentally unsound. The different components of cities can have different temporal aspects and dynamics—the cycles of the built environment, of the economy, and the life of infrastructures. The damage produced by a car's unclean motor spewing fumes is immediate and promptly visible; but when the car is not on, it is, strictly speaking, not producing damage. The greenhouse gases emitted by buildings never stop—emission is constant and relentless, but not as legible as a fuming car's motor. Combining these many different aspects helps us locate a particular negative or positive condition or process in a broader grid of spatial, temporal, and administrative scales.

When Finance Hits Urban Space

The financial sector has created complex instruments to extract profit from even very modest households. It used by now a well-established mechanism: securitization, a way of making liquid and hence subject to financial transactions what is, not strictly speaking, liquid, such as houses or credit card debt on cars and such. In the 1980s, securitization enabled financial firms to bundle up millions of credit cardholders' debts and home mortgages and develop investment instruments for the high-finance world. This is the prehistory of what we now refer to as the subprime mortgage crisis. In early 2000, a type of subprime mortgage was developed that became catastrophic for modest-income households. Subprime mortgages can be valuable instruments to enable modest-income households to buy a house or even get a second mortgage or a mortgage on an already-paid-for home. But what happened in the United States from 2001 to 2007 was an abuse of the concept, which led to a far higher than usual share of bankruptcies, mostly among modest-income households.

This subprime mortgage is just one case that serves to illustrate how financial experts can develop instruments that enable profit making on even very modest assets and on future losses of assets. Most importantly, this can be done with a disregard for social outcomes, for financial firms themselves, and for the "national economy." Finally, in our current legal system, this disregard is legal, no matter its enormously destructive effects, though criminal abuse of the law can also be present. Among the sharpest of these negative outcomes was the acute rise in foreclosures linked to subprime mortgages, not to prices. In 2008, for instance, on average 10,000 households in the United States lost their homes to foreclosure every day. An estimated ten to twelve million households in the United States will have lost their homes to foreclosures by 2011. Indeed, the available evidence for 2010 shows the highest levels of foreclosure yet in this current financial phase that began in the early 2000s. This is a brutal form of primitive accumulation achieved through an enormously complex sequence of instruments using vast talent pools in finance, law, accounting, mathematics, and so on.

The complexity of the meaning of "gains" in finance contrasts with traditional banking gains. In traditional banking, the gain is on the sale of money the bank actually owns and has, while in finance, the gains are on money the firm does not have. As a result, finance needs to "make" capital, and this means speculative instruments and the financializing of nonfinancial sectors, subjects I return to below and develop fuller elsewhere (Sassen 2008b: chap. 5; 2010).

Presented with the possibility (which turned out to be mostly a deception) of owning a house, modest-income people will put whatever few savings or future earnings they have into a down payment. The small savings or future earnings of modest-income households or the ownership of a modest house were used to enter into a contract necessary to develop a financial instrument that could make profits for investors. All that matters to the financial side was the contract, not the mortgage payments. By 2004, the success of the strategy with investors was such that the mortgage sellers did not even ask for a full credit report or down payment, just a signature on the contract. All that mattered in a financial world overwhelmed by speculative capital was the contract representing the material asset (the house). Indeed, the subprime mortgage sellers were, we now know, rather indifferent as to whether those households could meet the monthly payments. Speed also mattered, so the premium was on selling subprime mortgages even to households that could have qualified for a regular mortgage that would have given them more protections but taken much longer to process given all the documents they require. For the "innovation" to work, sellers had to get at least 500 contracts (mortgages) as fast as possible to construct an instrument by bundling these contracts up with high-grade debt and then sell on the high-finance circuit. The negative effects on households, on neighborhoods, on cities, were not part of the equation.

It becomes clear in the microcosm that is New York City. The table below shows how whites, who have a far higher average income than all the other groups in New York City, were far less likely to have subprime mortgages than all other groups, reaching just 9.1% of all mortgages taken by whites in 2006 compared with 13.6% of Asian-Americans, 28.6% of Hispanic-Americans, and 40.7% of African Americans. The table also shows that all groups, regardless of incidence, had high growth rates in subprime lending from 2002 to 2006. If we consider the most acute period, 2002 to 2005, it more than doubled for whites, tripled for Asians and Hispanics, and quadrupled for blacks. It also becomes evident in the estimated losses of cities due to the foreclosure crisis.

Exhibit 8.1   Rate of Conventional Subprime Lending by Race in New York City, 2002 to 2006

	2002	2003	2004	2005	2006
White	4.6%	6.2%	7.2%	11.2%	9.1%
Black	13.4%	20.5%	35.2%	47.1%	40.7%
Hispanic	11.9%	18.1%	27.6%	39.3%	28.6%
Asian	4.2%	6.2%	9.4%	18.3%	13.6%

Source: Furman Center for Real Estate & Urban Policy, 2007.

Exhibit 8.2   US Metro Areas With Largest GMP Losses, 2008 Estimates

Rank	2008	Revised Real GMP Growth, %	Loss in Real GMP Growth, %	Loss of GMP, Millions
1	New York-Northern New Jersey-Long Island, NY-NY-PA	2.13	–0.65	–$10,372
2	Los Angeles-Long Beach–Santa Ana, CA	1.67	–0.95	–$8,302
3	Dallas-Forth Worth-Arlington, TX	3.26	–0.83	–$4,022
4	Washington-Arlington-Alexandria, DC-VA-MD-WV	2.79	–0.60	–$3,957
5	Chicago-Naperville-Joliet. IL-IN-WI	2.23	–0.56	–$3,906
6	San Francisco-Oakland-Fremont, CA	1.88	–1.07	–$3,607
7	Detroit-Warren-Livonia, MI	1.30	–0.97	–$3,203
8	Boston-Cambridge-Qunincy, MA-NH	2.16	–0.99	–$3,022
9	Philadelphia-Camden-Wilmington, PA-NJ-	1.85	–0.63	–$2,597

Note: For an explanation of how these estimates were reached please see Global Insight 2007. This report contains a full list of GMP estimated losses for all 361 metros (Appendix, Table A2, pages 8–16). The estimate is that that 128 metros will see slow real GMP growth of less than 2% in 2008, and that growth will fall by more than a third in 65 metros, and more than a quarter in 143 metros.

From the investors' perspective, the key reason for even bothering to focus on mortgages for mostly modest-income households was the growing demand for asset-backed securities in an extremely speculative financial system. Its extreme character is made evident by its "value," as measured by the outstanding value of derivatives, which stood at well over US$600 trillion—fourteen times the value of global GDP (US$54 trillion). To address this demand, even subprime mortgage debt could be used as an asset because it represented a house. But the low quality of these mortgages meant cutting up each mortgage into multiple tiny slices and mixing these up with high-grade debt. The result was an enormously complex instrument that was also enormously opaque: tracing all the components of these bundled assets is difficult and, in many cases, evidently impossible. This is what happened with now-defunct Lehman, a financial firm whose value has still not been established by a team of top-level experts for the purposes of bankruptcy proceedings.

The lethal threat to the households buying these types of subprime mortgages was that payment of monthly mortgage dues mattered less to the sellers than securing a certain number of loans within a short time span to be bundled up into "investment products." Sellers of these mortgages used complex sequences of "products" aimed at delinking the creditworthiness of the homebuyer from investors' profit; further, the accelerated buying and selling of these instruments in the high-finance circuit enables profit making and passes on risk. Investors have made hundreds of billions of dollars in profits on these mixed instruments merely by including a bit of asset (those houses) in what were mostly purely speculative instruments but that could then be sold as *asset-*backed securities. Millions of those modest households went bankrupt and lost their homes and whatever savings they had put into this, even as many investors made vast profits.

As with the outsourcing of labor, the insidious element is that a very large number of mortgage sales to modest-income individuals (who mostly did not ask for them) can actually translate into profits for the high-finance investor. It took some serious financial engineering to make this possible, just as it did for corporate shareholder value through outsourcing jobs. The ensuing millions of bankruptcies among subprime mortgage holders in 2006 and 2007 mostly did not affect investors directly: only those who held onto these mortgages suffered. Most investors did not hold on and thus made profits. But within the logic of finance, it is also possible to make a good profit by betting against the success of an innovation, predicting failure.[5] And that type of profit making also happened.

In short, the so-called subprime crisis was not due to irresponsible households taking on mortgages they could not afford as is still commonly asserted in the United States and then onward to the rest of the world. The so-called subprime mortgage crisis was a foreclosure crisis for homeowners. But it was merely a crisis of *confidence* for the world of high finance: the numbers of foreclosures had grown to many millions by 2007 and it became evident that it was impossible to trace the toxic component (the foreclosed mortgage) in their investments, and hence could not be extracted.

The subprime mortgages turned out to be the little tail that wagged the huge dog of finance.

Crisis as Systemic Logic

Financial profit is a construction that can either be promptly materialized into a nonfinancial asset, such as an investment into building a dam or buying a telecommunications corporation, or can be used as a platform for further financial constructions, such as speculation. The latter is what has dominated the last twenty years and generated the extremely high levels of financialization now evident especially in several major developed countries, partly facilitated by the use of electronic networks, software instruments, and the invention of many new-derivative-based instruments (Sassen 2008a: chap. 7). More generally, and to give a sense of the orders of magnitude that the financial system has created over the last two decades, the total (notional) value of outstanding derivatives, which are a form of complex debt and the most common financial instrument, stood at more than $600 trillion. Financial assets have grown far more rapidly than the overall economy of developed countries, as measured by GDP.[6] In itself, this is not necessarily bad, especially if the growing financial capital is materialized in large-scale public-benefit projects—for example, a rapid transit system or development of solar energy, to mention a few attractive options. But in this current period that began in the 1980s, this was rare except for some extreme cases such as the building up of Dubai. Mostly, finance kept on developing more speculative and complex instruments. Historically, this does seem to be part of the logic organizing finance—as it grows and gains power, it does not govern its power well. Further, Arrighi (1994) has argued that when speculative finance becomes dominant in a historic period, it signals the decay of that period.

In the United States, the source of many of these organizational and financial innovations, the value of financial assets by 2006, right before the 2007 crisis takes off, had reached 450% to US GDP (McKinsey & Company 2008). In the European Union, it stood at 356% to GDP, with the UK at 440%, well above the EU average. More generally, the number of countries where financial assets exceeded the value of their gross national product more than doubled from thirty-three in 1990 to seventy-two in 2006.

These numbers illustrate that the period that begins in the late 1980s and continues today is an extreme moment. But is it an anomalous moment? I argue that it is not. Further, it is not created by exogenous factors, as the notion of "crisis" suggests. Having recurrent crises is the normal way this particular type of financial system functions. Our government has given finance the instruments to continue its leveraging stampede every time it has bailed out the financial system since the first crises of this phase in the 1980s, the savings and loans crisis, and the New York stock market crash of 1987. We have had five major bailouts since the 1980s, the decade when the new financial phase took off. Each time, taxpayers' money was used to pump liquidity into the financial system and finance used it to leverage, aiming at more speculation and gain; it did not use it to pay off its debt because finance *is* about debt.

The financializing of a growing number of economic sectors since the 1980s has become both a sign of the power of this financial logic and the sign of its autoexhaustion insofar as finance needs to use (invade?) other economic sectors in order to grow. Once it has subjected much of the economy to its logic, it reaches some type of limit, and the downward curve is likely to set in. One acute illustration of this is the development of instruments by some financial firms that bet on growth in a sector and simultaneously bet against that sector. This is clearly not made public, but every now and then, we get an insight into how this might work. One recent case is Goldman Sachs selling derivatives to the prior Greek government to help it handle its debt and then developing instruments for another client that would deliver profits if the Greek government went bankrupt. Goldman Sachs evidently engaged in similar practices with some of its clients, which led to a recent lawsuit by the US government against Goldman Sachs; the firm settled out of court to avoid making public too much information about its procedures and avoid having to admit it deceived some of its clients.

The current crisis has features that signal that financialized capitalism has reached the limits of its own logic, at least in the current phase. It has been extremely successful at extracting value from all economic sectors through their financializing. When everything has become financialized, finance can no longer extract value. It needs nonfinancialized sectors to build on. In this context, two of the last global frontiers for financial extraction are modest-income households, of which there are a billion or more worldwide, and bailouts through taxpayers' money—which is real, old-fashioned, not financialized money.[7]

Two Separate Crises

The critical factor in the current financial crisis is yet another innovation, credit default swaps. These had reached US$62 trillion by 2007 and launched the massive losses for high finance that exploded in September 2008, a full year after the subprime mortgage crisis of August 2007. The critical factor was not the millions of subprime mortgage foreclosures. The values in play due to the actual foreclosures were relatively small for global financiers.

It was the fact of not knowing what might next turn out to be a toxic asset given the impossibility of tracing the toxic component in complex investment instruments. As already indicated, this housing crisis for millions of people was merely a crisis of confidence among investors. Elsewhere, I have examined the importance of confidence and interpretation in our complex and accelerated global financial system (Sassen 2008b: chap. 7). The decline in house prices, the high rate of mortgage foreclosures, the declines in global trade, and the growth of unemployment all alerted investors that something was not right. This, in turn, led those who had bought credit default swaps as a sort of "insurance" to want to cash in. But the sellers of these swaps had not expected this downturn or the demand to cash in from those whom they had sold these credit swaps. They were not ready, and this catapulted much of the financial sector into crisis. Not everybody lost: investors such as Soros made large profits by going against the trend.

These credit default swaps are part of what has come to be referred to as the shadow banking system. According to some analysts, this shadow banking system accounted for 70% of banking at the time that the crisis exploded. The shadow banking system is not informal, illegal, or clandestine. Not at all: it is in the open, but it has thrived on the opaqueness of the investment instruments. This opaqueness has also facilitated the recoding of instruments (a derivative recoded as insurance), which allowed for practices that are now, after the fact, viewed as bordering on illegal. For instance, it is now clear that credit default swaps were sold as a type of insurance, though they were not, as I explained earlier. From the perspective of the financial system, this made a significant difference: if it is insurance, the law requires they be backed by capital reserves and be subject to considerable regulation. Making them into derivatives was a de facto deregulation and eliminated the capital reserves requirement. Credit default swaps could not have grown so fast and reached such extreme values if those capital reserves needed to be met, and it would have reduced much of the impact of the September 2008 crisis. Because they were actually derivatives, they could have an almost vertical growth curve beginning as recently as 2001. For that same reason, none of the financial firms had the capital reserves they would have needed to back $60 trillion in insurance.

There were, then, two very separate crises: the crisis of the people who had gotten these mortgages and the crisis of confidence in the investor community. The millions of home foreclosures were a signal that something was wrong, but in itself, it could not have brought down the financial system. The crisis of homebuyers was not a crisis for financial investors.

For finance, it was a crisis of confidence. It made visible the importance of the systems of trust that make possible the speed and orders of magnitude of this financial system. The crisis of homeowners (valued at a few hundred billion dollars) was the little tail that wagged the enormous dog of trust in the financial system. In other words, this type of financial system has more of the social in it than is suggested by the technical complexity of its instruments and electronic platforms, a subject I develop elsewhere (Sassen 2008a: chap. 7).

We all need debt, whether we are a firm, a household, or a country. But do we need this level of debt? And even more importantly, do we need such complex instruments to finance what are mostly rather basic needs for firms and households? No. Many of these needs can be met with traditional banking loans. We need finance because it "makes" capital, and large-scale projects need vast amounts of capital: at this point, only finance can reach these orders of magnitude. The problem is that finance has entered domains—such as consumer loans and home mortgages—where traditional banking would have been a safer option for consumers. We need to expand and strengthen regulated banking and make finance less invasive and aggressive.

The language of crisis remains ambiguous, as is evident in the following events and trends. A first point is the enormous variability of conditions that we call crisis. Since the 1980s, there have been several financial crises, some famous, such as the 1987 New York stock market crisis and the 1997 Asian crisis, and some obscure, such as the individual country financial crises that happened in more than seventy countries in the 1980s and 1990s as they deregulated their financial systems. These are usually referred to as adjustment crises; the language suggests they are good crises because they move a country towards economic development. Typically the term *financial crisis* is used for the first kind, that is to say, for a crisis to the leading sectors of finance rather than a country's institutions and people. The second, individual country "adjustment" crises, involved a far larger region of the globe given the vast number of countries involved. The miseries these adjustment crises brought to the middle sectors in each country and the destruction of often well-functioning economic sectors is largely an invisible history to the global eye. These individual country adjustment crises only intersected with global concerns and interests when there were strong financial links with global firms and investors, as was the case with the 1994 Mexican crisis and the 2001 Argentine crisis.

A second point arises from data that present the period after the 1997 so-called Asian financial crisis as a fairly stable one—until the current crisis.

One element in this representation is that after a country goes through an adjustment crisis, what follows can be measured as "stability" and even prosperity according to conventional indicators. This then produces a representation of considerable financial stability in the post-1997 period, except for a few major global crises, such as the dot-com crisis and the Argentine sovereign default.

But behind this "stability" is the savage sorting of winners and losers described in the prior section. Behind this stability also lies the fact that it is easier to track winners than to track the often slow sinking into poverty of households, small firms, and government agencies (such as health and education) that are not part of the new glamour sectors (finance and trade). The postadjustment losers became somewhat invisible to the global eye over the last twenty years. Every now and then, they became visible, as when members of the traditional middle class in Argentina went on food riots in Buenos Aires (and elsewhere) in the mid 1990s—after adjustment!—breaking into food shops just to get food—something unheard of in Argentina, which took many by surprise. Such mostly rare events also make visible the very partial character of postadjustment stability and the new "prosperity" so praised by global regulators and global media. Thus, we need to disaggregate the much-mentioned fact that in 2006 and 2007, most countries had a GDP growth rate of 4% a year or more, which is much higher than that of previous decades. Behind that measure lies the making of extreme forms of wealth and of poverty. In contrast, a 4% GDP growth rate in the Keynesian years described the massive growth of a middle class.

Also left out of this macro-level picture of relative stability in the post-Asian financial crisis decade is the critical fact that "crisis" is a structural feature of deregulated, interconnected, and electronic financial markets. Two points are worth mentioning in this regard. One is the sharp growth in the extent to which nonfinancial economic sectors were financialized, leading to overall extremely high financial deepening. That is to say, if crisis is a structural feature of current financial markets, then the more financialized nonfinancial economic sectors are, the more susceptible they become to a financial crisis. The overall outcome is extreme potentials for instability even in strong and healthy economic sectors, a likely possibility particularly in countries with highly developed financial systems and high levels of financialization, notably the United States and the UK.

Let me illustrate with an example from the current crisis and one from the 1997 Asian crisis. When the September 2008 crisis hit the United States, many healthy firms, with good capitalization, strong demand for their goods and services, and good profit levels, were brought down by the financial crisis. Large US corporations, from Coca-Cola and Pepsi to IBM and

Microsoft, were doing fine in terms of capital reserves, profits, market presence, and so on; but the financial crisis eventually hit them, largely via consumer demand and credit access. Highly financialized sectors such as the housing market and commercial property market suffered a direct and immediate impact. This is not the first time we saw this type of impact on basically healthy nonfinancial firms. It happened in many countries that underwent adjustment crises: they secured the conditions for globally linked financial markets but, in that process, ruined non-financial-sector firms. We saw this also in the 1997 Asian financial crisis, which destroyed thousands of healthy manufacturing firms in South Korea, whose products were in strong demand in national and foreign markets, which had the workforces and the machines to execute worldwide orders but had to close because credit dried up, preventing them from paying for all the up-front costs of production and causing the unemployment of more than a million factory workers (Sassen [1991] 2001: chap. 4).

When Pursuing National Security Is the Making of Urban Insecurity

The pursuit of national security has become the making of urban insecurity. Asymmetric war—war between a conventional army and armed insurgents— has made cities one site in the map for war. Cities worldwide are becoming key theaters for asymmetric war, regardless of what side of the divide they are on—allies or enemies.

Since 1998, most asymmetric attacks have been in cities. This produces a disturbing map. The US Department of State's Annual Report on Global Terrorism allows us to establish that over the last twenty years, cities have become the key targets for what the report defines as terror attacks— attacks by nonconventional combatants. This trend began before the September 2001 attacks on New York and the Pentagon. The report finds that from 1993 to 2000, cities accounted for 94% of the injuries resulting from all terrorist attacks and for 61% of the deaths. Secondly, in this period, the number of incidents doubled, rising especially sharply after 1998. In contrast, in the 1980s, hijacked airplanes accounted for a larger share of terrorist deaths and destruction than they did in the 1990s. Access to urban targets is far easier than access to military installations or to planes for terrorist hijacking. The report does not include conventional military action in and on cities; I consider this also part of the urbanizing of war.

A first feature of asymmetric war is that the new urban map of war is expansive: it goes far beyond the actual nations involved. The bombings in

Madrid, London, Casablanca, Bali, Mumbai, Lahore, Jakarta, and on are all part of this expansive map. Each of these bombings is specific and can be explained in terms of particular grievances and aims. As material practices, these are localized actions by local armed groups acting independently from each other. Yet they are also clearly part of a new kind of multisited war—a distributed and variable set of actions that gain larger meaning from a particular conflict with global projection.

A second key feature of asymmetric wars is that they are partial, intermittent, and lack clear endings. There is no armistice to mark their end. They are one indication of how the center no longer holds—whatever the center's format: the imperial power of a period or the national state, including in powerful countries. Asymmetric war found one of its sharpest enactments in the US war on Iraq. The US conventional military aerial bombing took only six weeks to destroy the Iraqi army and take over. But then asymmetric war set in, with Bagdad, Mosul, Basra, and other Iraqi cities the sites of conflict. And it has not stopped since.

A third feature is that they are enormously diverse. Consider, for instance, the case of Mumbai's attacks in 2008 and Gaza's bombing by Israel in December 2008. Both are places with long histories of conflict but representing sharply different trajectories and assemblages of elements. Mumbai got caught up in the older India–Pakistan conflict, with sharp fluctuations in its role as one site for asymmetric war. Gaza is part of a continuously live and open conflict with a modern state, Israel, a conflict that eventually fed a conflict with another asymmetric force, the Palestinian Authority. Both the Mumbai and Gaza cases are enormously complex and caught in very diverse assemblages of territory, authority, and rights, each with multiscalar dimensions. A question both these cases raise is whether they represent some of the future shapes of war.

A fourth feature is the activating by asymmetric war of older conflicts that evolve into armed conflict between two unconventional forces, as is the case with the Shia–Sunni conflicts in Iraq and with some of the wars among African tribal peoples that may have lived in relative peace for a long time but then find their old histories of conflict reactivated by novel types of conflict that have little to do with those older histories.

A fifth feature of contemporary wars generally, including wars that are not necessarily asymmetric, is that they often involve forced urbanization. This holds especially for the less developed areas. Contemporary conflicts produce significant population displacement both into and out of cities. In many cases, such as African conflicts or the Kosovo wars, displaced people swell urban populations. At the same time, in many of these conflicts, the warring bodies avoid battle or direct military confrontation, as

Mary Kaldor (2007; Beebe and Kaldor 2010) has described in her work on the new wars. Their main strategy is to control territory by getting rid of people of a different identity (ethnicity, religion, politics). The main tactic is terror—conspicuous massacres and atrocities pushing people to flee.

These types of displacement—with ethnic/religious "cleansing" the most virulent form—have a profound impact on the cosmopolitan character of cities. Cities have long had the capacity to bring together people of different classes, ethnicities, and religions through commerce, politics, and civic practices. Contemporary conflicts unsettle and weaken this cultural diversity of cities when they lead to forced urbanization or internal displacement. Belfast, Baghdad, or Mostar each is at risk of becoming a series of urban ghettoes, with huge implications for infrastructure and the local economy. Baghdad has undergone a deep process of such "cleansing," a critical component of the (relative) "peace" of the last two years.

Elsewhere, I have examined whether the systemic equivalent of these types of "cleansing" in the case of very large cities may well be the growing ghettoization of the poor and the rich—albeit in very different types of ghettoes. It leaves the middle classes, rarely the most diverse group in cities, to the task of bringing urbanity to these cities. The risk is that they will supplant traditional urban cosmopolitanisms with narrow defensive attitudes in a world of growing economic insecurity and political powerlessness. Under these conditions, displacement from countryside to town or within cities also becomes a source of insecurity rather than a source of rich diversity.

The urbanizing of war today is different from histories of cities and war in modern times. In older wars, such as the two so-called world wars of 1914 to 1918 and 1940 to 1945, large armies needed large open fields or oceans in which to meet and fight and to carry out invasions. These were the frontline spaces of war. In WWII, the city entered the war theater not as a site for war but as a technology for instilling fear: the full destruction of cities as a way of terrorizing a whole nation, with Dresden and Hiroshima the iconic cases.

Here, we can see a critical dimension that shows us the limits of power, and, perhaps, the power of basic norms. The countries with the most powerful conventional armies today cannot afford to repeat Dresden with firebombs or Hiroshima with an atomic bomb—whether in Baghdad, Gaza or the Swat valley.[8] They can engage in all kinds of activities, including violations of the law: rendition, torture, assassinations of leaders they don't like, excessive bombing of civilian areas, and so on in a history of brutality that can no longer be hidden and seems to have escalated the violence against civilian populations.

There seem to be limits for reasons that range from merely utilitarian to some tacit recognition of foundational norms: could be a touch of wisdom, some honest belief in those foundational norms, a practical tradeoff of some sort or another, such as access to armaments or oil, or the mere existence of a sticky web of constraints—a mix of law, reciprocal agreements, and the informal global court of public opinion. Over and over, history shows us the limits of power.[9] It would seem that unilateral decisions by the greater power are not the only source of restraint: in an increasingly interdependent world, the most powerful countries find themselves restrained through multiple interdependencies, a sort of sticky web that might be a function of systemic survival in a world where several countries have the capacity to destroy the planet (Sassen 2008: chap. 8).

Under these conditions, the city becomes a technology for containing conventional military powers and a technology of resistance for armed insurgencies. The physical and human features of the city are an obstacle for conventional armies—an obstacle wired into urban space itself.[10] Would Gaza have been completely rather than partially destroyed if it were not densely populated, if it was just occupied by factories, warehouses, and offices?

Notes

1   For a particularly strategic angle that cuts across all these factors, see *Ecological Economics:* by Daly and Farley 2003.

2   Jonkers, H. M. 2007. "Self Healing Concrete: A Biological Approach." Pp. 195–204 in *Self Healing Materials: An Alternative Approach to 20 Centuries of Materials Science.* Springer.

3   An experimental technology with a similar capacity to be deployed "globally at the local level" is the so-called carbon-negative cement (see http://www .novacem.com/docs/novacem_press_release_6_aug_2009.pdf). There are many other such uses of nature's capacity to address the environmental challenge in cities, although none as globally present as the challenge of greening buildings.

4   Yolo County, Planning and Public Works Dept. Full Scale Bioreactor Landfill for Carbon Sequestration and Greenhouse Emission Control March 2006.

5   They speculated against these instruments—that is to say, they bet against the sustainability of instruments based on getting low-income people to sign off on mortgage contracts regardless of their capacity to pay. This also suggests that many of the damaging aspects of these instruments for the households involved were known in the financial community.

6   More detail can be found in my "A Bad Idea: A Financial Solution to the Financial Crisis" at http://www.huffingtonpost.com/saskia-sassen/a-bad-idea-using -a-financ_b_145283.html.

7   Elsewhere (Sassen 2008b), I examine data that show the potential for global finance to use this particular type of subprime mortgage worldwide, given its features (delinking capacity to pay the mortgage from investors' profit).

8   Even if the nuclear threat to cities has remained hypothetical since 1945, cities have remained highly vulnerable to two kinds of very distinct threats. The first one is the specialized aerial attack of new computer-targeted weaponry, which has been employed "selectively" in places like Bagdad or Belgrade.

9   A separate source for unilateral restraint is tactical: thus theorists of war posit that also the superior military force should, for tactical reasons, signal to its enemy that it has not used its full power.

10   This dual process of urbanization of war and militarization of urban life unsettles the meaning of the urban. Marcuse (2009) writes that "the War on terrorism is leading to a continued downgrading of the quality of life in US cities, visible changes in urban form, the loss of public use of public space, restriction on free movement within and to cities, particularly for members of darker skinned groups, and the decline of open popular participation in the governmental planning and decision-making process." From a very different angle, Graham (2010) examines the strong presence of military imagery in cities. Second, it questions the role of cities as welfare providers. The imperative of security means a shift in political priorities. It implies a cut or a relative decrease in budgets dedicated to social welfare, education, health, infrastructure development, economic regulation, and planning. These two trends, in turn, challenge the very concept of citizenship (Sassen 2008a: chap. 6).

9

A New Geography of Centers and Margins

Summary and Implications

Three important developments that took off in the 1980s laid the foundation for the analysis of cities in the world economy presented in this book. They are captured in the four broad propositions organizing the preceding chapters.

1. *The territorial dispersal of corporate economic activities, of which globalization is one form, contributes to the growth of centralized functions and operations.* This entails a new logic for agglomeration and is a key condition for the renewed centrality of cities in advanced economies. Information technologies, often thought of as neutralizing geography, actually contribute to spatial concentration of central headquarters functions. These technologies are capabilities that enable the simultaneous geographic dispersal and integration of many activities. The particular conditions under which the utilities of such capabilities can be maximized have promoted centralization of the most advanced users and providers of information services in the most advanced urban economies. Parallel developments exist in cities that function as regional nodes—that is, at smaller geographic scales and lower levels of complexity than global cities.

2. *Centralized control and management over a geographically dispersed array of economic operations does not come about inevitably as part of a*

world system. It requires the production of a vast range of highly specialized services, telecommunications infrastructures, and industrial services. Major cities are centers for the servicing and financing of international trade, investment, the international art market, and many other activities that have complex requirements. Headquarters increasingly outsource some of their critical operations to this specialized service sector. This makes global cities strategic production sites for today's leading economic sectors. Cities that serve as regional centers exhibit similar developments but with lower levels of agglomeration and complexity. The built environments of cities partly represent the spatial effects of the growing service intensity in the organization of all industries.

3. *Economic globalization has contributed to a new geography of centrality and marginality.* This new geography assumes many forms and operates in many terrains, from the distribution of telecommunications facilities to the structure of the economy and of employment. Global cities become the sites of immense concentrations of economic power, while cities that were once major manufacturing centers suffer inordinate declines. Parallel inequalities develop inside cities. Professionals see their incomes rise to unusually high levels, while low- or medium-skilled workers see theirs sink. Financial services produce superprofits, while industrial services barely survive.

4. *Emergent transnational urban systems also enable a proliferation of sociopolitical networks.* The making of an infrastructure for the global operations of firms and markets is increasingly also used for purposes other than narrow corporate economic ones. Immigrants, diasporic groups, environmental and human-rights activists, global justice campaigns, and groups fighting the trafficking of people, among many others, are contributing to strengthen these emergent transnational urban systems. What distinguishes both the economic and sociopolitical networks examined in this book is that they constitute globalities centered in cities rather than running through the bureaucracies of national states or supranational agencies. Sociopolitical networks illuminate the ways in which powerlessness can become a complex condition in the concrete space of cities where multiple groups and projects intersect. The recurrence of such projects across cities contributes to an emergent horizontal multisited globality among growing numbers and types of disadvantaged groups.

Let us look more closely now at the two last and most encompassing propositions. They point to the emergence of two strategic geographies. One, inside global cities, brings the most powerful sectors of global capital together with some of the most disadvantaged workers from a large number of countries. The other, an increasingly developed intercity geography, produces transnational spaces that are beginning to be used by actors other than the firms and professionals who partly developed them.

The Locus of the Peripheral

The sharpening distance between the extremes evident in all major cities of developed countries raises questions about the notion of *rich* countries and cities. It suggests that the geography of centrality and marginality, which in the past was seen in terms of the duality of highly developed and less developed countries, is now also evident within developed countries and especially within their major cities.

One line of theorization posits that the intensified inequalities described in this book represent a transformation in the geography of center and periphery. They signal that peripheralization processes are occurring inside areas that were once conceived of as *core* areas—whether at the global, regional, or urban level—and that alongside the sharpening of peripheralization processes, centrality has also become sharper at all three levels.

The condition of being peripheral is installed in variable geographic terrains and institutional contexts depending on the prevailing economic dynamic. Beginning in the 1970s, we see new forms of peripheralization at the center of major cities in developed countries not far from some of the most expensive commercial land in the world: the inner city next to the central city or the downtown. These juxtapositions are evident not only in the United States and large European cities but also now in Tokyo (Sassen [1991] 2001: chap. 9), in Mumbai (Weinstein 2009), Shanghai (Gu and Tang 2002; Ren 2011), and just about all other cities becoming incorporated into the global economy (Gugler 2004). Peripheralization operates at the center also in organizational terms (e.g., garment sweatshops and the growing range of informal operations), a trend that began in the 1970s in US cities (Sassen-Koob 1982) and also in major European cities, such as Paris (Lazzarato 1997), Amsterdam (Russell and Rath 2002), and urban regions such as Northern Italy (Bagnasco 1977). We have long known about segmented labor markets, but today's downgrading of manufacturing sectors that are actually part of advanced urban economies and sharp devaluing of nonprofessional workers in leading industries go beyond segmentation and in fact represent an instance of peripheralization at the core.

Furthermore, the new forms of growth evident at the urban perimeter also mean crisis: violence in the immigrant ghetto of the *banlieues* (the French term for inner-ring suburbs), exurbanites clamoring for growth controls to protect their environment, and new forms of urban governance (Body-Gendrot 1999; Keil 1999; Rae 2003). The regional mode of regulation in many of these cities is based on the old city–suburb model and may, hence, become increasingly inadequate to deal with intraperipheral conflicts—conflicts between different types of constituencies at the urban perimeter or urban region (Frug 2001). Frankfurt, for example, is a city that cannot function without its region's towns; yet this particular *urban region* would not have emerged without the specific forms of growth in Frankfurt's center. Keil and Ronneberger (1992) noted the ideological motivation in the late 1980s in the call by politicians to officially *recognize* the region so as to strengthen Frankfurt's position in the global interurban competition (Brenner 2004). This call also provides a rationale for coherence and the idea of common interests among the many objectively disparate interests in the region: it displaces the conflicts between unequally advantaged sectors onto a project of regional competition with other regions. Regionalism then emerges as the concept for bridging the global orientation of leading sectors with the various local agendas of various constituencies in the region (Scott 2001; Brenner 2004).

In contrast, the city discourse rather than the ideology of regionalism dominates in cities such as Chicago or São Paulo (see Schiffer 2002) even when their regions are massive economic complexes. The challenge is how to bridge the inner city or the squatters at the urban perimeter with the center. In multiracial cities, multiculturalism has emerged as one form of this bridging. A *regional* discourse is perhaps beginning to emerge, but it has until now been totally submerged under the suburbanization banner, a concept that suggests both escape from and dependence on the city. The notion of conflict within the urban periphery between diverse interests and constituencies (Schiffer 2002) has not really been much of a factor in the United States. The delicate point at the level of the region has, rather, been the articulation between the residential suburbs and the city (Madigan 2004).

Contested Space

Large cities have emerged as strategic territories for these developments. *First, cities are the sites for concrete operations of the global economy.* For our purposes, we can distinguish two forms of such concrete operations: (1) In terms of economic globalization and place, cities are strategic places that concentrate command functions, global markets, and production sites for the advanced corporate service industries. (2) In terms of day-to-day work in the leading economic complex, a large share of the jobs involved are low paid and manual, and many are held by women and (im)migrants. Although these types of workers and jobs are never represented as part of the global economy, they are, in fact, as much a part of globalization as international finance is. We see at work here a dynamic of valorization that has sharply increased the distance between the devalorized and the valorized— indeed, overvalorized—sectors of the economy. These joint presences have made cities a contested terrain.

The structure of economic activity has brought about changes in the organization of work that are reflected in a pronounced shift in the job supply, with strong polarization occurring in the income distribution and occupational distribution of workers. Major growth industries show a greater incidence of jobs at the high- and low-paying ends of the scale than do the older industries now in decline. Almost half the jobs in the producer services are lower-income jobs, and the other half are in the two highest earnings classes. In contrast, large shares of manufacturing workers were in middle-earning jobs during the postwar period of high growth in these industries in the United States and most of Western Europe.

One particular concern here is to understand how new forms of inequality actually are constituted into new social forms, such as gentrified neighborhoods, informal economies, or downgraded manufacturing sectors. To what extent these developments are connected to the consolidation of an economic complex oriented to the global market is difficult to say. Precise empirical documentation of the linkages or impacts is impossible; the effort here was focused, then, on a more general attempt to understand the consequences of both the ascendance of such an international economic complex and the general move to a service economy.

Second, the city concentrates diversity. Its spaces are inscribed with the dominant corporate culture and also with a multiplicity of other cultures and identities, notably through immigration. The slippage is evident: the dominant culture can encompass only part of the city. And although corporate power inscribes noncorporate cultures and identities with *otherness*, thereby devaluing them, they are present everywhere. The immigrant communities and informal economy described in Chapters 6 and 7 are only two instances. Diverse cultures and ethnicities are especially strong in major cities in the United States and Western Europe, regions that also have the largest concentrations of corporate power.

We see here an interesting correspondence between great concentrations of corporate power and large concentrations of Others. It invites us to see that globalization is constituted not only in terms of capital and the new international corporate culture (international finance, telecommunications, information flows) but also in terms of people and noncorporate cultures.

There is a whole infrastructure of low-wage, nonprofessional jobs and activities that constitutes a crucial part of the so-called corporate economy.

A focus on the *work* behind command functions, *production* in the finance and services complex, and *marketplaces* has the effect of incorporating the material facilities underlying globalization and the whole range of jobs and workers typically not seen as belonging to the corporate sector of the economy: secretaries and cleaners, the truckers who deliver the software, the variety of technicians and repair workers, and all the people with jobs related to the maintenance, painting, and renovation of the buildings where the corporate economy is housed.

This expanded focus helps us recognize that a multiplicity of economies is involved in constituting the so-called global information economy. It recognizes types of activities, workers, and firms that have never been installed in the "center" of the economy or that have been evicted from that center in the various restructuring phases that began in the 1980s and have therefore been devalued in a system with a narrow conception of what is the center of the economy. But this expended focus also allows us to recognize segments of the workforce that are in the center but have been evicted from the *account about* that center. Economic globalization, then, can be seen as a process that involves multiple economies and work cultures.

In this book, I showed that cities are of great importance to the dominant economic sectors. Large cities in the highly developed world are the places where globalization processes assume concrete, localized forms. These localized forms are, in good part, what globalization is about. We can then think of cities also as one key place where the contradictions of the internationalization of capital either come to rest or to conflict. If we consider, further, that large cities concentrate a growing share of disadvantaged populations—immigrants in both Europe and the United States, African Americans and Latinos in the United States—then we can see that cities have become a strategic terrain for a whole series of conflicts and contradictions.

On the one hand, they concentrate a disproportionate share of corporate power and are one of the key sites for the overvalorization of the corporate economy; on the other, they concentrate a disproportionate share of the disadvantaged and are one of the key sites for their devalorization. This joint presence happens in a context in which (1) the globalization of the economy has grown sharply and cities have become increasingly strategic for global capital and the latter increasingly makes claims on these cities, and (2) marginalized people have come into representation and also are making claims on the city as well. This joint presence is further brought into focus by the sharpening of the distance between the two. The center, both as space and as social form, now concentrates immense power, a power that rests on the capability for global control and the capability to produce superprofits. And marginality, notwithstanding weak economic and political power, has become an increasingly strong presence through the new politics of culture and identity.

If cities were irrelevant to the globalization of economic activity, the key economic and political actors could simply abandon them and not be bothered by any of this. Indeed, this is precisely what some politicians argue—that cities have become hopeless reservoirs for all kinds of social despair. The dominant economic narrative argues that place no longer matters, firms can be located anywhere thanks to telematics, and major industries now are information-based and, hence, not placebound. This line of argument devalues cities at a time when they are major sites for the new cultural politics. It also allows the corporate economy to extract major concessions from city governments under the notion that firms can simply leave and relocate elsewhere, which is not quite the case for a whole complex of firms, as much of this book showed.

In seeking to show that (1) cities are strategic to economic globalization because they are command points, global marketplaces, and production sites for the information economy, and (2) many of the devalued sectors of the urban economy actually fulfill crucial functions for the center, in this book, I recover the importance of cities specifically in a globalized economic system and the importance of those overlooked sectors that rest largely on the labor of women, immigrants, and, in large US cities, African Americans and Latinos. In fact, the intermediary sectors of the economy (such as routine office work, headquarters that are not geared to the world markets, the variety of services demanded by the largely suburbanized middle class) and of the urban population (the middle class) can and have left cities. The two sectors that have stayed, the center and the *other*, find in the city the strategic terrain for their operations.

References and
Suggested Reading

A. T. Kearney, Inc. 2010. "The Global Cities Index." The Chicago Council on Global Affairs, and *Foreign Policy* Magazine. Chicago, IL: A. T. Kearney, Inc.

Aalbers, M.B. 2009. "The Gobalization and Europeanization of Mortgage Markets." *International Journal of Urban and Regional Research* 33(2): 389–410.

———, ed. 2012. *Subprime Cities*. Boston: Blackwell.

Abrahamson, Mark. 2004. *Global Cities*. New York and Oxford: Oxford University Press.

Abreu, A., M. Cocco, C. Despradel, E. G. Michael, and A. Peguero. 1989. *Las Zonas Francas Industriales: El Exito de una Politica Economica*. Santo Domingo: Centro de Orientacion Economica.

Abu-Lughod, Janet Lippman. 1980. *Rabat: Urban Apartheid in Morocco*. Princeton, NJ: Princeton University Press.

———. 1989. *Before European Hegemony: The World System A.D. 1250–1350*. New York and Oxford: Oxford University Press.

———. 1994. *From Urban Village to "East Village": The Battle for New York's Lower East Side*. Cambridge, MA: Blackwell.

———. 1999. *New York, Chicago, Los Angeles: America's Global Cities*. Minneapolis, MN: University of Minnesota Press.

Acemoglu, Daron. 2002. "Technical Change, Inequality, and the Labor Market." *Journal of Economic Literature* 40(1):7–72.

Acosta-Belen, Edna and Carlos E. Santiago. 2006. *Puerto Ricans in the United States: A Contemporary Portrait*. Boulder, CO: Lynne Reinner Publishers.

Adrian, C. 1984. *Urban Impacts of Foreign and Local Investment in Australia*. Publication 119. Canberra, Australia: Australian Institute of Urban Studies.

Aguiar, Luis L. M. and Andrew Herod, eds. 2005. *Cleaning Up the Global Economy*. Malden, MA: Blackwell.

Albrecht, Don E. and Scott G. Albrecht. 2009. "Economic Restructuring, The Educational Income Gap, and Overall Income Inequality." *Sociological Spectrum* 29(4): 519–47

Allen, John. 1999. "Cities of Power and Influence: Settled Formations." Pp. 181–228 in *Unsettling Cities*, edited by John Allen, Doreen Massey, and Michael Pryke. New York: Routledge.

———. 2003. *Lost Geographies of Power*. Malden, MA: Blackwell Publishers.

———, Doreen Massey and Michael Pryke, eds. 1999. *Unsettling Cities*. London, UK: Routledge.

Allison, Eric. 1996. "Historic Preservation in a Development-Dominated City: The Passage of New York City's Landmark Preservation Legislation." *Journal of Urban History* 22(3):350–76.

Alsayyad, N. and Ananya Roy. 2006. "Medieval Modernity: On Citizenship and Urbanism in a Global Era." *Space and Polity* 10:1–20.

Amen, Mark M., Kevin Archer and M. Martin Bosman, eds. 2006. *Relocating Global Cities: From the Center to the Margins*. New York: Rowman & Littlefield.

Amin, Ash, ed. 1997. *Post-Fordism*. Oxford, UK: Blackwell.

———. 2002. *Placing the Social Economy*. London: Routledge.

———. 2006. "The Good City." *Urban Studies* 43:10009–10023.

——— and Kevin Robins. 1990. "The Re-emergence of Regional Economies? The Mythical Geography of Flexible Accumulation." *Environment and Planning D: Society and Space* 8(1):7–34.

_____ and J. Roberts, eds. 2008. *Community, Economic Creativity and Organization*. Oxford: Oxford University Press.

Amin, S. 2010. "Exiting the Crisis of Capitalism or Capitalism in Crisis?" *Globalizations* 7(1–2):261–73.

AMPO. 1988. "Japan's Human Imports: As Capital Flows Out, Foreign Labor Flows In." Special issue of *Japan-Asia Quarterly Review* 19(1, Special issue).

Anderson, E. 1990. *Streetwise, Chicago*. Chicago, IL: University of Chicago Press.

Appadurai, Arjun. 1996. *Modernity at Large*. Minneapolis, MN: University of Minnesota Press.

———. 2000. *Globalization*. Raleigh, NC: Duke University Press.

Arias, E. D. 2004. "Faith in Our Neighbors: Networks and Social Order in Three Brazilian Favelas." *Latin American Politics and Society* 46:1–38.

Arrighi, G. 1994. *The Long Twentieth Century*. London: Verso.

Arroyo, Monica, Milton Santos, Maria Adelia A. De Souze and Francisco Capuano Scarlato, eds. 1993. *Fim de Seculo e Globalizacao*. São Paulo, Brazil: Hucitec.

Ascher, François. 1995. *Metapolis ou l'Avenir des Villes*. Paris, France: Editions Odile Jacob.

Asian Women's Association. 1988. *Women from Across the Seas: Migrant Workers in Japan*. Tokyo, Japan: Asian Women's Association.

Australian Government Foreign Investment Review Board. 1996. *Annual Report 1995–96*. Canberra, Australia: Australian Government Publishing Service.

———. 2004. *Annual Report 2003–04*. Canberra, Australia: CanPrint Communications.

Australia and New Zealand Banking Group Ltd. 2009. *Australia's 200 Biggest Companies: Standard & Poor's S&P/ASX 200 Index*. Retrieved March 18, 2010 (http://www.anz.com/resources/1/d/1d8a8b004e4a3a22a603af93c5571dd1/Australias-Biggest-200-Companies.pdf?CACHEID=93520f804e472ee49b39bf6672659df2).

Australian Bureau of Statistics. 2006. "2006 Census of Population and Housing, Cat. No. 2068.0—2006 Census Tables: Industry of Employment by Sex: Based on place of employment." Retrieved March 18, 2010 (http://www.abs.gov.au/).

Avgerou, Chrisanthi. 2002. *Information Systems and Global Diversity*. Oxford, UK: Oxford University Press.

Axel, Brian K. 2002. "The Diasporic Imaginary." *Public Culture* 14(2):411–28.

Bagnasco, Arnaldo. 1977. *Tre Italie: La Problematica Territoriale Dello Sviluppo Italiano*. Bologna, Italy: Il Mulino.

Bailey, Thomas. 1990. "Jobs of the Future and the Education They Will Require: Evidence from Occupational Forecasts." *Educational Researcher* 20(2):11–20.

Balbo, Laura and Luigi Manconi. 1990. *I Razzismi Possibili*. Milano, Italy: Feltrinelli.

Banerjee-Guha, Swapna, ed. 2010. *Accumulation by Dispossession: Transformative Cities in the New Global Order*. Thousand Oaks, CA: Sage Publications.

Bank for International Settlements. 1992. *62nd Annual Report*. Basel, Switzerland: BIS.

———. 1998. *Central Bank Survey*. Basel, Switzerland: BIS.

———. 1999. *69th Annual Report*. Basel, Switzerland: BIS.

———. 2002. *Central Bank Survey*. Basel, Switzerland: BIS.

———. 2004. *Quarterly Review—June 13, 2004*. Basel, Switzerland: BIS.

———. 2005. *Triennial Central Bank Survey*. Basel, Switzerland: BIS.

———. 2005. *Quarterly Review—December, 2005*. Basel, Switzerland: BIS.

———. 2007. *Triennial Central Bank Survey*. Basel, Switzerland: BIS. Retrieved March 18, 2010 (http://www.bis.org/publ/rpfxf07t.pdf?noframes=1).

Barr, J. B. and L. Budd. 2000. "Financial Services and the Urban System: An Exploration." *Urban Studies,* 37(3):593–610.

Bartlett, Anne. 2006. "Political Subjectivity in the Global City." Ph.D. Dissertation, Department of Sociology, University of Chicago.

———. 2007. "The City and the Self: The Emergence of New Political Subjects in London." Pp. 221–243 in *Deciphering the Global: Its Spaces, Scales and Subjects,* edited by S. Sassen. New York and London: Routledge.

Bauer, Thomas K. and Kunze, Astrid. 2004. "The Demand for High-skilled Workers and Immigration Policy," IZA Discussion Papers 999, Institute for the Study of Labor (IZA).

Bavishi, V. and Wyman, H. E. 1983. *Who Audits the World: Trends in the Worldwide Accounting Profession*. Storrs, CT: University of Connecticut, Center for Transnational Accounting and Financial Research.

Beck, Ulrich. 2000. *The Risk Society and Beyond: Critical Issues for Social Theory*. Thousand Oaks, CA: Sage

———. 2005. *Power in the Global Age*. Cambridge: Polity Press.

Beckfield, Jason and S. Alderson Arthur. 2004. Power and Position in the World City System. *American Journal of Sociology 109*(4): 811–851.

_____. and Arthur S. Alderson. 2006. "Whither the Parallel Paths? The Future of Scholarship on the World City System." *American Journal of Sociology* 112: 895–904.

Beebe, Shannon D. and Mary H. Kaldor. 2010. *The Ultimate Weapon is No Weapon.* London: Public Affairs.

Beneria, Lourdes. 1989. "Subcontracting and Employment Dynamics in Mexico City." Pp. 173–88 in *The Informal Economy: Studies in Advanced and Less Developed Countries,* edited by A. Portes, M. Castells, and L. Benton. Baltimore, MD: Johns Hopkins University Press.

—— and Marta Roldan. 1987. Crossroads of Class and Gender: Homework, Subcontracting, and Household Dynamics in Mexico City. Chicago, IL: University of Chicago.

—— and Shelley Feldman, eds. 1992. *Unequal Burden: Economic Crises, Persistent Poverty, and Women's Work.* Boulder, CO: Westview.

Benjamin, S. 2008. "Occupancy Urbanism: Radicalizing Politics and Economy beyond Policy and Programs." *International Journal of Urban and Regional Research* 32:719–29.

Benko, Georges and Mick Dunford, eds. 1991. Industrial Change and Regional Development: The Transformation of New Industrial Spaces. London and New York: Belhaven/Pinter.

Berger, Suzanne and Michael J. Piore. 1980. *Dualism and Discontinuity in Industrial Societies.* New York and London, UK: Cambridge University Press.

Berque, Augustin. 1987. *La Qualité de la Ville: Urbanite Française, Urbanite Nippone.* Tokyo, Japan: Maison Franco-Japonaise.

Bestor, Theodore. 1989. *Neighborhood Tokyo.* Stanford, CA: Stanford University Press

Bettencourt, M. A. Luis et al. 2007. "Growth, Innovation, Scaling, and the Pace of Life in Cities" *Proceedings of the National Academy of Sciences of the United Sates of America 2007* 104: 7301–06.

Beveridge, Andrew A. 2003. "The Affluent of Manhattan." *Gotham Gazette* June 2003.

Bhachu, Parminder. 1985. *Twice Immigrants.* London, UK: Tavistock.

Bhagwati, J. 1988. *Protectionism.* Boston, MA: MIT Press.

Bini, Paolo Calza. 1976. *Economia Periferica e Classi Sociali.* Napoli, Italy: Liguori.

Blaschke, J. and A. Germershausen. 1989. "Migration und Ethnische Beziehungen." *Nord-Sud Aktuell* 3–4(Special issue).

Bloomberg News. 2010. "China Suspends ETFs in Shanghai After Glitches, Oriental Says." Retrieved Dec. 30, 2010 (http://www.businessweek.com/news/2010-12-29/china-suspends-shanghai-etf-approvals-oriental-says.html).

Blumberg, P. 1981. *Inequality in an Age of Decline.* New York: Oxford University Press.

Bodnar, Judit. 2000. *Fin de Millénaire Budapest: Metamorphoses of Urban Life.* Minneapolis, MN: University of Minnesota Press.

Body-Gendrot, Sophie. 1993. *Ville et violence.* Paris, France: Presses Universitaires de France.

————. 1999. *The Social Control of Cities*. London, UK: Blackwell.

————, Emmanuel Ma Mung, and Catherine Hodier, eds. 1992. "Entrepreneurs entre Deux Mondes: Les Creations d'Entreprises par les Etrangers: France, Europe, Amerique du Nord." *Revue Européenne des Migrations Internationales* 8(1, Special issue):5–8.

————, Jacques Carré, and Romain Garbaye. 2008. *A City of One's Own: Blurring the Boundaries Between Private and Public*. Burlington, VT: Ashgate Publishing Company.

Boissevain, Jeremy. 1992. "Les Entreprises Ethniques aux Pays-Bas." *Revue Européenne des Migrations Internationales* 8(1, Special issue):97–106.

Bolin, Richard L., ed. 1998. *The Global Network of Free Zones in the 21st Century*. Flagstaff, AZ: The Flagstaff Institute.

Bonacich, Edna. 2000. *Behind the Label: Inequality in the Los Angeles Garment Industry*. Berkeley, CA: University of California Press.

Bonacich, Edna, Lucie Cheng, Nora Chinchilla, Norma Hamilton, and Paul Ong, eds. 1994. *Global Production: The Apparel Industry in the Pacific Rim*. Philadelphia, PA: Temple University Press.

Bonamy, Joel and Nicole May, eds. 1994. *Services et Mutations Urbaines*. Paris, France: Anthropos.

Bonilla, Frank, Edwin Melendez, Rebecca Morales, and Maria de los Angeles Torres, eds. 1998. *Borderless Borders*. Philadelphia, PA: Temple University Press.

Boonyabancha, Somsook. 2009. "Land for Housing the Poor—by the Poor: Experiences from the Baan Mankong Network Slum Upgrading Project in Thailand." *Environment and Urbanization* 21:309–22.

Booth, Cathy and Timothy Long. 1993. "Miami: the Capital of Latin America." *Time Magazine*. Retrieved Dec. 31, 2010 (http://www.time.com/time/magazine/article/0,9171,979733,00.html).

Boris, Eileen. 1994. *Home to Work*. Cambridge, UK: Cambridge University Press.

Bose, Christine E. 2001. *Women in 1900: Gateway to the Political Economy of the 20th Century*. Philadelphia, PA: Temple University Press.

———— and E. Acosta-Belen, eds. 1995. *Women in the Latin American Development Process*. Philadelphia, PA: Temple University Press.

Boston Consulting Group. 2011. Global Asset Management 2010: Building on Success. Boston: Boston Consulting Group. http://www.bcg.com/documents/file81068.pdf

Bourdeau-Lepage, L. and J. Huriot. 2008. "Megapolises and Globalization. Size Doesn't Matter." *Les Annales de la Recherche Urbaine* 105:81–93.

Bourgois, P. 1996. *In Search of Respect: Selling Crack in El Barrio*. Structural Analysis in the Social Sciences Series. New York: Cambridge University Press.

Bouzarovski, S. 2009. "Building Events in Inner-city Gdańsk, Poland: Exploring the Sociospatial Construction of Agency in Built Form." *Environment and Planning D: Society and Space*. 27:840–58.

Boyer, Christine. 1983. *Dreaming the Rational City*. Cambridge, MA: MIT Press.

Boyer, Robert, ed. 1986. *La Flexibilité du Travail en Europe*. Paris, France: La Découverte.

Bradshaw, Y., R. Noonan, L. Gash and C. Buchmann. 1993. "Borrowing Against the Future: Children and Third World Indebtedness." *Social Forces* 71(3): 629–56.

Braithwraite, John, Hilary Charlesworth, Peter Reddy and Leah Dunn. 2010. *Reconciliation and Architectures of Commitment: Sequencing Peace in Bougainville*. Canberra, Australia: Australian National University E Press.

Brand, Constant. 2006. "Belgian PM: Data Transfer Broke Rules" The Associated Press, *Washington Post*. Retrieved Jan. 9, 2011. (http://www.washingtonpost .com/wp-dyn/content/article/2006/09/28/AR2006092800585.html).

Braudel, Fernand. 1984. *The Perspective of the World, Vol. III*. London, UK: Collins.

Brauer, David, Beethika Khan and Elizabeth Miranda. 1998. *Earnings Inequality, New York–New Jersey Region*. New York: Federal Reserve Bank of New York (July).

Brettell, Caroline, and James F. Hollifield, eds. 2000. *Migration Theory: Talking Across the Disciplines*. New York: Routledge.

Brenner, Neil. 2004. *New State Spaces: Urban Governance and the Rescaling of Statehood*. Oxford: Oxford University Press.

———. 1998. "Global Cities, Glocal States: Global City Formation and State Territorial Restructuring in Contemporary Europe." *Review of International Political Economy* 5(1):1–37.

Bridge, Gary and Sophie Watson. 2011. *The New Blackwell Companion to the City*. Oxford, UK: Wiley-Blackwell.

———. 2004. *New State Spaces: Urban Governance and The Rescaling of Statehood*. Oxford, UK: Oxford University Press.

——— and Nik Theodore, eds. 2002. Spaces of Neoliberalism: Urban Restructuring in North America and Western Europe. Malden, MA: Blackwell Publishers.

——— and Roger Keil. 2006. *The Global Cities Reader*. London: Routledge.

Brookings Institute. "Living Cities Census Series" [Data file]. Retrieved May 2008 (http://www.brookings.edu/metro/living-cities/main.aspx).

Brosnan, P. and F. Wilkinson. 1987. *Cheap Labour: Britain's False Economy*. London, UK: Low Pay Unit.

Brotchie, J., M. Barry, E. Blakely, P. Hall, and P. Newton, eds. 1995. *Cities in Competition: Productive and Sustainable Cities for the 21st Spaces of Neoliberalism Century*. Melbourne, Australia: Longman Australia.

Brotherton, David and Philip Kretsedemas, eds. 2008. *Keeping Out the Other*. New York: Columbia University Press.

Brown, C. 1984. *Black and White Britain*. London, UK: Heinemann.

Brown, E., B. Derudder, C. Parnreiter, W. Pelupessy, P. J. Taylor and F. Witlox. 2010. "World City Networks and Global Commodity Chains: Towards a World Systems Integration." *Global Networks*, 10(1).

Brusco, Sebastiano. 1986. "Small Firms and Industrial Districts: The Experience of Italy." Pp. 182–202 in *New Firms and Regional Development*, edited by David Keeble and Francis Weever. London, UK: Croom Helm.

Bryson, J. R. and P. W. Daniels, eds. 2007. *The Service Industries Handbook*. Cheltenham, UK: Edward Elgar.

Buck, Nick, Matthew Drennan, and Kenneth Newton. 1992. "Dynamics of the Metropolitan Economy." Pp. 68–104 in *Divided Cities: New York & London in the Contemporary World,* edited by Susan Fainstein, Ian Gordon, and Michael Harloe. Oxford, UK: Blackwell.

Buechler, S. 2007. "Deciphering the Local in a Global Neoliberal Age: Three Favelas in Sao Paulo, Brazil." Pp. 95–112 in *Deciphering the Global: Its Scales, Spaces, and Subjects,* edited by Saskia Sassen. New York: Routledge.

Buntin, Jennifer. (In Process). "Transnational Suburbs? The Impact of Immigration Communities on the Urban Edge." Ph.D. Dissertation, Department of Sociology, University of Chicago.

Bunnell, T., H. Muzaini and J. D. Sidaway. 2006. Global City Frontiers: Singapore's Hinterland and the Contested Socio-political Geographies of Bintan, Indonesia. *International Journal of Urban and Regional Research. 30:*3–22.

Burdett, Ricky, ed. 2006. *Cities: People, Society, Architecture.* New York: Rizzoli.

_____ and Deyan Sudjic eds. 2011. *Living in the Endless City.* London: Phaidon Press.

Burgel, Guy. 1993. *La Ville Aujourd'hui.* Paris, France: Hachette, Collection Pluriel.

Burgess R., M. Carmona and T. Kolstee, eds. 1997. *The Challenge of Sustainable Cities: Neoliberalism and Urban Strategies in Developing Countries.* London and New York: Zed Books.

Cadena, Sylvia. 2004. "Networking for Women or Women's Networking." A report for the Social Science Research Council's Committee on Information Technology and International Cooperation. Accessible at http://www.ssrc .org/programs/itic/publications/civsocandgov/cadena.pdf.

Canadian Urban Institute. 1993. *Disentangling Local Government Responsibilities: International Comparisons.* Urban Focus Series 93–1. Toronto, Canada: Canadian Urban Institute.

Canevari, Annapaola. 1991. "Immigrati Prima Accoglienza: E Dopo?" Dis T Rassegna di Studi e Ricerche del Dipartimento di Scienze del Territorio del Politecnico di Milano 9(September):53–60.

Cardew, R. V., J. V. Langdale and D. C. Rich, eds. 1982. *Why Cities Change: Urban Development and Economic Change in Sydney.* Sydney, Australia: Allen and Unwin.

Carleial, L. and M. R. Nabuco. 1989. *Transformacoes na DiviSao Inter-regional no Brasil.* São Paulo, Brazil: Anpec/Caen/Cedeplar.

Castells, Manuel. 1972. La Question Urbaine. Paris: Maspero

———. 1983. *The City and the Grassroots: A Cross-Cultural Theory of Urban Social Movements.* Berkeley, CA: University of California Press.

———. 1989. *The Informational City.* London, UK: Blackwell.

———. 1996. *The Rise of the Network Society.* Oxford: Blackwell.

———. 1998. *The Information Age: Economy, Society, and Culture. Vol. 3: End of Millennium.* Malden/Oxford, UK: Blackwell.

——— and Yuko Aoyama. 1994. "Paths Toward the Informational Society: Employment Structure in G-7 Countries, 1920–1990." *International Labour Review* 133(1):5–33.

———— and P. Hall. 1994. *Technopoles of the World: The Making of Twenty-First-Century Industrial Complexes*. London, UK: Routledge.

Castles, S. and M. Miller. 2003. *The Age of Migration: International Population Movements in the Modern World*. 3rd ed. London, UK: Macmillan.

Castro, Max, ed. 1999. *Free Markets, Open Societies, Closed Borders*. Coral Gables, FL: University of Miami, North-South Center Press.

CEMAT (European Conference of Ministers Responsible for Regional Planning). 1988. *Draft European Regional Planning Strategy*. Vols. 1 and 2. Luxembourg: CEMAT.

Center on Housing Rights and Evictions. 2009. *Global Survey: Forced Evictions, Violations of Human Rights*. Author.

Chaney, E. and M. Garcia Castro. 1993. *Muchacha Cachifa Criada Empleada Empregadinha Sirvienta Y...Mas Nada*. Caracas, Venezuela: Nueva Sociedad.

Chang, Grace. 1998. "Undocumented Latinas: The New 'Employable Mothers.'" Pp. 311–19 in *Race, Class, and Gender*, 3d ed., edited by M. Andersen and Patricia Hill Collins. Belmont, CA: Wadsworth.

———— and Mimi Abramovitz. 2000. *Disposable Domestics: Immigrant Women Workers in the Global Economy*. Boston, MA: South End Press.

Chant, Sylvia H. and Nikki Craske. 2002. *Gender in Latin America*. New Brunswick, NJ: Rutgers University Press.

———— and Lisa Ann Richey. 2010. *The International Handbook of Gender and Poverty: Concepts, Research, Policy*. Northampton, MA: Edward Elgar Publishing, Inc.

Chase-Dunn, C. 1984. "Urbanization in the World System: New Directions for Research." Pp. 111–20 in *Cities in Transformation*, edited by M. P. Smith. Beverly Hills, CA: Sage.

Chen, Xiangming. 2005. *As Borders Bend: Transnational Spaces on the Pacific Rim*. New York: Rowman & Littlefield.

————. 2009. Shanghai Rising: *State Power and Local Transformations in a Global Megacity*. Minneapolis, MN: University of Minnesota Press.

———— and Tomas de'Medici. 2010. "Research Note—The 'Instant City' Coming of Age: Production of Spaces in China's Shenzhen Special Economic Zone." *Urban Geography* 31(8):1141–47.

Cheshire, P. C. and D. G. Hay. 1989. *Urban Problems in Western Europe*. London, UK: Unwin Hyman.

Chinchilla, Norma and Nora Hamilton. 2001. *Seeking Community in the Global City: Salvadorans and Guatemalans in Los Angeles*. Philadelphia, PA: Temple University Press.

Chuang, Janie. 1998. "Redirecting the Debate over Trafficking in Women: Definitions, Paradigms, and Contexts." *Harvard Human Rights Journal* 10 (Winter):65–108.

CIA World Factbook, Hong Kong. 2010. Retrieved Dec. 30, 2010 (https://www.cia .gov/library/publications/the-world-factbook/geos/hk.html).

Ciccolella, Pablo. 1998. "Territorio de Consumo: Redefinición del Espacio en Buenos Aires en el Fin de Siglo." Pp. 201–30 in *Ciudades y Regiones al Avance de la Globalización*, edited by S. Sorenstein and R. Bustos Cara. UNS (Universidad Nacional del Sur), Bahia Blanca, Argentina.

———— and Mignaqui. 2002. "Buenos Aires: Sociospatial Impacts of the Development of Global City Functions." Pp. 309–26 in *Global Networks, Linked Cities*, edited by Saskia Sassen. New York and London: Routledge.

City of Frankfurt. 2011. "Population." Frankfurt, Germany. Retrieved July 12, 2011 (http://www.frankfurt.de/sixcms/detail.php?id=437171&_ffmpar%5b_id_inhalt%5d=258871).

City of Sydney. 2011. "Sydney as a Global City." http://www.cityofsydney.nsw.gov.au/AboutSydney/CityResearch/GlobalSydney.asp

City of Toronto. 1990. *Cityplan '91: Central Area Trends Report.* Toronto, Canada: City of Toronto, Planning and Development Department.

————. 2001. *Toronto's Financial Services Cluster: A Review.* Toronto, Canada: City of Toronto, Economic Development. Retrieved December 7, 2005 (http://www.city.toronto.on.ca/business_publications/finance_review.pdf).

————. 2005a. Business and Economic Development facts. Toronto, Canada. Retrieved December 7, 2005 (http://www.city.toronto.on.ca/toronto_facts/business_econdev.htm).

————. 2005b. *Toronto's Economic Profile.* Toronto, Canada. Retrieved December 7, 2005 (http://www.city.toronto.on.ca/economic_profile/index.htm).

————. 2010. Retrieved Dec. 31, 2010 (http://www.toronto.ca/invest-in-toronto/finance.htm) (http://www.toronto.ca/business_publications/pdf/TOREcoDevOverview 27845.pdf) (http://www.toronto.ca/business_publications/pdf/TOREcoDevIT&New2783C .pdf)

Clark, Terry Nichols, ed. 2003. *The City as an Entertainment Machine.* St. Louis, MO: Elsevier.

———— and Vincent Hoffman-Martinot, eds. 1998. *The New Political Culture.* Oxford, UK: Westview.

Clavel, P. 1986. *The Progressive City.* New Brunswick, NJ: Rutgers University Press.

Cobos, Emilio Pradilla. 1984. *Contribución a la Critica de la "Teoria Urbana": Del "Espacio" a la "Crisis Urbana."* Mexico, D.F.: Universidad Autonoma Metropolitana Xochimilco.

Cohen, R. 1987. *The New Helots: Migrants in the International Division of Labour.* London, UK: Avebury.

Cohen, Stephen S. and John Zysman. 1987. *Manufacturing Matters: The Myth of the Post-industrial Economy.* New York: Basic Books.

Colomina, Beatriz, ed. 1992. *Sexuality & Space.* Princeton Papers on Architecture. Princeton, NJ: Princeton Architectural Press.

Colon, Alice, Marya Munoz, Neftali Garcia, and Idsa Alegria. 1988. "Trayectoria de la Participación Laboral de las Mujeres en Puerto Rico de los Años 1950 a 1985." In *Crisis, Sociedad y Mujer: Estudio Comparativo entre Paises de America 1950–1985).* Havana: Federación de Mujeres Cubanas.

Connell, J. 2000. *Sydney: The Emergence of a World City.* Melbourne, Australia: Oxford University Press.

Consalvo, Mia and Susanna Paasonen, eds. 2002. *Women and Everyday Uses of the Internet: Agency and Identity.* New York: Peter Lang.

———. 2010. "Parliament Rejects Bank Transfer Data Deal" Retrieved Jan. 10, 2011. (http://www.europeanvoice.com/article/2010/02/parliament-rejects-bank-transfer-data-deal/67144.aspx).

Copjec, Joan and Michael Sorkin, eds. 1999. *Giving Ground*. London, UK: Verso.

Corbridge, S. and J. Agnew. 1991. "The U.S. Trade and Budget Deficit in Global Perspective: An Essay in Geopolitical Economy." *Environment and Planning: Society and Space* 9:71–90.

———, Ron Martin, and Nigel Thrift, eds. 1994. *Money, Power, and Space*. Oxford, UK: Blackwell.

Cordero-Guzman, Hector R., Robert C. Smith, and Ramon Grosfoguel, eds. 2001. *Migration, Transnationalization, and Race in a Changing New York*. Philadelphia, PA: Temple University Press.

Cornelius, Wayne A., Philip L. Martin, and James F. Hollifield, eds. 1994. *Controlling Immigration: A Global Perspective*. Stanford, CA: Stanford University Press.

———, Takeyuki Tsuda, Philip L. Martin, and James F. Hollifield, eds. 2004. *Controlling Immigration: A Global Perspective* (2nd Ed.). Stanford, CA: Stanford University Press.

Crichlow, Michaeline A. 2004. *Negotiating Caribbean Freedom: Peasants and The State in Development*. Lanham, MD: Lexington Books.

Cybriwsky, R. 1991. *Tokyo. The Changing Profile of an Urban Giant*. World Cities series, edited by R. J. Johnson and P. L. Knox. London, UK: Belhaven.

da Gama Torres, Haraldo. 2008. *Social and Environmental Aspects of Peri-Urban Growth in Latin American Megacities*. United Nations Expert Group Meeting on Population Distribution, Urbanization, Internal Migration and Development. United Nations Secretariat, Department of Economic and Social.

Daly, H. E. and J. Farley. 2003. *Ecological Economics: Principles and Applications*. Washington, DC: Island Press.

Daly, M. T. and R. Stimson. 1992. "Sydney: Australia's Gateway and Financial Capital." pp 18.1–18.42 in *New Cities of the Pacific Rim*, edited by E. Blakely and T. J. Stimpson. Berkeley, CA: University of California, Institute for Urban & Regional Development.

Daniels, J. 2009. *Cyber Racism: White Supremacy Online and the New Attack on Civil Rights*. Lanham, MD: Rowman & Littlefield Publishers.

Daniels, Peter W. 1985. *Service Industries: A Geographical Appraisal*. London, UK, and New York: Methuen.

———. 1991. "Producer Services and the Development of the Space Economy." Pp. 108–17 in *The Changing Geography of Advanced Producer Services*, edited by Peter W. Daniels and Frank Moulaert. London, UK, and New York: Belhaven.

Dauhajre, A., E. Riley, R. Mena, and J. Guerrero. 1989. *Impacto Economico de las Zonas Francas Industriales de Exportación en la Republica Dominicana*. Santo Domingo, Dominican Republic: Fundacion Economia y Desarrollo.

Davis, Mike. 1999. *Ecology of Fear: Los Angeles and the Imagination of Disaster*. New York: Vintage Editions.

———. 2006. *Planet of the Slums*. London: Verso.

Dawson, A. 2009. "Surplus City." *Interventions: International Journal of Postcolonial Studies* 11:16–34.

Dear, Michael. 2001. "Los Angeles and the Chicago School: Invitation to a Debate." *Cities and Communities* (1)1:5–32.

Dean, J., J. W. Anderson and G. Lovink. 2006. *Reformatting Politics: Information Technology and Global Civil Society*. London: Routledge.

Debrah, Yaw A., Ian McGovern, and Pawan Budhwar. 2010. "Complementarity or competition: the development of human resources in the South-East Asian Growth Triangle: Indonesia, Malaysia and Singapore." *International Journal of Human Resource Management* 11:314–35.

Deecke, H., T. Kruger, and D. Lapple. 1993. "Alternative Szenarien der Wirtschaftlichen Strukturentwicklung in der Hamburger Wirtschaft unter Raumlichen Gesichtspunkten." Final Report for the City of Hamburg. Hamburg, Germany: Technische Universität Hamburg Harburg.

Deere, Carmen Diana, Peggy Antrobus, Lynn Bolles, Edwin Melendez, Peter Phillips, Marcia Rivera, and Helen Safa. 1990. *In the Shadows of the Sun: Caribbean Development Alternatives and U.S. Policy*. Boulder, CO: Westview.

Delauney, Jean Claude and Jean Gadrey. 1987. *Les Enjeux de la Societé de Service*. Paris, France: Presses de la Fondation des Sciences Politiques.

Demographia. 2005. "Western Europe: Metropolitan Area & Core Cities 1965 to Present." Belleville, IL: Wendell Cox Consultancy. Retrieved December 7, 2005 (http://www.demographia.com/db-metro-we1965.htm).

Derudder, B. and P. J. Taylor. 2005. "The cliquishness of world cities." *Global Networks* 5(1):71–91.

———, P. Taylor, P. Ni, A. De Vos, M. Hoyler, H. Hanssens, D. Bassens, J. Huang, F. Witlox, W. Shen and X. Yang. 2010. "Pathways of Change: Shifting Connectivities in the World City Network, 2000–2008." *Urban Studies*, 47(9):1861–77.

Desfor, Gene and Roger Keil. 2004. *Nature and the City: Making Environmental Policy in Toronto and Los Angeles*. Tempe, AZ: University of Arizona Press.

Dietz T., E. A. Rosa and R. York. 2009. "Environmentally Efficient Well-being: Rethinking Sustainability as the Relationship Between Human Well-being and Environmental Impacts." *Human Ecology Review* 16(1):114–23.

Dogan, M. and J. D. Kasarda, eds. 1988. *A World of Giant Cities*. Newbury Park, CA: Sage.

Domhoff, G. W. 1991. *Blacks in White Establishments: A Study of Race and Class in America*. New Haven: Yale University Press.

Dore, Ronald. 1986. *Flexible Rigidities: Industrial Policy and Structural Adjustment in the Japanese Economy, 1970–1980*. London, UK: Athlone.

Drache, D. and M. Gertler, eds. 1991. *The New Era of Global Competition: State Policy and Market Power*. Montreal, Canada: McGill-Queen's University Press.

Drainville, Andre. 2004. *Contesting Globalization: Space and Place in the World Economy*. London, UK: Routledge.

Drennan, Mathew P. 1989. "Information Intensive Industries in Metropolitan Areas of the United States." *Environment and Planning A* 21:1603–18.

———. 1992. "Gateway Cities: The Metropolitan Sources of U.S. Producer Service Exports." *Urban Studies* 29(2):217–35.

Duarte, R. 1989. "Heterogeneidade no Setor Informal: Um Estudo de Microunidades Produtivas em Aracaju e Teresina." *Estudios Economicos,* Fipe 19(Numero Especial):99–123.

Dubet. Francois and Henri Lustiger-Thaler. 2004. The Sociology of Collective Action Reconsidered. Special Issue, *Current Sociology,* 52(4). Thousand Oaks, CA: Sage Publishing.

Duneier, M. 1999. *Sidewalk.* New York: Farrar, Strauss & Giroux.

duRivage, Virginia L., ed. 1992. *New Policies for the Part-Time and Contingent Workforce.* Washington, DC: Economic Policy Institute.

Eade, John. 1997. *Living the Global City: Globalization as a Local Process.* New York: Routledge.

Economist Intelligence Unit. 2008. "Global Migration Barometer." Retrieved July 11, 2011 (http://mighealth.net/eu/images/6/66/GMB.pdf).

Economic Policy Institute (EPI). 2005a. *The State of Working America 2004–05.* Washington, DC: EPI.

———. 2005b. Income Picture: August 31, 2005. Washington, DC: EPI. Retrieved December 7, 2005 (http://www.epi.org/pages/books_swa2004/).

———. 2008a. "Hourly and Weekly Earnings of Production and Nonsupervisory Workers, 1947–2007 (2007 dollars)." Datazone National Data from *The State of Working America 2004–05.* Washington, DC: EPI. Retrieved March 19, 2010 (http://www.epi.org/resources/datazone_dznational/).

———. 2008b. "Real Hourly Wage for All by Education, 1973–2007 (2007 dollars)." Datazone National Data from *The State of Working America 2004–05.* Washington, DC: EPI. Retrieved March 19, 2010 (http://www.epi.org/resources/datazone_dznational/).

———. 2008c. *Analysis of U.S. Bureau of the Census Current Population Survey data described in Appendix B of the source publication.* Reprinted with permission from the Economic Policy Institute, www.epinet.org.

———. 2008d. *Analysis of U.S. Bureau of the Census Current Population Survey data described in Appendix B of the source publication.*

Edel, Matthew. 1986. "Capitalism, Accumulation and the Explanation of Urban Phenomena." Pp. 19–44 in *Urbanization and Urban Planning in Capitalist Society,* edited by Michael Dear and Allen Scott. New York: Methuen.

Ehrenreich, Barbara and Arlie Hochschild, eds. 2003. *Global Woman.* New York: Metropolitan Books.

El-Shakhs, Salah. 1972. "Development, Primacy and Systems of Cities." *Journal of Developing Areas* 7(October):11–36.

Elyachar, J. 2005. *Markets of Dispossession: NGOs, Economic Development and the State in Cairo.* Durham, NC: London: Duke University Press.

Enterprise Florida. 2005a. Global Advantages: Florida's Foreign Affiliated Companies. Retrieved December 7, 2005 (http://www.eflorida.com/ContentSubpage.aspx?id =348).

———. 2005b. Global Advantages: Global Linkages. Retrieved December 7, 2005 (http://www.eflorida.com/Why_Florida.aspx?id=358).

Environment and Urbanization. 2007. "Special Issue: Reducing the Risk to Cities from Disasters and Climate Change." 19(1). Retrieved from: http://eau.sagepub .com/content/vol19/issue1/.

Ernst, Dieter. 2005. "The New Mobility of Knowledge: Digital Information Systems and Global Flagship Networks." Pp. 89–114 in *Digital Formations: IT and New Architectures in the Global Realm,* edited by Robert Latham and Saskia Sassen. Princeton, NJ: Princeton University Press.

———. 2010. "Indigenous Innovation and Globalization—the Challenge for China's Standardization Strategy." Draft scheduled for Publication by the East-West Center and National Bureau of Asian Research (2011).

_____. 2010. "A Smart Response to China's `Indigenous Innovation' Policies." Honolulu, HI: East-West Center, Retrieved July 11, 2011(http://www.eastwestcenter.org/news-center/east-west-wire/a-smart-response-to-chinas-indigenous-innovation-policies/).

Ernst and Young. 2010. "Reinventing European Growth: Ernst & Young's 2009 European Attractiveness Survey." Retrieved July 11, 2011 (http://www.ey.com/ Publication/vwLUAssets/European_Attractiveness_Survey_2009/$FILE/EY_ European_Attractiveness_Survey_2009.pdf).

Espinoza, V. 1999. "Social Networks Among the Poor: Inequality and Integration in a Latin American City." Pp. 147–184 in *Networks in the Global Village: Life in Contemporary Communities,* edited by Barry Wellman. Boulder, CO: Westview Press.

Etsy, D. C. and M. Ivanova. 2005. "Globalisation and Environmental Protection: A Global Governance Perspective." In F. Wijen et al., eds., *A Handbook of Globalisation and Environmental Policy: National Government Interventions in a Global Arena.* Cheltenham, UK: Edward Elgar.

EU Council, Representatives of the Governments of the Member States. 1998. "Resolution of the Council and the Representatives of the Governments of the Member States, Meeting Within the Council of 1 December 1997 on a Code of Conduct for Business Taxation." *Official Journal of the European Communities,* C 002:1–6.

Eurocities. 1989. *Documents and Subjects of Eurocities Conference.* Barcelona, Spain, April 21–22.

EUROSTAT. 2005. *The Urban Audit.* Retrieved October 14, 2005 (http://www .urbanaudit.org).

———. 2010. *The Urban Audit.* Retrieved March 19, 2010 (http://www.urbanaudit.org).

European Institute of Urban Affairs. 1992. Urbanisation and the Functions of Cities in the European Community: A Report to the Commission of the European Communities, Directorate General for Regional Policy (XVI). Liverpool, UK: John Moores University.

Fainstein, S. 1993. *The City Builders.* Oxford, UK: Blackwell.

———. 2001. *The City Builders.* 2nd ed. Lawrence, KS: University of Kansas Press.

———. 2010. *The Just City.* Ithaca: Cornell U.P.

——— and Campbell. 2011. "Theories of Urban Development and Their Implications for Policy and Planning." Pp. 1–15 in *Urban Theory.* 3rd ed. Oxford, UK: Wiley-Blackwell.

—— and Dennis Judd, eds. 1999. *Urban Tourism.* New Haven, CT: Yale University Press.

——, N. Fainstein, R. C. Hill, D. R. Judd, and M. P. Smith. 1986. *Restructuring the City,* 2nd ed. New York: Longman.

——, I. Gordon and M. Harloe. 1992. *Divided Cities: Economic Restructuring and Social Change in London and New York.* New York: Blackwell.

Farrer, G. L. 2007. "Producing Global Economies from Below: Chinese Immigrant Transnational Entrepreneurship in Japan." Pp. 179–98 in *Deciphering the Global: Its Spaces, Scales and Subjects,* edited by Saskia Sassen. New York and London: Routledge.

Fawaz, M. 2008. "An Unusual Clique of City-Makers: Social Networks in the Production of a Neighborhood in Beirut." *International Journal of Urban and Regional Research* 32:565–85.

Feldbauer, P., E. Pilz, D. Runzler, and I. Stacher, eds. 1993. *Megastädte: Zur Rolle von Metropolen in der Weltgesellschaft.* Vienna, Austria: Boehlau Verlag.

"Feminism and Globalization: The Impact of the Global Economy on Women and Feminist Theory." 1996. *Indiana Journal of Global Legal Studies* 4(1, Special issue).

Fernandes, S. 2010. *Who Can Stop the Drums: Urban Social Movements in Chavez's Venzuela.* Durham, NC: London: Duke University Press.

Fernandez-Kelly, M. P. 1984. *For We are Sold, I and My People.* Albany, NY: SUNY Press.

Fernandez-Kelly, M. P. and A. M. Garcia. 1989. "Informalization at the Core: Hispanic Women, Homework, and the Advanced Capitalist State." Pp. 247–64 in *The Informal Economy: Studies in Advanced and Less Developed Countries,* edited by A. Portes, M. Castells, and L. Benton. Baltimore, MD: Johns Hopkins University Press.

—— and S. Sassen. 1992. "Immigrant Women in the Garment and Electronic Industries in the New York–New Jersey Region and in Southern California." Final Research Report presented to the Ford, Revson, and Tinker Foundations, June, New York.

—— and J. Shefner. 2005. *Out of the Shadows.* University Park, PA: Penn State University Press.

Fernando, Vincent. 2010. "Think Tank Warns that Hong Kong's Dangerous Dependence on Finance Could Result in Catastrophe." Retrieved Dec. 30, 2010 (http://www.businessinsider.com/hong-kong-financial-sector-too-big-2010-6).

Firman, T. 2002. "Urban Development in Indonesia, 1990–2001: From the Boom to the Early Reform Era through the Crisis." *Habitat International* 26:229–49.

Fiscal Policy Institute. 2010. "Grow Together or Pull Further Apart? Income Concentration Trends in New York." New York, NY: Fiscal Policy Institute. Retrieved December 13, 2010.

Fisher, Melissa. 2004. "Corporate Ethnography in the New Economy: Life Today in Financial Firms, Corporations, and Non-profits." *Anthropology News* 45(4):294–320.

Fitzgerald, R. 2005. "Welcome to the World's Favourite Metropolis." *The Australian,* July 27, 2005.

Michael, Demetrios G. Papademetriou, Jeanne Batalova, Aaron Terrazas, Serena Yi-Ying Lin, and Michael Mittelstadt. 2009. *Migration and the Global Recession.* Washington, DC: Migration Policy Institute. Retrieved July 11, 2011 (http://www.migrationpolicy.org/pubs/MPI-BBCreport-Sept09.pdf).

Florida Agency for Workforce Innovation. 2005. *Labor Market Statistics, Current Employment Statistics Program.* Miami-Dade County, Department of Planning and Zoning, Research Section (July). Retrieved December 7, 2005 (http://www.labormarketinfo.com/library/ces/current/miamidiv.xls).

Florida, Richard. 2004. *Cities and the Creative Class.* New York: Routledge.

———. 2006. *The Flight of the Creative Class.* New York: Collins.

"The Forbes Global 2000." 2005. *Forbes Magazine.* March 31, 2005. (http://www.forbes.com/2005/03/30/05f2000land.html).

———. 2009. *Forbes Magazine.* April 8, 2009. (http://www.forbes.com/2009/04/08/worlds-largest-companies-business-global-09-global_land.html).

Fortin, N. M. and T. Lemieux. 1997. "Institutional Changes and Rising Wage Inequality: Is There a Linkage?" *Journal of Economic Perspectives* 11(2):75–96.

Fraser, Nancy. 2007. "Transnationalizing the Public Sphere." *European Institute for Progressive Cultural Policies: Publicum.* Available at (http://eipcp.net/transversal/0605/fraser/en)

———. 2009. *Scales of Justice: Reimagining Political Space in a Globalizing World.* New York: Columbia U.P.

Freeman, R., ed. 1994. *Working under Different Rules.* New York: Russell Sage Foundation.

Friedmann, John. 1986. "The World City Hypothesis." *Development and Change* 17:69–84.

——— and G. Wolff. 1982. "World City Formation: An Agenda for Research and Action." *International Journal of Urban and Regional Research* 15(1):269–83.

———. 2007. "The Wealth of Cities: Towards an Assets-based Development of Newly Urbanizing Regions." *Development and Change* 38:987–998.

"From Chatham House Man to Davos Man." 1997. *The Economist,* 342(February 1):18ff.

Frost, Martin and Nigel Spence. 1992. "Global City Characteristics and Central London's Employment." *Urban Studies* 30(3):547–58.

Frug, Gerald E. 2001. *City Making: Building Communities without Building Walls.* Princeton, NJ: Princeton University Press.

FSF. 2000. *Report of the Working Group on Offshore Financial Centres.* Basel: Financial Stability Forum.

Fujita, Kuniko. 1991. "A World City and Flexible Specialization: Restructuring of the Tokyo Metropolis." *International Journal of Urban and Regional Research* 15(1):269–84.

Furman Center for Real Estate & Urban Policy. 2007. "New Housing Data Continue to Show Signs of Danger for New York City's Homeowners, Furman Center Analysis Concludes." October 15. New York: New York University Press. (http://furmancenter.org/files/FurmanCenterHMDAAnalysis_000.pdf).

Gad, Gunther. 1991. "Toronto's Financial District." *Canadian Urban Landscapes* 1:203–207.

Gandy, M. 2008. "Landscapes of Disaster: Water, Modernity, and Urban Fragmentation in Mumbai." *Environment and Planning* A(40): 108–30.

Gans, Herbert. 1984. "American Urban Theory and Urban Areas." Pp. 308–26 in *Cities in Recession,* edited by Ivan Szelenyi. Beverly Hills, CA: Sage.

Garcia, D. Linda. 2002. "The Architecture of Global Networking Technologies." Pp. 39–69 in *Global Networks/Linked Cities,* edited by Saskia Sassen. New York and London, UK: Routledge.

Garofalo, G. and M. S. Fogarty. 1979. "Urban Income Distribution and the Urban Hierarchy-Inequality Hypothesis." *Review of Economics and Statistics* 61:381–88.

GaWC (Globalization and World Cities Study Group and Network). Retrieved April 15, 2011 from (http://www.lboro.ac.uk/gawc/).

Gereffi, Gary, John Humphrey, and Timothy Sturgeon. 2005. "The Governance of Global Value Chains." *Review of International Political Economy (Special Issue: Aspects of Globalization)* 12(1):78–104.

——— and Miguel Korzeniewicz. 1994. *Commodity Chains and Global Capitalism.* Westport, CT: Praeger.

Gerlach, Michael. 1992. *Alliance Capitalism: The Social Organization of Japanese Business.* Berkeley, CA: University of California Press.

Gershuny, Jonathan and Ian Miles. 1983. *The New Service Economy: The Transformation of Employment in Industrial Societies.* New York: Praeger.

Ghertner, D. A. 2010. "Calculating Without Numbers: Aesthetic Governmentality in Dehli's Slums." *Economy and Society* 39:185–217.

Giarini, Orio, ed. 1987. *The Emerging Service Economy.* Oxford, UK, and New York: Pergamon.

Giddens, A. 1991. *The Consequences of Modernity.* Oxford, UK: Polity.

Giesecke, Gerald. 2005. "The Day after Tomorrow." Retrieved December 7, 2005 (http://www.zdf.de/ZDFde/inhalt/1/0,1872,2342977,00.html).

Gilbert, Allan, ed. 1996. *Cities in Latin America.* Tokyo, Japan: United Nations University Press.

Gillette, A. and A. Sayad. 1984. *L'immigration Algerienne en France.* 2d ed. Paris, France: Editions Entente.

Girardet, H. 2008. *Cities People Planet: Urban Development and Climate Change* (2nd ed.). Amsterdam: John Wiley & Sons.

Glaeser, A. 2000. *Divided in Unity: Identity, Germany and the Berlin Police.* Chicago, IL: University of Chicago Press.

Glickman, N. J. 1979. *The Growth and Management of the Japanese Urban System.* New York: Academic Press.

——— and A. K. Glasmeier. 1989. "The International Economy and the American South." Pp. 60–89 in *Deindustrialization and Regional Economic Transformation: The Experience of the United States,* edited by L. Rodwin and H. Sazanami. Winchester, MA: Unwin Hyman.

——— and D. P. Woodward. 1989. *The New Competitors: How Foreign Investors Are Changing the U.S. Economy.* New York: Basic Books.

"Global 500." 2005. *Fortune,* July 25, 2005.

————. 2009. *Fortune*, July 20, 2009. Available at: http://money.cnn.com/magazines/fortune/global500/2009/index.html.

Global Finance. 2003. "Features: The World's Biggest Banks 2003." Retrieved Feb. 18, 2010 (http://www.gfmag.com/archives/80–80-october-2003/2107-features-the-worlds-biggest-banks-2003.html).

————. 2009. "World's Biggest Banks 2009." Retrieved Feb. 18, 2010 (http://www.gfmag.com/tools/best-banks/2523-worlds-biggest-banks.html).

"Global City: Zitadellen der Internationalisierung." 1995. *Wissenschafts Forum* 12(2, Special Issue).

Global Insight, Inc. 2007. "The Mortgage Crisis: Economic and Fiscal Implications for Metro Areas." Research Paper, United States Conference of Mayors and the Council for the New American City. Lexington MA: Global Insight, Inc. Retrieved July 11, 2011 (http://www.usmayors.org/metroeconomies/1107/report.pdf).

Global Networks. 2010. Special Issue on Commodity Chains and World-City Networks. (Nr. 1).

Goddard, J. B. 1993. "Information and Communications Technologies, Corporate Hierarchies and Urban Hierarchies in the New Europe." Presented at the Fourth International Workshop on Technological Change and Urban Form: Productive and Sustainable Cities, April 14–16, Berkeley, CA.

Goldsmith, Stephen and Linda Greene. 2010. *What We See: Advancing the Observations of Jane Jacobs* . NEW YORK: New Village Press.

Goldsmith, William V. and Edward J. Blakely. 1992. *Separate Societies: Poverty and Inequality in U.S. Cities.* Philadelphia, PA: Temple University Press.

Goldthorpe, John, ed. 1984. *Order and Conflict in Contemporary Capitalism.* Oxford, UK: Clarendon.

Gordon, I. R. 1996. "The Role of Internationalization in Economic Change in London over the Past 25 Years." Paper presented to the World Cities Group, CUNY Graduate School, New York.

———— and Saskia Sassen. 1992. "Restructuring the Urban Labor Markets." Pp. 105–28 in *Divided Cities: New York and London in the Contemporary World,* edited by S. Fainstein, I. Gordon, and M. Harloe. Oxford, UK: Blackwell.

————, Nick Buck, Alan Harding, and Ivan Turok, eds. 2005. *Changing Cities: Rethinking Urban Competitiveness, Cohesion, and Governance.* New York: Palgrave Macmillan.

Gottschalk, P. and T. Smeeding. 1997. "Cross-National Comparisons of Earnings and Income Inequality." *Journal of Economic Literature* 35:633–87.

Graham, Edward M. and Paul R. Krugman. 1989. *Foreign Direct Investment in the United States.* Washington, DC: Institute for International Economics.

Graham, Stephen. 2003. *The Cybercities Reader.* London: Routledge.

————.2010. *Cities Under Siege: The New Military Urbanism.* London: Verso.

———— and Simon Marvin. 1996. Telecommunications and the City: Electronic Spaces, Urban Places. London, UK: Routledge.

Granovetter, Mark. 1985. "Economic Action and Social Structure: The Problem of Embeddedness." *American Journal of Sociology* 91:481–510.

Gravesteijn, S. G. E., S. van Griensven, and M. C. de Smidt, eds. 1998. "Timing Global Cities." *Nederlandse Geografische Studies* 241(Special issue).

Greene, R. P., et al., eds. 2006. *Chicago's Geographies: Metropolis for the 21st Century*. Washington, D.C.: Association of American Geographers.

Gregory, Derek and John Urry, eds. 1985. *Social Relations and Spatial Structures*. London, UK: Macmillan.

Grosfoguel, Ramon. 1993. "Global Logics in the Caribbean City System: The Case of Miami and San Juan." Pp. 156–70 in *World Cities in a World System*, edited by P. Knox and P. Taylor. New York: Cambridge University Press.

Grosz, E. 1992. "Bodies Cities." Pp. 241–53 in *Sexuality & Space*, edited by Beatriz Colomina. Princeton Papers on Architecture. Princeton, NJ: Princeton Architectural Press.

Gu, Felicity Rose and Zilai Tang. 2002. "Shanghai: Reconnecting to the Global Economy." Pp. 273–308 in *Global Networks/Linked Cities*, edited by Saskia Sassen. New York and London, UK: Routledge.

Gugler, Joseph. 2004. *World Cities beyond the West*. Cambridge, UK: Cambridge University Press.

Gund Institute for Ecological Economics, University of Vermont. (2009). http://www.uvm.edu/giee/.

Hagedorn, John, ed. 2006. *Gangs in the Global City: Exploring Alternatives to Traditional Criminology*. Chicago, IL: University of Illinois at Chicago.

Hajnal, Peter I. 2002. "Civil Society Encounters the G7/G8." Pp. 215–42 in *Civil Society in the Information Age*, edited by Peter I. Hajnal. Aldershot, UK: Ashgate.

Hall, Peter. 1964. *Greater London*. London, UK: Faber & Faber.

———. 1966. *The World Cities*. New York: McGraw-Hill.

———. 1988. *Cities of Tomorrow*. Oxford, UK: Blackwell.

———. 2002. *Cities of Tomorrow*. 3rd ed. Oxford, UK: Blackwell.

——— and D. Hay. 1980. *Growth Centers in the European Urban System*. London, UK: Heinemann Educational Books.

Hall, Rodney Bruce. *National Collective Identity*. 1999. New York: Columbia University Press.

Hall, S. 1991. "The Local and the Global: Globalization and Ethnicity." Pp. 19–40 in Current Debates in Art History 3. *Culture, Globalization and the World-System: Contemporary Conditions for the Representation of Identity*, edited by Anthony D. King. New York: State University of New York at Binghamton, Department of Art and Art History.

Hancock, Marguerite Gong, Henry S. Rowen and William F. Miller, eds. 2007. "China's Quest for Independent Innovation." Shorenstein Asia Pacific Research Center and Brookings Institution Press.

Hardoy, J. E. 1975. *Urbanization in Latin America*. Garden City, NJ: Anchor.

——— and D. Satterthwaite. 1989. *Squatter Citizen: Life in the Urban Third World*. London, UK: Earthscan.

Harris, R. 1991. "The Geography of Employment and Residence in New York Since 1950." Pp. 129–52 in *Dual City: Restructuring New York*, edited by J. Mollenkopf and M. Castells. New York: Russell Sage.

Harrison, B. and B. Bluestone. 1988. *The Great U-Turn.* New York: Basic Books.

Hartmann, Heidi, ed. 1987. *Computer Chips and Paper Clips: Technology and Women's Employment.* Washington, DC: National Academy Press.

Harvey, David. 1985. *The Urbanization of Capital.* Oxford, UK: Blackwell.

———. 1989. *The Condition of Postmodernity.* Oxford, UK: Blackwell.

———. 1996. *Justice, Nature, and the Geography of Difference.* Cambridge, MA: Blackwell Publishers.

———. 2000. *Spaces of Hope.* Berkeley, CA: University of California Press.

Harvey, Rachel. 2008. "The Sub-National Constitution of Global Markets: London's Gold Fix." Ph.D. Dissertation, Department of Sociology, University of Chicago.

———. 2007. "The Sub-National Constitution of Global Markets." In *Deciphering the Global: Its Spaces, Scales and Subjects,* edited by Saskia Sassen. New York and London: Routledge.

Hausserman, Hartmut and Walter Siebel. 1987. *Neue Urbanität.* Frankfurt: Suhrkamp Verlag.

Healy, P. 2007. *Urban Complexity and Spatial Strategies: Towards a Relational Planning for Our Times.* London: Routledge.

Heine, Jorge, ed. 2011. *The Dark Side of Globalization.* Tokyo: United Nations University.

Henderson, Jeffrey. 2005. "Governing Growth and Inequality: The Continuing Relevance of Strategic Economic Planning." Pp. 227–36 in *Towards a Critical Globalization Studies,* edited by R. Appelbaum and W. Robinson. New York: Routledge.

——— and Manuel Castells, eds. 1987. *Global Restructuring and Territorial Development.* London, UK: Sage.

Herzog, Lawrence A. 1990. *Where North Meets South: Cities, Space, and Politics on the United States–Mexico Border.* Austin, TX: University of Texas Press.

———. 2001. *From Aztec to High Tech: Architecture and Landscape across the Mexico-United States Border (Creating the North American Landscape).* The Johns Hopkins University Press.

———. 2006. *Return to the Center: Culture, Public Space, and City-Building in a Global Era.* Austin, TX: University of Texas Press.

Hill, R. C. 1989. "Comparing Transnational Production Systems: The Case of the Automobile Industry in the United States and Japan." *International Journal of Urban and Regional Research* 13(3):462–80.

Hino, Masateru. 1984. "The Location of Head and Branch Offices of Large Enterprises in Japan." *Science Reports of Tohoku University* (Senday, Japan), Geography Series 34(2):1–22.

Hirst, Paul and Jonathan Zeitlin. 1989. *Reversing Industrial Decline?* Oxford, UK: Berg.

Hitz, H., R. Keil, U. Lehrer, K. Ronneberger, C. Schmid and R. Wolff, eds. 1995. *Capitales Fatales.* Zurich, Switzerland: Rotpunkt.

Hodson, M. and Marvin, S. 2009. "Urban Ecological Security: A New Urban Paradigm?" *International Journal of Urban and Regional Research* 33: 193–215.

Hollifield, James F. 1992. *Immigrants, Markets, and States: The Political Economy of Postwar Europe*. Cambridge, MA: Harvard University Press.

⸻ and Dietrich Thränhardt. 2006. *Beyond Exceptionalism: Immigration and National Traditions in the United States and Germany*. New York: Palgrave Macmillan.

Holston, J. 2008. *Insurgent Citizenship: Disjunctions of Democracy and Modernity in Brazil*. Princeton: Princeton University Press.

⸻ and A. Appadurai. 1996. "Cities and Citizenship." *Public Culture* 8(2):187–204.

Hondagneu-Sotelo, Pierrette, ed. 2003. *Gender and U.S. Immigration: Contemporary Trends*. Berkeley, CA: University of California Press.

⸻. 1994. *Gendered Transitions: Mexican Experiences of Immigration*. Berkeley, CA: University of California Press.

Hoover's Handbook of World Business. 1998. Austin, TX: Reference Press.

Hume, Christopher. 2010. "Hume: Toronto's Chief Planner 'not afraid of heights.'" *Toronto Star*. Retrieved Dec. 31, 2010 (http://www.thestar.com/news/article/904754—hume-toronto-s-chief-planner-not-afraid-of-heights).

Hymer, Stephen and Robert Rowthorn. 1970. "Multinational Corporations and International Oligopoly." Pp. 57–91 in *The International Corporation*, edited by Charles P. Kindleberger. Cambridge, MA: MIT Press.

Hunt, S. 2009. "Citizenship's Place: The State's Creation of Public Space and Street Vendors' Culture of Informality in Bogotá, Colombia." *Environment and Planning D: Society and Space* 27:331–51.

Hyatt, Susan Brin. 2008. "An Alliance of Women: Immigration and the Politics of Race." *American Anthropologist* Mar. 2008 110(1):130.

ICLEI Climate Program. www.iclei.org/index.

ICLEI: Local Governments for Sustainability. 2011. "Local Solutions to Global Challenges." Retrieved July 11, 2011 (http://www.iclei.org/fileadmin/user_upload/documents/Global/About_ICLEI/brochures/ICLEI-intro-2009.pdf).

IFPRI "Land Grabbing" by Foreign Investors in Developing Countries: Risks and Opportunities. April 2009. http://www.ifpri.org/sites/default/files/publications/bp013all.pdf

Inda, Jonathan Xavier, Louis F. Miron, and Rodolfo D. Torres. 1999. *Race, Identity, and Citizenship*. Oxford, UK: Blackwell.

⸻. 2005. *International Bank Lending by Country*. Washington, DC: IMF.

Industrial Institute for Economic and Social Research (Stockholm, Sweden). 2005. Retrieved December 7, 2005 (http://www.iui.se).

Inter-Agency and Expert Group on MDG Indicators, United Nations Statistics Division (IAEG). 2009a. "Millennium Development Goals Indicators: Debt Service as a Percentage of Exports of Goods and Services and Net Income." Last updated 14 July. (http://mdgs.un.org/unsd/mdg/SeriesDetail.aspx?srid1/4655).

IMF (International Monetary Fund). 1999. *International Capital Markets Report*. Washington, DC: IMF.

⸻. 2006. "Household Credit Growth in Emerging Market Countries." *In Global Financial Stability Report, Market Developments and Issues*. Washington DC: IMF.

_____. 2008. "Containing Systemic Risks and Restoring Financial Soundness." *IMF World Economic and Financial Surveys: Global Financial Stability Report, Market Developments.* Washington, DC: IMF. Retrieved August 28, 2008 (http://www.imf.org/external/pubs/ft/gfsr/2008/01/index.htm).

———. 2009. "Cayman Islands: Off-Shore Financial Center Assessment Update—Assessment of Financial Sector Supervision and Regulation December." Country Report No. 29/323 Retrieved Jan. 10, 2011 (http://www.imf.org/external/pubs/ft/scr/2009/cr09323.pdf).

———. 2009a. "Factsheet: Poverty Reduction Strategy Papers (PRSP)." 14 August. (https://www. imf.org/external/np/exr/facts/prsp.htm).

———. 2009b. "Factsheet: Debt Relief Under the Heavily Indebted Poor Country (HIPC) Initiative," 22 September. (http://www.imf.org/external/np/exr/facts/hipc.htm).

———. 2010. *LABORSTA Internet*: Online Statistics. Geneva, Switzerland: ILO. Available at http://laborsta.ilo.org/STP/guest (retrieved 12 March 2010).

International Labor Organization. 2005. *LABORSTA: On-line Statistics.* Geneva, Switzerland: ILO. Retrieved December 7, 2005 (http://laborsta.ilo.org/).

International Organization for Migration (IOM). 1998. *Trafficking in Migrants.* Geneva, Switzerland: IOM.

INURA, ed. 2003. *The Contested Metropolis.* New York: Birkhauser.

Ishizuka, H. and Ishida, Y. 1988. *Tokyo: Urban Growth and Planning, 1968–1988.* Tokyo, Japan: Tokyo Metropolitan University, Center for Urban Studies.

Isin, Engin F., ed. 2000. *Democracy, Citizenship and the Global City.* London, UK, and New York: Routledge.

Istanbul Metropolitan Municipality. 2011. Istanbul, Turkey. Retrieved July 11, 2011 (http://www.ibb.gov.tr/en-US/Pages/Home_Page.aspx).

Ito, Tatsuo and Masafumi Tanifuji. 1982. "The Role of Small and Intermediate Cities in National Development in Japan." Pp. 71–100 in *Small Cities and National Development,* edited by O. P. Mathur. Nagoya, Japan: United Nations Centre for Regional Development.

Iyotani, Toshio. 1989. "The New Immigrant Workers in Tokyo." Typescript, Tokyo University of Foreign Studies. Tokyo, Japan.

———. 1998. "Globalization and Immigrant Workers in Japan." In NIRA Review (Winter 1998). Tokyo: National Institute for Research Advancement. Retrieved December 13, 2005 (http://www.nira.or.jp/past/publ/review/98winter/iyo.html).

———, Naoki Sakai and Brett de Bary, eds. 2005. *Deconstructing Nationality.* Ithaca, NY: Cornell University East Asia Program.

——— and Toshio Naito. 1989. "Tokyo no Kokusaika de Tenkan Semarareru Chusho Kigyo" [Medium- and small-sized corporations under pressure of change by Tokyo's internationalization]. *Ekonomisuto,* September 5:44–49.

Japan Ministry of Internal Affairs and Communications, Statistics Bureau. 2005. *Monthly Statistics of Japan* No. 530. Tokyo: MIAC. Retrieved December 7, 2005 (http://www.stat.go.jp/english/data/geppou/#g).

Japan Ministry of Labor. Various Years. *Monthly Labor Statistics and Research Bulletin.* Tokyo, Japan: Ministry of Labor.

Jenkins, Rhys. 1991. "The Political Economy of Industrialization: A Comparison of Latin American and East Asian Newly Industrializing Countries." *Development and Change* 11:197–231.

Jessop, Robert. 1999. "Reflections on Globalization and Its Illogics." Pp. 19–38 in *Globalization and the Asian Pacific: Contested Territories,* edited by Kris Olds, Peter Dicken, Philip F. Kelly, Lilly Kong, and Henry Wai-Chung Yeung. London, UK: Routledge.

———. 2003. *The Future of the Capitalist State.* Cambridge, UK: Polity Press.

Jonas, S. 1992. *The Battle for Guatemala: Rebels, Death Squads, and U.S. Power.* Boulder, CO: Westview.

Jones, Steve and Philip N. Howard, eds. 2004. *Society Online: The Internet in Context.* London: Sage Publications.

Jonkers, H. M. 2007. "Self Healing Concrete: A Biological Approach." Pp. 195–204 in *Self Healing Materials: An Alternative Approach to 20 Centuries of Materials Science.* Dordrecht, The Netherlands: Springer.

Jubilee Debt Campaign UK. 2007. "Debt and Women." (http://www.jubileedebtcam paign.org.uk/Debt%20and% 20Womenþ3072.twl).

———. 2008. Angola, country information, (http://www.jubileedebtcampaign.org .uk/ Angolaþ4038.twl).

———. 2009a. "How Big is the Debt of Poor Countries?" (http://www.jubileedebt campaign.org.uk/2%20How%20big%20is%20the%20debt%20of%20poor% 20countries%3Fþ2647.twl).

———. 2009b. "Hasn't All the Debt been Cancelled?" (http://www.jubileedebtcam paign.org.uk/4% 20Hasn%27t%20all%20the%20debt%20been%20cancelled %3Fþ2651.twl)

Kahnert, Friedrich. 1987. "Improving Urban Employment and Labor Productivity." World Bank Discussion Paper No. 10. Washington, DC: World Bank.

Kaldor, Mary H. 2007. *New and Old Wars: Organized Violence in a Global Era,* 2nd ed. Palo Alto, CA: Stanford University Press.

Kasarda, John D. and Edward M. Crenshaw. 1991. "Third World Urbanization: Dimensions, Theories and Determinants." *Annual Review of Sociology* 17:467–501.

Kasinitz, Philip. 1992. *Caribbean New York.* Ithaca, NY: Cornell University Press.

Kazepov, Yuri, ed. 2005. *Cities of Europe: Changing Contexts, Local Arrangements, and the Challenge to Urban Cohesion.* London, UK: Blackwell.

Keil, Roger. 1999. *Los Angeles: Globalization, Urbanization and Social Struggles.* Hoboken, NJ: John Wiley & Sons.

——— and Klaus Ronneberger. 1992. "Going up the Country: Internationalization and Urbanization on Frankfurt's Northern Fringe." Presented at the UCLA International Sociological Association, Research Committee 29, *A New Urban and Regional Hierarchy? Impacts of Modernization, Restructuring and the End of Bipolarity,* April 24–26, Los Angeles, CA.

Kelly, Maryellen R. 1989. "Alternative Forms of Work Organization under Programmable Automation." Pp. 235–46 in *The Transformation of Work?* edited by Stephen Wood. London, UK: Unwin-Hyman.

Kerbo, H. R. 2005. *World Poverty: The Roots of Global Inequality and the Modern World-System*. New York: McGraw-Hill.

King, A. D. 1990. *Urbanism, Colonialism, and the World Economy; Culture and Spatial Foundations of the World Urban System*. International Library of Sociology. London, UK, and New York: Routledge.

————, ed. 1996. *Re-presenting the City. Ethnicity, Capital and Culture in the 21st Century*. London, UK: Macmillan.

Kipfer, S. 2007. "Fanon and Space: Colonization, Urbanization, and Liberation from the Colonial to the Global City." *Environment and Planning D: Society and Space* 25:701–726.

Klier, Thomas and William Testa. 2002. "Locational Trends of Large Company Headquarters during the 1990s." *Federal Reserve Bank of Chicago: Economic Perspectives* (26)2. Chicago, IL: Federal Reserve Bank of Chicago.

Klinenberg, E. 2003. *Heat Wave : A Social Autopsy of Disaster in Chicago*. Chicago: University of Chicago Press.

Klopp, Brett. 1998. "Integration and Political Representation in a Multicultural City: The Case of Frankfurt am Main." *German Politics and Society* 16(4): 42–68.

Knight, R. V. and G. Gappert, eds. 1989. *Cities in a Global Society*, vol. 35. Urban Affairs Annual Reviews. Newbury Park, CA: Sage.

Knox, P. and P. Taylor, eds. 1995. *World Cities in a World-System*. New York: Cambridge University Press.

———— and Linda McCarthy. 2005. *Urbanization: An Introduction to Urban Geography*. New York: Prentice Hall.

Komai, Hiroshi. 1992. "Are Foreign Trainees in Japan Disguised Cheap Laborers?" *Migration World* 10(1):13–17.

Komlosy, A., C. Parnreiter, I. Stacher and S. Zimmerman, eds. 1997. *Ungeregelt und Unterbezahlt: Der Informelle Sektor in der Weltwirtschaft*. Frankfurt, Germany: Brandes & Apsel/Sudwind.

Komori, S. 1983. "Inner City in Japanese Context." *City Planning Review* 125: 11–17.

Konings, P., R. van Dijk and D. Foeken. 2006. The African Neighborhood: An Introduction. In P. Konings and D. Foeken, eds., *Crisis and Creativity: Exploring the Wealth of the African Neighborhood*. Leiden: Brill.

Kopczuk, Saez E. and J. Song. 2007. "Uncovering the American Dream: Inequality and Mobility in Social Security Earnings Data since 1937." Longer version: NBER WP #13345, revision requested by *Quarterly Journal of Economics*.

Kothari, Uma. 2006. *A Radical History of Development Studies: Individuals, Institutions and Ideologies*. London: Zed Books.

Kotkin, J. 2005. *The City: A Global History*. New York: The Modern Library.

Kowarick, L., A. M. Campos and M. C. de Mello. 1991. "Os Percursos de Desigualdade." In *São Paulo, Crise e Mudanca*, edited by R. Rolnik, L. Kowarick, and N. Somekh. São Paulo, Brazil: Brasiliense.

Krause, Linda and Patrice Petro, eds. 2003. *Global Cities: Cinema, Architecture, and Urbanism in a Digital Age*. New Brunswick, NJ, and London, UK: Rutgers University Press.

Kresl, Peter, & Ni, Pengfei. 2010. *Economic Strategies for Nature Industrial Economies*. Cheltenham, UK: Edward Elgar.

Kunzmann, K. R. and M. Wegener. 1991. "The Pattern of Urbanisation in Western Europe 1960–1990." Report for the Directorate General XVI of the Commission of the European Communities as part of the study *Urbanisation and the Function of Cities in the European Community*. Dortmund, Germany: Institut für Raumplanung.

KUPI (Kobe Urban Problems Institute). 1981. *Policy for Revitalization of Inner City*. Kobe, Japan: KUPI.

Kuttner, Robert. 1991. *The End of Laissez Faire*. New York: Knopf.

Landell-Mills, Pierre, Ramgopal Agarwala, and Stanley Please. 1989. *Sub-Saharan Africa: From Crisis to Sustainable Growth*. Washington, DC: World Bank.

Lang, Robert. 2000. *Office Sprawl: The Evolving Geography of Business (Data Sets Appendix)*. Washington, D.C.: The Brookings Institution. Retrieved December 7, 2005 (http://www.brookings.edu/es/urban/officesprawl/13regions.pdf).

Lash, Scott M. 2002. *Critique of Information*. London: Sage Publications.

—— and John Urry. 1987. *The End of Organized Capitalism*. Cambridge, UK: Polity.

—— and ——. 1994. *Economies of Signs and Space*. London, UK: Sage.

——. 2010. *Intensive Culture: Religion and Social Theory in Contemporary Culture*. London: Sage.

Latham, Robert and Saskia Sassen, eds. 2005. *Digital Formations: IT and New Architectures in the Global Realm*. Princeton, NJ: Princeton University Press.

Latour, Bruno. 2004. *Politics of Nature: How to Bring the Sciences into Democracy*. Harvard University Press.

Lavinas, Lena and Maria Regina Nabuco. 1992. "Economic Crisis and Flexibility in Brazilian Labor Markets." Presented at the UCLA International Sociological Association, Research Committee 29, *A New Urban and Regional Hierarchy? Impacts of Modernization, Restructuring and the End of Bipolarity*, April 24–26, Los Angeles, CA.

Lazzarato, Maurizio. 1997. *Lavoro Immateriale*. Verona, Italy: Ombre Corte.

Leborgne, D. and A. Lipietz. 1988. "L'après-Fordisme et son Espace." *Les Temps Modernes* 43:75–114.

Lee, Kyu Sik. 1989. The Location of Jobs in a Developing Metropolis: Patterns of Growth in Bogota and Cali, Colombia. New York: Oxford University Press.

LeGates, R. T. and F. Stout, eds. 2003. *The City Reader*. New York: Routledge.

Leontidou, L. 2010. "Urban Social Movements in 'Weak' Civil Societies: The Right to the City and Cosmopolitan Activism in Southern Europe." *Urban Studies* 47:1179–1203.

Leung, Jimmy C. F. 2009. "Hong Kong's Search for a Sustainable Land Use-Transport Planning Strategy." The Institution of Engineers, Malaysia: Green Workshop on Engineering A Sustainable Economic Development Model for Malaysia, November 2–3, 2009.

Levine, Marc V. 1990. *The Reconquest of Montreal: Language Policy and Social Change in a Bilingual City*. Philadelphia, PA: Temple University Press.

Levy, Frank and Richard Murname. 1992. "U.S. Earnings Levels and Earnings Inequality: A Review of Recent Trends and Proposed Explanations." *Journal of Economic Literature* 30(3):1333–81.

Leyshon, A., P. Daniels, and N. Thrift. 1987. "Large Accountancy Firms in the U.K.: Spatial Development." Working Paper, St. David's University College, Lampeter, UK, and University of Liverpool.

———, Roger Lee, and Colin C. Williams, ed. 2003. *Alternative Economic Spaces.* London: Sage Publications.

Light, Ivan. 2006. *Deflecting Immigration: How Los Angeles Tamed Globalization.* New York: Russell Sage Foundation Publications.

——— and E. Bonacich. 1988. *Immigrant Enterprise.* Berkeley: University of California Press.

Lim, L. Y. C. 1982. "Women Workers in Multinational Corporations: The Case of the Electronics Industry in Malaysia and Singapore." Pp. 109–36 in *Transnational Enterprises: Their Impact on Third World Societies and Cultures,* edited by Kumar Krishna. Boulder, CO: Westview Press.

Lindell, I. 2010. "Informality and Collective Organizing: Identities, Alliances and Transnational Activism in Africa." *Third World Quarterly* 31:207–22.

Linn, Johannes F. 1983. *Cities in the Developing World: Policies for Their Equitable and Efficient Growth.* New York and Oxford: Oxford University Press.

Lipietz, A. 1988. "New Tendencies in the International Division of Labor: Regimes of Accumulation and Modes of Regulation." Pp. 16–40 in *Production, Work, Territory,* edited by A. Scott and M. Storper. Boston, MA: Allen and Unwin.

Lloyd, Richard. 2005. *Neo-Bohemia: Art and Commerce in the Post-Industrial City.* New York and London: Routledge.

———. 2007. "How Middle Class Kids Get Working Class Jobs." Harvard/MIT Workshop on Economic Sociology. Harvard University, March 2007.

———. 2010. *Neo-Bohemia: Art and Commerce in the Postindustrial City* (Revised Edition). New York: Routledge.

Lo, Fu-chen and Y. Yeung, eds. 1996. *Emerging World Cities in Pacific Asia.* Tokyo, Japan: United Nations University Press.

Logan, J. R. and H. Molotch. 1987. *Urban Fortunes.* Berkeley, CA: University of California Press.

——— and T. Swanstrom, eds. 1990. *Beyond the City Limits: Urban Policy and Economic Restructuring in Comparative Perspective.* Philadelphia, PA: Temple University Press.

Lomnitz, Larissa. 1985. "Mechanisms of Articulation between Shantytown Settlers and the Urban System." *Urban Anthropology* 7(2):185–205.

Lovink, Geert. 2008. *Zero Comments: Blogging and Critical Internet Culture.* London: Routledge.

Lovink, Geert and J. Dean. 2010. *Blog Theory: Feedback and Capture in the Circuits of Drive.* London: Polity.

Low N. P. & B. Gleeson, eds. 2001. *Governing for the Environment: Global Problems, Ethics and Democracy.* Basingstroke, United Kingdom: Palgrave Publishers Ltd.

Lozano, Beverly. 1989. *The Invisible Work Force: Transforming American Business with Outside and Home-Based Workers.* New York: Free Press.

Lozano, Wilfredo and Isis Duarte. 1991. "Proceso de Urbanización, Modelos de Desarrollo y Clases Sociales en Republica Dominicana: 1960–1990." Paper presented at the seminar on Urbanization in the Caribbean in the Years of Crisis, May 29–June 1, Florida International University, Miami, FL.

Lucas, L. ed. 2005. *Unpacking Globalisation: Markets, Gender and Work.* Kampala, Uganda: Makerere University Press.

Lustiger-Thaler, Henri, ed. 2004. "Social Movements in a Global World." *Current Sociology* (52)4:657–74.

Machimura, Takashi. 1992. "The Urban Restructuring Process in the 1980s: Transforming Tokyo into a World City." *International Journal of Urban and Regional Research* 16(1):114–28.

———. 2003. "Narrating a 'Global City' for 'New Tokyoites': Economic Crisis and Urban Boosterism in Tokyo." Pp. 196–212 in *Japan and Britain in the Contemporary World: Responses to Common Issues*, edited by Hugo Dobson and Glenn D. Hook. London: Routledge Curzon.

Madigan, Charles ed. 2004. *Global Chicago.* Chicago: University of Illinois Press.

Mahler, Sarah. 1995. *American Dreaming: Immigrant Life on the Margins.* Princeton, NJ: Princeton University Press.

Manpower Inc. 2007. "Manpower Employment Outlook Survey: Global Q1/2008." Milwaukee, WI. Manpower Inc. Retrieved July 13, 2011(https://candidate.manpower.com/wps/wcm/connect/a519de004ec2f59cb8abf9ee16aecd97/30 MEOS_08Q1.pdf?MOD=AJPERES).

Mansell, Robin and Uta When. 1998. *Knowledge Societies: Information Technology for Sustainable Development.* Oxford: Oxford University Press.

Marcotullio, Peter and Fu-Chen Lo. 2001. *Globalization and the Sustainability of Cities in the Asia Pacific Region.* New York: United Nations University Press.

Marcuse, Peter. 1986. "Abandonment, Gentrification, and Displacement: The Linkages in New York City." Pp. 153–77 in *Gentrification of the City*, edited by Neil Smith and Peter Williams. Boston, MA: Allen and Unwin.

———. 2003. *Of States and Cities: The Partitioning of Urban Space.* New York: Oxford University Press.

——— and Ronald Van Kempen. 2000. *Globalizing Cities: A New Spatial Order.* Oxford, UK: Blackwell.

———. 2009. Comments at "Conference on Cities and the New Wars." Columbia University September 28, 2009. (http://cgt.columbia.edu/events/cities_and_new_wars/)

Marie, Claude-Valentin. 1992. "Les Etrangers Non-Salaries en France, Symbole de la Mutation Economique des Années 80." *Revue Européenne des Migrations Internationales* 8(10):27–38.

Markusen, A. 1985. *Profit Cycles, Oligopoly, and Regional Development*. Cambridge, MA: MIT Press.

———. 1994. "Multipolarity and the Layering of Functions in the World Cities: New York City's Struggle to Stay on Top." Working Paper #55. New Brunswick, NJ: Rutgers University, Center for Urban Policy Research.

———, P. Hall, S. Campbell, and S. Deitrick, eds. 1991. *The Rise of the Gunbelt*. New York: Oxford University Press.

———, P. Hall, and A. Glasmeier. 1986. *High Tech America: The What, How, Where and Why of the Sunrise Industries*. London, UK, and Boston, MA: Allen and Unwin.

———, Yong-Sook Lee, and Sean Digiovanna, eds. 1999. *Second Tier Cities: Rapid Growth beyond the Metropolis*. Minneapolis, MN: University of Minnesota Press.

Marlin, John Tepper, Immanuel Ness, and Stephen T. Collins. 1986. *Book of World City Rankings*. New York: Macmillan.

Marshall, J. N., N. Thrift, P. Wood, P. Daniels, A. Mackinnon, J. Batchelor, P. Damesick, A. Gillespie, A. Leyshon and A. Green. 1986. "Uneven Development in the Service Economy: Understanding the Location and Role of Producer Services." Report of the Producer Services Working Party, Institute of British Geographers and the ESRC, August.

Martin, Philip. 1997. "Economic Integration and Migration: The Case of NAFTA." In *Proceedings of the Conference on International Migration at Century's End: Trends and Issues*, Barcelona Spain, May 7–10, 1997. Liege, Belgium: The International Union for the Scientific Study of Population.

Martinelli, Flavia and Erica Schoenberger. 1991. "Oligopoly Is Alive and Well: Notes for a Broader Discussion of Flexible Accumulation." Pp. 117–33 in *Industrial Change and Regional Development: The Transformation of New Industrial Spaces,* edited by Georges Benko and Mick Dunford. London, UK, and New York: Belhaven/Pinter.

Masser, I., O. Sviden, and M. Wegener. 1990. "Europe 2020: Long-Term Scenarios of Transport and Communications in Europe." Unpublished paper for the European Science Foundation.

Massey, Doreen. 1984. Spatial Divisions of Labour: Social Structures and the Geography of Production. London, UK: Macmillan.

———. 2005. *For Space*. London: Sage Publications.

Massey, Douglas S. and Nancy Denton. 1998. *American Apartheid: Segregation and the Making of the Underclass*. Cambridge, MA: Harvard University Press.

MasterCard. 2008. "Fact Sheet: 2008 Worldwide Centers of Commerce Index Overview of Global Findings." Retrieved July 13, 2011 (http://www.mastercard.com/us/company/en/insights/pdfs/2008/MCWW_WCoC_Global_Fact_Sheet.pdf).

Mayer, Margit. 1992. "The Shifting Local Political System in European Cities." Pp. 255–74 in *Cities and Regions in the New Europe*, edited by Mick Dunford and Grigoris Kafkalas. London: Belhaven Press.

———. 1999. "Urban Movements and Urban Theory in the Late 20th Century." Pp. 209–39 in *The Urban Moment*, edited by Sophie Body-Gendrot & Bob Beauregard. Thousand Oaks, CA: Sage Publications.

Mayne, S. 2005. "The Complete Demise of Corporate Melbourne." *Crikey Daily,* June 15, 2005.

McCann, E. and K. Ward. 2010. *Mobile Urbanism: Cities and Policy-making in a Global Age.* Minneapolis; London: Minnesota University Press.

McDowell, Linda. 1997. *Capital Culture.* Oxford, UK: Blackwell.

———. 2005. *Hard Labour: The Forgotten Voices Of Latvian Migrant "Volunteer" Workers.* London: University College London Press.

McFarlane, C. 2009. "Translocal Assemblages: Space, Power and Social Movements." *Geoforum* 40:461–67.

McGee, Terry. 2009. *The Spatiality of Urbanization and the Policy Challenges of Mega-Urban and Desakota Regions of Southeast Asia.* United Nations University–IAS Working Paper 161.

McKinsey Report. August 2011: http://www.mckinsey.com/mgi/publications/Mapping_global_capital_markets/index.asp

McKinsey & Company. 2008. "Mapping Global Capital Markets Fourth Annual Report." McKinsey Global Institute, January. (http://www.mckinsey.com/mgi/reports/pdfs/Mapping_Global/MGI_Mapping_Global_full_Report.pdf).

McMichael, Philip. 2004. *Development and Social Change: A Global Perspective, 3rd ed.* Thousand Oaks, CA: Pine Forge Press.

McRoberts, O. 2005. *Streets of Glory: Church and Community in a Black Urban Neighborhood.* Chicago, IL: University of Chicago Press.

Meagher, K. 2010. "The Tangled Web of Associational Life: Urban Governance and the Politics of Popular Livelihoods in Nigeria." *Urban Forum* 21:299–313.

Megacities Foundation. 2011. *Megacities Jubileess.* The Hague: Megacities Foundation.

Mele, Christopher. 1999. "Cyberspace and Disadvantaged Communities: The Internet as a Tool for Collective Action." Pp. 264–89 in *Communities in Cyberspace,* edited by Marc A. Smith and Peter Kollock. New York and London: Routledge.

Melendez, E., C. Rodriguez, and J. B. Figueroa. 1991. *Hispanics in the Labor Force.* New York: Plenum.

Meridian Securities Markets. 1998. *World Stock Exchange Fact Book.* Morris Plains, NJ: Electronic Commerce.

Meyer, David R. 1991. "Change in the World System of Metropolises: The Role of Business Intermediaries." *Urban Geography* 12(5):393–416.

———. 2002. "Hong Kong: Global Capital Exchange." Pp. 249–72 in *Global Networks/Linked Cities,* edited Saskia Sassen. London: Routledge.

Meyer, John R. and James M. Gustafson, eds. 1988. *The U.S. Business Corporation: An Institution in Transition.* Cambridge, MA: Ballinger.

Mgbeogi, I. 2006. *Biopiracy: Patents, Plants, and Indigenous Knowledge.* Vancouver: University of British Columbia Press.

Miami-Dade County, Florida. 2003. *General Statistical Data.* Retrieved December 7, 2005 (http://www.co.miami-dade.fl.us/finance/library/genstat03.pdf).

———. 2010. "Economic and Demographic Profile." Retrieved Jan. 1, 2011.(http://www.miamidade.gov/oedit/library/10–10-economic_profile.pdf).

Mignaqui, Iliana. 1998. "Dinamica Immobiliaria y Transformaciones Metropolitanas." Pp. 255–84 in *Ciudades y Regiones al Avance de la Globalización,* edited by

S. Sorenstein and R. Bustos Cara. Bahia Blanca, Argentina: UNS (Universidad Nacional del Sur).

Migrant Remittances. 2008. "Worldwide Trends in International Remittances." May, 5(2), Electronic newsletter jointly sponsored by DFID and USAID, (http://pdf .usaid.gov/pdf_docs/PNADN335.pdf).

Migration Policy Institute. 2011. "Global City Migration Map." Washington, DC: Migration Policy Institute. Retrieved July 13, 2011 (http://www.migrationinfor- mation.org/DataHub/gcmm.cfm).

Milkman, R. and Dwyer, R. 2002. "Growing Apart: The 'New Economy' and Job Polarization in California, 1992–2000." University of California Institute for Labor and Employment, Multi-Campus Research Unit, 2000; p. 12.

Mingione, E. 1991. *Fragmented Societies: A Sociology of Economic Life beyond the Market Paradigm.* Oxford, UK: Blackwell.

———— and E. Pugliese. 1988. "La Questione Urbana e Rurale: Tra Superamento Teorico e Problemi di Confini Incerti." *La Critica Sociologica* 85:17–50.

Mioni, Alberto. 1991. "Legittimita ed Efficacia del Progetto Urbano." Dis T Rassegna di Studi e Ricerche del Dipartimento di Scienze del Territorio del Politecnico di Milano 9(September):137–50.

Mishel, L. 2004. "Unfettered markets, income inequality, and religious values." *Viewpoints*, 25 May. Washington, D.C.: Economic Policy Institute. Retrieved July 26, 2008 (http://www.epi.org/publications/entry/webfeatures_viewpoints_ moral_markets_presentation/).

————. 2007. "Who's grabbing all the new pie?" *Economic Snapshots*, 1 August. Washington, DC: Economic Policy Institute. Retrieved July 26, 2008. (http:// www.epi.org/content.cfm/webfeatures_snapshots_20070801).

————. 2008. "Surging Wage Growth for Topmost Sliver." *Economic Snapshots*. June 18, 2008. Economic Policy Institute. Retrieved July 26, 2008. (http://www .epi.org/content.cfm/webfeatures_snapshots_20080618).

Mitchell, Matthew and Saskia Sassen. 1996. "Can Cities Like New York Bet on Manufacturing?" In *Manufacturing Cities: Competitive Advantage and the Urban Industrial Community*, a symposium given by the Harvard Graduate School of Design and the Loeb Fellowship, May 1996.

Mitter, S., ed. 1989. *Information Technology and Women's Employment: The Case of the European Clothing Industry.* Berlin and New York: Springer-Verlag.

Miyajima, Takashi. 1989. *The Logic of Receiving Foreign Workers: Among Dilemmas of Advanced Societies* (Gaikokujin Rodosha Mukaeire no Ronri: Senshin shakai no Jirenma no naka de). Tokyo, Japan: Akashi Shoten.

Mol, Arthur P. J. and David Sonnenfeld. 2000. *Ecological Modernization Around the World: Perspectives and Critical Debates.* New York: Routledge.

Mongin, O. 2004. "Globalization and Urban Metamorphosis. 'Mega-cities,' 'Global cities' and Metropoles." *Esprit* 303:175–200.

Montgomery, Cynthia A. and Michael E. Porter, eds. 1991. *Strategy: Seeking and Securing Competitive Advantage.* Boston, MA: Harvard Business School Press.

Morello-Frosch R. et al. (2009). *The Climate Gap: Inequalities in How Climate Change Hurts Americans & How to Close the Gap.* Los Angeles: USC Program for Environmental and Regional Equity. Retrieved from http://college.usc.edu/geography/ESPE/documents/The_Climate_Gap_Full_Report_FINAL.pdf.

Mori Foundation. 2011. *Global Power City Index 2010.* Tokyo: Mori Foundation.

Morita, Kiriro. 1990. "Japan and the Problem of Foreign Workers." Research Institute for the Japanese Economy, Faculty of Economics. Tokyo, Japan: University of Tokyo-Hongo.

———. 1993. "Foreign Workers." Unpublished paper, Department of Economics, University of Tokyo, Tokyo-Hongo.

——— and Saskia Sassen. 1994. "The New Illegal Immigration in Japan, 1980–1992." *International Migration Review* 28(1):153.

Morris, M. 1992. "Great Moments in Social Climbing: King Kong and the Human Fly." Pp. 1–51 in *Sexuality and Space,* edited by Beatriz Colomina. Princeton Papers on Architecture. Princeton, NJ: Princeton Architectural Press.

Moser, C. 1989. "The Impact of Recession and Structural Adjustment Policies at the Micro-level: Low Income Women and Their Households in Guayaquil, Ecuador." *Invisible Adjustment* 2:137–66. New York: UNICEF.

Mowery, David, ed. 1988. *International Collaborative Ventures in U.S. Manufacturing.* Cambridge, MA: Ballinger.

Munger, Frank, ed. 2002. *Laboring Under the Line.* New York: Russell Sage Foundation.

Nabuco, M. R., A. F. Machado, and J. Pires. 1991. *Estrategias de Vida e Sobrevivencia na Industria de Confeccoes de Belo Horizonte.* Belo Horizonte, Brazil: Cedeplar/UFMG.

Nakabayashi, Itsuki. 1987. "Social-Economic and Living Conditions of Tokyo's Inner City." *Geographical Reports of Tokyo Metropolitan University* 22: 275–92.

Nanami, Tadashi and Yasuo Kuwabara, eds. 1989. *Tomorrow's Neighbors: Foreign Workers* (Asu no Rinjin: Gaikokujin Rodosha). Tokyo, Japan: Toyo Keizai Shimposha.

Naim, M. 2006. *Illicit: How Smugglers, Traffickers, and Copycats are Hijacking the Global Economy.* New York: Anchor Books.

Nelson, J. I. and J. Lorence. 1985. "Employment in Service Activities and Inequality in Metropolitan Areas." *Urban Affairs Quarterly* 21(1):106–25.

Nashashibi, Rami. 2007. "Ghetto Cosmopolitanism: Making Theory at the Margins." Pp. 241–62 in *Deciphering the Global: Its Spaces, Scales and Subjects.* Edited by S. Sassen. New York and London: Routledge.

National Academy of Sciences. 2003. *Cities Transformed: Demographic Change and Its Implications in the Developing World.* Washington, DC: National Academies Press, Panel on Urban Population Dynamics.

Nepomnyaschy, Lenna and Irwin Garfinkel. 2002. "Wealth in New York City and the Nation: Evidence from the New York Social Indicators Survey and the Survey of Income and Program Participation." *Social Indicators Survey Center Working Paper.* New York: Columbia University School of Social Work.

Neuwirth, Robert. 2004. *Shadow Cities: A Billion Squatters, A New Urban World.* London: Routledge.

New South Wales Department of State and Regional Development. 2005. "Facts & Statistics: B17. Australian and Foreign-Owned Banks—Australian Cities, 2005." Retrieved December 7, 2005 (http://www.business.nsw.gov.au/facts Reports.asp? cid=31&subCid=69).

———. 2009. "Australian and Foreign Owned Banks." Retrieved March 18, 2010. (http://www.business.nsw.gov.au/invest-in-nsw/about-nsw/trade-and-investment/australian-and-foreign-owned-banks).

New South Wales Government (NSW). 2010. "Sydney and New South Wales Financial Services." Retrieved April 15, 2011 (http://www.business.nsw.gov.au/__data/assets/pdf_file/0006/5685/nsw_financial_services_profile_20101014.pdf).

Nijman, Jan. 2000. "The Paradigmatic City." *Annals of the Association of American Geographers* 90(1):135–45.

———. 1996. "Breaking the Rules: Miami in the Urban Hierarchy." *Urban Geography* 17(1):5–22.

———. 2010. *Miami: Mistress of the Americas.* Philadelphia, PA: University of Pennsylvania Press.

Noyelle, T. and A. B. Dutka. 1988. *International Trade in Business Services: Accounting, Advertising, Law and Management Consulting.* Cambridge, MA: Ballinger.

O'Connor, K. 1990. *State of Australia.* Clayton, Australia: National Centre for Australian Studies, Monash University.

———. 2002. "Rethinking Globalisation and Urban Development: The Fortunes of Second-ranked Cities." *Australasian Journal of Regional Studies* 8 (3):247–60.

OECD (Organization for Economic Cooperation and Development). 1993. *Main Economic Indicators.* Paris: OECD.

———. 1996. *Main Economic Indicators.* Paris: OECD.

———. 1998. *Harmful Tax Competition. An Emerging Global Issue.* Paris: OECD.

———. 2001. *The OECD's Project on Harmful Tax Practices: The 2001 Progress Report.* Paris: OECD.

———. 2004. *The OECD's Project on Harmful Tax Practices: The 2004 Progress Report.* Paris: OECD.

———. 2005. *Main Economic Indicators.* Paris: OECD.

OECD-CFA. 2000. *Towards Global Tax Cooperation.* Paris: OECD.

OECD-CTPA. 2006. *The OECD's Project on Harmful Tax Practices: 2006 Update on Progress in Member Countries.* Paris: Organization for Economic Cooperation and Development.

Office for National Statistics. 2002. *Census 2001.* London: ONS.

Olds, Kris, Peter Dicken, Philip F. Kelly, Lilly Kong, and Henry Wai-Chung Yeung, eds. 1999. *Globalization and the Asian Pacific: Contested Territories.* London, UK: Routledge.

Oliver, Nick and Barry Wilkinson. 1988. *The Japanization of British Industry.* Oxford, UK: Blackwell.

O'Neill, P. M. and P. McGuirk. 2002. "Prosperity Along Australia's Eastern Seaboard: Sydney and the Geopolitics of Urban and Economic Change." *Australian Geographer* 33(30):241–61.

Ong, Aihwa. 2003. *Buddha Is Hiding: Refugees, Citizenship, the New America.* Berkeley, CA: University of California Press.

——— and Donald Nonini, eds. 1997. *Underground Empires.* New York: Routledge.

——— and A. Roy, eds. 2010. *Worlding Cities: Asian Experiments and the Art of Being Global.* Oxford: Blackwell.

Orozco, M., B. L. Lowell, M. Bump and R. Fedewa. 2005. *Transnational Engagement, Remittances and their Relation-ship to Development in Latin America and the Caribbean.* Washington, DC: Georgetown University, Institute for the Study of International Migration.

Orr, J. and Rae Rosen. 2000. "New York–New Jersey Job Expansion to Continue in 2000." Federal Reserve Bank of New York: *Current Issues in Economics and Finance* 6(5, April 2000):1–6.

Orr, and Rosen. 2000. "New York-New Jersey Job Expansion to Continue in 2000." Federal Reserve Bank of New York: *Current Issues in Economics and Finance* 6(5, April 2000):1–6.

Orum, Anthony and Xianming Chen. 2002. *Urban Places.* Malden, MA: Blackwell.

Paddison, Ronan, ed. 2001. Introduction. *Handbook of Urban Studies.* London, UK: Sage.

Palumbo-Liu, David. 1999. *Asian/American.* Stanford, CA: Stanford University Press.

Park, R. E., E. W. Burgess and R. D. McKenzie, eds. 1967. *The City.* Chicago: University of Chicago Press.

Parkinson, M., B. Foley, and D. R. Judd, eds. 1989. *Regenerating the Cities: The U.K. Crisis and the U.S. Experience.* Glenview, IL: Scott, Foresman.

Parnreiter, Christof. 2002. "Mexico: The Making of a Global City." Pp. 145–82 in *Global Networks/Linked Cities,* edited by Saskia Sassen. New York: Routledge.

———. 2010. "Global cities in Global Commodity Chains: exploring the role of Mexico City in the geography of governance of the world economy." *Global Networks,* 10(1).

Parnell, S. and E. Pieterse. 2010. "The 'Right to the City': Institutional Imperatives of a Developmental State." *International Journal of Urban and Regional Research* 34:146–62.

Parrenas, Rhacel Salazar, ed. 2001. *Servants of Globalization: Women, Migration and Domestic Work.* Stanford, CA: Stanford University Press.

Parsa, Ali, Ramin Keivani, Loo Lee Sim, Seow Eng Ong, Adeesh Agarwal and Bassem Younes. 2003. *Emerging Global Cities: Comparisons of Singapore and the cities of United Arab Emirates.* London: RICS Foundation. Retrieved Jan. 4, 2010 (http://www.rics.org/site/download_feed.aspx?fileID=2944&fileExtension=PDF).

Pasternak, Sean B. 2010. "Toronto's financial district returning to normal after G20." *Financial Post.* Retrieved Dec. 31, 2010 (http://www.financialpost.com/news/Toronto+financial+district+returning+normal+after/3211393/story.html).

Pathak B. (1999). "Sanitation is the Key to Healthy Cities: A Profile of Sulabh International." *Environment and Urbanization* 11(1).

Peraldi, M. and E. Perrin, eds. 1996. *Reseaux Productifs et Territoires Urbains.* Toulouse, France: Presses Universitaires de Mirail.

Perez-Sainz, J. P. 1992. *Informalidad Urbana en America Latina: Enfoques, Problematicas e Interrogantes.* Caracas, Venezuela: Editorial Nueva Sociedad.

Perez-Stable, Marifeli and Miren Uriarte. 1993. "Cubans and the Changing Economy of Miami." Pp. 133–59 in *Latinos in a Changing U.S. Economy: Comparative Perspectives on Growing Inequality,* edited by Rebecca Morales and Frank Bonilla. Sage Series on Race and Ethnic Relations, Vol. 7. Newbury Park, CA: Sage.

Pessar, P. R. and S. J. Mahler. 2003. "Transnational Migration: Bringing Gender In." *International Migration Review* 37(3):812–46.

Perlman, J. 2007. "Elusive Pathways Out of Poverty: Intra and Inter-Generational Mobility in the Favelas of Rio de Janeiro." In D. Narayan and P. Petesch, eds., *Moving out of Poverty: Cross-Disciplinary Perspectives on Mobility.* Washington, DC: Palgrave and the World Bank.

Petrella, R. 1990. "Technology and the Firm." *Technology Analysis & Strategic Management* 2(2):99–110.

Pickvance, C. and Preteceille, E., eds. 1991. *State Restructuring and Local Power: A Comparative Perspective.* London, UK: Pinter.

Pieterse, E. 2008. *City Futures: Confronting the Crisis of Urban Development.* London: Zed.

Polanyi, Karl. 1975. *The Great Transformation: The Political and Economic Origins of Our Time.* Boston, MA: Beacon.

Population Division of the Department of Economic and Social Affairs of the United Nations Secretariat. 2007. *World Urbanization Prospects: The 2007 Revision* (Data Set). Retrieved Feb. 27, 2010 (http://esa.un.org/unup).

Porter, J. et al. 2009. "The Value of Producing Food, Energy, and Ecosystem Services within an Agro-ecosystem." *Ambio* 38(4): 186–93.

Portes, Alejandro, ed. 1988. *The Economic Sociology of Immigration: Essays on Networks, Ethnicity and Entrepreneurship.* New York: Russell Sage Foundation Publications.

———, M. Castells, and L. Benton, eds. 1989. *The Informal Economy: Studies in Advanced and Less Developed Countries.* Baltimore, MD: Johns Hopkins University Press.

——— and S. Sassen-Koob. 1987. "Making It Underground: Comparative Material on the Informal Sector in Western Market Economies." *American Journal of Sociology* 93(1):30–61.

——— and Alex Stepick. 1993. *City on the Edge: The Transformation of Miami.* Berkeley, CA: University of California Press.

——— and Min Zhou. 1992. "Gaining the Upper Hand: Economic Mobility among Immigrant and Domestic Minorities." *Ethnic and Racial Studies* 15(October): 492–522.

Portes, Alejandro and M. Lungo, eds. 1992a. *Urbanización en Centroamerica.* San José, Costa Rica: Facultad Latinoamericana de Ciencias Sociales.

———, eds. 1992b. *Urbanización en el Caribe.* San José, Costa Rica: Facultad Latinoamericana de Ciencias Sociales.

Portes, Alejandro and Ruben G. Rumbaut. 2001. *Legacies: The Story of the Immigrant Second Generation*. Berkeley, CA: University of California Press.

———, eds. 1997. *Immigrant America: A Portrait*. Berkeley, CA: University of California Press.

Powell, Walter. 1990. "Neither Market nor Hierarchy: Network Forms of Organization." Pp. 295–336 in *Research in Organizational Behavior*, edited by Barry M. Straw and Larry L. Cummings. Greenwich, CT: JAI.

Pozos Ponce, Fernando. 1996. *Metropolis en Reestructuración: Guadalajara y Monterrey 1980–1989*. Guadalajara, Mexico: Universidad de Guadalajara, con Apoyo de El Fondo para la Modernización de la Educación Superior.

Prader, T., ed. 1992. *Moderne Sklaven: Asyl und Migrationspolitik in Österreich*. Vienna, Austria: Promedia.

PREALC (Regional Employment Program for Latin America and the Caribbean). 1982. *Mercado de Trabajo en Cifras: 1950–1980*. Santiago de Chile: International Labour Office.

———. 1987. *Ajuste y Deuda Social: Un Enfoque Estructural*. Santiago de Chile: International Labour Office.

Preteceille, E. 1986. "Collective Consumption, Urban Segregation, and Social Classes." *Environment and Planning D: Society and Space* 4:145–54.

Price, Marie and Lisa Benton-Short. 2007. "Counting Immigrants in Cities Across the Globe." *Migration Information Source* Retrieved Jan. 4, 2011 (http://www.migrationinformation.org).

PricewaterhouseCoopers. 2009. *Which Are the Largest City Economies in the World and How Might This Change by 2025?* UK Economic Outlook.

Prigge, Walter. 1991. "Zweite Moderne: Modernisierung und Städtische Kultur in Frankfurt." Pp. 97–105 in *Frankfurt am Main: Stadt, Soziologie und Kultur*, edited by Frank-Olaf Brauerhoch. Frankfurt, Germany: Vervuert.

Primarolo Report. 1999. *Report of the Code of Conduct Group (Business Taxation) to ECOFIN Council*, 29 November 1999.

Pugliese, Enrico. 1983. "Aspetti dell' Economia Informale a Napoli." *Inchiesta* 13(59–60):89–97.

———. 2002. *L'Italia tra Migrazioni Internazionali e Migrazioni Interne*. Bologna, Italy: Il Mulino.

Pyle, Jean L. and Kathryn Ward. 2003. " Recasting our Understanding of Gender and Work During Global Restructuring." *International Sociology* 18(3): 461–89.

Queiroz Ribeiro, Luis Cesar de. 1990. "Restructuring in Large Brazilian Cities: The Center/Periphery Model in Question." Research Institute of Urban and Regional Planning, Federal University of Rio de Janeiro, Brazil.

Rae, Douglas W. 2003. *City: Urbanism and Its End*. New Haven, CT: Yale University Press.

Rakatansky, M. 1992. "Spatial Narratives." Pp. 198–221 in *Strategies in Architectural Thinking*, edited by J. Whiteman and R. Burdett. Chicago, IL, and Cambridge, MA: Chicago Institute for Architecture and Urbanism and MIT Press.

Ramirez, Nelson, Isidor Santana, Francisco de Moya, and Pablo Tactuk. 1988. *Republica Dominicana: Población y Desarrollo 1950–1985*. San José, Costa Rica: Centro Latinoamericano de Demografia (CELADE).

Ratha, D., Mohapatra, S. and Silwal, A. 2009. "Migration and Development Brief 11: Migration and Remittance Trends 2009: A Better-than-expected Outcome for Migration and Remittance Flows in 2009, but Significant Risks Ahead." 3 November. Washington, DC: World Bank, Migration and Remittances Team, Development Prospects Group. (http://siteresources.worldbank.org/INTPROSPECTS/Resources/334934-1110315015165/MigrationAndDevelopmentBrief11.pdf).

RECLUS. 1989. *Les villes européennes*. Rapport pour la DATAR. Paris, France: RECLUS.

Redclift, M. 2000. "The Environment and Carbon Dependence: Landscapes of Sustainability and Materiality. *Current Sociology*, 57(3): 369–87.

Rees, W. E. 2006. "Ecological Footprints and Bio-Capacity: Essential Elements in Sustainability Assessment." In J. Dewulf and H. Van Langenhove, eds. *Renewables-Based Technology: Sustainability Assessment* 143–58. Chichester, UK: John Wiley and Sons.

Regional Planning Association (RPA). 2007. *Economic Megaregions*. Princeton: Policy Research Institute for the Region, Woodrow Wilson School of Public and International Affairs, Princeton University.

Reich, Robert B. 1991. *The Work of Nations: Preparing Ourselves for 21st Century Capitalism*. New York: Knopf.

Ren, Xuefei. 2011. *Building Globalization: Transnational Architecture Production in Urban China*. Chicago: University of Chicago Press.

Renooy, P. H. 1984. "Twilight Economy: A Survey of the Informal Economy in the Netherlands." Research Report, Faculty of Economic Sciences, University of Amsterdam, The Netherlands.

Reuveny R. 2008. "Ecomigration and Violent Conflict: Case Studies and Public Policy Implications." *Human Ecology*, 361–13.

Ribas-Mateos, Natalia. 2005. *The Mediterranean in the Age of Globalization: Migration, Welfare, and Borders*. Somerset, NJ: Transaction.

Ribera-Fumaz, R. 2009. "From Urban Political Economy to Cultural Political Economy: Rethinking Culture and Economy in and Beyond the Urban." *Progress in Human Geography* 33:447–65.

Richburg, Keith B. 2010. "Shanghai Poised to Take on Hong Kong as China's Financial Hub." *Washington Post*. Retrieved Dec. 31, 2010 (http://www.washingtonpost.com/wp-dyn/content/article/2010/09/25/AR2010092501884.html).

Rimmer, P. J. 1986. "Japan's World Cities: Tokyo, Osaka, Nagoya or Tokaido Megalopolis?" *Development and Change* 17(1):121–58.

———. 1988. "Japanese Construction and the Australian States: Another Round of Interstate Rivalry." *International Journal of Urban and Regional Research* 12(3):404–24.

Robbins, Paul and Julie Sharp. 2003. "The Lawn-Chemical Economy and Its Discontents" *Antipode* 10(2):955–979

Roberts, B. 1973. *Organizing Strangers: Poor Families in Guatemala City*. Austin, TX: University of Texas Press.

———. 1976. *Cities of Peasants*. London, UK: Edward Arnold.

———. 1995. *The Making of Citizens: Cities of Peasants Revisited.* New York: Edward Arnold.

——— and A. Portes. 2006. "Coping with the Free Market City: Collective Action in Six Latin American Cities at the End of the Twentieth Century." (On file with author).

Roberts, Susan. 1994. "Fictitious Capital, Fictitious Spaces: The Geography of Off-Shore Financial Flows." Pp. 91–115 in *Money, Power and Space,* edited by S. Corbridge, R. Martin, and N. Thrift. Oxford, UK: Blackwell.

Rodgers, D. 2009. "Slum Wars of the 21st Century: Gangs, 'Mano Dura,' and the New Urban Geography of Conflict in Central America." *Development and Change* 40:949–76.

Rodriguez, N. P. and J. R. Feagin. 1986. "Urban Specialization in the World System." *Urban Affairs Quarterly* 22(2):187–220.

Rodríguez-Pose, Andrés. 2011. "Economists as Geographers and Geographers as Something Else: On the Changing Conception of Distance in Geography and Economics." *Journal of economic geography* 11(2): 347–56.

Rolnik, R., L. Kowarick, and N. Somekh, eds. 1991. *São Paulo Crise e Mudanca.* São Paulo, Brazil: Brasiliense.

Roncayolo, M. 1990. *L'imaginaire de Marseille.* Marseille, France: Chambre de Commerce et d'Industrie de Marseille.

Rosen, F. and D. McFadyen, eds. 1995. *Free Trade and Economic Restructuring in Latin America* (NACLA reader). New York: Monthly Review Press.

Ross, R. and K. Trachte. 1983. "Global Cities and Global Classes: The Peripheralization of Labor in New York City." *Review* 6(3):393–431.

Rotzer, Florian. 1995. *Die Telepolis: Urbanität im Digitalen Zeitalter.* Mannheim, Germany: Bollman.

Roulleau-Berger, Laurence. 1999. *Le Travail en Friche.* La Tour d'Aigues, France: Editions de l'Aube.

Roulleau-Berger, ed. 2003. *Youth and Work in the Post-Industrial City of North America and Europe.* Boston, MA: Brill Academic Publishers.

Roy, Olivier. 1991. "Ethnicité, bandes et communautarisme." *Esprit* (February): 37–47.

Russell, Alan and Jan Rath. 2002. *Unravelling the Rag Trade: Immigrant Entrepreneurship in Seven World Cities.* Oxford, UK: Berg.

Rutherford, Jonathan. 2004. *A Tale of Two Global Cities: Comparing the Territorialities of Telecommunications Developments in Paris and London.* Aldershot, UK, and Burlington, VT: Ashgate.

SAIS Review. 2009. Special Issue on The City. Vol. XXIX (nr. 1) Spring–Summer. 29(1): 1–173

Sachar, A. 1990. "The Global Economy and World Cities." Pp. 149–60 in *The World Economy and the Spatial Organization of Power,* edited by A. Sachar and S. Oberg. Aldershot, UK: Avebury.

———. 1996. "European World Cities." Pp. 135–52 in *The Spatial Impact of Economic Changes in Europe,* edited by W. Lever & A. Bailly. Aldershot, UK: Avebury.

Saidam, Sabri. 2004. "On Route to an E-Society: Human Dependence on Technology and Adaptation Needs." A report for the Social Science Research Council's Committee on Information Technology and International Cooperation. (http://www.ssrc.org/programs/itic/publications/knowledge_ report/memos/sabri.pdf).

Safi, M. A. 1998. An integrated approach to sanitation and health in Kabul. In John Pickford (ed.) Sanitation and Water for All. Proceedings of the 24th WEDC Conference, Islamabad, Pakistan.

Salmon, Scott. 2006. "Gentrification, Globalization and Governance: The Reterritorialization of Sydney's City-State." Chapter 7 in *Relocating Global Cities: From the Center to the Margins*, edited by Mark M. Amen, Kevin Archer, and M. Martin Bosman. New York: Rowman & Littlefield.

Salzinger, Leslie. 1995. "A Maid by Any Other Name: The Transformation of 'Dirty Work' by Central American Immigrants." Pp. 139–60 in *Ethnography Unbound: Power and Resistance in the Modern Metropolis*, edited by Michael Burawoy. Berkeley, CA: University of California Press.

———. 2003. *Genders in Production: Making Workers in Mexico's Global Factories*. Berkeley, CA: University of California Press.

Samers, Michael. 2002. "Immigration and the Global City Hypothesis: Towards an Alternative Research Agenda." *International Journal of Urban and Regional Research* 26(2, June):389–402.

Sanchez, Roberto and Tito Alegria. 1992. "Las Cuidades de la Frontera Norte." Departamento de Estudios Urbanos y Medio Ambiente, El Colegio de la Frontera Norte, Tijuana, Mexico.

Sandercock, Leonie. 2003. *Cosmopolis II: Mongrel Cities in the 21st Century*. New York and London, UK: Continuum.

Sands, Oonagh. 2004. Temporary Movement of Labor Fuels GATS Debate, June 2004. Retrieved Jan. 16, 2011. (http://www.migrationinformation.org/Feature/display.cfm?ID=231).

Santos, Milton, Maria Adelia A. De Souze, and Maria Laura Silveira, eds. 1994. *Territorio Globalizacao e Fragmentacao*. São Paulo, Brazil: Hucitec.

Santoso, Oerip Lestari Djoko. 1992. "The Role of Surakarta Area in the Industrial Transformation and Development of Central Java." *Regional Development Dialogue* 13(2):69–82.

Saskai, Nobuo. 1991. *Tocho: Mo Hitotsu no Seifu* (The Tokyo Metropolitan Government: Another Central Government). Tokyo, Japan: IwanamiShoten.

Sassen, Saskia. 1988. *The Mobility of Labor and Capital: A Study in International Investment and Labor Flow*. New York: Cambridge University Press.

———. [1991] 2001. *The Global City: New York, London, and Tokyo*, 2nd ed. Princeton, NJ: Princeton University Press.

———. 1995. "Immigration and Local Labor Markets." Pp. 87–127 in *The Economic Sociology of Immigration: Essays on Networks, Ethnicity, and Entrepreneurship*, edited by Alejandro Portes. New York: Russell Sage.

———. 1996. *Losing Control? Sovereignty in an Age of Globalization*. The 1995 Columbia University Leonard Hastings Schoff Memorial Lectures. New York: Columbia University Press.

———. 1998. *Globalization and Its Discontents: Selected Essays*. New York: New Press.

———. 1999. "Global Financial Centers." *Foreign Affairs* 78(1):75–87.

———, ed. 2002. *Global Networks, Linked Cities*. London and New York: Routledge.

———. 2003. "The Repositioning of Citizenship: Emergent Subjects and Spaces for Politics." *Berkeley Journal of* Sociology 46:4–26.

———. 2004a. "The migration fallacy." *The Financial Times* December 27, 2004.

———. 2004b. "Local Actors in Global Politics." *Current Sociology* 52(4): 657–674.

———. 2005. "The Ecology of Global Economic Power: Changing Investment Practices to Promote Environmental Sustainability." *Journal of International Affairs* 58(2) 11–33.

———. 2006. Human Settlement and the Environment. *EOLSS Encyclopaedia of the Environment* (Vol. 14). Oxford: EOLSS and UNESCO.

———. 2007. *A Sociology of Globalization*. New York: W. W. Norton & Co.

———. 2008a. *Territory, Authority, Rights: From Medieval to Global Assemblages*, revised 2nd ed. Princeton: Princeton University Press.

———. 2008b. "Mortgage Capital and Its Particularities: A new Frontier for Global Finance." *Journal of International Affairs* 62(1):187–212.

———. 2008c. "Two stops in today's new global geographies: shaping novel labor supplies and employment regimes." *American Behavioral Scientist* 52(3):457–96.

———. 2010. "Novel spatial formats: Megaregions and Global Cities" Pp. 101–126 in *Governance and Planning of Mega-City Regions: An International Comparative Perspective*, Edited by Xu, J. and A.O.H Yeh. UK: Routledge.

———. 2011. "The Global City and the Global Slum." http://blogs.forbes.com/mega cities/2011/03/22/the-global-city-and-the-global-slum/#more-33

——— and Robert Latham. 2005. *Digital Formations: IT and New Architectures in the Global Realm*. Princeton, NJ: Princeton University Press.

——— and Natan Dotan. 2011. "Delegating, not Returning, to the Biosphere: How to Use the Multi-scalar and Ecological Properties of Cities." *Global Environmental Change* 21(3).

———— with Olivia Nicol and Marta Walinska. 2011. *The Global Labor Market at a Tipping Point*. Prepared for The Economist Intelligence Unit. New York: The Economist Intelligence Unit.

Sassen-Koob, Saskia. 1980. "Immigrants and Minority Workers in the Organization of the Labor Process." *Journal of Ethnic Studies* 8(Spring):1–34.

———. 1982. "Recomposition and Peripheralization at the Core." Pp. 88–100 in *The New Nomads: Immigration and Change in the International Division of Labor*, edited by Marlene Dixon and Susanne Jonas. San Francisco, CA: Synthesis. (Reprinted in *Contemporary Marxism*, vol. 4.).

———. 1984. "The New Labor Demand in Global Cities." Pp. 139–71 in *Cities in Transformation*, edited by M. P. Smith. Beverly Hills, CA: Sage.

Satler, Gail. 2006. *Two Tales of a City: Rebuilding Chicago's Architectural and Social Landscape, 1986–2005*. DeKalb, IL: Northern Illinois University Press.

Satterthwaithe, D. 1999. "Sustainable Cities or Cities That Contribute to Sustainable Development?" Pp. 80–107 in D. Satterthwaithe, ed., *The Earthscan Reader in Sustainable Cities*. London: Earthscan.

—— and Saleemul Huq, Mark Pelling, Hannah Reid, and Patricia Romero Lankao. 2007. "Adapting to climate change in urban areas: the possibilities and constraints in low- and middle-income nations." Human Settlements Discussion Paper Series, London: IIED. http://www.iied.org/pubs/pdfs/10549IIED.pdf.

Saxenian, Anna-lee. 1996. Regional Advantage: Culture and Competition in Silicon Valley and Route 128. Cambridge, MA: Harvard University Press.

Savitch, H. 1988. *Post-Industrial Cities*. Princeton, NJ: Princeton University Press.

——. 1996. "Cities in a Global Era: A New Paradigm for the Next Millennium." Pp. 39–65 in *Preparing for the Urban Future: Global Pressures and Local Forces*, edited by M. Cohen, B. Ruble, J. Tulchin, and A. Garland. Washington, DC: Woodrow Wilson Center Press (Distributed by Johns Hopkins University Press).

Sayer, Andrew and Richard Walker. 1992. *The New Social Economy: Reworking the Division of Labor*. Cambridge, MA: Blackwell.

Schiffer, Sueli Ramos. 2002. "Sao Paulo: Articulating a Cross-border Regional Economy." Pp. 209–36 in *Global Networks/Linked Cities*, edited by Saskia Sassen. New York and London, UK: Routledge.

Schwartz, Moshe. 2009. "Department of Defense Contractors in Iraq and Afghanistan: Background and Analysis." *Congressional Research Service Report* December 14, 2009 (http://books.google.com/books?hl=en&lr=&id=F5xB0r3qw0QC&oi= fnd&pg=PA1&dq=Moshe+Schwartz+%E2%80%9CDepartment+of+Defense+ Contractors+in+Iraq+and+Afghanistan:+Background+and+Analysis%E2%80% 9D+Congressional+Research+Service+Report+December+14,+2009&ots=OvX biu-Pqv&sig=9rzDP4RmwVU-uAhT85_I5UOKb88#v=onepage&q&f=false).

Sclar, Elliott D. and Walter Hook. 1993. "The Importance of Cities to the National Economy." Pp. 48–80 in *Interwoven Destinies: Cities and the Nation*, edited by Henry G. Cisneros. New York: Norton.

Scott, Allen J. 2001. *Global City-Regions*. Oxford, UK: Oxford University Press.

——. 1988. *Metropolis: From the Division of Labor to Urban Form*. Berkeley, CA: University of California Press.

—— and Michael Storper, eds. 1986. *Production, Work, Territory*. Boston, MA: Allen and Unwin.

Sennett, R. 1990. *The Conscience of the Eye: The Design and Social Life of Cities*. New York: Knopf.

——. 1996. *Flesh and Stone: The Body and the City in Western Civilization*. New York: Norton.

——. 2006. *The Culture of the New Capitalism*. New Haven, CT: Yale University Press.

——. 2008. *The Craftsman*. London: Penguin.

"The Service 500." 1993, May 31. *Fortune* 199–230.

Shanghai Stock Exchange. 2010. Retrieved Dec. 30, 2010 (http://www.sse.com.cn/ sseportal/en/c05/c02/c01/c02/p1113/c1505020102_p1113.shtml).

Shank, G., ed. 1994. "Japan Enters the 21st Century." *Social Justice* 21(2, Special issue).

Sharman, Jason. 2006. *Havens in a Storm. The Struggle for Global Tax Regulation.* Ithaca: Cornell U.P.

Shatkin, G. 2008. "The City and the Bottom Line: Urban Megaprojects and the Privatization of Planning in Southeast Asia." *Environment and Planning A* 40:383–401.

Sheets, R. G., S. Nord, and J. J. Phelps. 1987. The Impact of Service Industries on Underemployment in Metropolitan Economies. Lexington, MA: D. C. Heath.

Sherman, Arloc and Chad Stone. 2010. "Income Gaps Between Very Rich and Everyone Else More Than Tripled in Last Three Decades, New Data Show." Washington, DC: Center on Budget and Policy Priorities, Retrieved July 13, 2011 (http://www.cbpp.org/cms/index.cfm?fa=view&id=3220).

Short, John Rennie. 2005. *Global Metropolitanism.* London: Routledge.

———— and Y. H. Kim. 1999. *Globalization and the City.* New York: Longman.

Siebel, W. 1984. "Krisenphänomene der Stadtentwicklung." *arch + d* 75/76:67–70.

Silver, H. 1984. "Regional Shifts, Deindustrialization and Metropolitan Income Inequality." Presented at the Annual Meeting of the American Sociological Association, August, San Antonio, TX.

————. 1993. "National Conceptions of the New Urban Poverty: Social Structural Change in Britain, France and the United States." *International Journal of Urban and Regional Research* 17(3):336–54.

———— and R. Bures. 1997. "Dual cities? Sectoral shifts and metropolitan income inequality, 1980–90." *Service Industries Journal* 17(1):69–90.

Simon, David. 1995. "The World City Hypothesis: Reflections from the Periphery." Pp. 132–55 in *World Cities in a World-System,* edited by P. Knox and P. Taylor. New York: Cambridge University Press.

Sinclair, Timothy. 2008. *The New Masters of Capital: American Bond Rating Agencies and the Politics of Creditworthiness.* Cornell Studies in Political Economy. Ithaca, NY: Cornell University Press.

————. 2004. *Global Governance: Critical Concepts in Political Science.* London: Routledge.

Singelmann, J. 1974. "The Sectoral Transformation of the Labor Force in Seven Industrialized Countries, 1920–1960." Ph.D. dissertation, University of Texas, Austin, TX.

———— and H. L. Browning. 1980. "Industrial Transformation and Occupational Change in the U.S., 1960–70." *Social Forces* 59:246–64.

Singh, Surjit. 1994. *Urban Informal Sector.* Jaipur, India: Rawat.

Singtel. 2001. *Subsidiaries and Associated Companies.* Retrieved Dec. 31, 2010 (http://info.singtel.com/about-us/subsidiaries-associated-companies).

Skeldon, R. 1997. "'Hong Kong: Colonial City to Global City to Provincial City?" *Cities* (14)5:265–71.

————, ed. 1994. *Reluctant Exiles?: Migration from Hong Kong and the New Overseas Chinese.* Armonk, NY: M. E. Sharpe.

————. 2000. "Trends in international migration in the Asian and Pacific region." *International Social Science Journal* 52(165):369–82.

Sklair, Leslie. 1985. "Shenzhen: A Chinese 'Development Zone' in Global Perspective." *Development and Change* 16:571–602.

———. 1991. *Sociology of the Global System: Social Changes in Global Perspective.* Baltimore, MD: Johns Hopkins University Press.

———. 2001. *The Transnational Capitalist Class.* Malden, MA: Blackwell Publishers.

Smeeding, T. 2002. "Globalization, Inequality, and the Rich Countries of the G-20: Evidence from the Luxembourg Income Study (LIS)." *Luxembourg Income Study Working Paper No. 320.* Prepared for the G-20 Meeting, Globalization, Living Standards and Inequality: Recent Progress and Continuing Challenges, Sydney, Australia, May 26–28, 2002.

Smith, Anthony, ed. 1992. *The Apartheid City and Beyond: Urbanization and Social Change in South Africa.* London, UK: Routledge/Witwatersrand University Press.

Smith, Carol A. 1985. "Theories and Measures of Urban Primacy: A Critique." Pp. 87–116 in *Urbanization in the World-Economy,* edited by M. Timberlake. Orlando, FL: Academic Press.

Smith, David. 2004. "Global Cities in East Asia: Empirical and Conceptual Analysis." *International Social Science Journal* 56(3):399–412.

———. 1995. "The New Urban Sociology Meets the Old: Rereading Some Classical Human Ecology." *Urban Affairs Review* 30(3):432–57.

——— and Michael Timberlake. 2001. "World City Networks and Hierarchies, 1977–1997: An Empirical Analysis of Global Air Travel Links." *American Behavioral Scientist* 44(10):1656–79.

———, S. Solinger, and S. Topik, eds. 1999. *States and Sovereignty in the Global Economy.* London, UK: Routledge.

Smith, Etienne. 2009. *L'Afrique: histoire et défis: 50 cartes et fiches.* Paris: Ellipses.

Smith, M. P. and J. R. Feagin. 1987. *The Capitalist City: Global Restructuring and Territorial Development.* London, UK: Sage.

———. 1996. *The New Urban Frontier; Gentrification and the Revanchist City.* London: Routledge.

——— and P. Williams. 1986. *Gentrification of the City.* Boston, MA: Allen and Unwin.

Smith, Robert C. 1997. "Transnational Migration, Assimilation, and Political Community." Pp. 110–32 in *The City and the World,* edited by Margaret Crahan and Alberto Vourvoulias-Bush. New York: Council on Foreign Relations.

———. 2005. *Mexican New York: Transnational Lives of New Immigrants.* Berkeley. CA: University of California Press.

Smith, R.G. 2007. "Poststructuralism, Power and the Global City." p. 258–70 in *Cities in Globalization: Practices, Policies and Theories,* edited by Taylor, P. J., Derudder, B., Saey, P. & Witlox, F., eds. London: Routledge.

Soja, Edward W. 2000. *Postmetropolis: Critical Studies of Cities and Regions.* Oxford: Blackwell.

Solinger, Dorothy. 1999. *Contesting Citizenship in Urban China: Peasant Migrants, the State, and the Logic of the Market.* Berkeley, CA: University of California Press.

Sonnenfeld, David A., and Arthur P.J. Mol. 2011. Special Issue on "Social Theory and the Environment in the New World (dis)Order," *Global Environmental Change* 21(3), August 2011.

Sonobe, M. 1993. "Spatial Dimension of Social Segregation in Tokyo: Some Remarks in Comparison with London." Paper presented at the meeting of the Global City Project, Social Science Research Council, March 9–11, New York.

SOPEMI (Systeme d'Observation Permanente pour les Migrations). 1999–2005. *Trends in International Migration*. Paris, France: OECD, Directorate for Social Affairs, Manpower and Education.

Soysal, L. 2010. "Intimate Engagements of the Public Kind." *Anthropological Quarterly* 83:373–89.

Stanback, T. M., Jr., P. J. Bearse, T. J. Noyelle, and R. Karasek. 1981. *Services: The New Economy*. Montclair, NJ: Allenheld, Osmun.

———— and T. J. Noyelle. 1982. *Cities in Transition: Changing Job Structures in Atlanta, Denver, Buffalo, Phoenix, Columbus (Ohio), Nashville, Charlotte*. Montclair, NJ: Allenheld, Osmun.

Statistics Canada. 2005. "Employment by Industry." Table 282–0008. Ontario: Statistics Canada. Retrieved December 7, 2005 (http://www40.statcan.ca/101/cst01/econ40.htm?sdi=employment%20sector).

Stimson, Robert J. 1993. "The Process of Globalisation and Economic Restructuring and the Emergence of a New Space Economy of Cities and Regions in Australia." Presented at the Fourth International Workshop on Technological Change and Urban Form: Productive and Sustainable Cities, April 14–16, Berkeley, CA.

Stopford, John M., ed. 1992. *Directory of Multinationals*. London, UK: Macmillan.

Stren, R. E. and R. R. White. 1989. *African Cities in Crisis: Managing Rapid Urban Growth*. Boulder, CO: Westview.

Stren, R. 1996. "The Studies of Cities: Popular Perceptions, Academic Disciplines, and Emerging Agendas." In *Preparing for the Urban Future: Global Pressures and Local Forces*, edited by M. Cohen, B. Ruble, J. Tulchin and A. Garland. Washington D.C.: Woodrow Wilson Center Press (distributed by The Johns Hopkins University Press).

————, Richard, Barney Cohen, Holly E. Reed, and Mark R. Montgomery, eds. 2003. *Cities Transformed: Demographic Change and Its Implications in the Developing World*. Washington, DC: National Academies Press.

Susser, Ida. 1982. *Norman Street, Poverty and Politics in an Urban Neighborhood*. New York: Oxford University Press.

————. 2002. "Losing Ground: Advancing Capitalism and the Relocation of Working Class Communities." Pp. 247–90 in *Locating Capitalism in Time and Space: Global Restructurings, Politics, and Identity*, edited by David Nugent. Stanford, CA: Stanford University Press.

Swyngedouw, Eric and Heynen, C Nikolas. 2003. "Urban Political Ecology, Justice, and the Politics of Scale." http://onlinelibrary.wiley.com/doi/10.1111/anti.2003.35.issue-5/issuetoc.

Tabak, Faruk and Michaeline A. Crichlow, eds. 2000. *Informalization: Process and Structure*. Baltimore, MD: The Johns Hopkins Press.

Tardanico, Richard and Mario Lungo. 1995. "Local Dimensions of Global Restructuring in Urban Costa Rica." *International Journal of Urban and Regional Research* (19)2:223–249.

Tax Justice Network. 2007. "Identifying Tax Havens and Offshore Finance Centers." Retrieved July 13, 2011 (http://www.taxjustice.net/cms/upload/pdf/Identifying_Tax_Havens_Jul_07.pdf).

Taylor, Peter J. 2000. "World Cities and Territorial States Under Conditions of contemporary Globalization." *Political Geography* (19)5:5–32.

———. 2004. World City Network: A Global Urban Analysis. New York: Routledge.

———, D. R. F. Walker, and J. V. Beaverstock. 2002. "Firms and Their Global Service Networks." Pp. 93–116 in *Global Networks, Linked Cities,* edited by Saskia Sassen. New York: Routledge.

———, Gilda Catalano and Michael Hoyler. 2002. "Diversity and Power in the World City Network." *Cities* (19)4:231–42.

——— and Knox, P. L., eds. 1995. *World Cities in a World-System.* Cambridge: Cambridge University Press.

———, B. Derudder, P. Saey, and F. Witlox, eds. 2007. *Cities in Globalization: Practices, Policies and Theories.* London: Routledge.

———, P. Ni, B. Derudder, M. Hoyler, J. Huang and F. Witlox, eds. 2010. *Global Urban Analysis: A Survey of Cities in Globalization.* London, UK: Earthscan.

Teresaka, Akinobu, Itsuki Wakabayashi, and Abe Kazutoshi. 1988. "The Transformation of Regional Systems in an Information-Oriented Society." *Geographical Review of Japan* 61(1):159–73.

The Annals of the American Academy of Political and Social Science. 2010. Special Issue on The New American City. (Forthcoming).

Thomas, Margaret. 1983. "The Leading Euromarket Law Firms in Hong Kong and Singapore." *International Financial Law Review* (June):4–8.

Thomasson, Lynn. 2010. "Hong Kong Tops Japan as Asia's Biggest Market for Short Selling." Retrieved Dec. 30, 2010 (http://www.businessweek.com/news/2010-10-12/hong-kong-tops-japan-as-asia-s-biggest-market-for-short-selling.html).

Thomson Financials. 1999. *International Target Cities Report.* New York: Thomson Financial Investor Relations.

Thrift, N. 1987. "The Fixers: The Urban Geography of International Commercial Capital." Pp. 219–47 in *Global Restructuring and Territorial Development,* edited by J. Henderson and M. Castells. London, UK: Sage.

———. 2005. *Knowing Capitalism.* London: Sage Publications.

——— and Ash Amin. 2002. *Cities: Reimagining the Urban.* Cambridge, UK: Polity Press.

Timberlake, M., ed. 1985. *Urbanization in the World Economy.* Orlando, FL: Academic Press.

Tinker, I., ed. 1990. *Persistent Inequalities: Women and World Development.* New York: Oxford University Press.

TMX Group. 2010. "TMX Group—Equity Financing Statistics November 2010." Retrieved Dec. 31, 2010 (http://www.tmx.com/en/pdf/month_stats/FinancingStats_Nov10.pdf).

Todd, Graham. 1993. The Political Economy of Urban and Regional Restructuring in Canada: Toronto, Montreal and Vancouver in the Global Economy, 1970–1990.

Ph.D. dissertation, Department of Political Science, York University, Toronto, Canada.

————. 1995. "'Going Global' in the Semi-periphery: World Cities as Political Projects. The Case of Toronto." Pp. 192–214 in *World Cities in a World-System*, edited by P. Knox and P. Taylor. New York: Cambridge University Press.

Toly, Noah J. (2008). "Transnational Municipal Networks in Climate Politics: From Global Governance to Global Politics." *Globalizations* 5(3):341–56.

Topel, Robert. 1997. "Factor Proportions and Relative Wages: The Supply Side Determinants of Wage Inequality." *Journal of Economic Perspectives*. Spring: 55–74.

Toronto Financial Services Alliance (TSFA). 2010. Retrieved Dec. 31, 2010 (http://www.tfsa.ca/downloads/resources/Perspectives_Magazine_2010_new.pdf).

Torres, R., L. Miron, and J. X. Inda, eds. 1999. *Race, Identity, and Citizenship*. Oxford: Blackwell.

Toulouse, Christopher. 1992. "Thatcherism, Class Politics and Urban Development in London." *Critical Sociology* 18(1):57–76.

Trejos, J. D. 1991. "Informalidad y Acumulación en el Area Metropolitana de San José, Costa Rica." In *Informalidad Urbana en Centroamerica: Entre la Acumulación y la Subsistencia*, edited by J. P. Perez-Sainz and R. Menjivar Larin. Caracas, Venezuela: Editorial Nueva Sociedad.

Tribalat, M., J.-P. Garson, Y. Moulier-Boutang, and R. Silberman. 1991. *Cent Ans d'Immigration: Etrangers d'Hier, Français d'Aaujourd'hui*. Paris, France: Presses Universitaires de France, Institut National d'Etudes Demographiques.

Turkish Government Statistical Institute. 2000. "Turkish Government's Statistical Records: Annual Report." DIE (Turkish Government Statistical Institute). Ankara, 2000. Retrieved July 11, 2007 (http://www.turkstat.gov.tr).

Turkish Statistical Institute. 2009. Retrieved July 13, 2011. http://www.tepav.org.tr/tur/admin/dosyabul/upload/TR-TEPAV-Ticaretin%20Finansmani%20Raporu.pdf

Tyner, James. 1999. "The Global Context of Gendered Labor Emigration from the Philippines to the United States." *American Behavioral Scientist*. 42(40): 671–94.

Union Bank of Switzerland. 2009. *Prices and Earnings: A Comparison of Purchasing Power around the Globe, 2009 ed.* Zurich, Switzerland: UBS.

UNCTC (United Nations Center on Transnational Corporations). 1991. *World Investment Report: The Triad in Foreign Direct Investment*. New York: United Nations.

————. 1992. *The Determinants of Foreign Direct Investment: A Survey of the Evidence*. New York: United Nations.

UNCTAD (United Nations Conference on Trade and Development). 1992. *World Investment Report 1992: Transnational Corporations as Engines of Growth*. New York: United Nations.

————. 1993. *World Investment Report 1993: Transnational Corporations and Integrated International Production*. New York: United Nations.

————. 1997. *World Investment Report 1997: Transnational Corporations, Market Structure and Competition Policy.* New York: United Nations.

————. 1998. *World Investment Report 1998: Trends and Determinants.* New York: United Nations.

————. 2004. *World Investment Report 2004: The Shift Towards Services.* New York: United Nations.

————. 2008. *World Investment Directory Volume X: Africa.* New York: United Nations.

————. 2009a. "Major FDI Indicators (WIR 2009)." *FDI Stat Online Database.* Retrieved Feb. 19, 2010 (http://stats.unctad.org/FDI/TableViewer/tableView .aspx?ReportId=3084).

————. 2009b. *World Investment Report 2009: Transnational Corporations, Agricultural Production and Development.* New York: United Nations.

United Nations. Department for Economic and Social Affairs, Policy Analysis. 2003. *Urban and Rural Areas, 2003.* New York: United Nations.

————. 1994. *Urban Agglomerations and Rural Agglomerations, 1994.* New York: United Nations.

United Nations, Department of Economic and Social Affairs, Population Division. 2010. *World Urbanization Prospects: The 2009 Revision.* New York. Retrieved January 6, 2010 (http://esa.un.org/unpd/wup/index.htm).

United Nations, Department of Economic and Social Affairs, Population Division. 2002. *World Urbanization Prospects, the 2001 Revision.* New York. Accessed January 6, 2010 (http://www.un.org/esa/population/publications/wup2001/WUP 2001report.htm).

United Nations, Department of Economic and Social Affairs, Population Division. 2008. *World Urbanization Prospects: The 2007 Revision.* New York: United Nations. Available at http://www.un.org/esa/population/publications/wup2007/ 2007wup.htm. Accessed 21 March 2010.

————. 2004. *Urban Agglomerations, 2003.* New York: United Nations.

————. 1996. *Urban Agglomerations, 1996.* New York: United Nations.

United Nations, Department of Economic and Social Affairs, Population Division. 2010. *World Urbanization Prospects: The 2009 Revision.* New York. Retrieved Jan. 6, 2010. (http://esa.un.org/unpd/wup/index.htm).

————. 2002. *World Urbanization Prospects, the 2001 Revision.* New York. Retrieved Jan. 6, 2010. (http://www.un.org/esa/population/publications/wup 2001/WUP2001report.htm)

United Nations Department for International Economic and Social Affairs. 1988. *Prospects of World Urbanization.* New York: United Nations.

————. 2003. *Prospects of World Urbanization.* New York: United Nations.

UNDP (United Nations Development Programme). 2005. "A Time for Bold Ambition: Together We Can Cut Poverty in Half." UNDP Annual Report. New York: UNDP.

————. 2008. "Human Development Report 2007–2008." UNDP Annual Report. New York: UNDP.

Urban Geography. 2008. *Chicago and Los Angeles: Paradigms, Schools, Achetypes, and the Urban Process.* Vol 29(2). February 15-March 31, 2008.

Urban Age. 2008. *The Future of Cities Conference Series.* London: The Cities Program, London School of Economics (http://www.urban-age.net).

US Department of State, Bureau of Public Affairs. 2010a. *Trafficking in Persons: Ten Years of Partnering to Combat Modern Slavery.* Washington, DC: Bureau of Public Affairs: Strategic Communications.

———. 2010b. Fact Sheet. (http://www.state.gov/r/pa/scp/fs/2010/143115.htm).

US Bureau of the Census. 2004a. *Income, Poverty, and Health Insurance Coverage in the United States: 2003.* Washington, DC: U.S. Government Printing Office.

———. 2004b. *Money Income in The U.S.: 2001.* Washington, DC: U.S. Government Printing Office.

———. 2009a. Current Population Reports, P60–236, *Income, Poverty, and Health Insurance Coverage in the United States: 2008.* Washington, D.C.: U.S. Government Printing Office.

———. 2009b. Current Population Survey, Annual Social and Economic Supplements: Table F-2: "Share of Aggregate Income Received by Each Fifth and Top 5 Percent of Families, All Races: 1947 to 2008 (Families as of March of the following year)." Retrieved April 15, 2011. (http://www.stateofworkingamerica.org/files/files/2%20Family%20Income_Fast%20and%20fair%20vs%20slow-and-skewed.xlsx).

———. 2009c. Current Population Survey, Annual Social and Economic Supplements: Table IE-2: "Measures of Individual Earnings Inequality for Full-Time Year-Round Workers by Sex." Retrieved 20 March 2010. (http://www.census.gov/hhes/www/income/histinc/incqtoc.html).

———. 1997. *U.S. Census Update.* Washington, DC: U.S. Government Printing Office.

US Bureau of Labor Statistics. 1998. *U.S. Bureau of Labor Statistics Data.* Washington, DC: U.S. Government Printing Office.

———. 2005. *U.S. Bureau of Labor Statistics: Labor Force Statistics from the Current Population Survey.* Washington, DC: U.S. Bureau of Labor Statistics. Retrieved December 7, 2005 (http://www.bls.gov/home.htm).

US Department of Commerce, Office of the U.S. Trade Representative. 1983. *U.S. National Study on Trade in Services.* Washington, DC: U.S. Government Printing Office.

US Department of Commerce. 1992. *U.S. Direct Investment Abroad: 1989 Benchmark Survey, Final Results.* Washington, DC: U.S. Government Printing Office.

———. 1985. *U.S. Direct Investment Abroad: 1982 Benchmark Survey Data.* Washington, DC: U.S. Government Printing Office.

US Department of Housing and Urban Development. 2005. *State of the Cities Data Systems.* Washington DC: HUD. Retrieved December 6, 2005. (http://socds.huduser.org/index.html).

US Department of State. 2004. *Trafficking in Persons Report,* released by the Office to Monitor and Combat Trafficking in Persons. Washington, DC: U.S. Department of State. (http://www.state.gov/r/pa/scp/fs/2010/143115.htm).

Valle, Victor M. and Rodolfo D. Torres. 2000. *Latino Metropolis*. Minneapolis, MN: University of Minnesota Press.

van den Berg, L., R. Drewett, L. H. Klaassen, A. Rossi and C. H. T. Vijverberg. 1982. *Urban Europe: A Study of Growth and Decline*. Oxford, UK: Pergamon.

Van Dijk, Michiel, Francis Weyzig and Richard Murphy. 2006. *The Netherlands—A Tax Haven?* Amsterdam: Centre for Research on Multinational Organisations (SOMO).

Van Veenhuizen, R. and G. Danso. 2007. *Profitability and Sustainability of Urban and Peri-urban Agriculture*. Rome: Food and Agriculture Organization of the United Nations. Retrieved from http://www.ruaf.org/sites/default/files/2838.pdf.

Varchaver, N. and K. Benner. 2008. "The $55 Trillion Question: Special Report Issue 1: America's money crisis." CNNMoney.com. (http://money.cnn.com/2008/09/30/magazines/fortune/varchaver_derivatives_short.fortune/index.htm).

Von Braun, J. and R. S. Meinzen-Dick. 2000. "'Land Grabbing' by Foreign Investors in Developing Countries: Risks and Opportunities." IFPRI Policy Brief 13. Washington, DC: International Food Policy Research Institute. (www.ifpri.org/publication/land-grabbing-foreign-investors-developing-countries).

Vecchio, Diane C. 2007. "Cleaning Up: The Transformation of Domestic Service in Twentieth Century New York City." *The Journal of American History* 93(4):1279.

Veltz, Pierre. 1996. *Mondialisation Villes et Territoires*. Paris, France: Presses Universitaires De France.

Vidal, Sarah, Jean Viard, et al. 1990. *Le Deuxième Sud, Marseille ou le Present Incertain*. Arles, France: Editions Actes Sud, Cahiers Pierre-Baptiste.

Vieillard-Baron, Herve. 1991. "Le Risque du Ghetto." *Esprit* (February):14–22.

Von Petz, U. and K. Schmals, eds. 1992. *Metropole, Weltstadt, Global City: Neue Formen der Urbanisierung*. Dortmund: Dortmunder Beiträge zur Raumplanung Vol. 60. Dortmund, Germany: Universität Dortmund.

Wacquant, L. 1997. "Inside the Zone." *Theory, Culture, and Society* (15)2:1–36.

———. 2006. *Deadly Symbiosis: Race and the Rise of Neoliberal Penalty*. London: Polity Press.

———. 2007. *Urban Outcasts*. London: Polity Press.

Waldinger, Roger. 1996. *Still the Promised City? African-Americans and the New Immigrants in Postindustrial New York*. Cambridge, MA: Harvard University Press.

Walter, I. 1989. *Secret Money*. London, UK: Unwin Hyman.

Walters, Pamela Barnhouse. 1985. "Systems of Cities and Urban Primacy: Problems of Definition and Measurement." Pp. 63–86 in *Urbanization in the World-Economy*, edited by M. Timberlake. Orlando, FL: Academic Press.

Walton, John and David Seddon. 1994. *Free Markets & Food Riots: The Politics of Global Adjustment*. Cambridge, MA: Blackwell.

Wang, Lan, Ratoola Kundu and Xiangming Chen. 2010. "Building for What and Whom? New Town Development as Planned Suburbanization in China and India." *Research in Urban Sociology* 10:319–45.

Wang, Y. P., Y. Wang and J. Wu. 2009. "Urbanization and Informal Development in China: Urban Villages in Shenzhen." *International Journal of Urban and Regional Research* 33:957–73.

Ward, K. 1991. *Women Workers and Global Restructuring.* Ithaca, NY: Cornell University Press.

—— and Jean Pyle. 1995. "Gender, Industrialization and Development." Pp. 37–64 in *Women in the Latin American Development Process: From Structural Subordination to Empowerment,* edited by Christine E. Bose and Edna Acosta-Belen. Philadelphia, PA: Temple University Press.

Warkentin, Craig. 2001. *Reshaping World Politics: NGOs, the Internet, and Global Civil Society.* Lanham, MD: Rowman & Littlefield.

Warner K. et al. 2009. *In Search of Shelter: Mapping the Effects of Climate Change on Human Migration and Displacement.* CARE International. Retrieved from http://www.ehs.unu.edu/file.php?id=621.

Warnock, Veronica Cacdac and Francis E. Warnock. 2008. "Markets and Housing Finance." Retrieved August 24, 2008 (http://ssrn.com/abstract=981641).

Weinstein, Liza. 2008. "Mumbai's Development Mafias: Organized Crime, Land Development, and Globalization." *International Journal of Urban and Regional Research* 32(1): 22–39.

_____. and Xuefei Ren. 2009. "The Changing Right to the City: Urban Renewal and Housing Rights in Globalizing Shanghai and Mumbai." *City & Community* 8(4): 407–32.

Wentz, Martin, ed. 1991. *Stadtplanung in Frankfurt: Wohnen, Arbeiten, Verkehr.* Frankfurt, Germany, and New York: Campus.

Werth, M. and H. Korner, eds. 1991. *Immigration of Citizens from Third Countries into the Southern Member States of the European Community. Social Europe.* Supplement 1/91. Luxembourg: Office for Official Publications of the European Communities.

Whiteman, J., J. Kipnis, and R. Burdett. 1992. *Strategies in Architectural Thinking.* Chicago, IL, and Cambridge, MA: Chicago Institute for Architecture and Urbanism/MIT Press.

WIACT (Workers' Information and Action Centre of Toronto). 1993. "Trends in Employee Home Employment." Toronto, Canada: WIACT (Mimeo).

Wigle, J. 2010. "Social Relations, Property and 'Peripheral' Informal Settlement: The Case of Ampliación San Marcos, Mexico City." *Urban Studies* 47:411–36.

Wigley, M. 1992. "Untitled: The Housing of Gender." Pp. 327–90 in *Sexuality and Space,* edited by Beatriz Colomina. Princeton Papers on Architecture. Princeton, NJ: Princeton Architectural Press.

Wihtol de Wenden, Catherine, ed. 1988. *La Citoyenneté.* Paris, France: Edilic, Fondation Diderot.

Willoughby, K. W. 1990. *Technology Choice.* Boulder, CO, and San Francisco, CA: Westview.

Wilpert, Czarina. 1998. "Migration and Informal Work in the New Berlin: New Forms of Work or New Sources of Labor?" *Journal of Ethnic and Migration Studies* 24(2):269–94.

Wilson, A. 2008. "The Sacred Geography of Bangkok's Markets." *International Journal of Urban and Regional Research* 32:631–42.

Wilson, W. J. 1997. *The Truly Disadvantaged: The Inner City, the Underclass and Public Policy.* Chicago, IL: University of Chicago Press.

———. 1987. *When Work Disappears.* New York: Alfred A. Knopf.

Wonders, Nancy A. and Raymond Michalowski. 2001. "Bodies, Borders, and Sex Tourism in a Globalized World: A Tale of Two Cities—Amsterdam and Havana." *Social Problems* 48(4):545–71.

World Bank. 1991. *Urban Policy and Economic Development: An Agenda for the 1990s.* Washington, DC: World Bank.

———. 1998. *World Development Indicators.* Washington, DC: World Bank.

———. 2005. *World Development Indicators.* Washington, DC: World Bank.

———. 2006. *Global Economic Prospects: Economic Implications of Remittances and Migration.* Washington, DC: World Bank.

———. 2008. *Migration and Remittances: Top Ten.* March, (http://econ.worldbank.org/WBSITE/EXTERNAL/EXTDEC/EXTDECPROSPECTS/0,,content MDK:21352016 pagePK:64165401 piPK:64401 piPK:64165026 theSitePK:476883,00.html).

———. 2009. *World Development Indicators Online*, Database.

"World Business." 1989. *Wall Street Journal.* September 22, R23.

———. 1992. *Wall Street Journal.* September 24, R27.

———. 1998. *Wall Street Journal.* September 28, R25–27.

———. 2004. *Wall Street Journal.* September 27, R20.

World Federation of Exchanges. 2003. *Annual Statistics for 2003.* Paris: World Federation of Exchanges.

———. 2004. *Annual Statistics for 2004.* Paris: World Federation of Exchanges.

———. 2005. *Annual Statistics for 2004.* Paris: World Federation of Exchanges.

———. 2008a. *Statistics: Time Series: Total Value of Share Trading.* Paris: World Federation of Exchanges. Retrieved January 21, 2009 (http://www.world-exchanges.org/statistics/time-series/value-share-trading).

———. 2008b. *Statistics: Time Series: Total Number of Listed Companies.* Paris: World Federation of Exchanges. (http://www.world-exchanges.org/statistics/time-series/number-listed-companies).

———. 2009. *Annual Statistics.* Paris: World Federation of Exchanges.

World Health Organization. 2009. *Megacities and Urban Health.*

Worldscope Global. 2011. http://www.lib.umich.edu/database/worldscope-global European Trade Commission. 2006.

Wright, E. O. and R. E. Dwyer. 2007. "The Patterns of Job Expansions in the USA: A Comparison of the 1960s and 1990s." *Socio-Economic Review* 1:302.

Wright, Talmadge. 1997. *Out of Place.* Albany, NY: State University of New York Press.

Xu, J. and A. O. H. Yeh. 2010. *Governance and Planning of Mega-City Regions: An International Comparative Perspective.* London: Routledge.

Yamanaka, Keiko. 2004. "New Worlds, New Lives: Globalization and People of Japanese Descent in the Americas and From Latin America in Japan." *Journal of Asian Studies* 63(4):1080–2.

Yeoh, Brenda S. A. 2007. *Singapore: Hungry for Foreign Workers at All Skill Levels, January 2007.* Accessible at http://www.migrationinformation.org/Profiles/display.cfm?id=570.

Yeung, Yue-man. 2000. *Globalization and Networked Societies.* Honolulu, HI: University of Hawaii Press.

Young, D. and R. Keil. 2010. "Reconnecting the Disconnected: The Politics of Infrastructure in the in-between City." *Cities* 27:87–95.

Yuval-Davis, N. 1999. "Ethnicity, Gender Relations and Multiculturalism." Pp. 112–25 in *Race, Identity, and Citizenship,* edited by R. Torres, L. Miron and J. X. Inda. Oxford, UK: Blackwell.

———. 2006. *Gender and Nation* (updated 2nd ed.). London: Sage Publications.

Zelinsky, Wilbur. 1991. "The Twinning of the World: Sister Cities in Geographic and Historical Perspective." *Annals of the Association of American Geographers* 81(1):1–31.

Zoromé, Ahmed. 2007. *Concept of Offshore Financial Centers: In Search of an Operational Definition.* Working Paper 07/87. Washington DC: IMF.

Zukin, Sharon. 1991. *Landscapes of Power.* Berkeley, CA: University of California Press.

———. 2005. *Point of Purchase: How Shopping Changed American Culture.* New York: Routledge.

Index

Pages followed by "*e*" indicate Exhibits.

About the Author

Saskia Sassen is the Robert S. Lynd Professor of Sociology and Co-Chair of the Committee on Global Thought, Columbia University (www.saskiasassen .com). Her recent books are *Territory, Authority, Rights: From Medieval to Global Assemblages* (2008) and *A Sociology of Globalization* (2007). She is currently working on *When Territory Exits Formalized Frameworks*. Recent edited books are *Deciphering the Global: Its Spaces, Scales and Subjects* (2007), and *Digital Formations: New Architectures for Global Order* (2005). For UNESCO, she organized a five-year project on sustainable human settlement with a network of researchers and activists in over thirty countries; it is published as one of the volumes of the *Encyclopedia of Life Support Systems* (2006; http://www.eolss.net). *The Global City* came out in a new fully updated edition in 2001. Her books are translated into twenty-one languages. She has received multiple honors and awards. She has written for *The Guardian, The New York Times, Le Monde, Newsweek International*, among others, and contributes regularly to www.OpenDemocracy.net and www .HuffingtonPost.com.